CHECHNYA'S TERRORIST NETWORK

**Recent Titles in
PSI Guides to Terrorists, Insurgents, and Armed Groups**

The ETIM: China's Islamic Militants and the Global Terrorist Threat
J. Todd Reed and Diana Raschke

The Phinehas Priesthood: Violent Vanguard of the Christian Identity Movement
Danny W. Davis

The Militant Kurds: A Dual Strategy for Freedom
Vera Eccarius-Kelly

The Palestine Liberation Organization: Terrorism and Prospects for Peace in the Holy Land
Daniel Baracskay

Armed for Life: The Army of God and Anti-Abortion Terror in the United States
Jennifer Jefferis

The IRA: The Irish Republican Army
James Dingley

The Khmer Rouge: Ideology, Militarism, and the Revolution That Consumed a Generation
Boraden Nhem

The Lord's Resistance Army
Lawrence E. Cline

17N's Philosophy of Terror: An Analysis of the 17 November Revolutionary Organization
Ioanna K. Lekea

The Taliban: Afghanistan's Most Lethal Insurgents
Mark Silinsky

CHECHNYA'S TERRORIST NETWORK

The Evolution of Terrorism in Russia's North Caucasus

Elena Pokalova

PSI Guides to Terrorists, Insurgents, and Armed Groups
James J. F. Forest, Series Editor

PRAEGER

AN IMPRINT OF ABC-CLIO, LLC
Santa Barbara, California • Denver, Colorado • Oxford, England

Copyright © 2015 by Elena Pokalova

All rights reserved. No part of this publication may be reproduced, stored in a retrieval system, or transmitted, in any form or by any means, electronic, mechanical, photocopying, recording, or otherwise, except for the inclusion of brief quotations in a review, without prior permission in writing from the publisher.

Library of Congress Cataloging-in-Publication Data

Pokalova, Elena.
 Chechnya's terrorist network : the evolution of terrorism in Russia's North Caucasus / Elena Pokalova.
   pages cm. — (Praeger security international) (PSI guides to terrorists, insurgents, and armed groups)
 Includes bibliographical references and index.
 ISBN 978–1–4408–3154–6 (hardback) — ISBN 978–1–4408–3155–3 (ebook) 1. Terrorism—Prevention—Russia (Federation)—Chechnia. 2. Terrorism—Russia (Federation)—Chechnia . 3. Terrorism—Prevention—Russia (Federation)—Caucasus, Northern. 4. Terrorism—Russia (Federation)—Caucasus, Northern. 5. Caucasus, Northern (Russia)—Autonomy and independence movements. I. Title.
 HV6433.R9P646 2015
 363.32509475'2—dc23   2014038634

ISBN: 978–1–4408–3154–6
EISBN: 978–1–4408–3155–3

19 18 17 16 15   1 2 3 4 5

This book is also available on the World Wide Web as an eBook.
Visit www.abc-clio.com for details.

Praeger
An Imprint of ABC-CLIO, LLC

ABC-CLIO, LLC
130 Cremona Drive, P.O. Box 1911
Santa Barbara, California 93116-1911

This book is printed on acid-free paper ∞

Manufactured in the United States of America

The views expressed in this book are those of the author and do not reflect the official policy or position of the National Defense University, the Department of Defense, or the U.S. Government.

Contents

Introduction	vii
1. Russia and the North Caucasus: Evolution of the Relationship	1
2. Russia Confronts Terrorism	33
3. Interwar Years: Ideological Developments behind Chechen Terrorism	67
4. Counterterrorist Operation: The Second Chechen Campaign	105
5. The Caucasus Emirate	143
6. Conclusion	173
Appendix A: Chechen Leaders (Dates in Power)	185
Appendix B: Terrorist Attacks Associated with the North Caucasus	187
Notes	217
Selected Bibliography	247
Index	251

Introduction

In 2013 Russia was busy preparing to host the Winter Olympic Games in Sochi in February 2014. The decision to hold the games in Sochi was controversial. The city is located in direct proximity to the North Caucasus—a region that has been engulfed in unrest and insurgency since 1991. Numerous security concerns haunted the preparation for the games as Doku Umarov, leader of the Caucasus Emirate—designated in Russia as a terrorist organization—urged his followers to attack the site of the games to prevent the Olympics from taking place. Umarov called for the peoples of the North Caucasus to boycott the Olympics that would demonstrate President Putin's glory in Sochi—a site at which Russia had exterminated a number of Caucasus ethnicities throughout history.[1]

Despite Putin's assurances that Sochi was perfectly safe, panic and fear set in as a series of terrorist attacks took place in the southern Russian city of Volgograd just weeks before the opening of the games. On October 21, in a suicide bombing of a public bus, six people were killed and 37 injured. On December 29 another suicide bombing claimed the lives of 18 people; another 44 were injured. The next day, on December 30, ten people were killed and 23 injured in a third suicide terrorist attack. These attacks continued the string of suicide bombings that had been staged by members of the Caucasus Emirate across Russia for years. The attacks taking place on the verge of the Olympics turned out to be among the more severe terrorist attacks of the last few years. Vilayat Dagestan, a division of the Caucasus Emirate, claimed responsibility for the attacks and warned that the group was prepared to carry out more attacks during the Olympics.[2] After this, international Olympic committees received electronic threats.[3]

Russia's security services frantically engaged in a search for a suspected suicide bomber—Ruzanna Ibragimova, a widow of an insurgent—who was reportedly involved in a plot to attack Sochi.[4]

The threats to attack the Sochi Olympics did not materialize. However, even though no terrorist attacks took place during the Olympics, the declared intentions to sabotage the games demonstrated the scope of the threat emanating from Russia's North Caucasus. In 2007 the Caucasus Emirate became an umbrella organization that united terrorist cells that had formed in the North Caucasus and beyond. Today the Emirate no longer exclusively represents the Chechen ethno-nationalist separatist project. Instead, the organization has expanded to unite the extremist cells of the North Caucasus, as well as Tatarstan and Bashkortostan, against occupation by Russian infidels. Further, under Umarov's leadership, the organization has transitioned to encompass the rhetoric of global Islamist jihadi groups. In 2007 Umarov declared that Russia was no longer the only enemy against whom he was waging war. In addition to Russia, anyone who had attacked Islam became Umarov's enemy as well.[5] Umarov has been implicated in terrorist attacks that include the bombings of the Nevsky Express train, the 2010 suicide bombings at the Moscow metro stations of Lubianka and Park Kultury, and the 2011 suicide attack at Moscow's international Domodedovo airport. In 2012 North Caucasus–inspired terrorism reached Kazan, the capital of Russia's Tatarstan.

THE CAUCASUS EMIRATE: STRATEGIC THREATS

Despite being a terrorist organization on UN and U.S. terrorist lists, the Caucasus Emirate has not attacked foreign targets. Umarov's call to sabotage the Olympic Games appears to have been more of a propaganda move than an indication that the group wanted to attack international actors. While Umarov's rhetoric grew to appeal to global jihadis, including radicalized Islamist cells present in Russia and the former Soviet Union, his insurgency, network of support, funding, and terrorist attacks have remained predominantly local. Umarov's attempt to situate the Caucasus Emirate within global jihadi networks came at a time when the organization was experiencing an existential crisis and needed to strategically adapt in order to survive. Umarov was able not only to preserve the organization but also to expand it to the territories of Russia's Tatarstan and Bashkortostan. However, no known Caucasus Emirate cells have been created outside Russia.

The activities and targets of the Caucasus Emirate have remained predominantly local. The group finds supporters among the peoples of the North Caucasus who have become disgruntled over the socio-economic and political conditions created by the local pro-Russian governments in the North Caucasus republics. The only terrorist attack with explicitly international implications committed by the Caucasus Emirate was the 2011 bombing of Moscow's Domodedovo international airport. Besides this attack, no targets with international significance have come under attack from the Caucasus Emirate. Neither has the organization committed any terrorist attacks outside Russia, even though individuals with links to the North Caucasus have been implicated in international terrorist plots. In fact, the leaders of the Caucasus Emirate were adamant in disassociating themselves from any international terrorism after the attack on the Boston Marathon.

The global community became acutely aware of the existence of the terrorist threat in Russia's North Caucasus on April 15, 2013, when two pressure cooker bombs detonated close to the Boston Marathon finish line in the United States. Brothers Tamerlan and Dzhokhar Tsarnaev were identified as suspects involved in the bombing. As the media traced the biographies of the brothers, it appeared that they had roots in Russia's North Caucasus; the brothers came from a family that lived in Dagestan. Immediately suspicions arose that the brothers had been radicalized by the Dagestani branch of the Caucasus Emirate, Vilayat Dagestan. Adding to such suspicions were reports that Russia's Federal Security Service (FSB) contacted American Federal Bureau of Investigation (FBI) in 2011 providing the agency with information suggesting that Tamerlan Tsarnaev was an adherent of radical Islam. According to the FSB, Tamerlan Tsarnaev had been trying to make contact with underground Dagestani Islamist organizations.[6]

The leadership of Vilayat Dagestan, however, emphatically denied any links to the Tsarnaev brothers. In a statement that appeared on the Vilayat website, Umarov's colleagues reminded the world that their struggle was intrinsically local, aimed against Russia. The statement explicitly reported that "the Caucasus mujahedeen are not engaged in military action with the United States of America."[7] The Caucasus Emirate has embraced some of the global jihadi rhetoric but at the same time remained true to local goals and aspirations. In this respect the group more resembles the Palestinian group Hamas rather than global or regional Al Qaeda groups. It has changed and adapted to the local, regional, and international climate but has retained its local North Caucasus roots. The structural and ideological transformations of the North Caucasus terrorist strain present valuable lessons for the global counterterrorism community in terms of the adaptability capabilities of terrorist movements.

IDEOLOGICAL TRANSFORMATIONS OF NORTH CAUCASUS TERRORISM

The first terrorist attack perpetrated by the Chechen separatists was staged by Shamil Basayev on November 9, 1991. The attack came as an immediate response to President Yeltsin's decision to impose a state of emergency in the republic after it unilaterally declared independence. Since then such terrorist attacks as the 1995 hostage crisis in Budennovsk, 1996 raid on Kizlyar, and 1996 explosions in Moscow were committed in the name of Chechen independence. Terrorists who carried out these attacks demanded the termination of the war in Chechnya, the withdrawal of Russian troops from the republic, and the start of peace negotiations between Moscow and Grozny. As the first Chechen war started in 1994, the separatist tactic of terrorism was instrumental in forcing the Kremlin to negotiate with Grozny. Moreover, the tactic of terrorism helped the Chechen separatists secure in August 1996 the Khasavyurt peace agreement. The Khasavyurt Accords marked the beginning of Chechnya's de facto independence that lasted till 1999.

While not explicitly religious, separatist terrorism of the first Chechen war exhibited certain religious connotations. For instance, former Soviet general Dzhokhar Dudayev declared jihad against Russia back in the early 1990s. Green headbands with inscriptions from the Quran became widely known to the Russian public from the Budennovsk attack of 1995. By the mid-1990s Shamil Basayev already described himself as a warrior of Islam.[8] Over time, as Shamil Basayev emerged as the mastermind behind the Chechen terrorist campaign, he realized the unifying force of Islam and increasingly adopted Islamist rhetoric in his justifications for terrorism. Subsequently, in 1999 Basayev was ready to wage a "holy war" against Russia to liberate the territories stretching "from the Volga to the Don," even if it meant the world had to be "engulfed in blue flames."[9]

The use of Islam for political purposes is not new in the North Caucasus. Historically Islam united diverse ethnic and cultural groups in liberation movements against Russia. For example, in the nineteenth century, with the help of Islam, Imam Shamil was able to unite representatives from Adygs, Chechens, Dagestanis, Balkars, Cherkess, Ingush, Kabardins, Karachai, and Ossetians against Russia's conquest. Declaring sharia law, Imam Shamil founded a theocratic state uniting these groups as the Caucasus Imamate. What started as a religious purification movement in the eighteenth century in the presence of political oppression from Russia transformed into the liberation ideology of Muridism. Under the banner of Muridism the diverse peoples of the North Caucasus rose up against the Russian Empire; the Murid insurgency lasted until Shamil's surrender in 1859.

Similar processes accompanied the rise of Wahhabism in the North Caucasus in the twentieth century.[10] The first Chechen war coincided with a period of religious revival that filled the spiritual void left by the demise of the Soviet Union. In the North Caucasus this period signified the reopening of mosques and religious schools, and the return of calls to restore sharia law. Calls to purify Islam became widespread in the post-Soviet territories.

Salafism, which in Russia became known as Wahhabism, quickly became a popular alternative to Soviet secularism, and many new Wahhabi converts organized in religious communities, or jamaats. Many local religious figures were now able to travel abroad and receive religious education in the countries of the Middle East. They organized religious jamaats and turned their attention toward the crime, corruption, and economic decline associated with local pro-Russian secular authorities. Local North Caucasus governments, in turn, responded to the rise of the religious jamaats with repression.

Government persecution, poor economic conditions, growing crime and corruption, and the lack of effective governance provided enough local grievances for Wahhabi followers to turn to violence. Dagestani Wahhabis sought support from the successful Chechen separatists, which led to the formation of the union of Chechen and Dagestani forces encouraged by Shamil Basayev. On the verge of the second Chechen war, Chechen separatists were ready to stage terrorist attacks not only for the independence of Chechnya but also for the liberation of Dagestan, and the unification of the two into a state similar to the historical Imamate of Imam Shamil. Apartment bombings that provoked Russia's counterterrorist operation started in the territory of Dagestan on September 4, 1999.

The second Chechen campaign began in Dagestan but almost immediately moved back to Chechnya. According to the Russian government, Russia was at war with the forces of international Islamist terrorists that had established safe havens in Chechnya. As a result, the renewed military action in the republic was justified as an attempt to eradicate the terrorist threat there. However, instead of eradicating the terrorist threat, the second Chechen campaign displaced the terrorist cells from Chechnya to the neighboring republics of the North Caucasus. By the early 2000s as the newly founded North Caucasus Wahhabi jamaats saw their Muslim brothers attacked by federal forces in both Dagestan and Chechnya, many of them set a course for radicalization. Many jamaats converted to terrorist cells that were eventually organized under the umbrella of the Caucasus Emirate in 2007.

Today Russia's North Caucasus remains one of the most violent spots in Europe. Despite the Kremlin's continued declarations that the situation is under federal control, violence continues to destabilize the region. Contrary to official claims, since the end of the counterterrorist operation in Chechnya in 2009, the number of people who have become victims of violence remains high. In the period between 2010 and 2013, there were 5,291 victims of the violence.[11] Among them, 2,728 people were killed, and 2,563 were injured. Dagestan has seen the most victims; over half of them, or 2,845 people, were killed or injured there. Chechnya today also still suffers from violence; 726 people were killed or injured there between 2010 and 2013. Following Dagestan and Chechnya are Ingushetia (695 victims),

Kabardino-Balkaria (613 victims), North Ossetia (226 victims), the Stavropol region (136 victims), and Karachaevo-Cherkessia (50 victims).

Despite the resolutely hardline response of Russia to the terrorist threat coming from the North Caucasus, it has failed to defeat the sources of violence. The terrorist command has successfully adapted and changed its ideology, goals, and structures and has thus sustained its potential to challenge Russia's security. On New Year's Eve 2014 President Putin vowed to continue methodically fighting the terrorists until he achieved "their complete extermination."[12] From Chechnya zones of counterterrorist operations have spread to every republic of the North Caucasus. And yet, Russia remains far from victory over the North Caucasus terrorists. This book examines in detail the shifts, adaptations, and transformations of the Chechen and North Caucasus terrorists, drawing the lessons from such dynamics for the counterterrorism community.

NORTH CAUCASUS MODES OF TERRORIST ATTACKS

Chechen hostage-takings in Budennovsk in 1995, in Kizlyar in 1996, at Dubrovka in 2002, and in Beslan in 2004 became widely known throughout the world. As Russian security services made it more difficult to carry out such large-scale attacks, the terrorist command switched to other modes. Explosions have been frequent both in the region and in Moscow itself, targeting the capital's metro and transportation system. Attacks on infrastructure and railway bombings have also been common tactics, as have hijackings and suicide bombings. This book analyzes such terrorist tactics, paying specific attention to the terrorist organizations that emerged to stage such attacks: Riyad us-Saliheyn Martyrs Brigade, Special Purpose Islamic Regiment, Islamic International Peacekeeping Brigade, and the Caucasus Emirate.

Terrorism in the North Caucasus is especially worthy of examination due to the number of innovations the movement has introduced. Basayev became one of the first terrorists in the world to carry out an act of radiological terrorism. He also became the first Islamist terrorist leader to strategically implement the tactic of female suicide terrorism. By employing women, his Black Widows, Basayev transformed the traditional female roles as perceived by violent Islamist jihadi groups. Further, the North Caucasus terrorist command was also a pioneer in terms of recruiting people of Slavic ethnicities to carry out acts of terrorism on behalf of the North Caucasus movement. This tactic has been especially effective, and many Slavs who converted to Wahhabi Islam have taken part in terrorist attacks against fellow Slavs.

Such innovations have not remained in the North Caucasus. Following Basayev's example, other terrorist groups have sought to acquire weapons of mass destruction, at times with help from the Chechens. Emulating Basayev's use of female suicide bombers, groups such as Hamas and Al Qaeda in Iraq have resorted to the same tactic. Seeking out converted Muslims and locally radicalized extremists for terrorist purposes has become a common global jihadi strategy. This has been an especially dangerous trend because terrorist groups themselves do not always have control over all the terrorist attacks committed in their name. This was demonstrated with the Boston Marathon bombing, where it seems the alleged perpetrators were driven by some of the extremist ideas from the North Caucasus but were not sanctioned by the Caucasus Emirate leadership.

NORTH CAUCASUS TERRORISM AND GLOBAL JIHAD

The relationship between Al Qaeda and the North Caucasus terrorist groups has long been a contentious issue. When it began its counterterrorist operation in 1999, Russia announced that it was facing a threat from international Islamist elements that operated from Chechnya. After September 11, 2001, Russia became one of the most vocal supporters of the war on terror because, as the Kremlin claimed, Russia had suffered from international terrorism enough to realize the danger the world was facing.[13] Moscow described Chechen terrorists as Al Qaeda emissaries, operating on orders from Osama bin Laden. Many controversial reports have emerged allegedly providing proof of such connections. This book examines the nature of such links through analyzing the existing factual evidence connecting Al Qaeda to the North Caucasus. While Afghan Arab and other foreign mujahedeen have indisputably helped North Caucasus leaders acquire foreign funding and support, empirical evidence analyzed in this book suggests that the stated links between Al Qaeda and the North Caucasus are somewhat exaggerated. As the strategy and actions of the Caucasus Emirate suggest, the group has not yet joined forces with Al Qaeda to wage global jihad.

What has emerged in recent years, however, is the increased circulation of North Caucasus mujahedeen. At the outset of the first Chechen war, mujahedeen were mainly flowing into the republic. Afghan Arab mujahedeen who had fought against the Soviets in Afghanistan started arriving in Chechnya around 1995 to assist their Muslim brothers in fighting an infidel, occupying regime. These mujahedeen, associated mainly with Khattab, became highly instrumental in training North Caucasus fighters in unconventional tactics that they excelled in while resisting the Soviets. Since the start of the second war, as it became increasingly difficult for foreign mujahedeen to reach the North Caucasus, Afghan Arabs instead chose to join jihad in Afghanistan and Iraq. This was the case with some of the terrorists who planned and executed the 9/11 attacks.[14]

While the flow of foreign mujahedeen into the North Caucasus decreased over time, the movement of North Caucasus mujahedeen out of the region increased. Since the beginning of Operation Enduring Freedom, North Caucasus fighters have been spotted in Afghanistan. A number of individuals from the North Caucasus that were implicated in criminal activities there emerged as detainees at Guantanamo. Since Afghanistan, North Caucasus mujahedeen have surfaced in Iraq and Syria. Today one of the prominent leaders of the Islamic State of Iraq and the Levant, a group originally linked to Al Qaeda, is an ethnic Chechen, Omar al-Shishani. Al-Shishani comes from Georgia's Pankisi Gorge, which was once famous as a safe haven for North Caucasus militants. In Syria, al-Shishani is fighting for a very different goal than his counterparts in the North Caucasus—the restoration of the global Islamic caliphate.[15] According to Alexander Bortnikov, Russia's FSB head, around 500 militants from Russia are fighting along with al-Shishani in Syria.[16]

One of the North Caucasus volunteer mujahedeen fighting in Syria today made the following promise: "Jihad in Syria is being strengthened and will continue, Inshallah. And this jihad will definitely arrive in Russia, Inshallah."[17] In Syria mujahedeen are acquiring firsthand battle experience. At the same time in Syria, they are being radicalized further under the influence of jihadi extremists from all over the world. When these mujahedeen make their way back to Russia, they will have the potential to completely change the nature of North Caucasus terrorism. As a result, counterterrorist interventions today are more important than ever. Russia has been fighting North Caucasus terrorism for over 20 years. In the course of this war, Moscow has implemented numerous approaches and tactics to combat terrorism. This book analyzes Russia's major counterterrorism initiatives, examining which measures are the most promising and which tend to be counterproductive.

This book presents an analysis of the dynamics behind North Caucasus terrorism. It traces the origins and evolution of the terrorist threat and Russia's responses to it. By analyzing the threat over time, the book presents a complete picture of terrorism in the North Caucasus through tracing both its local and foreign roots. The book analyzes Russia's responses to terrorism and their impact on the threat, examining Moscow's successes and failures. Learning from these experiences can help the global counterterrorism community contain the terrorist threat that grew out of the North Caucasus by avoiding Russia's mistakes that led to the emergence of the threat in the first place.

1

Russia and the North Caucasus: Evolution of the Relationship

RUSSIA'S INTEGRATION OF THE NORTH CAUCASUS

Russia's absorption of the North Caucasus has been a long and tumultuous endeavor.[1] In this process the North Caucasus territories have undergone numerous status changes and land transfers. One of the most diverse areas of the world due to its kaleidoscope of ethnic groups, languages, cultures, and territorial arrangements, the North Caucasus has been home to such historical territorial formations as Caucasian Albania, Great Bulgaria, the Khazar Khaganate, and the medieval kingdom of Alania. A series of khanates, kingdoms, principalities, and other territories arose here, succeeded each other, and changed loyalties. These territories have evolved to represent diverse histories, grievances, and aspirations that have often conflicted with each other. The contemporary Russian republics of Chechnya, Dagestan, Ingushetia, Kabardino-Balkaria, Karachaevo-Cherkessia, and North Ossetia are relatively new territorial formations. Some of these administrative units appeared on political maps only during the twentieth century.

Territories in the North Caucasus have developed unique structural arrangements, leading to major differences in social organization between the mountainous and lowland areas of Chechnya, Dagestan, and Ingushetia. While lowland societies have tended to consolidate around specific geographical boundaries, mountainous areas have traditionally organized in numerous *teips*. Teips, or family clan structures of common descent, focus on kinship rather than borders and represent a model of societal organization in which traditions of governance evolve based on common origins. Teips usually span several villages and are led by an elder who controls the life of the community and serves as a judge for contentious issues.[2] Contemporary Chechnya includes anywhere from 134 to 164 teips with one of the largest of them—Benoi teip—accounting for as much as 15 percent of the Chechen population.[3] Structurally, teips could be further organized into clusters that form *tukhums* in Chechnya or *jamaats* in Dagestan, which has further complicated the ephemeral issue of territorial borders. Such differences in societal arrangements throughout the centuries have greatly affected the relationship between Russia and the territories of the North Caucasus.

As a consequence of such inherent diversity, borders and loyalties in the North Caucasus have shifted constantly over time. Up to the twentieth century the struggle for power among princes, khans, emirs, and sheikhs was as common as conquest and counterconquest campaigns. Alliances were fickle and allegiances often changed. As a result, reactions to Russia's encroachment upon the region have varied tremendously through time and geographic location, and it would be incorrect to claim that the North Caucasus has engaged in a unified resistance campaign against Russia's actions.

Russia's military campaigns in the region can be traced back to the tenth century, when Prince Sviatoslav directed his attention to the Khazar Khaganate. In 1556 Russia conquered the Khanate of Astrakhan. A more concerted effort to bring the North Caucasus into Russia's sphere of control began when Peter the Great conquered Derbent in 1722 and Baku in 1723 to secure trade routes on the Caspian Sea. This wave of military conquest differed from previous historical campaigns because it was accompanied by efforts to secure and hold territory. To fulfill this goal, Russia initiated population transfers of Cossacks into the region. In the course of these transfers, Russian-held territories became marked by what became known as the Cossack Line stretching from the Caspian to the Azov Sea. Dagestan was added to Russia under the Treaty of Gulistan signed with Persia.

Despite Russia's military involvement in the region, not all of the North Caucasus territories initially joined Russia through force. Influenced by the great power competition over control of the region, some territories appealed to Russia for protection against either Persian or Ottoman rule. For instance, in 1557 the Adyg peoples of Cherkessia opted to align themselves with Russia. In the same year Russia concluded a treaty with Kabarda. To further solidify the Russian-Kabardin alliance, Russia's Tsar Ivan IV (the Terrible) married a Kabardin princess, who became known as Maria Temryukovna after her conversion to Russian Orthodoxy. Russia and Kabarda together participated in several joint campaigns against the Crimean Khanate. The late eighteenth century saw other Caucasian alliances with Russia: in 1771 the Ingush pledged allegiance to Russia, followed by the Ossetians in 1774 and the Chechens in 1781.[4]

Russia's absorption of the North Caucasus followed different patterns; some territories were conquered through force, while others joined the empire peacefully. The diversity of territorial aspirations, combined with changes in ethnic composition, identities, and historical paths, resulted in an ambiguous set of borders with many remaining in constant flux. Some borders remain disputed to this day. The disparity in territorial aspirations and statehood projects has prevented the emergence of a permanent anti-Russian front in the region. Instead, anti-Russian alliances have formed and dissolved over centuries. When such unions have arisen, they have been spurred by common religious ground and grievances created by Russia's rule in the North Caucasus.

THE SPREAD OF RESISTANCE AND THE RISE OF MURIDISM

One of the first major movements against Russia's advance in the North Caucasus was the uprising led by Sheikh Mansur in 1785. While little is known today about Sheikh Mansur's biography, his movement became the first political movement against Russian occupation that relied on religious rhetoric. Living in the Chechen village of Aldy, Mansur initiated a movement of spiritual purification. His message predominantly focused on what he perceived as an impious way of life full of sin, evil intentions, and a propensity to lie, steal, and kill, with such widespread destructive habits as drinking alcohol and smoking tobacco. "O believers!" Mansur addressed his followers, "Know that your life is full of ignorance, and that you have committed sins by drinking alcohol and smoking tobacco. Now you have an opportunity to rectify your mistakes and to find a way out."[5] Mansur urged his followers to give up sinful ways of life and turn to religion for salvation.

In the eyes of Mansur, these sins were associated with Russia's presence. As a result, the sheikh preached against practicing norms and traditions imposed by the Russians. For instance, Sheikh Mansur called for the replacement of the local customary law, or *adat*, with sharia law, becoming one of the first North Caucasus leaders to unite adherents with a religious cause.[6] Chechens, Dagestanis, Kabardins, Kumyks, and Adygs all joined in his quest for religious revival under the banner of establishing the rule of sharia. While Mansur's movement failed to significantly destabilize Russia's position in the North Caucasus, it became a precursor for future liberation campaigns based on similar justifications grounded in the goals of religious revival.

In response to Mansur's uprising, Russia initiated a concerted subjugation campaign. The mastermind behind the subjugation plan was General

Aleksey Yermolov. As a governor of the Caucasus Gubernia, Yermolov began implementing a series of reforms to ensure Russia's control of the North Caucasus. Yermolov devised a comprehensive strategy, moving away from trying to control individual locations to a campaign of total subjugation. According to Yermolov's plan, control over the territory had to spread into mountainous areas through subduing rebellious villages and cutting down forests on the way to increase the advantages for his regular army. His methods of dealing with local populations included scorched earth actions, repression, cleansing operations and punitive campaigns, deportations, and forced assimilation. Entire villages were burnt, houses and property were destroyed, livestock was confiscated, and new fines and taxes were imposed.[7] As Yermolov himself proclaimed, he preferred that "the terror of [his] name should guard our [Russia's] frontiers more potently than chains of fortresses, that [his] word should be for the natives a law more inevitable than death." The general continued, "Condescension in the eyes of Asiatics is a sign of weakness, and out of pure humanity I am inexorably severe. One execution saves hundreds of Russians from destruction, and thousands of Mussulmans from treason."[8]

Yermolov's policies became widely despised by the locals for their severity. Frequent revolts against his campaign led to the start of Russia's Caucasus war in 1817. The war ushered in a period of unrest that was finally put down only in 1864. The war spread from Kabarda, where the population began rioting in response to Russia's forced relocations, the building of Russian fortresses, and replacement in 1822 of sharia courts with administrative institutions controlled by Russia. Uprisings then spread to Chechnya, where the population revolted under the leadership of Beibulat Taimazov and Abdul-Kadyr in 1825–1826. These revolts preceded the emergence of Muridism, which unified many of the North Caucasus peoples against Russia.

Anti-Russian uprisings across the region received much support from local religious leaders. Among them was Mullah Muhammad of Yaraghi, a Sufi scholar of the Naqshbandi order who revived Sheikh Mansur's call for spiritual purification. He urged fellow Muslims to avoid common sins: "Drive away lewdness, mortify passions by fasting and abstention. Do not drink wine, this produce of the devil, do not follow the examples set by the infidels, who smoke pipes but weep in repentance, swear that you will never commit sins again."[9] Many of the sins and temptations were again associated with Russian infidels. As Mullah Muhammad claimed, "All your ablutions, prayers and pilgrimages to Mecca, your repentance and sacrifices, all your holy deeds are invalid as long as the Muscovites supervise your life ... So how can you serve God if you are serving the Russians?"[10] The movement to impose sharia first spread in Dagestan, a pattern that would later emerge in the twentieth century as well. From there, Mullah

Muhammad of Yaraghi started rallying people to defy the Russian administration, which did not support sharia.

The preaching of Mullah Muhammad of Yaraghi lay the spiritual grounds for the call for liberation from Russia. His disciple, or murid, Ghazi Muhammad (also known as Ghazi Mullah) took the teachings a step further by declaring holy war, or *gazavat*, against Russia, thus consolidating the spiritual component with a political call for independence. According to one account, on a night in 1825 Mullah Muhammad woke Ghazi Muhammad up, and, with the Quran in his hand, gave his murid a blessing: "In the name of Allah I urge you to lead a holy war for the purity of faith."[11] In 1828 Ghazi Muhammad became the first imam of the Caucasus Imamate, a theocratic political unit comprising the territories of Dagestan and Chechnya that declared its independence from Russia and initiated a concerted effort to liberate its lands from the Russian rule. Gazavat had begun; Muridism was born.

The term *Muridism* derives from the word *murid*, meaning a committed one, or a disciple of a murshid, or teacher, in a spiritual path in Sufism.[12] The Sufi order, or *tariqa*, of Naqshbandiyya spread to the North Caucasus in the eighteenth century from Bukhara, where Baha al-Din Naqshband lived in the fourteenth century.[13] Some scholars believe Sheikh Mansur was the first religious leader to preach the Naqshbandi tradition in the North Caucasus.[14] However, the Naqshbandi order only grew in popularity there with the spread of the teachings of Mullah Muhammad of Yaraghi. One of the main tenets of the Naqshbandi order was the belief that the Muslim community went astray and as a result needed to be returned to the true path. The decline of the North Caucasus was seen as a result of the failure to strictly adhere to sharia law. The role of Sufi sheikhs then was to guide the populace to spiritual purification through avoidance of alcohol, tobacco, blood feuds, and other institutionalized impurities and adats.

Ghazi Muhammad relied on these religious concepts to consolidate his resistance movement against Russia. Along with urging his followers to stop drinking, playing music, and dancing, Ghazi Muhammad declared gazavat against Russia: "God calls all those who accept Islam as a true faith to fight against the infidels in order to recover the pearl of freedom from the dirt of slavery. Those who do not use the opportune moment sent by God Himself will never have it again and eternal slavery will be their destiny."[15] This way, Sufi religious revivalist ideas became combined with the political ideals of equality for Muslims and liberation from Russian invaders.

The call to gazavat resulted in an era of Murid wars against Russia. While Russia at the time attributed the outbreaks of resistance to religious fundamentalism (as it did again in the 1990s), as Baddeley explains, religion was secondary in justifications for violence. Instead,

It was in the role of invaders, oppressors, conquerors—or, to use the current euphemism, civilisers—that excited such bitter resentment... zeal for the religion of Muhammad, though mighty the part it played henceforth, was but as air in a blow-pipe feeding a flame that already existed. The Ghazavat would never have been preached in the Caucasus had the Russians been peaceful and friendly neighbors.[16]

The call to violence not only expressed the political aspect of the Murid wars but also substantially departed from the principle of Sufi nonviolence. In this regard, Muridism came to be criticized by more traditional Sufi clerics who disagreed with the need for violence.[17] Even the spiritual mentor of Ghazi Muhammad—Jamal al-Din Ghumuqi, one of the first North Caucasus sheikhs to codify the Naqshbandi doctrine and practices—explicitly forbade warfare.[18] Thus, Muridism became an innovation brought about by Ghazi Muhammad to rally the peoples of the North Caucasus against Russia. Similarly, centuries later religious interpretations of Wahhabism would cause splits among the Muslim communities and would rally peoples of the region against the Russian federal center.

The appeal of the tenets of Muridism led to its spread beyond Dagestan and Chechnya to other territories, including Kabarda and Ossetia. The movement, however, did not reach its peak under its founder. Ghazi Muhammad's campaign, although impressive, proved to be rather short lived. Muhammad was killed in a battle in his native Gimry in 1832. The Murid cause was carried on by his successor Gamzat-Bek. But it was not until the rule of Imam Shamil, however, that the Murid wars spread across the Caucasus to their greatest extent. Under Imam Shamil, the Murid resistance gained its widest reach, and the unifying power of Muridism became explicit in the foundation of the Caucasus Imamate.

IMAM SHAMIL AND THE CAUCASUS IMAMATE

The Murid resistance to Russia's conquest reached its peak under the leadership of Imam Shamil. Succeeding Gamzat-Bek in 1834, Shamil became the third imam of the Caucasus Imamate and achieved great successes due to his outstanding military and administrative skills. The first imam, Ghazi Muhammad, had inspired Shamil to continue the Murid quest: "No matter what way we pray nor what miracles we perform, relying on tariqa alone will not save us: we will not get to heaven without gazavat... Let's do gazavat, Shamil."[19] With this incentive, Imam Shamil rallied enough support to successfully resist Russia for about a quarter of a century.

The rise of Shamil was a direct outcome of local reactions to Russia's policies in the conquered territories. As it would centuries later, Russia attempted to install its own version of Islam in the North Caucasus. Muslim clerics from the Crimea and Tatarstan were utilized in such propaganda efforts. For instance, a Tatar mufti from Kazan was commissioned to the Caucasus to persuade the local population of the falseness of the precepts advocated by adherents of Muridism.[20] Alternative religious schools for Sunni and Shia Muslims were opened throughout the Caucasus during the mid-1840s to educate students to be loyal subjects to the Russian government.[21] Along with these measures, policies of ruthlessly putting down rebellions, relocating populations, and eliminating villages initiated by Yermolov continued. Such policies fostered the conditions that created fertile ground for the ideas of Muridism to gain more popularity.

Shamil's Murid struggle occupies a significant place in the history of the North Caucasus. His most significant achievement became the consolidation of rebellious territories in the Caucasus Imamate, a theocratic state based on sharia law. The Caucasus Imamate was first established by Shamil's predecessors in 1828, but it was Shamil's effective administrative reform of the lands under his control that united Dagestan and Chechnya in a statehood project that served as an alternative to the administrative divisions imposed by Russia. Under Shamil's leadership, the Imamate expanded and reached the peak of its glory in the 1840s and 1850s. In this theocratic state, Shamil wielded supreme temporal and religious authority until his surrender in 1859 to the Russians.

Shamil's success with the Imamate was partially driven by the administrative reforms he initiated. Three features distinguished Shamil's undertakings: the Sufi religious framework, the Ottoman administrative structure, and the Russian centralized autocracy.[22] First, within the Sufi religious framework and justified through Naqshbandi tradition, the imam represented the supreme religious authority of the Imamate, allowing the imam to wield complete control over the disparate populations of the area. Second, the entire territory of the Imamate was divided into districts—*naibstvo*, or vilayat—governed by Shamil's representatives—*naibs*. A similar structure was used within the Ottoman Empire. Throughout the existence of the Imamate, scholars counted as many as 50 such districts formed at different periods in time.[23] The imam ensured subordination of naibs by clearly delineating their spheres of responsibility and further diluting their authority through the empowerment of religious clerics.

After consolidating his rule in Dagestan and Chechnya, Shamil worked to expand the Imamate into further territories. During the 1840s and 1850s he staged numerous incursions into Adyg and Kabardin territories and even into Christian Georgia. Shamil's capture of two Georgian princesses became a legend in itself.[24] He planned to unite his territories with Adyg lands by cutting through the Georgian Military Highway. Through persuasion and diplomacy Shamil was able to establish his rule in the Adyg territory. As one Adyg explained in 1847, "The rule over us . . . is entrusted to Shaykh Shamil, the ruler of the entire area from Temir Kapi [the iron gate of Derbent] to Anapa."[25] Shamil's naib Muhammad Emin ruled in Adygea for over a decade. At certain times, Shamil's sphere of influence grew to include Adyg, Chechen, Dagestani, Balkar, Cherkess, Ingush, Kabardin, Karachai, and Ossetian territories.

To support the functioning of the Imamate, Shamil created numerous government and military institutions that he held under tight control, a feature that made his rule similar to that of Russian autocracy. He raised well-trained and disciplined armed forces and built economic institutions to oversee taxation and the development of industries. His judiciary system was based on sharia law. However, Imam Shamil advanced his own interpretations of sharia, which became codified in an administrative codex, or *nizam*, that he compiled to run the Imamate. The codex, which consisted of 13 rulings, was unveiled in 1847.[26] It contained provisions covering areas such as the organization of armed forces, judiciary, the economic sphere, and family law. The codex banned tobacco, alcohol, music, singing, and dancing. Even the traditional Sufi *zikr* involving voiced recitation of prayers was replaced with silent prayers.[27] The supreme judicial and legislative body was represented by the Divan-Khaneh, or the supreme council that consisted of the imam's trusted people. The council served as a consultative assembly and met every day except Friday to discuss issues of governance.[28] To further monitor administrative and religious affairs, Shamil also created his own secret police.[29]

The Caucasus Imamate became the first successful statehood project in the North Caucasus that effectively governed significant territories and resisted Russia's rule. Driven by the principles of Muridism, which were derived from Sufi Islam, and the political call to gazavat, Imam Shamil succeeded in temporarily uniting the diverse peoples of the North Caucasus against the invader—Russia. Based on sharia law, Shamil's Imamate encompassed diverse ethnic groups held together by Islam. Shamil's state became a prototype that many future generations have tried to emulate.

THE END OF TSARIST RULE

Imam Shamil eventually surrendered to Russia in 1859. The capture of Shamil largely ended the Caucasus war, with the victorious Russian government then proceeding to stamp out the last vestiges of resistance. This era brought about one of the first major waves of deportations of the peoples of the North Caucasus.

The tsarist deportation mostly affected the Adyg peoples of Cherkessia.[30] The Muslim Adyg people were either forced to move to the Ottoman Empire or were ethnically cleansed by the Russian Imperial Army. A Russian officer, Ivan Drozdov, described the deportation process, saying, "Mankind has rarely experienced such disasters and to such extremes, but only horror could have an effect on the hostile mountaineers and drive them from the impenetrable mountain thickets."[31] Aiming to increase the number of people loyal to the empire, the Russian government confiscated Adyg lands and redistributed them among the Cossacks and other pro-Russian settlers. Many deportees, also called *muhajir*, or Muslim refugees, died of hunger and disease in the resettlement process, thus causing the number of Adyg people to sink to a historic low. A foreign observer noted in 1864 that "Circassia [was] gone."[32]

The Cherkess issue has remained one of the most controversial issues reverberating throughout the Caucasus until this day. The forceful removal of Cherkess from the Caucasus constitutes one of the most important historical traumas for this people. The Adyg people have organized around the issue and since the breakup of the Soviet Union have made numerous appeals to the Russian government to recognize the nineteenth-century expulsion of Adygs as genocide. Numerous Cherkess organizations addressed petitions to the Russian president and the European Parliament. Addressing the Russian president on the verge of May 21, 2013—a day that the Adygs mourn as a Cherkess Genocide Memorial Day—Cherkess representatives stated that "a century of heroic resistance to the aggression of the Russian Empire between 1763 and 1864 remains the main historical era in the Adyg history."[33]

Neighboring Georgia became the first country in the world to recognize the Cherkess genocide in 2011 in the wake of the Russia-Georgia War. Russia, however has still not granted the request. Moreover, Russia's actions toward the issue continue to provoke further criticisms from the Adyg community. For instance, many appeals for the recognition of the genocide reached President Putin on the verge of the 2014 Sochi Olympics that were held on historic Adyg lands.[34] In anticipation of the Olympics, Adyg organizations staged protests in Russia as well as in Turkey and even the United States.[35] The Cherkess issue circulated in the media as one of the potential reasons for boycotting the games. Despite the mounting activism, Russia avoided addressing the issue. Furthermore, as May 21, 2014, the 150-year anniversary of the Adyg deportation, approached, Russian authorities in Moscow detained Beslan Teuvazhev. An activist, Teuvazhev was implicated in preparing over 70,000 traditional green ribbons that had become a symbol associated with the Cherkess issue. The ribbons were confiscated on the grounds of spreading extremist activity. Such a response from Russia has prompted Adyg activists to call Moscow's actions "the continuation of the policy of oppression of ethnic minorities."[36]

After Shamil's surrender Russia transferred the mountainous peoples of the North Caucasus from the purview of the Ministry of Foreign Affairs to that of Military Affairs. This signified that from the point of view of the Russian Empire, the conquest was over; the North Caucasus became an internal issue. Shamil's successors, however, continued their resistance campaigns against Russia. The history of the North Caucasus conquest produced a number of chosen traumas that, similar to the issue of Cherkess genocide, keep reverberating through the politics of the region today.[37] For instance, General Yermolov's name has become synonymous with Russia's brutal policies of subjugation. In the 1990s parallels were drawn between Yermolov's strategy and Russia's contemporary handling of the Chechen quest for independence.[38] As Chechen separatists claimed, "modern ideologists of conquest of Chechnya are sticking to Yermolov's tactics."[39]

The figure of Imam Shamil in turn became one of the leading symbols of Chechen separatists. For instance, the second capital of Shamil's Imamate[40]—Vedeno, a village in Chechnya—became symbolic during the twentieth-century resistance campaign. Chechnya's Shamil Basayev, who became Russia's most wanted terrorist, was born in Vedeno and was thus immensely proud of his connection to Imam Shamil through both this geographical location and their shared first name. Basayev was convinced that he had inherited Shamil's quest for liberating the North Caucasus from the Russian invaders.[41] Subsequently, contemporary declarations of jihad have been justified as a continuation of the struggle started by Sheikh Mansur and Imam Shamil.[42] The founding of the contemporary Caucasus Emirate has also been proclaimed as an effort to re-establish the "Sharia legitimacy and revival of the united Islamic State of Muslims of Chechnya and the Caucasus, which our ancestors [Sheikh Mansur and Imam Shamil] were striving for throughout all times."[43] In this way, the events of the tsarist era continue to live on in the contemporary narratives circulating in the North Caucasus.

THE BEGINNING OF THE SOVIET ERA AND THE 1920S SEPARATIST PROJECTS

Due to the growing resentment toward the tsarist policies in the North Caucasus, the region became especially receptive to the leftist ideas widely circulating across Europe at the start of the twentieth century. Socialist left-wing ideals became a popular alternative to the perceived injustices imposed by Imperial Russia. As a result, the fall of the Russian monarchy and two subsequent revolutions were initially greeted with enthusiasm and hope in the North Caucasus.[44] In fact, the Caucasus played a crucial role in defining the future of the Soviet state. The Caucasus was one of the central battlefields between the White and Red Armies during the Russian Civil War. The Caucasus provided Joseph Stalin with his first experiences in the capacity of the Commissar of Nationalities and thus helped shape the entire future approach to Soviet nationalities policies. It was also the Caucasus that later produced the most bitter resistance to the Soviet rule and continued to challenge the Soviet power structures until the final collapse of the Soviet Union.

The separatist tendencies in the North Caucasus found a receptive track in the turbulent processes that began to take place across the Russian Empire. In fact, attempts to establish sovereignty in the North Caucasus actually preceded the October Bolshevik Revolution. An initiative to unite local peoples in a sovereign entity resulted in the First Congress of the United Mountain Peoples of the North Caucasus and Dagestan that took place in May 1917 in Vladikavkaz. At this stage the Congress discussed the formation of an autonomous entity not necessarily insubordinate to the Russian government. However, by September 1917 the Second Congress advanced their ideas, and debated and adopted a temporary constitution laying out the foundations of a future independent state. The founding of a sovereign Mountainous Republic of the North Caucasus was announced in 1918. While the republic was officially recognized by the Ottoman Empire, Germany, Austro-Hungary, Azerbaijan, and Georgia, it soon collapsed under attacks both from Denikin's White Army and the Bolshevik Red forces.[45]

Along with attempts to establish an independent Mountainous Republic during the formative years of the Soviet state, North Caucasus leaders reintroduced the idea of religious revival. Religious separatism during this time resulted in an attempt to restore Imam Shamil's Caucasus Imamate. Shamil's ideals of religious revival and political independence were continued by his own grandson Said Bey, Sheikh Uzun Khadzhi, and Imam Nazhmutdin Gotsinskii. Said Bey continued his grandfather's quest and became one of the symbols of the first anti-Soviet revolts. Nazhmutdin Gotsinskii acted as a political and spiritual leader of the movement, and Uzun Khadzhi served as the main spiritual authority behind the efforts to restore the theocratic state.

In 1919 Uzun Khadzhi founded his theocratic state—the Emirate of the North Caucasus—and placed it under the formal authority of the Ottoman Caliph.[46] The Emirate was modelled on Imam Shamil's Imamate. Despite the fact that the Emirate's religious agenda contradicted the principles of communism, the Bolsheviks initially acknowledged the state so that it could be used as an instrument for countering Denikin's White Army. However, as soon as Denikin's forces were defeated in February 1920, the Bolsheviks turned against their former ally and dismantled the Emirate. Uzun Khadzhi himself died shortly thereafter. His successors now had a new enemy—the Bolsheviks.

Imam Nazhmutdin Gotsinskii, an Avar, was initially pronounced spiritual leader of the United Mountain Peoples in 1917.[47] However, he soon broke away from the Union politics and set out to fight the Soviets, promoting Uzun Khadzhi's legacy of the Emirate. As the next imam, Gotsinskii continued to strive for the restoration of sharia law. He cooperated closely with Shamil's grandson Said Bey in mounting a full-scale anti-Bolshevik revolt in the North Caucasus in 1920–1921. His political structures were called a Council of Sheikhs and Said Bey, while his armed forces became known as the Sharia Army of the Mountainous Peoples.[48] This period of gazavat lasted until its defeat in 1921, when Soviet power was finally firmly established in the region.

THE SOVIET POLICIES IN THE NORTH CAUCASUS

The victorious Bolshevik forces proceeded cautiously to integrate the North Caucasus into the Soviet Union. They were initially welcomed by such slogans as "Long live the Soviet power, sharia, and unification of people!"[49] and tried to capitalize on locals willing to cooperate. As historian Abdurakhman Avtorkhanov explained,

> In national regions the very "padishahs" and their electorate had the voice that Moscow had to consider. That is why the Bolsheviks proceeded with especially flexible and cautious politics in the Caucasus. That was done so as to persuade the people of the North Caucasus that they were seriously granted the coveted independence that they had fought for for centuries. This required suppleness and flexibility in tactics.[50]

As a result, the Soviet People's Commissariat for Nationalities paid special attention to developing ways of co-opting local leaders. In 1918 the Commissariat established a special division to deal with affairs of the peoples of the mountainous Caucasus. One of the first policies adopted by the division was the approval of the display of images of Imam Shamil in public offices. In the early Soviet period Imam Shamil became celebrated as a hero of antitsarist resistance[51] and therefore became a symbol of cooperation between the Bolsheviks and the peoples of the North Caucasus.

The Bolsheviks further tried to empower local Muslim leaders that cooperated with the new regime. As a result, in the formative years of Soviet rule, the Bolsheviks treated Islam as one of their instruments for consolidating power. Consequently, in the early Soviet years, sharia law was not only allowed but was also promoted as an inalienable right of the locals. The majority of Muslim cities relied on functioning sharia courts that combined features of sharia along with adat norms. By the end of the Civil War, sharia courts were fully institutionalized in Dagestan, Chechnya, Ingushetia, North Ossetia, Kabarda, and Karachai.[52] Speaking in Dagestan in 1920, then-commissar of nationalities Joseph Stalin explained the significance of sharia law as follows:

> Dagestan should be governed according to its peculiarities, its customs, traditions. We are being informed that sharia plays an important role among the Dagestani peoples. It was also made known to us that the enemies of the Soviet power are spreading rumors that the Soviet government bans sharia.

Here on the part of the government of the Russian Soviet Federative Socialist Republic I am authorized to state that such rumors are false. The government of Russia grants every people full power to govern itself based on its laws and traditions. The Soviet government considers sharia equally legitimate regular law that other peoples of Russia have.[53]

In 1921 a decree on sharia jurisprudence made sharia courts official institutions of the Mountain Autonomous Soviet Socialist Republic (ASSR).

Such religious freedoms, however, were short lived. As the Soviets embarked on an antireligious campaign in 1923, freedoms gave way to persecution. In the North Caucasus the antireligious campaign first of all turned against the sharia courts. The first to ban them was Christian North Ossetia in 1924. That same year sharia courts were banned in the Mountain ASSR, and after the ASSR dissolution they were closed down in 1925 in Adygea and Kabardino-Balkaria and in 1926 in Ingushetia and Chechnya.[54] Sharia courts survived the longest in Dagestan, where they were eventually closed down in 1927. The 1920s and 1930s ushered in an era of purges; Muslim clergy became one of the primary targets of repression in the North Caucasus. Former sharia court members were prosecuted, and Muslim communities were forcefully converted to collective farms.

The period of Bolshevik innuendos with local cultures and traditions was further complicated by the Soviet policy of *korenizatsiia*. Collectivization and industrialization efforts increased the number of disagreements between Moscow and local territories, which fed into the grievances against Soviet power. Korenizatsiia was introduced in the 1920s as a concerted effort on the part of the new Soviet government to win over the different ethnic groups of the former Russian Empire. Korenizatsiia became a way to promote titular cultures and traditions as a method of filling government positions with representatives of titular nationalities.[55] As part of the new Soviet order, the effort was meant to gain greater political legitimacy among the local populations in the periphery of the Soviet Union. It became a way of indigenizing Soviet government institutions that were meant to function in languages comprehensible to the local populations. The policy of Chechenization during the 1990s bore several resemblances to the korenizatsiia attempt.

In the process of korenizatsiia, the North Caucasus territories were arranged in new territorial administrative units. By 1924 the redrawing of Soviet borders gave rise to the following ethno-national units within the Russian Soviet Federative Socialist Republic (RSFSR): Dagestan ASSR and the Autonomous Regions of Karachaevo-Cherkessia, Kabardino-Balkaria, Adygea, Chechnya, North Ossetia, and Ingushetia. These territories were further placed under the auspices of the North Caucasus Krai in an effort to better accommodate the ethno-nationalist aspirations. Similar territorial rearrangements were later implemented in the 2000s when federal districts were introduced as a means to better control the restive North Caucasus.

By the late 1920s reactions to Soviet policies started provoking unrest. Co-optation of local political and spiritual leaders combined with the persecution of local religious and cultural traditions brought to the surface renewed fears of continued Russian oppression. The outcomes of korenizatsiia, collectivization, and industrialization resulted in an increase in crime and poverty, and economic decline, which were attributed to Soviet attempts to exploit local resources. As a result, uprisings and anti-Soviet revolts became common in the North Caucasus by the 1930s. In addition to locally generated unrest, by the verge of the Second World War, the North Caucasus had also become a target of subversive activities by Nazi Germany. A number of German units began operations with the explicit aim of inciting anti-Soviet uprisings across the region.

In the 1940s most of the major uprisings in the Checheno-Ingushetia ASSR were led by Mairbek Sheripov and Khasan Israilov. Sheripov's insurgent activities were carried out under the auspices of an organization called the Chechen Mountaineer National-Socialist Underground Organization. The group was short lived because Sheripov was killed by the NKVD in 1942, and the group was eliminated. Israilov's group was created as the anti-Soviet United Party of the Caucasus Brethren and was later renamed the National-Socialist Party of the Caucasus Brethren. The organization's goal of liberating the North Caucasus from the Soviet rule attracted nearly 1,000 members,[56] and the campaign presented a serious challenge to the Soviets in the course of World War II. This insurgency was terminated only through the deportation of the North Caucasus peoples and Israilov's own elimination in 1944. In fact, the resistance campaigns and collaboration with Nazi Germany became the primary reasons cited by the Soviet government in justifying its decision to relocate large portions of the North Caucasus population. The North Caucasus insurgencies led the way to the next tragic chapter in the North Caucasus history—Stalin's deportations.

WORLD WAR II DEPORTATIONS

In the North Caucasus the World War II era became synonymous not only with Soviet patriotism and the unification of all Soviet peoples against Nazi Germany but also with the next ethnic trauma inflicted on local ethno-nationalist groups by the Soviet regime. The 1940s saw an era of deportation of thousands of individuals from local ethnic groups to the lands of Siberia and Central Asia. Despite the evidence that many North Caucasus people fought on the side of the Red Army against the Nazi occupation, the predominant reason given for the forced relocation of many was their collaboration with Nazi Germany.[57] Local banditry, crime, and Nazi collaboration gave Moscow enough reason to forcefully remove almost entire ethnicities from their historic lands, including Karachai, Chechens, Ingush, and Balkars.

The first group to be deported from the North Caucasus was the Karachai. The reason for deportation was cited as follows:

> many Karachai during the German occupation conducted themselves in a traitorous manner, many participated in German detachments to combat Soviet power, betrayed to the Germans honourable Soviet citizens, accompanied and acted as guides for German forces and, after the expulsion of the occupiers, opposed the Soviet authorities, and concealed and abetted enemies of the state and German agents.[58]

As a result, in October 1943 the Soviet government issued a decree declaring the liquidation of the Karachai Autonomous Region and the deportation of its inhabitants into the Kazakh and Kyrgyz Soviet Socialist Republics (SSR). The relocation affected 69,207 people.[59] After their departure from the Karachai region, the territory was divided between Russia's Stavropol and Krasnodar regions, and parts of the Karachai mountainous areas were transferred to the Georgian SSR.

The next to be deported were the Chechen and Ingush populations. Their deportation plan was approved in 1943. On January 31, 1944, the State Committee on Defense issued a decree confirming the Chechen and Ingush deportation to the Kazakh and Kyrgyz SSRs. This deportation was overseen by Lavrentiy Beria, who served as the commissar responsible for dealing with ethnic minorities under Stalin. Beria arrived in Grozny on February 20, 1944. The operation itself, called *Chechevitsa* (or *Lentil*), commenced on February 23, 1944; a total of 459,486 Chechens and Ingush were singled out in Chechnya, Ingushetia, and neighboring Dagestan to be moved.[60] After their departure the Checheno-Ingushetia ASSR ceased to exist. Its territory was divided between the Grozny district, the Dagestan ASSR, the North Ossetian ASSR, and the Georgian SSR. During this land redistribution North Ossetia received the Ingush Prigorodnii District that in 1992 became the object of an armed conflict between Ingushetia and North Ossetia.

While directing the deportation of the Chechens and Ingush, Beria received reports on the situation in Kabardino-Balkaria. According to Beria, the Balkars had collaborated with Nazi Germany and conspired with the Karachai insurgency.[61] As a result, the decision to deport the Balkar people from the North Caucasus soon followed in March 1944. In the course of the deportation, 44,415 Balkars were forcefully removed and sent mainly to Kazakhstan and Kyrgyzstan.[62] To complete the deportation the Kabardino-Balkaria ASSR was renamed Kabardin ASSR, and some of the Balkar lands were transferred to Georgia.

According to Beria's calculations, the three deportation operations resulted in the removal of 650,000 from the North Caucasus to the eastern parts of the Soviet Union. The people were predominantly moved to the Kazakh, Kyrgyz, Uzbek, and Tajik Soviet Socialist Republics. According to official reports, 608,749 Chechen, Ingush, Karachai, and Balkar deportees were registered at their new homes by 1948.[63] As per NKVD figures, from the total number of deported Chechens, Ingush, Karachai and Balkars, 144,704 people (or 23.7 percent) died between 1944 and 1948.[64] People were transported to their new homes in cattle train cars not equipped for human transfers. During the trip that lasted about a month, deportees traveled to their destination with no electricity or running water. Epidemic disease often struck the passengers, and many died from infection or hunger in transit. Many more deportees died upon arrival due to poor housing conditions, hunger, and disease.

Stalin's deportations during World War II became one of the most significant ethnic traumas of the Soviet period. The deportation resulted in the physical elimination of thousands of people of certain ethnic groups. The policy disrupted ongoing political, economic, and social processes in the North Caucasus and led to the oppression of cultural traditions of the deported peoples. The memory of the deportation remains firm in the national consciousness of the peoples of the North Caucasus. The inflicted trauma is so deep that even today disturbances in the region invoke fear of renewed deportations. Consequently, the deportation figures prominently in the rhetoric of the North Caucasus insurgent groups. Personal accounts of the deportation often appear in insurgent leaders' narratives. For instance, Chechnya's Shamil Basayev referred to his 40 relatives who died during the deportation.[65] Further, Aslan Maskhadov, president of Ichkeriia, stated in an interview that February 23—the day of the deportation of Chechens and Ingush—remained one of the most tragic dates for his people. According to Maskhadov, over 60 years after Stalin's deportation, and despite the changes in the Russian government, the goal of the Kremlin has always stayed the same: "to physically exterminate the Chechen people" under the same slogan "Chechnya without Chechens."[66]

The memory of the deportation thus transcends time and has continued into the twenty-first century. Rumors that the Russian government had designed new Stalin-like plans for another wave of deportations circulated in the Chechen media at the time it announced independence. To this effect the separatist website Kavkaz Center published a whole list of deportations carried out by the Russian government. According to the site, Russia's actions of the 1990s and 2000s were at least the tenth attempt to completely annihilate the Chechen nation.[67] In another posting, Russia's Prime Minister Chernomyrdin was accused of planning a new deportation under an order On Relocating Forced Settlers to Regions of Russia during the 1990s. According to the posting, the Russian government had devised a new plan to move all Chechen people to Yakutia, Russia's region in Siberia in a matter of just nine days.[68] Stalin's deportations still resonate with the experiences of the North Caucasus peoples, and the trauma of the deportation remains one of the strongest justifications for contemporary animosity toward Russia's rule.

THE END OF SOVIET RULE

After Stalin's death the Soviet government acknowledged some of the flaws of the Soviet nationalities policies, and Khrushchev tried to reverse some of their negative effects. In 1954 Khrushchev embarked on a rehabilitation initiative. On November 24, 1956, the Soviet government adopted a decree to restore the national autonomy of the Balkar, Chechen, Ingush, and Karachai peoples. However, the border changes that accompanied the deportation process significantly complicated the subsequent return of the deportees. As people returned to their homelands, now occupied by new inhabitants, clashes ensued between the old and new homeowners. Thus, the return of the deportees provoked varying levels of violence across the North Caucasus. The restoration of the Balkar and Karachai autonomies and the return of these peoples appeared to be relatively free of hostilities. The return of Chechens and Ingush, on the other hand, was riddled with numerous challenges.

The partial reversal of the policies of deportation contributed to the formation of some of the long-standing ethno-nationalist issues in the North Caucasus. For instance, the restoration of Checheno-Ingushetia ASSR in 1957 returned the territorial borders to their pre-1944 status. However, in this process some territories were only partially returned. For instance, the North Ossetian ASSR kept the Prigorodnii District that had previously been part of the Checheno-Ingushetia ASSR. In its place Checheno-Ingushetia received as compensation Cossack areas: Naurskii and Shelkovskii regions. As a result, the process of rehabilitation resulted in sporadic violence and led to territorial conflicts that persist until this day.

On November 14, 1989, the Supreme Soviet issued a declaration in which it recognized the Soviet acts against the deported peoples as illegal. Based on this declaration, on April 26, 1991, Russia issued a law on the political, cultural, social, and territorial rehabilitation of the peoples repressed during the Soviet era. However, such laws did not create the means for addressing territorial grievances. As a result, the collapse of the Soviet Union was accompanied by attempts by some ethno-nationalist groups to take territorial matters into their hands.

An armed conflict broke out between the Ingush and North Ossetians over the Prigorodnii District between October 31 and November 5, 1992. The conflict claimed the lives of 583 people; in addition, 939 people were injured, 261 people disappeared, and 1,093 were kept as hostages.[69] The conflict was sparked after Russia adopted a law on June 4, 1992, that confirmed the establishment of the Ingush Republic but once again failed to delineate its borders. Several thousand Ingush were left without the means of returning to their homes in North Ossetia. Tired of the inability of the government to adequately deal with the issue, the Ingush organized into armed groups to defend their rights through force. Despite the outbreak of violence and future attempts to settle this territorial dispute, the conflict between the Ingush and North Ossetians remains unresolved.

Another area that was affected by territorial redistribution during the deportation era and that was later beset by violence is the Novolakskii district of Dagestan. The district was created in 1944 in place of the Aukhovskii district previously populated by Chechen Akkin groups. After the deportation of the Chechens, the area was repopulated by Dagestani Laks. This redistribution also became problematic after the deported Chechens began to return to their historic lands. Just as in the Prigorodnii issue, the Novolakskii dispute has persisted and has created significant grievances in the region. Notably, the Novolakskii grievance was exploited by Chechen separatists in 1999. In September 1999 Chechnya's Shamil Basayev and Khattab led their armed divisions to the Novolakskii district of Dagestan hoping that the disgruntled Chechens of the district would join forces with them.

The collapse of the Soviet Union was accompanied by renewed turbulence in the North Caucasus. At the same time, in the 1990s such phenomena as separatism, terrorism, and insurgency did not become pervasive. The North Caucasus territories had different visions for their future, and the quest for independence that started in Chechnya in 1991 did not spread across the region. The six North Caucasus territories that emerged after the collapse of the Soviet Union—Chechnya, Dagestan, Ingushetia, Kabardino-Balkaria, Karachaevo-Cherkessia, and North Ossetia—pursued different self-determination routes. Certain territories became susceptible to sovereignty slogans popular at the time. Many ethnic groups felt entitled to participate in the parade of sovereignties encouraged by President Yeltsin as he urged territories to grab as much sovereignty as they could. However, after the breakup of the Soviet Union, independence calls outside Chechnya did not lead to violence, and declarations of sovereignty implied a change of status within the Russian Federation, rather than secession from it. By the time of the first Chechen war, most territories of the North Caucasus claimed loyalty to Russia, indicating little support for Chechen separatism.

Among the North Caucasus republics, North Ossetia, Kabardino-Balkaria, and Karachaevo-Cherkessia were more integrated with Russia than other territories. As a result, they experienced fewer calls for independence from the parent state. For instance, in the 1990s North Ossetia did not experience separatist tendencies; violence in North Ossetia was associated with the Prigorodnii District and was the result of a territorial dispute rather than an issue of sovereignty or independence. Independence from Russia was not on the agenda. As the president of North Ossetia, Akhsarbek Galazov stated on independence: "Our main goal is to maintain unity with Russia. In this direction we all need to join effort and act in concert."[70] Furthermore, North Ossetia was prepared to assist Russia in fighting the separatist tendencies in its neighboring republics. During the first Chechen war the territory of North Ossetia, primarily its two major cities of Vladikavkaz and Mozdok, served as a base for Russian forces and a safe zone for operational command.[71] Through this, North Ossetia demonstrated its dedication to the territorial unity of the Russian Federation.

Kabardino-Balkaria and Karachaevo-Cherkessia, in turn, while choosing the pro-Russia position, went through a number of sovereignty conflicts. In 1996 Kabardino-Balkaria's leader Valery Kokov affirmed:

> The development of statehood of Kabardin and Balkar peoples is inextricably tied to the development and consolidation of their connection with the destiny of the great Russian people and the Russian state. The voluntary accession to Russia saved our peoples from slavery imposed by foreign occupying powers, from fratricide and endless wars. It created favorable conditions for further economic and cultural development, and, therefore for progressing movement towards state self-determination.[72]

In 2012 Kabardino-Balkaria proceeded with a celebration of two significant anniversaries—185 years since Balkaria's voluntary accession to Russia and 455 years since that of Kabarda. The celebrations once again demonstrated that both Balkaria and Kabarda joined Russia willingly and to this day are its staunch allies.

While Kabardino-Balkaria did not share the Chechen separatist insurgent aspirations of the 1990s, it did experience its share of declarations of sovereignty. In 1991 the Balkar people declared their sovereignty within the Russian Federation and announced the founding of a Balkar Republic, thus stating the decision to secede from Kabardino-Balkaria. This was backed by a referendum held on December 29, 1991. According to the results, out of 85 percent of the Balkars who took part in the referendum, 94.5 percent supported this move.[73] Following the decision to secede, the Balkars formed their own National Council of the Balkar People. In response to the Balkar sovereignty initiative, Kabardins in turn convened a conference of their own. On January 12, 1992, the conference announced the founding of a sovereign Kabardin Republic within the Russian Federation.[74] The Congress of the Kabardin People was created to represent the new republic. While disputes over the border between the Balkar and Kabardin Republics followed suit, the dissolution initiative soon lost public support; a public poll conducted in 1994 indicated that 86 percent of the population no longer supported separation.[75] The Republic of Kabardino-Balkaria thus continued as a natural successor of the Kabardino-Balkaria ASSR, with minor controversies over renewed calls for Balkar sovereignty arising again in 1996.

Similar processes were underway in neighboring Karachaevo-Cherkessia. In July 1991 the status of the autonomous region was elevated to that of a republic within the Russian Federation. At the same time representatives of different ethnic groups within Karachaevo-Cherkessia began appealing to the Russian government for recognition of their sovereignty. Between 1990 and 1992 congresses of various ethnic groups announced the founding of their respective territories. Among them were the Karachai and Cherkess Republics that stated their intent to separate from Karachaevo-Cherkessia. By January 1992 the Russian government was considering a bill on the recognition of Karachai and Cherkess autonomies within the Russian Federation and was ready to approve the dissolution. However, a referendum held on March 28, 1992, indicated that the majority of the population was against the split of Karachaevo-Cherkessia. As a result, sovereignty initiatives in Karachaevo-Cherkessia did not lead to its dissolution. Looking back at the 1990s former head of the republic Vladimir Khubiev stressed his efforts in resolving ethnic issues peacefully. Khubiev was very critical of the violence in neighboring Chechnya and pointed out that separatism was not on the republic's agenda; instead it was the preservation of the "unity of the brethren peoples of the North Caucasus."[76]

A more contentious ethno-nationalist situation was prevalent in Dagestan. Many of the Dagestani identity groups were not content with their status at the end of the Soviet era. However, in the 1990s Dagestan managed to control the separatist tendencies and, unlike its neighbor, did not plunge into separatist violence. While some ethnic groups within Dagestan, for instance Lezgins, did voice calls for sovereignty, Dagestan managed to preserve its unity peacefully. Addressing representatives of the peoples of Dagestan in 1992, Dagestani leader Magomedali Magomedov clearly stated his position against secession from Russia or the creation of Dagestan's own armed forces.[77] In 2013 Dagestan marked 200 years of alliance with Russia with the celebration of the anniversary of the 1813 Gulistan treaty. On this occasion Ramazan Abdulatipov, the leader of Dagestan, reminded his people of the unity with Russia once again: "The government is extensively preoccupied with culture and traditions and the integration of Dagestan into Russia's cultural and economic space. It is important that Dagestanis perceive themselves as citizens of great Russia. We are a people of Russian destiny."[78]

Lastly, Ingushetia was in the most precarious position in the 1990s as the territory that was most likely to be affected by Chechen independence campaigns. In addition to sharing history and traditions with Chechnya, Ingushetia became the target of a steady influx of refugees from its neighbor. Despite the existing links, the Ingush declared their desire for sovereignty before the start of the first Chechen war and pursued the pro-Russia stance. This marked the end of the Checheno-Ingushetia Republic. In December 1991 Ingushetia held a referendum in which 92.5 percent of the voters supported a sovereign Ingushetia within the Russian Federation.[79] On June 4, 1992, the creation of the Ingush Republic within the Russian Federation was finalized. As Ingushetia's former leader Ruslan Aushev confirmed: "Ingushetia will remain within Russia. We held a referendum and said that we are hands down in favor of staying with Russia."[80]

At the time of the Soviet Union's collapse, the North Caucasus republics did not exhibit uniform sovereign or separatist tendencies. Despite pervasive demands for sovereignty, violence over independence ensued only in Chechnya. In 1992 Chechnya became one of the two Russian republics that refused to sign the Federation Treaty of March 31.[81] The rest of the territories willingly affirmed their status within the Russian Federation. Moreover, many of Chechnya's neighbors expressed concern over violence and urged the Russian government to solve the situation. In November 1994 some of the North Caucasus leaders, including North Ossetia's Akhsarbek Galazov, Kabardino-Balkaria's Valery Kokov, and Karachaevo-Cherkessia's Vladimir Khubiev, sent a letter to President Yeltsin encouraging him to address the crisis in Chechnya. This controversial letter came to play a significant role in justifying what followed. By urging the president to undertake any measures possible to restore constitutional order, the letter implicitly showed support for a heavy-handed solution. The letter was not signed by Ingushetia's Ruslan Aushev or Dagestan's Magomedali Magomedov. As Aushev later recalled, he refused to sign the letter because its wording encouraged military action in Chechnya.[82]

Such differences in opinion, as well as differences in territorial and administrative goals and aspirations, indicated a lack of unity among the North Caucasus territories in the 1990s. Both leadership statements and indicators of popular opinion signaled that the Chechen cause was not widely supported. Violence remained confined to Chechnya, and the outbreak of the first Chechen war was not accompanied by the spread of its ideological underpinnings across the region. In fact, the only exercise in unity in the 1990s became the failed Confederation of the Mountain Peoples of the Caucasus. The organization, which initially united 14 peoples of the Caucasus was a rather unsuccessful endeavor. Internal divisions as well as differences in opinion regarding the beginning of violence in Chechnya soon led to the organization's demise.

CONFEDERATION OF THE MOUNTAIN PEOPLES OF THE CAUCASUS

While the political and territorial motivations of the North Caucasus territories differed, the collapse of the Soviet Union presented the next opportunity for unification endeavors. The Confederation of the Mountain Peoples of the Caucasus was the next attempt to build a common independent state in the North Caucasus. An Assembly of the Mountain Peoples of the Caucasus was initially convened during the first Congress of the North Caucasus Peoples held in August 1989 in Sukhumi, Georgia. The Assembly was then renamed the Confederation of the Mountain Peoples of the Caucasus. During the second Congress of the Caucasus peoples that took place in October 1990 in Nalchik, Kabardino-Balkaria, the Confederation was announced as a successor state to the Mountainous Republic of 1918. The Confederation was conceived as a sovereign nation-state that would defy Russia's federal arrangement.

During the third Congress in November 1991, representatives of 14 peoples of the North Caucasus republics signed a confederate treaty formally founding the Confederation. The representatives included peoples from the territories of Chechnya, Dagestan, Ingushetia, Kabardino-Balkaria, and North Ossetia, as well as Abkhazia and South Ossetia. It was later reported, although later disputed, that Osama bin Laden attended the founding conference of the Confederation.[83] Following the founding of the Confederation, *Mountain* was dropped from its name and after 1992 it became known as the Confederation of the Peoples of the Caucasus.

The purpose of the organization was to create a space for the peoples of the North Caucasus free of Russia's influence. In a way it was the continuation of Imam Shamil's efforts to become independent of Russia's domination. Unlike Shamil's undertakings, however, the confederate project was not driven by religious ideology. The founders of the organization justified their call for independence by focusing on Russia's injustices in the North Caucasus. To this end the founders cited actions such as the colonial policies of the tsarist regime, the brutalities of the Caucasus wars, and the ethnic traumas of the Bolshevik totalitarian system.[84] In trying to break away from Russia, the Confederation followed the secular pattern of the Mountainous Republic of 1918 rather than the religious project of the Emirate of 1919.

Similar to the Mountainous Republic of the early twentieth century, the Confederation was preoccupied with creating its own governing bodies, including legislative, executive, judicial, and defense institutions. Sukhumi became the capital city of the Confederation. The Confederation was headed by President Musa (Yuri) Shanibov and 14 vice presidents, each of whom represented a constituent nationality. The Confederation established a Parliament and Yusup Soslambekov, a Chechen independence activist who later joined Dudayev's opposition camp, was appointed its leader. Similar to its predecessor states, the Confederation devised its own judiciary system and even considered the issue of official religion. However, unlike its theocratic predecessors—Imam Shamil's Imamate of the nineteenth century or the Emirate of the North Caucasus of the twentieth century—the

Confederation rejected Islam as a state religion.[85] Because the organization included non-Muslim members, the idea of a theocratic state did not appeal to the Confederation founders.

The Confederation institutions competed with the governments of the North Caucasus republics that supported Russia. As a result, confederate ministries played a rather marginal role in regional politics. The only institution that became significant was the Confederation's defense ministry. Headed by Yusup Soslambekov, the ministry created its own armed forces, comprised of volunteers. It was the Confederation armed forces that made the organization known to wider audiences.

As the Georgian conflicts of the 1990s broke out, the Confederation recognized the sovereignty of breakaway South Ossetia and Abkhazia. In the wake of secession announcements, the Confederation leadership addressed the Georgian government with a petition to "stop the genocide of the Ossetian people."[86] In 1992, ready to support separatist causes in the region, the armed forces of the Confederation set out to help the Abkhaz separatists. At the outset of violence in Abkhazia, Yusup Soslambekov appeared on Grozny TV encouraging his followers to gather to defend the Abkhaz people from the "Georgian invaders."[87] Shanibov and Soslambekov subsequently issued a decree ordering a transfer of volunteer divisions from the Confederation to support fellow Abkhaz separatists.[88] These calls rallied hundreds of Chechens, who went to Sukhumi to fight for the separatist cause. Among these volunteer fighters were Shamil Basayev, Ruslan Gelayev, and Khamzat Gitsba—individuals who became widely known to the Russian public in the course of the Chechen conflict.

It was the conflict in Abkhazia that provided initial military training to Shamil Basayev, who later became known as Russia's "terrorist number one." It was also the Abkhaz conflict that, according to some sources, revealed Basayev's connections with Russia's special services. According to these accounts, Basayev's battalion in Abkhazia was trained by Russia's own 345th Airborne Division and representatives of the intelligence services.[89] Such accounts, however, remain uncorroborated by the Russian government. The conflict in Abkhazia also revealed Basayev's propensity toward banditry, kidnapping, and murder. Such activities led the Republic of Abkhazia to list Basayev as a wanted person and to appeal to Russia for assistance in efforts to apprehend him.[90]

The Confederation's involvement in the Abkhaz conflict thus placed the organization in the crosshairs of politicians in Moscow. The participation of its armed forces in Abkhazia was widely criticized in Russia. In response to the organization's activities, President Yeltsin encouraged the peoples of the North Caucasus not to get involved in violence. In his address the president urged them to "restrain emotions and not let themselves be driven into a dangerous exploit."[91] The very legitimacy of the Confederation came into question. Russia's minister of justice at the time, Nikolai Fedorov, described the founding of the organization as unconstitutional. He classified the "attempt to create a parliament, defense council, armed forces, ... [and] commander-in-chief" as actions that clearly breached the constitution of the Russian Federation.[92]

At the same time, aside from its role in the Abkhaz conflict, the organization did not have much influence in the North Caucasus. By the time the first Chechen war started in 1994, the Confederation seemed to be split in terms of its opinion on Chechen independence. On the one hand, the Confederation leadership encouraged the Russian government to resolve the Chechen conflict peacefully. For instance, vice president of the Confederation of the Peoples of the Caucasus Zhantemir Gubachikov in 1994 addressed the Russian Duma, urging it to solve the problem in Chechnya through political means. As Gubachikov stated, a peaceful solution was a priority:

> Comrades, who needs this war? ... The political problem cannot be resolved with fire and sword; we need negotiations, we need compromise. We are convinced that the leadership of the Chechen Republic is ready for it. Regardless of whether we want it or not, Dudayev today heads the legitimately elected government in Chechnya. I have already stated that this government at the time was not recognized by the Supreme Soviet of the Russian Federation or the President of the Russian Federation. Comrades, Stalin did not go to the extent of physically exterminating the Chechen people. He only managed to deport the Chechen people. But today, due to irresponsible reactions from certain circles headed by the party of war that started this war, the extermination of the Chechen people is on the agenda again.[93]

On the other hand, more radical members of the organization were ready to support the separatist camp of Chechnya's Dzhokhar Dudayev. Even the Confederation president Shanibov pointed out that his organization was divided in opinion over policies toward Dudayev.[94] After all, Dudayev was one of the most active members of the Confederation. Dudayev urged his colleagues to stand up to the evil empire, expel Russia's forces from their territories, and terminate its oppression of the Muslim people.[95] Many of his colleagues shared the general's opinion. As a result, some factions within the Confederation supported Dudayev's fight for independence. Among the supporters ready to use violence was Shamil Basayev's Abkhaz battalion. Basayev not only provided military support to Dudayev but also turned his Confederation division into one of the strongest fighting components of Dudayev's force. Basayev's Abkhaz battalion became one of Dudayev's best fighting units.

As the war progressed in Chechnya, the Confederation's influence steadily diminished. In 1996 Yusup Soslambekov, who replaced Shanibov in the presidential post, unsuccessfully attempted to revive the decaying organization. Another attempt to bring back the Confederation followed in 2006, when Musa Shanibov convened a Union of Veterans of the Confederation of the Peoples of the Caucasus in Sukhumi. Further, during the 2008 war in Abkhazia, news sources provided reports of the Confederation of the Peoples of the Caucasus resurfacing yet again. According to these sources, the Confederation was ready to come to Abkhazia's rescue once again.[96] While the Confederation lost much of its political clout, it produced a valuable lesson for future unification projects. It demonstrated the significance of a unifying ideology; without it, independence projects were doomed to succumb to individual nationalisms, resulting in the dissolution of confederate states.

CHECHNYA'S SLIDE TO INDEPENDENCE

While diverse ethno-nationalist aspirations were pervasive in the North Caucasus at the time of the Soviet Union's collapse, Chechnya was the only republic that pursued its independence project through violence. While Moscow tried to prop up its dwindling influence in the republic through the promotion of a Soviet official, Doku Zavgayev, as the head of the Checheno-Ingushetia ASSR, the opposition forces consolidated around the National Congress of the Chechen People. In November 1990, in Grozny, the Congress appointed General Dzhokhar Dudayev as its leader and adopted a declaration on the founding of the Chechen Republic. Dzhokhar Dudayev was born in 1944—the year of the Chechen deportation. He was able to return to Chechnya in 1957, proceeded with his career, and became a Soviet general. Before his return to Chechnya in the 1990s, Dudayev served at a Tartu air base in Estonia. Under Dudayev's leadership, the Congress announced the sovereignty of the Chechen Republic during its second meeting in July 1991, beginning Chechnya's independence campaign.

Chechnya's fate was further affected by the changes happening at the same time in Moscow. In June 1991 Boris Yeltsin was elected president of Russia. In August a communist coup in Moscow attempted to depose the reformist government of Mikhail Gorbachev, to preserve the Soviet Union. Yeltsin denounced the putsch as an illegitimate move to grab power. In the first hours of the putsch, Dudayev sided with Yeltsin in condemning the coup attempt, creating an image of his loyalty to Yeltsin's regime. As a result, Dudayev was initially supported by Russia's president as an emerging leader of Chechnya. As a former head of presidential administration, Sergei Filatov later recalled, Yeltsin's advisors Gennadiy Burbulis and Mikhail Poltoranin vetted Dudayev as Russia's loyal ally.[97]

Doku Zavgayev, on the other hand, failed to condemn the putsch, thus exhibiting his pro-communist leanings. This gave Dudayev a reason to call for the resignation of Zavgayev's Supreme Soviet. At the same time Dudayev indicated the existence of his own agenda, independent of Yeltsin's, as he also called for the sovereignty of the Chechen Republic both from Russia and the Soviet Union. Dudayev proceeded to depose the Supreme Soviet of the Checheno-Ingushetia ASSR; Doku Zavgayev resigned his position. In place of the Supreme Soviet, Yeltsin's administration tried to prop a Provisional Supreme Soviet to prepare and hold new elections. However, Dudayev's National Congress of the Chechen People overthrew this institution on September 17, 1991, and pronounced itself the only legitimate government of the Chechen Republic.

In response to Dudayev's actions, Russia's Supreme Soviet issued a declaration on October 8, 1991, in which it denounced the general's National Congress. To Moscow, the Provisional Supreme Soviet remained the only legitimate governing institution in Grozny. Despite Moscow's disapproval, Dudayev proceeded with parliamentary and presidential elections in Chechnya. On October 27, 1991, Dzhokhar Dudayev was elected president of the breakaway republic. His first decisions as president were the declaration of the sovereignty of the Chechen Republic on November 1, followed by the declaration of independence of the state of Ichkeriia on November 2.[98] Dudayev justified this decision as follows: "The territorial integrity of the Chechen Republic is inviolable... The Chechen Republic has the right to militarily defend its sovereignty. Our goal is freedom and independence. Our way is law along with faith in God."[99]

Yeltsin's administration, however, disagreed and pronounced Dudayev's elections illegal. On November 7 Yeltsin declared a state of emergency in Chechnya. This was followed by Yeltsin's order to deploy military force. Troops of the Ministry of Internal Affairs (MVD) were sent into the republic. This was Yeltsin's first attempt to resolve the Chechen crisis militarily. This military action, however, proved to be rather shortlived. On November 11 the Supreme Soviet of the Russian Federation refused to affirm the state of emergency and annulled Yeltsin's decree. The troops withdrew.

In Chechnya, Yeltsin's actions provoked a strong reaction; Dudayev imposed martial law in response. The general called on his people to come together against Russia's involvement in the republic. Dudayev also issued his first call to a holy war against Russia—gazavat, or jihad—in the post-Soviet North Caucasus. To resist Russia, Dudayev was ready to employ all means necessary. In addition, he also issued the first post-Soviet call to commit terrorist acts against Russia. To the general, events in Chechnya represented a state of war, and he encouraged his citizens to be prepared to engage in "acts of terror, including explosions against nuclear power stations" all over Russia.[100] The first terrorist attacks followed shortly thereafter. Thus, Yeltsin's very first policies toward breakaway Chechnya resulted in the emergence of the terrorist threat that over the next couple of decades grew into one of Russia's biggest security challenges.

The Chechen leadership used the opportunity created by the uncertainties of the post-Soviet transition to declare its independence. At this time Moscow used military force in the republic only very briefly. The second attempt to pacify Chechnya militarily came in 1992 during the Prigorodnii conflict between Ingushetia and North Ossetia. Despite Dudayev's declaration of neutrality during the conflict, Russian troops crossed into Chechnya. However, again Russia backed away from the military campaign there. Preoccupied with more pressing concerns, including the collapse of the Soviet Union, Yeltsin's government came to largely view the Chechen issue as peripheral by the end of 1991. Chechnya gained de facto independence that lasted up until the beginning of the war in 1994.

DUDAYEV'S CHECHNYA AND THE START OF THE WAR

While Dudayev came to power with virtually no opposition inside Chechnya, his rule soon became associated with rapid economic decline and the rise of criminal activities. Following the collapse of the Soviet Union, crime rates skyrocketed in many regions of Russia. Yet the Chechen case became unique due to its de facto independent existence. In the absence of oversight from Moscow, Dudayev's presidential decisions contributed to the escalation of crime. For instance, in the fall of 1991 Dudayev decided to order the release of inmates from Chechen correctional facilities. According to Russian statistics, 1,123 inmates were released from prison; 1,500 inmates were freed from juvenile facilities; and another 1,500 were discharged from detention.[101] Along with joining Dudayev's freedom fighting forces, many of these individuals returned to criminal activities. In another decree, Dudayev legalized the possession of firearms in Chechnya, regardless of the origin of the weapons.[102] As a result, Chechnya became flooded with arms, and crime rates increased drastically. According to Ruslan Khasbulatov, a Russian politician who came to play a central role in consolidating Dudayev's opposition, between 1991 and 1994 over 10,000 people either were killed or disappeared in Chechnya.[103]

The wide availability of weapons was also a byproduct of Russia's departure from the republic. By June 1992 Moscow had pulled all federal forces out of Chechnya, leaving large amounts of Soviet weapons behind at the former military bases. For instance, troops leaving the Grozny district training center left behind large volumes of equipment, weapons, and ammunition, including 42 tanks; 38 infantry combat vehicles; 14 armored vehicles; 31,738 automatic rifles; 12,813 guns; 460 rifles; 1,011 machine guns; and 1,012 grenade launchers.[104] Grozny became one of the biggest black market centers for weapons in the former Soviet Union. At the same time weapons were not the only commodities freely sold in Chechnya; drugs also flooded the republic. Grozny emerged as one of the largest post-Soviet drug trafficking hubs.

The economic situation under Dudayev's rule deteriorated rapidly. During the Soviet era the Chechen budget was heavily dependent on subsidies from the federal center. Despite the development of the oil industry, the Checheno-Ingushetia ASSR received about 90 percent of its budget from allocations from Moscow.[105] As the post-Soviet economic crisis progressed in Russia and federal allocations decreased and eventually stopped in 1993, the situation in Chechnya worsened. Under Dudayev, between 1991 and 1993 Chechnya's gross national product declined by 68 percent, its gross domestic product declined by 65 percent, trade was down 68 percent, the production of manufactured goods declined by 58 percent, and the production of food was reduced by 52 percent.[106] Many factories in the republic stopped functioning. By 1993, reportedly 80 percent of the population lived below or near the poverty line.[107] By 1994, seventy-five percent of the workforce was unemployed, and 80–90 percent of industrial facilities ceased operation.[108] Pensions and social payments lagged behind schedule, and the infrastructure began to crumble.

As legal venues for income decreased, criminal ventures replaced many failed legitimate economic enterprises. The shadow economy flourished under Dudayev's leadership as Russian federal regulations no longer reached Grozny. Because it was not subject to taxation or federal customs control over exports and imports, Chechnya was transformed into a virtually free economic zone between 1991 and 1994. Chechnya became the center of financial fraud and a major producer of counterfeit currencies, with money laundering becoming one of the most lucrative businesses. In 1993 alone, 9.4 billion counterfeit rubles were circulating in Russia, 3.7 billion of which originated in Chechnya.[109] The Grozny airport was no longer monitored by federal authorities and as a result, numerous unauthorized flights from foreign countries came with contraband goods. Syphoning of Chechen oil also became a lucrative activity. Although legal oil production dropped more than 50 percent by 1992 when compared to 1980,[110] illegal oil deals boomed in the republic. Sales of stolen oil benefited many Chechen criminal groups, as well as Chechen leadership and Russian officials.[111]

Against this background, opposition to Dudayev's rule began to grow. The first coup attempt was in March 1992 and notably, many of those who emerged to oppose Dudayev were his former supporters. Among them was Yusup Soslambekov, who had previously acted as Dudayev's minister of defense, and Beslan Gantamirov, who served under Dudayev as mayor of Grozny. Yaragi Mamodaev was Dudayev's prime minister but turned against Dudayev's government and criticized it for the embezzlement of oil revenues. Other opposition leaders included Umar Avturkhanov, Salambek Khadzhiev, Ruslan Labazanov, and Moscow's Ruslan Khasbulatov, who later attempted to broker negotiations between Dudayev and his opposition. One of the key issues of disagreement between Dudayev and his opposition was cooperation with Russia. While some called for a complete blockade of Russia, other opposition leaders went so far as to form secret pacts with Moscow. For instance, in 1994 Duma deputy Ella Pamfilova estimated that besides weapons, Moscow had provided Dudayev's opposition with approximately150 billion rubles in assistance.[112]

By 1993 substantial disagreements had developed between Dudayev and his Parliament in reaction to Dudayev's efforts to strengthen his executive powers at the expense of parliamentary authority. To justify such efforts legally, in February 1993 Dudayev tried to hold a referendum on a new edition of the republic's constitution. The Parliament, however, blocked this initiative and pronounced Dudayev's efforts unconstitutional.[113] These confrontations led to rallies in Grozny where Dudayev's opposition called for his resignation. The power crisis culminated in April 1993, when Dudayev announced the beginning of direct presidential rule and the dissolution of Parliament. This move was condemned by Chechnya's constitutional court, which in turn was also dismissed. Dudayev's actions aroused much discontent among his opposition, who demanded that a referendum take place on June 5 to decide the fate of the republic. The referendum did not take place. Instead, Dudayev announced a state of emergency in Chechnya. Mass protests followed in Grozny, which eventually led to open clashes between opposition forces and Dudayev's supporters.

The situation continued to deteriorate and by the summer of 1994 opposition groups were organized under the auspices of Umar Avturkhanov's Temporary Council, which was originally convened in December 1993. Even though Dudayev restored parliamentary functions in August 1994, the Temporary Council proceeded with creating parallel governing bodies in the republic. The rise of the Temporary Council was also supported by Moscow as an alternative to Dudayev's regime because the latter refused to cooperate with the Kremlin. Initially cooperative with Moscow, when he came to power, as Dudayev consolidated his hold on Chechnya he defied Russian attempts to restore federal power in the republic. In 1992 Dudayev refused to sign the Federation Treaty with Russia, and in January 1993 he rejected a protocol produced through a series of negotiations between the Chechen and Russian delegations.

In the context of these actions, Russia began to prepare for more serious measures to pacify the restive republic. As it later did in preparation for the counterterrorist|operation of 1999, Russia first became preoccupied with updating its legislative arsenal. In November 1993 Yeltsin issued a document on the basic principles of the military doctrine of the Russian Federation. The document delineated the major threats to the Russian Federation, including internal dangers, pacification of which required the deployment of troops. Among such threats the document listed establishment of illegal armed formations, the rise of organized crime threatening the livelihood of people, as well as illegal arms and drug trafficking.[114] Thus, the document laid out the conditions that by then were widespread in Chechnya.

This way, the document created a legal instrument that allowed Russia to justify its future deployment of troops in the republic.

At the same time, at the beginning of 1994 the State Duma of the Russian Federation was still urging the president to attempt a political solution to the Chechen crisis to avoid a military confrontation. On March 25 it issued a decree calling for the government to engage in peaceful consultations between Moscow and the Chechen Republic. However, during the first half of 1994, crime levels in Chechnya increased even further, and the first wave of Chechen terrorism reached Russia. In May, June, and July, a wave of bus hijackings, all of which were committed using similar methods, were carried out by Chechen individuals. These hijackings, which are further discussed in the next chapter, equipped the Russian government with a formal reason to intervene in a Chechnya governed by Dudayev's criminal clique. Dudayev's opposition, on the other hand, was treated by Moscow as the means of restoring law and order in Chechnya.

As the clashes between Dudayev's supporters and his opposition intensified, Moscow initially decided to intervene in Chechnya covertly. With Moscow's support, Dudayev's opposition attempted to storm Grozny on November 26, 1994. The attempt, however, was put down by Dudayev's forces, and many captured soldiers and officers confessed that they had been clandestinely recruited by Russia's Federal Counterintelligence Service (a predecessor of the Federal Security Service, or FSB). It was only in December that Russia eventually admitted the involvement of its forces in the failed storming of Grozny.[115]

After the failed clandestine operation to depose Dudayev, the Kremlin made a decision to move onto Grozny with an open military operation to restore constitutional order. On November 29, 1994, Russia's Security Council decided in favor of a military intervention in Chechnya. On that same day President Yeltsin addressed the conflicting sides in Grozny and issued an ultimatum to lay down arms within 48 hours. In the case of noncompliance, Yeltsin threatened to declare another state of emergency. Legally, the declaration of a state of emergency would have allowed Yeltsin to lawfully engage in military action in the republic. However, Yeltsin's previous declaration of a state of emergency in 1991 had been widely criticized, and his decision had been annulled by the Supreme Soviet of the Russian Federation. Hence, the president was cautious about declaring another state of emergency, and as a result, the first Chechen war of 1994–1996 proceeded without it.

Instead, on November 30, 1994, President Yeltsin signed secret decree 2137 on measures to restore constitutional law and order on the territory of the Chechen Republic. The decree, although not made public until 1995, allowed for the use of military force without the declaration of a state of emergency. In public decree 2142 of December 1 on measures to support law and order in the North Caucasus, Yeltsin demanded that factions fighting in Grozny lay down arms by December 15. In the meantime, Russia's State Duma was critical of Yeltsin's position on the conflict and urged him to resolve the issue through political processes. The president, however, proceeded with adopting yet another decree, number 2166, on December 9. This decree allowed for all means necessary to be used against illegal armed formations operating in the territory of Chechnya. On December 11 Yeltsin replaced his previous decree 2137 with a new decree, number 2169. This law avoided any reference to a state of emergency but did sanction the deployment of federal troops for an unlimited period of time. Divisions of Russia's Ministry of Defense and the MVD crossed the border to Chechnya on New Year's Eve to begin the siege of Grozny that marked the beginning of the first Chechen war. The era of Chechnya's de facto independence was over.

2

Russia Confronts Terrorism

TERRORISM BEGINS

The very first terrorist attack staged by the Chechen rebels came in response to Russia's use of troops in Chechnya. In reaction to Yeltsin's imposition of a state of emergency on November 7, 1991, two days later a group of three Chechens carried out their first terrorist attack. The group hijacked a TU-154 plane with 178 passengers at the airport at Mineralnye Vody in the Stavropol region. Together with Said-Ali Satuyev and Lom-Ali Chachayev, Shamil Basayev demanded the plane be directed to Turkey, where upon landing the hijackers negotiated a press conference. The goal of the press conference was to inform the world via international media, uninhibited by Russian censorship, of the situation in Chechnya. Basayev explained that his action was provoked by President Yeltsin's decision to use military force in his homeland. After the meeting with journalists, the group arranged for safe passage back to Chechnya. All the hostages were released unharmed, but the first terrorist statement had been made.

While this terrorist attack received relatively little close attention, it remains a significant event in the history of North Caucasus terrorism for a number of reasons. First, the daring act helped Shamil Basayev emerge as a liberation hero in Grozny. Due to the success of the operation, Basayev gained much respect and credence among the governing circles in separatist Chechnya. From that point on, Basayev played an important role in the struggle for Chechen independence and staged numerous similarly spectacular terrorist acts and raids against Russia until his death in 2006. Second, the act of November 9, 1991, laid out a script for many future terrorist raids. Hostage-taking became a popular tactic used by Chechen separatists. Upon taking hostages the group would make their demands known and would negotiate safe passage. Hostages were generally released unharmed unless the Russian government resisted a safe escape for the hostage-takers. This dynamic changed significantly only during the second Chechen war when the Russian government stopped negotiating with terrorists at any level. After that terrorist raids such as the 2002 Moscow theater attack and the 2004 Beslan school attack resulted in hundreds of hostage deaths.

Third, the attack of November 9 was a peculiar event in terms of the history of aviation hijackings. Not only did the act involve the hijacking of a civilian aircraft, it also involved a professional pilot—Said-Ali Satuyev. Interestingly, the attack relied on the expertise of an aviation professional nearly 10 years prior to the events of September 11, 2001. Finally, Basayev's first terrorist act set the current campaign for independence in the North Caucasus apart from previous iterations. The terrorist attack was an immediate reaction to President Yeltsin's first attempt to resolve the Chechen issue militarily; it was an unconventional response to a conventional move on the part of the Russian government. Previous declarations of independence in the North Caucasus had been associated with conventional confrontations between Russia and insurgent armies. Military detachments of Imam Shamil had been engaged in regular positional warfare and at the turn of the twentieth century, North Caucasus military forces had been fighting conventional battles against both the White and Red Armies. Yeltsin's introduction of conventional troops, however, resulted in the immediate use of unconventional tactics by Chechen separatists—terrorism. Since then, the tactic of terrorism has become a permanent feature of the contemporary insurgency that has spread from Chechnya to the entire region of the North Caucasus.

While the act of November 9, 1991, signified the willingness of Chechen separatists to resort to terrorist tactics, other terrorist attacks of the early 1990s were less remarkable. Terrorist acts in the North Caucasus had started even before the declaration of Chechnya's independence. For instance, one of the very first airplane hijackings in Grozny took place in June 1990. A terrorist hijacked a TU-154 en route to Moscow. The plane was diverted to Turkey, where the terrorist was shot in a hostage rescue operation. Terrorist demands to escape to Turkey became quite popular. In another instance, on March 27, 1992, three criminals hijacked a bus with over 20 construction workers in the city of Lermontovo in Russia's Stavropol region. Threatening to blow up the bus, the hijackers requested a plane ready to fly to Turkey. In this case the Turkish authorities refused to receive the plane, and the hijacked bus instead proceeded toward Chechnya. The criminals surrendered to Dzhokhar Dudayev's representatives in Nazran, Ingushetia, and the hostages were released. On May 26, 1994, four armed Chechens hijacked a bus with over 30 people traveling in the vicinity of Mineralnye Vody. The majority of the hostages in this case were schoolchildren on a field trip. The hijackers demanded $10 million, drugs, weapons, and a helicopter.[1] Such criminal acts at the time were not unique to the North Caucasus region. According to official statistics, between 1990 and 1993 alone, Russian authorities experienced 160 acts of terrorism, which resulted in the deaths of 21 people.[2] As opposed to Basayev's act, however, such attacks had no political motivation and were driven by criminal, rather than ethno-nationalist, aspirations.

According to Moscow, terrorist attacks linked to Chechnya were a direct outcome of Dudayev's rule there. President Yeltsin blamed Dudayev for allowing lawlessness to emerge:

> Violence and banditry have become the order of the day and arbitrariness the main principle in life... Just imagine that more than a thousand criminals wanted on the federal level have found refuge in the Chechen Republic. The regime established in the republic has become a major source of crime, especially in Russia... The main conclusion is that the situation in the Chechen Republic was exerting an increasingly destructive influence on stability in Russia. It became one of the main internal threats to the security of our [Russian] state.[3]

Yeltsin portrayed Chechnya as a breeding ground for violent criminals, and in the eyes of Moscow the lawlessness of Dudayev's regime required federal intervention to restore constitutional order in the republic. The wave of terrorist attacks of the early 1990s became the catalyst for Russia's military intervention in Chechnya.

SHAMIL BASAYEV

In Russia the name of Shamil Basayev, who was also known as Abdallah Shamil Abu Idris, became synonymous with terrorism. Basayev was the mastermind behind the first terrorist operation carried out by Chechen separatists in November 1991, and he was the figure responsible for the most spectacular terrorist attacks associated with the Chechen campaign, including the act of radiological terrorism, the Budennovsk raid, and the Beslan school attack. Basayev also claimed responsibility for many terrorist attacks, including the Dubrovka theater attack, the assassination of Akhmad Kadyrov, bombings that included Kryl'ia and the National Hotel, and many airplane and metro attacks. In separatist Chechnya, Basayev was treated as a national liberation hero. In Russia, Basayev became notorious as a "terrorist number one."

Similar to many prominent terrorists, Basayev's biography does not strike one as extraordinary. He was born in 1965 in a village in the Chechen

Vedeno region, finished high school in 1982, and tried to apply to study at the law department of Moscow State University. Basayev's ambition was to "become a detective and catch criminals since [his] father was a real communist and taught [him] the same."[4] However, as he claimed, the bribe of $5,000 required to enter the university prevented him from becoming a lawyer. Instead, Basayev settled on attending the Moscow State University of Land Use Planning. According to some accounts, Basayev finished the university, while others claim he was expelled due to poor academic performance.

Surprisingly for many, Basayev started his political career on Boris Yeltsin's side. While in Moscow, Basayev defended the White House along with Yeltsin during the August putsch of 1991. He justified his decision to resist the attempted Communist coup d'état by explaining that if Communists had prevailed, "you [could] kiss Chechnya's independence goodbye."[5] A few months later Basayev competed with General Dzhokhar Dudayev in the Chechen presidential elections of October 1991. Following Dudayev's victory, Basayev formed a military unit to support Dudayev's struggle for independence. Shortly thereafter Basayev demonstrated his will to use violence for the goal of independence through the staging of his first terrorist attack on November 9, 1991.

Basayev's military training began during his military service in the Soviet Air Force. His practical experience came primarily from his participation in the independence campaigns in Nagorno-Karabakh and Abkhazia between 1991 and 1993. In Nagorno-Karabakh, Basayev fought on the side of Azerbaijan for the purpose of "jihad in order to help in the name of God."[6] When war broke out in Georgia, Basayev headed the detachments of the Confederation of the Peoples of the Caucasus to support separatist Abkhazia. There, according to some accounts, Basayev's Abkhaz battalion received training from Russian special services.[7] Basayev himself claimed his knowledge of military strategy was a product of his own studies based on Russian textbooks. Basayev explained: "I started studying because I had a goal. We were about 30 guys who understood that Russia would not let Chechnya go easily. Freedom is an expensive thing and you have to pay for it with blood. That's why we thoroughly prepared."[8] While Basayev was contradictory about his connections to mujahedeen training camps in Pakistan and Afghanistan, in one account, he claimed he received additional military training in the Khost province of Afghanistan in 1994. "I sold some weapons and borrowed some money and we went [to Afghanistan]," he explained.[9]

Under Dudayev, Basayev emerged as one of the most prominent leaders of the Chechen resistance. After Dudayev's death Basayev once again ran for the presidency, this time competing against Aslan Maskhadov. In January 1997 Basayev came in second to Maskhadov with 23.5 percent of the vote.[10] Maskhadov appointed Basayev his prime minister, but Basayev soon resigned to join Maskhadov's opposition. Basayev publicly acknowledged a rift between himself and the elected president of Ichkeriia. Basayev once again accepted a political post in 2006 when he served as vice president of Ichkeriia under the presidency of Doku Umarov.

Shamil Basayev's biography is closely linked to that of Ibn al-Khattab, an Arab mujahed fighting in Chechnya. While many accounts tell of Basayev becoming a Wahhabi adherent under Khattab's influence, the alliance between the two seems less straightforward. Basayev was a Sufi of the Qadiriyya order and often spoke against the spread of Wahhabism in Chechnya. For instance, after the first Chechen war Basayev acknowledged he had Wahhabi friends but was himself not a Wahhabi. Speaking at a conference, Basayev encouraged his followers to revive Sufism in the Republic of Ichkeriia along the lines of Imam Shamil's path. In fact, Basayev reminded his audience that his ancestors fought for the imam's cause and referred to himself as the Imam's murid.[11] Basayev was proud to share the same name with the famous imam and declared that it was his goal to bring back to life the imam's Imamate. In one of his last interviews, Basayev stated:

> The Russian serfs, like many Russian soldiers, escaped to Imam Shamil from Russian slavery. Little has changed since then. The Islamic state of Imam Shamil was a just state in which everyone had a sense of their own dignity. If alongside Russia were to appear a country where justice and the dignity of the people were fundamental to it, Russia in its present form would not last long and its criminal rulers would be severely punished.[12]

At the same time the opportunistic alliance with Khattab to secure funding for the independence struggle did influence Basayev's religious rhetoric. By 1998 Basayev proclaimed it was an obligation of every Muslim to defend sharia. He cited this principle as his justification for preparing to go to Dagestan to protect Wahhabi communities there.[13] As the Dagestani operation began in August 1999, Basayev expressed a willingness to wage "holy war even if the world is engulfed in blue flames" in order to liberate Muslims "from the Volga to the Don."[14] Basayev's rhetoric evolved from the explicit goal of Chechen independence to aspiring to create a common state that would encompass territory from the Black Sea to the Caspian.

Another contentious issue in Basayev's biography is his connection to Al Qaeda. While Russian sources widely claimed links between Basayev and Osama bin Laden, Basayev himself refuted any association. As he stated sarcastically, "I have always said that I am not acquainted with Bin Laden and have had no contact with him, although I would very much like to meet him. Anyway, Putin has already 'appointed' him as my commander."[15]

Basayev's inspiration came from many sources, including the Russian media. He skillfully adjusted his rhetoric to reflect Russian accounts of him waging jihad against Russia. Along with Imam Shamil, Basayev admired other revolutionary strategists; a poster of Che Guevara hung in his dorm room. Thinking of himself as a revolutionary, Basayev wrote his own Book of Mujahiddeen in 2004. Motivated by Paolo Coelho, Basayev wrote his advice to the warriors of Allah, citing the Quran and the Sunna extensively.

In 2000 Basayev lost his leg in a minefield while his forces were withdrawing from Grozny. After that his media appearances became less frequent, and he relied more on the Internet, namely the Kavkaz Center website, to disseminate his messages. The Russian FSB opened a criminal case against Basayev after his staging of the Budennovsk attack in 1995, and his name was placed on Interpol's international wanted list. The U.S. Department of State listed Basayev as a terrorist in February 2003.[16] Shamil Basayev died in an explosion on July 10, 2006. The FSB services claim the explosion was a result of a special operation, while Chechen separatists insist the explosion was an accident.

STRATEGIC ADAPTATIONS OF CHECHEN FIGHTERS DURING THE FIRST CHECHEN CAMPAIGN

When he began the operation to restore constitutional order in Chechnya in December 1994, President Yeltsin was counting on a short victorious campaign. Despite the president's expectations, however, the operation turned into a protracted conflict. Even though they used overwhelming force, federal troops failed to secure an easy victory. In response to Russia's heavy-handed methods, Chechen separatists adapted their campaign. Failing at positional warfare, the Chechen side switched to irregular tactics and announced the start of a subversive action campaign in Russia. By taking the war to Russian territory, Chechen separatists managed to change the course of the war and eventually forced Russia into negotiations. The year 1995 marked the time terrorism became a consciously used tool in the arsenal of Chechen fighters.

Russia's overt involvement in Chechnya under the banner of the restoration of constitutional order began on December 11, 1994. On that day troops of the Ministry of Defense and the MVD were deployed to the republic. According to the Kremlin's calculations, the swift victorious operation needed to be over by December 19. Moscow calculated that taking control of Grozny would effectively restore its rule in Chechnya. To that end, the Russian government had already planned the restoration of federal power in Grozny. On December 17 Yeltsin signed his Decree 2200, restoring federal authorities in the Chechen Republic. By that date, however, Russian troops had failed to even reach Grozny. The troops traveling to Chechnya were halted by protesting civilians blocking their way in Dagestan and Ingushetia. The storming of Grozny began only on New Year's Eve of 1995. In the course of the storming attempt, the Russian military suffered a humiliating defeat: the 131 Maikop brigade and the 81 Samara regiment were almost entirely massacred in unfamiliar to them urban combat.[17]

Despite the initial failures, Russian forces soon managed to regain the initiative. By March 1995 federal troops secured complete control over Grozny. On March 23 Yeltsin signed his Decree 309, restoring constitutional government authorities in the separatist republic. After ousting Dudayev from Grozny, a parallel Moscow-backed provisional government was formed, primarily from members of Dudayev's opposition, and it started to function in the Chechen capital. Dudayev's forces retreated and were mainly scattered across southern Chechnya. By the end of April, Russian forces controlled the majority of lowland Chechnya and were successfully advancing in several mountainous regions. In May 1995 Defense Minister Pavel Grachev initiated a surge to eliminate the remnants of the illegal armed formations.[18] Following an indiscriminate bombing campaign on June 3, Vedeno fell under federal control. By June, Chechnya was almost entirely under Russian control, with the exception of the hard to access mountainous areas in the south of the republic. Chechen separatists were forced out of their bases and seemed to be on the verge of losing their independence campaign.

Under such circumstances negotiation initiatives advanced by the separatists did not lead to a political solution. Russia's choice of the military approach and use of overwhelming military force left little option for separatist forces to rely on conventional tactics. Facing certain defeat in Chechnya if they continued using conventional tactics, the Chechen separatists initiated strategic adaptations to their campaign. The separatist command decided to relocate the fighting onto Russia's own territory. This move signified the beginning of the terrorist campaign against Russian targets, which should not have been altogether unexpected. Dzhokhar Dudayev was known for calling for terrorist acts against Russia as early as 1991. By January 1995 he expressed a readiness to carry out raids against Moscow.[19] In June 1995, only three days before the terrorist raid on Budennovsk, Dudayev stated: "We do not need war. The spread of war to the territory of Russia is not only terrorism, but is also a corollary that is not dependent on me."[20] The Budennovsk attack of June 14, 1995, marked a different phase in the Chechen campaign—the beginning of strategically planned terrorist attacks against Russian cities.

The concerted shift in tactics was announced in May 1995 when Shamil Basayev proclaimed the start of a subversive action campaign. According to Basayev, irregular tactics were the only means available to the Chechen fighters to withstand the military superiority of Russia. As Basayev explained, "we rely on subversive activities aimed to eliminate them [federal troops] and impede their movement." The purpose behind this campaign, Basayev expanded, was to force the "Russian leadership [to] sit down at the negotiating table."[21] To mark the shift, Basayev started referring to his force as the Intelligence and Sabotage Battalion.

To train Chechen separatists in unconventional insurgent tactics, the Chechen leadership primarily relied on the veterans of the Soviet-Afghan war. After the end of the Soviet-Afghan war in 1989, many Afghan mujahedeen who had fought against the Soviet invasion in Afghanistan joined other liberation struggles that were springing up in the 1990s. Tajikistan, Algeria, Yemen, and Bosnia were only a few of the places where the mujahedeen went to continue their struggle of liberation against oppressors of Muslims. During the decade-long struggle against the superior Soviet military, they had become experts in guerilla warfare, subversive tactics, and terrorism, and they were ready to offer their knowledge and skills to Muslims worldwide. In the Caucasus the mujahedeen first arrived as the conflict broke out in Nagorno-Karabakh. It was there that Afghan mujahedeen came in contact with some of the Chechen fighters.

The first Afghan mujahedeen arrived in Chechnya in the early 1990s. One of the first people with mujahedeen links to arrive in Chechnya was Sheikh Fathi, a Jordanian of Chechen descent.[22] Fathi was instrumental not only in recruiting foreign mercenaries but also in securing foreign money for the Chechen struggle. Sheikh Fathi was one of the first Wahhabi adherents to appear in the North Caucasus, and it was Fathi who introduced Afghan-style jihad to Chechnya. With the help of other mujahedeen, Sheikh Fathi formed his Islamic Battalion, also known as Jamaat, placing it under the leadership of another Afghan Arab mujahed—Khattab. Khattab himself appeared in Chechnya in the midst of the Russian attack on Grozny of January 1995 with a group of fighters who formed the core of the Jamaat.[23] With the arrival of Fathi and Khattab, the Chechen struggle acquired new symbols that later came to be associated with it—the Afghan Arab notions of mujahedeen, jihad, jamaat.

To train Chechen separatists in unconventional tactics, Basayev, together with Khattab, established training schools. Khattab's training camp, Kavkaz, started in 1995 in Serzhen-Yurt. Styled along the lines of Pakistani and Afghan training centers and madrasas, such training camps provided both military training and religious education. And while the role of ideological and religious education did not play a significant role in the first Chechen conflict, the influence of Afghan mujahedeen shaped the future evolution of the insurgent movement.

May 1995 became the turning point in the Chechen fight for independence. When Basayev staged his first terrorist act in November 1991, it was a single act in protest of Yeltsin's declaration of a state of emergency. This time, though, Basayev's declaration indicated an entire shift from positional to guerilla warfare. From this moment on the Chechen side was ready to use terrorism to counter Russia's decisive military superiority. By the end of May 1995, Chechen forces formed suicide brigades ready to deploy, even though suicide terrorism was not used in the first war. This was the only way for the Chechen armed forces, much smaller and less well equipped than their Russian opponents, to shift the balance toward a political solution. The Budennovsk attack of June 1995 ushered in a new era for Chechen separatists.

BUDENNOVSK

Shamil Basayev implemented his idea of taking the war to Russia on June 14, 1995.[24] On that day he led a group of some 200 camouflaged Chechen fighters to the town of Budennovsk in Russia's Stavropol region. Five days of panic, chaos, and horror followed. The group raided the town, firing machine guns and launching grenades. A spectacular massacre of police officers was staged at the local police headquarters. Elsewhere in town, the group rampaged through the streets, killing people and taking hostages. The group ended up at a local hospital along with around 2,000 people as hostages. In the course of the following five days, the raid left over 100 people dead and more than 400 injured. At the time the raid on Budennovsk became one of the worst terrorist attacks in the world in regards to its scope and consequences.

"It grieves me that things turned out like this. I don't know how to apologize to the population of Budennovsk, but especially I don't regret my actions," said Shamil Basayev from the hospital where he held the hostages for five days.[25] By the time of Budennovsk, Basayev had many reasons for the raid, including personal ones. Some accounts suggest that a number of Basayev's relatives were killed in the federal bombardments of Vedeno on June 3, 1995.[26] That month Russia engaged in numerous indiscriminate raids on the Chechen territory that resulted in hundreds of civilian deaths.[27] As Basayev explained, Chechen separatists got tired of watching peaceful civilians being killed in Chechnya by the Russian forces: "We target the military, and they fire at our villages," he said.[28] According to Basayev, it was time for the Russian side to experience the same.

While planning the operation, Budennovsk was not the end goal for Basayev. Rather, he was planning an attack against Russia's own capital—Moscow.[29] According to Basayev's calculations, such an attack would have given Russian citizens the taste of what was happening in Chechnya. However, Basayev's group never reached Moscow, settling instead for carrying out the terrorist attack in the city of Budennovsk. One explanation for why the separatists had to target Budennovsk was the issue of money. The Chechen group was traveling on trucks that were routinely stopped at checkpoints along the way. To cross these checkpoints Basayev had to pay bribes in the amount of 5,000 rubles for every Chechen fighter.[30] Once the group ran out of money, they could not travel as far as Moscow and had to pick the closest city—Budennovsk. According to this explanation, Budennovsk became the target of Basayev's group due to the greed of checkpoint officers.

An alternative explanation for the choice of Budennovsk as a target also had to do with road checkpoints. According to this explanation, Basayev's group told officers at checkpoints that the trucks were carrying bodies of Russian troops killed in combat in Chechnya, or Cargo 200.[31] The group was able to travel as far as Budennovsk, but once Basayev reached the city the guards at the traffic police checkpoint there wanted to inspect the cargo. As the former police head in Budennovsk Nikolai Liashenko recalled, he was the one to order the suspicious procession to stop and be inspected:

> I was informed of the procession of a suspicious convoy. I was informed that three military trucks are moving with a police "shesterka."[32] By the looks of it all seemed normal—people were in uniform. But think of it: in the 40-degree summer heat they are transporting Cargo 200 on several KAMAZ trucks and not planes. It seemed strange at the very least. They tried to check them on the spot—outside of the city at the checkpoint. They did not cooperate, started yelling. They said we fought, and are transporting our dead friends, and you are going to search us! So I, according to the protocol, ordered to escort them to the police headquarters for further investigation. That's how it all started...[33]

The trucks with Chechen fighters proceeded into the city. There the armed group amassed around 2,000 hostages and barricaded themselves with explosives in a local hospital.

Receiving news of the attack, Moscow immediately dispatched its main special forces, including the Alpha group, to Budennovsk. Shamil Basayev demanded to meet with journalists and threatened to kill hostages if his demands were not met. To demonstrate the seriousness of his intentions, Basayev executed five people on the spot—three pilots and two police officers. Under pressure, authorities agreed to convene a press conference, where Basayev laid out his demands: "the main aim of our operation is to end the war in Chechnya, the withdrawal of Russian troops and resolution of all questions through talks."[34] Budennovsk became the first among many terrorist attacks—including Kizlyar and Pervomaiskoe, Dubrovka, and Beslan—that tried to force federal troops out of Chechnya through terrorism.

In response to Basayev's demands, Prime Minister Chernomyrdin conceded to the terms of the hostage-takers on June 16: "The Russian government guarantees an immediate ceasefire in Chechnya. A government delegation flew out to Grozny to negotiate with the Chechen Prosecutor General Isman [Imaev], as was demanded by Basayev. After release, Basayev and his people will be guaranteed transportation and a convoy to ensure the safety of the fighters."[35] At the same time, however, the Kremlin was planning a rescue operation. The decision to storm the hospital building was discussed with Minister of Internal Affairs Viktor Yerin before President Yeltsin left for a meeting with world leaders in Halifax, Nova Scotia. The crisis in Budennovsk did not prevent the Russian president from traveling to Halifax, where he informed global audiences of people with green headbands taking hostages in a hospital in Budennovsk.[36] Before he left, Yeltsin explained that the storming of the hospital was planned to begin one or two days after the capture of the hostages so that there would be enough time to "get ready and not do anything that could cause harm."[37]

Along with preparing for storming the hospital, the Russian government tried to sway Basayev by other means. To prevent Basayev from executing any more hostages, the local authorities, with Moscow's approval, started rounding up local ethnic Chechens, threatening to execute them in return. In the course of the crisis, Cossacks and special police forces proceeded to harass and interrogate the Chechen population of Budennovsk. Following the raid the majority of ethnic Chechens were forced to leave the area.[38]

Despite Chernomyrdin's promise, the storming of the hospital started on June 17. Contrary to the president's expectations, it did result in many hostage fatalities; the planning and execution of the storming was a failure. As the leader of the Alpha group later pointed out, "The storm was a failure from the very beginning... Too little time was given to prepare the storm."[39] Another participant of the storming attributed its failure to the lack of adequate support: "We asked for equipment... We were given some equipment but in the course of the storm it turned out it was from the Afghanistan era and was almost nonfunctional."[40] Survivors of the hostage crisis were also critical. As one former hostage recalled, it was only the thick walls of the hospital that prevented everyone there from being killed by Russian forces.[41] Some former hostages pointed out that even Chechen hostage-takers made more effort to protect them from the Russian fire than their own government did.[42]

After realizing the futility of the storming operation, the Russian government finally conceded to negotiations with Basayev. As Yeltsin was still in Nova Scotia, Prime Minister Viktor Chernomyrdin represented the Russian government in the negotiations. By June 18 a direct telephone line was established between the prime minister and Shamil Basayev. As soon as the negotiations started, Basayev initiated several waves of hostage releases. Among the first to leave the hospital building were the patients of the maternity ward with their newborn babies. Basayev went even further and agreed to let Anatoly Kashpirovsky—a widely popular Russian psychic— into the building. This was done in response to pleas from female hostages who were asking to see the famous healer.

The negotiation process itself was public; it was closely followed by the media and was widely broadcast by TV channels. To secure the release of the hostages, Basayev requested an immediate cease-fire in Chechnya and the start of peace talks. Basayev and Chernomyrdin also discussed safe passage for Basayev's group back to Chechnya. Basayev demanded that a group of hostages be allowed to proceed with him. Basayev warned Chernomyrdin: "I will not go anywhere unless journalists and deputies who want to come with us will be allowed to do so."[43] In response, Chernomyrdin appeared on TV agreeing to Basayev's terms: "Hello Shamil Basayev! Yes, I agree. Yes, we are terminating the war in Chechnya and you are releasing the hostages. We are providing transportation, and you are leaving."[44] The worst of the crisis was over. The agreement between the sides met all of Basayev's demands. The Russian government agreed to an immediate cease-fire by the Russian forces, the start of negotiations, and the provision of transportation for the Chechen group to travel back to Chechnya.

As agreed, on June 19 six buses with Basayev's group accompanied by over 100 remaining hostages drove off in the direction of Chechnya. The group of hostages was comprised of volunteers and included government officials, journalists, medical workers, and previously freed hostages. On the way, however, the procession was stopped at the North Ossetian border. General Anatolii Kulikov ordered the border closed so that the buses could not get through. As Yulii Rybakov, one of the volunteer hostages, a human rights activist, and a State Duma deputy recalled, hostages traveling with Basayev had a suspicion that the government was trying to eliminate the buses with terrorists and everyone else in them along the way.[45] Indeed, the existence of such a plan was confirmed 10 years after Budennovsk by Viktor Chernomyrdin himself. As Chernomyrdin revealed, Russian security services were planning an operation to eliminate Basayev on the way from Budennovsk to Chechnya. "No one was planning to just let them go," Chernomyrdin explained.[46] Basayev, however, was able to prevent the operation by turning the buses around and reaching Chechnya through neighboring Dagestan. The Budennovsk raid finally ended in a Chechen village of Zandak in the Vedeno region, when the remaining hostages were released.

THE AFTERMATH OF BUDENNOVSK

Basayev came back from Budennovsk victorious. His daring raid demonstrated that the Chechen side possessed the means of countering Russia's military superiority. It not only challenged Russia's military achievements in Chechnya but also forced the superior opponent to sit down at the negotiating table. Through demanding a press conference, Basayev made the war in Chechnya visible to wider audiences. Starting with Budennovsk, Chechen separatists' green headbands emblazoned with inscriptions from the Quran became recognized both in Russia and in the West. Budennovsk became a significant success for the Chechen side and was a turning point in the Chechen campaign.

The Budennovsk raid was one of the few terrorist acts committed by the Chechen side that demonstrated Basayev's focus on subversive action. After announcing a shift toward unconventional tactics in May 1995, Basayev was initially careful in distinguishing between subversive action and terrorism, claiming he would engage only in the former. This was seen during the Budennovsk crisis, where Basayev was resolved not to harm women and children. Despite taking them hostage, Basayev did not execute women and children, only men working for the Russian government. In this respect, Basayev treated his victims as opponents in war: "I did not shoot hostages, but firstly prisoners who put up opposition, secondly military pilots, with whom we basically have a special relationship, and thirdly people sent here after we had fortified our position, that is, special services personnel."[47] At these early stages of Chechen terrorism, such distinctions were important. In later terrorist attacks, especially with the advent of suicide terrorism, Russian women and children would become regular targets.

The Budennovsk raid showed the Russian side's complete unpreparedness to face unconventional attacks by the Chechen separatists on its own territory. It was a great shock for President Yeltsin and his supporters, who had expected a swift victory in Chechnya. As Yeltsin explained:

> The appearance of the terrorists in Budyonnovsk became a total surprise for everyone, including intelligence officers, the Federal Security Service, and so on. As a matter of fact, the decisions of the Security Council of January 6, 1995, prescribing the security service, the Ministry of the Interior and the office of the Prosecutor General to take measures to expose attempts of shifting military operations and acts of subversion and terror beyond the boundaries of Chechnya, have not been fulfilled.[48]

The raid also exposed Russia's utter lack of preparedness to deal with terrorist attacks in general. In fact, at that time Russia did not even possess appropriate legislation to counter the terrorist threat. The subsequent failure to deal with the attack caused resignations throughout Russia's governing circles. Among those who resigned were Minister of Internal Affairs Viktor Yerin, FSB head Sergei Stepashin, Minister of Nationalities Nikolai Yegorov, and the governor of the Stavropol region, Yevgeny Kuznetsov.

Further, the attack on Budennovsk demonstrated the dismal state of Russia's military and security services. The operation revealed that chaos predominated among Russian security agencies and that their decision-making processes were inadequate. The storming of the hospital building was highly unsuccessful and exposed many problems that existed in Russia's bureaucratic and military structures. It demonstrated a lack of cohesion and shortfalls in training among military and security personnel. The Kremlin failed to provide adequate support to those on the ground. As a result, the storming led to an unprecedented number of victims, among both hostages and military personnel. In Budennovsk, Russia's special force Alpha suffered the worst casualties in the history of the group.[49] These failures prompted the president to reorganize the Russian federal security services. On June 23, 1995, Yeltsin issued Decree 633 in which he ordered a reorganization of the FSB, formerly known as the Federal Counterintelligence Service. The law also updated Russia's counterterrorist services, establishing, under FSB auspices, the Department on the Fight against Terrorism.

In Budennovsk, Russia also lost the media campaign to the Chechen side. The televised course of the hospital storming and the subsequent negotiations process greatly affected Russian public opinion. The anger of the Russian people in response to the atrocities in Budennovsk was turned toward the Russian government, not the Chechen hostage-takers. According to polls, more people blamed the Russian government for the events in Budennovsk than the Chechen separatists: 49 percent considered Moscow responsible for the attack; only 32 percent blamed Chechnya's General Dudayev.[50] Russia's power ministries, including the Ministry of Defense and the Ministry of Security, were criticized for allowing trucks full of Chechen fighters to even reach Budennovsk. The botched attempts to storm the hospital turned many Russians against their government for causing so many casualties.

Following Budennovsk, President Yeltsin's popularity plummeted. Viktor Chernomyrdin, on the other hand, emerged with more favorable ratings due to his actions as peace broker. In September 1995 only 13 percent of Russians trusted the Russian president; Chernomyrdin enjoyed a slightly greater level of trust at 27 percent.[51] Discontent over the war in Chechnya continued to grow after Budennovsk. The Russian population was growing increasingly weary of Yeltsin's actions in Chechnya, and more people demanded a change in the handling of the Chechen issue. A majority of Russians were against military action in Chechnya at the very outset of the first campaign.[52] After Budennovsk over 70 percent of Russians considered peaceful negotiations with Dudayev to be the appropriate solution to the Chechen crisis. Only 12 percent favored continued military action.[53] Even Russia's own State Duma issued Decree 893-I in which it described the terrorist attack on Budennovsk as an outcome of ineffective actions on the part of Russian federal forces. As a result, the Duma encouraged the government to switch to negotiations. Negotiations became the biggest achievement of Basayev's Budennovsk raid.

NEGOTIATIONS

The attack on Budennovsk was a highly successful operation for the Chechen separatists. The terrorist act strategically reversed the situation in Chechnya. The Kremlin was forced to the negotiating table; after Budennovsk, President Yeltsin for the first time expressed his readiness to resolve the Chechen crisis through political means. The first round of negotiations between the Russian and Chechen delegations, which were followed by many more, began in Grozny on June 19, 1995. The negotiations, aimed at resolving the crisis in Chechnya, took place under the auspices of the Organization for Security and Co-operation in Europe (OSCE).

The negotiations revealed many existing problems between the sides and focused exclusively on transitioning to the peace process while leaving the very cause of the Chechen problem—its independence—unaddressed. On July 5 Moscow made it clear that discussions of the change of status of the republic would be unconstitutional and refused to tackle this key issue. As Dzhokhar Dudayev described it, "our delegation does not have the power to lay down the nature of links with Russia and the Russian delegation does not have the power to recognise Chechenia's independence."[54] Dudayev did not place much hope on the negotiation process in general. Moscow attempted to use the political space to convince Dudayev to resign and replace his government with a new pro-Moscow administration.

One accomplishment of the post-Budennovsk peace process was the questioning of the very legitimacy of Russia's military action in Chechnya. As the Russian public increasingly demanded to end the war in Chechnya, the Russian government initiated investigations into the decision to send troops to the republic. The Constitutional Court of the Russian Federation embarked on the review of presidential decisions that precipitated the military action. Yeltsin's secret Decree 2137 of November 30, 1994, on the restoration of constitutional order in Chechnya and Decree 2166 of December 9, 1994, on the measures to counter illegal armed formations came under close scrutiny. While the constitutionality of Yeltsin's actions was upheld on July 31, 1995, the very act of questioning the presidential resolve to engage in a military campaign was unprecedented. This became one of the few cases in the history of Russian democracy when the lack of confidence in its president led to official investigations of the decision-making process.

The main concrete achievement of the post-Budennovsk negotiations was the military agreement signed between the Russian and Chechen sides on July 30, 1995. The agreement outlined several important steps. First, the agreement announced an immediate cease-fire. Second, the agreement discussed the disarmament process and a schedule for federal troop withdrawals from Chechnya. Finally, the agreement assumed the termination of terrorist and subversive activities. Commenting on the agreement, Vyacheslav Mikhailov, who became the new minister of nationalities, confirmed that "all the participants of the negotiations came to the conclusion that there is no other way to stop the bloodshed." General Kulikov agreed with his colleague: "We, the military, understand better than anyone else the futility of continuing military action in the republic."[55] While the status of Chechnya was not part of the negotiations, the sides agreed to decide the future of the republic after conducting free and fair elections there. The elections were supposed to take place after the withdrawal of Russian troops.

The post-Budennovsk achievements did not have a long-lasting effect. By the fall of 1995 the negotiation process was effectively derailed. In October 1995 an assassination attempt was carried out against General Romanov. Following the attack Russia suspended its implementation of the military agreement, and military action resumed. Despite previously agreeing to hold elections after the withdrawal of forces was complete, Moscow proceeded with measures to restore its oversight over Grozny. Doku Zavgayev was reintroduced into Chechen politics. The Kremlin tried to revive the Chechen Supreme Soviet of the revolutionary era of the 1990s and appointed Zavgayev as its leader. In November the Supreme Soviet appointed Zavgayev as head of the Chechen Republic—a newly created government position. Elections for the new head of the Chechen Republic were scheduled for December 1995.

Reaction from the separatists was immediate. Doku Zavgayev was highly unpopular in Chechnya and was seen in the region as Moscow's political puppet. An assassination attempt against him using a remotely detonated bomb in Grozny followed on November 20, 1995. As Shamil Basayev's brother, field commander Shirvani Basayev, explained, the terrorist act against Zavgayev represented a subversive action to prevent the Moscow-orchestrated elections. He considered the possibility of holding elections unrealistic, as such elections could not be free or fair: "We will not allow any elections. Today around 150,000 Russian soldiers are deployed on the territory of Chechnya. According to your [Russian] laws, they can take part in elections, and their number is enough to pronounce the elections as legitimate."[56] Shamil Basayev agreed with his brother in that while Russian troops were on the ground, it was impossible to ensure fair voting. "We don't need elections now. When Russia leaves we will hold the elections ourselves," Shamil Basayev explained.[57]

Shamil Basayev was also critical of Russia's renewed military action. He warned of more subversive acts if Russia continued its military involvement in Chechnya:

> I have said unambiguously and I repeat once again: we do not intend to fight longer on our own territory. It's enough. After all, only the mountains remain untouched here. I have radioactive material. This is a good weapon. I will spray it anywhere in the centre of Moscow and to the glory of God I will turn that city into an eternal desert. That can be done. With this, everything we have experienced, everything they have done here, can be revenged. If the Russians lengthen this war, we will have to resort to what I have been speaking of.[58]

Just as with his previous warnings, Basayev was not bluffing. This time, an experience with radiological terrorism was in store for the Kremlin.

RADIOLOGICAL TERRORISM

Basayev's act of radiological terrorism became seminal in the history of weapons of mass destruction (WMD) terrorism. Following the end of the Cold War, WMD terrorism has emerged as one of the most dangerous security concerns facing the world. Counterterrorism experts have been preoccupied with the possibility of terrorists acquiring nuclear, biological, and/or chemical weapons and striking with them. Scenarios of WMD attacks have envisioned consequences much more devastating than those of a conventional terrorist attack. As a result, many security professionals have been engaged in efforts to protect WMD facilities from being accessed by terrorists. For instance, Russia and the United States have embarked on joint programs to secure vulnerable nuclear facilities in the former Soviet Union. The Nunn-Lugar Cooperative Threat Reduction program represented mutual security efforts to ensure WMD safety in Russia.

While the danger of WMD terrorism has preoccupied many security specialists, the threat itself has not materialized to the extent predicted. To date, there have been no registered nuclear terrorist attacks. According to the Global Terrorism Database (GTD), which records terrorist incidents around the world, the largest share of WMD attacks comes from chemical weapons—220 incidents across the world. The number of biological weapons attacks amounts to 32, while the number of radiological weapons terrorist acts is much smaller at 13.[59] Compared to conventional terrorist attacks, very few WMD terrorist attacks have been committed to date.

Moreover, even in the world of terrorism, very few terrorist groups have made explicit threats to commit WMD terrorism. Few groups have actively sought to acquire a WMD capability; Aum Shinrikyo, Lashkar-e-Taiba, and Al Qaeda and its cooperatives have made threats. Even so, very few actual terrorist acts have occurred with the use of WMD agents. One such attack was Aum Shinrikyo's 1995 attack on the Tokyo metro. This religious group used sarin gas to orchestrate a chemical terrorist attack. This attack reportedly provoked much interest from other groups. For instance, Al Qaeda carefully examined the Aum Shinrikyo attack and initiated its own WMD program. Thus, in 1999 Al Qaeda's Ayman Zawahiri started his own *al-Zabadi* ("yogurt") program dealing with chemical and biological weapons.[60]

In this respect, Al Qaeda remains one of the few terrorist groups that has persistently pursued the development of weapons of mass destruction. According to *The 9/11 Commission Report*, Al Qaeda had been preoccupied with acquiring nuclear weapons capability for at least 10 years before its attacks on the United States.[61] In his 1998 Nuclear Bomb of Islam statement, Osama bin Laden referred to the acquisition of weapons of mass destruction as a religious duty. He declared it "the duty of Muslims to prepare as much force as possible to terrorize the enemies of God."[62] In 2003 Al Qaeda–affiliated Saudi cleric Nasir al-Fahd issued a religious ruling on the use of WMD. Al-Fahd justified the use of weapons of mass destruction as a means of defending the Islamic community.[63] However, despite such declared intentions to use WMDs and elaborate justifications for the declarations, Al Qaeda's actual involvement with WMD terrorism has been rather limited.

Here is where Shamil Basayev broke new ground in terrorist tactics. While Basayev's attack is not recorded in the GTD database, it remains one of the few known terrorist attacks involving a radioactive substance. His act became one of the first radiological terrorist attacks in the world and thus paved the way for imitation by other terrorist organizations. In the world of terrorist organizations, Basayev's attack on Moscow provided an example of the successful use of radiological agents for terrorist purposes.

Similar to his previous attacks, Basayev's act of radiological terrorism was a statement against Russia's military involvement in Chechnya. As the post-Budennovsk negotiations broke down and military action in Chechnya resumed, Basayev grew weary of the ongoing war. At the time even Aslan Maskhadov, who was committed to the peace process, became ready to set diplomacy aside and use "actions and measures that would be more effective under the circumstances."[64]

On November 21, 1995, Shamil Basayev contacted Elena Masiuk, a correspondent working for Russian television network NTV in Chechnya. He informed the reporter that he had buried a radioactive container in Moscow's Izmailovsky Park. Following Basayev's instructions, Masiuk's crew arrived in Moscow on November 23 and was able to uncover the container with the help of a radiation meter. The 30-pound package contained radioactive cesium 137. As per Basayev's account, there were a total of four such containers. All of them were supposedly wrapped in trinitrotoluene TNT and could be detonated at any time.[65] Basayev explained the purpose behind the container found by the journalists as follows: "Giving back this container we want to show the Russian side that we have radioactive substances that we are capable of transporting to Moscow. There we can hide them so that no one would be able to find them, and, if you do not stop the war, we can detonate them, then it will be your fault."[66]

Once again the Russian government was caught unaware by Basayev's action. Just as Budennovsk raised concerns over security checkpoints, the act in Moscow puzzled security experts as they wondered how a radioactive container had reached Russia's capital. As Elena Masiuk later found out, the container had arrived by air. Bypassing all security installations, the container traveled from Grozny on a plane carrying State Duma deputies.[67] The Russian government once again failed to protect its citizens by allowing Basayev to carry out his radiological plot in Moscow's Izmailovsky Park.

In response to the attack, the park was encircled by military, security, and health services. The Russian Ministry of Emergency Situations activated its radiation monitoring system, and defense agencies in Moscow installed 46 radiation meters.[68] However, the government tried to diminish the significance of the attack. According to the official reports, the installed meters registered no changes in radiation levels. Basayev's container was described as not dangerous to the population. As a security service representative claimed: "The first tests showed that beyond one meter from the package there was no threat to health. Initial tests show that the package does not pose a serious threat to the environment or health."[69]

While the Russian government tried to play down the significance of the attack, Basayev's act was a very serious terrorist event both to Russia and the world. The act revealed that Chechen separatists had seriously embarked on a WMD program. Back in 1992 Dzhokhar Dudayev allocated $350,000 from the Ichkeriia budget for "acquisitioning materials of strategic significance."[70] Reportedly, Grozny used these funds to acquire over 148 tons of zirconium E110 from a factory in the Russian region of Udmurtia. In the territory of Chechnya itself, there was an industrial complex, Radon, that was built in the vicinity of Grozny in 1965 and that specialized in the transportation and burial of radioactive waste. After the collapse of the Soviet Union, Radon was closed down and left largely unattended. In the course of the two Chechen wars, radioactive material from the complex was spotted in different Chechen locales.[71] Radon could have been the source of Basayev's cesium container. According to some estimates, during the first Chechen war alone, 450 cubic meters of radioactive waste—including plutonium 239, uranium 235, cesium 137, and strontium 90—went missing from Radon.[72] It remains unclear which exact substances and in what quantities have disappeared from the complex since the first war and which of those could be in the hands of Basayev-like terrorists.

Thus, the attack had significant implications for Russia's security. It showed that Chechen separatists had the means of acquiring WMDs and were prepared to use them. Further, the significance of the attack reached beyond the North Caucasus and Russia. Planting the radioactive container was not only Basayev's next attempt to stop the war in Chechnya, but it also signaled to the world that the danger of terrorists using WMD was real. In this respect, the Chechens' strategic use of a radioactive substance suggested that other terrorist groups would be tempted to imitate Basayev's daring act. In fact, in 2003 British and French special services traced a terrorist plot involving the deadly toxin ricin back to Chechnya.[73] Just like Aum Shinrikyo's sarin gas attack inspired Al Qaeda to develop its own WMD program, Chechen experiments with WMD could also inspire future generations of terrorists. Replications of Basayev's daring act of radiological terrorism remain a persistent danger.

ELECTIONS AND REACTIONS: KIZLYAR, PERVOMAISKOE, AND AVRASYA

Regardless of Basayev's radiological escapade, Moscow proceeded with preparations for elections in Chechnya. The Kremlin was ready to restore its control in the republic. On December 8, 1995, Prime Minister Chernomyrdin and Doku Zavgayev signed an agreement that laid down the basic principles for a federation agreement between Russia and Chechnya. As Dudayev had previously refused to sign the federation treaty, the Kremlin was counting on the fact that it could finalize the agreement with a newly elected government along the lines of the Tatarstan scenario. Accordingly, the Chechen Republic was to receive a large degree of autonomy within the Russian Federation. Thus, the elections were another step on the way to pacifying separatist tendencies in Chechnya.

Elections took place on December 14–17, 1995. To ensure their success, the Moscow-backed Chechen government adopted a law stating that elections would be recognized as valid with a turnout as low as 25 percent of the population.[74] The actual turnout was reported to be much higher; official reports claimed over 50 percent of the Chechen population took part in the elections, with 90 percent of the voters casting their vote for Zavgayev.[75] Doku Zavgayev became the undisputed winner of the elections, affirming his position as the head of the Chechen Republic. Concerns over electoral irregularities were disregarded, and Moscow proceeded with justifying its presence in Grozny while General Dudayev was ousted from his government seat. The Moscow-staged elections completely derailed the negotiation process, and fighting on both sides resumed with new force. Further terrorist actions followed the elections.

This time the attack struck Dagestan. In the early hours of January 9, 1996, a group of 300–400 Chechen separatists entered the city of Kizlyar. The group, led by Dzhokhar Dudayev's son-in-law Salman Raduyev, proceeded with a hostage-taking operation similar to the attack on Budennovsk the previous year.[76] As with the Budennovsk raid, Kizlyar was not the end goal for the Chechen group. Instead, the intention was to attack a military airfield near Kizlyar. As Raduyev explained, "There is a military base in Kizlyar and our mission was to destroy eight helicopters. We found three and destroyed them and smashed the military base."[77] The operation proceeded on orders from Dzhokhar Dudayev. As Dudayev confirmed, "Everything that is taking place in this war is under my tight control,"[78] and he was closely monitoring the progress of Raduyev's raid.

According to Raduyev, he did not initially plan to take hostages. However, the situation became complicated as his forces withdrew from the airfield and Raduyev headed into Kizlyar. Again, as with Budennovsk, Raduyev's group took around 2,000 hostages from throughout the city and eventually barricaded themselves in a local hospital. The occupied hospital included a maternity ward, after which Raduyev received the nickname "Gynecologist." Many contradictory reports followed on the number of casualties and executions of hostages during the raid. Learning from its failures with the media coverage of the Budennovsk campaign, Moscow restricted media access to the epicenter of the attack. As a result, fewer media personnel were allowed onto the front lines, and many decisions were taken behind closed doors. This was the beginning of Moscow's censorship campaign on information regarding the Chechen conflict.

Demanding a meeting with journalists, Raduyev declared his demands: the annulment of the election results, an immediate withdrawal of federal forces, and an end to the war in Chechnya. "As long as there is a single Russian soldier on our [Chechen] territory there will be no talks, no peace with Russia," Raduyev warned.[79] President Yeltsin was furious at the news of another terrorist attack and appeared on Russian TV, scolding his military and security personnel for allowing Kizlyar to happen. This time, the Kremlin was facing much more pressure: Yeltsin's presidential term was expiring, and stakes were being raised ahead of the presidential elections scheduled for June 1996.

In anticipation of the elections, Yeltsin tried to avoid a repeat of the humiliating failures of the government's response to the Budennovsk attack. As a result, the president immediately rejected the demands of the hostage-takers. This time he was not willing to negotiate with Raduyev's group; it was clear the president was set on a military crackdown against the rebels. The Kremlin dispatched over 4,000 troops, detachments of the MVD, as well as police and other security professionals to Kizlyar to seal off the city. Moscow deployed a convoy of 48 tanks and armored vehicles and sent its elite forces Alpha and Vympel to Kizlyar. This time the operation against the hostage-takers was also coordinated by the newly reorganized FSB Department on the Fight against Terrorism. As General Anatoly Kulikov promised, "this time, nobody will walk out of there alive."[80]

Contrary to Moscow's militant stance, the local Dagestani authorities were more willing to negotiate a peaceful resolution to the crisis. Overall, compared to Budennovsk, the Kizlyar attack resulted in much more local involvement as the federal government tried to distance itself from the disaster. As President Yeltsin explained, "it is beneficial for us to transfer this case from the federal to the regional level."[81] Despite Raduyev's demands of negotiations at the federal level, negotiations were offered only at the level of the Dagestani regional government. After several hours of overnight negotiations, Raduyev dropped the political demands and settled on accepting safe passage back to Chechnya. The authorities agreed to provide Raduyev's group with transportation for him to travel back.

Just as after Budennovsk, on January 10 Raduyev's group boarded 11 buses and two trucks and set out for Chechnya. The procession was again accompanied by a group of over 160 hostages serving as human shields. The hostages included volunteers who were previously released hostages and senior Dagestani politicians. However, the group did not travel far. Russian security services again planned to eliminate the terrorists in the course of their retreat. This time the group was halted at the village of Pervomaiskoe as the procession came under Russian fire. Fearing an attack from the Russian side, Raduyev's group acted preemptively and prepared for a siege. The Chechens dispersed throughout the village and built a line of defense using hostage labor. The ensuing standoff lasted for several days, until the village was stormed by Russian troops on January 15.

In support of Raduyev's forces surrounded at Pervomaiskoe, the first international terrorist attack was staged in the name of Chechen separatists. On January 16 a group of around 12 terrorists sympathetic to the Kizlyar/Pervomaiskoe events hijacked the Russia-bound ferryboat *Avrasya* in the Turkish port of Trabzon. The majority of the passengers were Russian citizens, but citizens of Turkey, Georgia, Jordan, Kyrgyzstan, and Ukraine were also traveling on the ferryboat. Echoing Raduyev's demands in Kizlyar, the leader of the group, Mohammed Tokcan, demanded that the Russian government end the blockade of Pervomaiskoe, allow Raduyev safe passage to Chechnya, withdraw federal forces from the North Caucasus, and end the war in Chechnya. Tokcan separated the Russians from the rest of the passengers and threatened to execute them if the Russian government failed to meet his demands. In his message to President Yeltsin, Tokcan stated, "We are not terrorists, we are freedom fighters. If our Chechen brothers are not freed, Russia will be the murderer of these passengers— no one else."[82]

Unlike Raduyev's raid, the Avrasya operation was not sanctioned by Grozny. As Dudayev's Foreign Minister Yusuf explained upon arriving in Istanbul, the attack "is against our interests and it is against the law to take civilian hostages, especially in Turkey which is our friend." Yusuf condemned the actions of Tokcan's group, stating that "they think they are helping us but they are doing wrong."[83] Tokcan himself was an Abkhaz and claimed he met Shamil Basayev in Abkhazia, where they fought together against the Georgian government. Another participant in the events—Khamzat Gitsba—also knew Basayev from Abkhazia. The attack on Avrasya became one of the first terrorist operations committed not directly by Chechen separatists, but by individuals inspired by the Chechen cause.

The ferryboat proceeded to Istanbul, where the Turkish authorities, much more experienced in dealing with terrorism due to their exposure to attacks by the Kurdistan Workers' Party (PKK), negotiated with Tokcan. Tokcan agreed to release the hostages in return for holding a press conference. Sonmez Koksal, head of Turkey's National Intelligence Organization, assured Tokcan that authorities would not intervene,[84] and *Avrasya* dropped anchor on the Asian side of the Bosporus in Istanbul on January 19. Following the resolution of the Pervomaiskoe siege, the Tokcan group surrendered to the Turkish authorities. The Turkish incident was resolved with no violence or casualties. As the attack unfolded, President Yeltsin offered assistance to the Turkish authorities in handling the crisis. However, his offer, along with his insistence on a more hard-line response, was rejected. As Turkey's Prime Minister Tansu Ciller commented, "We could have handled [the crisis] definitely a lot easier and faster, but it might have meant loss of blood." She added, "That was something we did not want."[85]

In several ways, the hijacking of *Avrasya* became another seminal event in the evolution of North Caucasus terrorism. The Turkish counterterrorist operation against the *Avrasya* hijackers revealed the inadequacy of Russia's counterterrorism approach. Contrary to the declarations of the Russian government, the incident illustrated that a hostage crisis could be resolved peacefully without bloodshed. Further, the incident indicated the potential danger of the spread of a terrorist cause. The attack was not the first act linked to Chechen terrorism to involve Turkey. It followed the wave of plane hijackings in the 1990s that demanded passage into Turkey. However, it was one of the first attacks perpetrated not by Chechen separatists but by their sympathizers: the attack was not sanctioned by Dudayev, nor was it committed by Chechen separatists. Instead, the attack was committed on behalf of the Chechen cause, thus signaling the potential of terrorism to inspire followers that might not be direct participants in the cause.

Back in Russia the Pervomaiskoe siege culminated with a bombardment campaign on January 18. Commenting on Russia's methods, a Federal Security Service spokesman explained, "What we are facing today is not an operation to liberate hostages... We are liberating a town here."[86] Federal forces proceeded with firing Grad rockets toward the village. Despite this onslaught, Raduyev's group managed to escape. A diversionary group of Chechen separatists arrived from Grozny and attacked the outer encirclement of federal forces. In the meantime, Raduyev's group escaped from the siege with a group of hostages. These hostages were not released until February 1996, after Russia's State Duma agreed to officially offer amnesty to Raduyev's group.[87]

AFTER KIZLYAR/PERVOMAISKOE

Similar to the Budennovsk attack, the Kizlyar/Pervomaiskoe episode further exposed Russia's unpreparedness to deal with terrorist attacks. Despite having the experience of the Budennovsk attack, Russia's security services were once again caught unawares. President Yeltsin himself pointed out the inadequacy of the response preparedness of his security services:

> One emergency situation was not enough for us. The lessons from that case were not enough for our defense agencies, ministries, the government, security services, border patrol. Not enough. We received another blow, so to say. And to cover such a distance, given that the information about Dudayev coming with his group was available beforehand. But no, border patrol overslept.[88]

In this case, the indignation of the president was even greater because numerous accounts suggested that information about the planning of the Kizlyar raid was available to Russian security services prior to the attack.

According to some accounts, the idea of the Kizlyar raid was conceived by Chechen separatists in December 1995, when Dzhokhar Dudayev received intelligence on a forthcoming arms shipment to the Kizlyar airfield.[89] In turn, intelligence on Dudayev's plan reached the Russian authorities. The Moscow-backed Chechen government in Grozny confirmed their awareness of the planned raid. As a representative of Zavgayev's administration described, "The terrorist attack in Kizlyar was not unexpected for us. Neither were there any riddles in the planning of its execution."[90] Despite having knowledge of the Chechen plan, Russian authorities failed to prevent or even effectively deal with the attack. Thus, the incompetence of Russia's security services was illustrated to the fullest extent.

The Russian government perceived the negotiation process in Budennovsk as a humiliating failure that cast the perception that they were soft on terrorism. In trying to avoid producing a similar impression in Kizlyar, the Kremlin refused to hold any negotiations at the federal level. This was Russia's initial attempt to assume the position of being tough on terrorism by refusing to negotiate with terrorists. Since Kizlyar/Pervomaiskoe, the Russian government has persisted with forceful resolution of hostage crises by refusing to negotiate and simultaneously limiting media access to their storming operations so that hostage deaths inflicted by Russia's rescue teams are not broadcast.

On the Chechen side, the Kizlyar/Pervomaiskoe raid signified another achievement. Even though the operation did not lead to negotiations as Budennovsk did, it did signify that terrorism had emerged as a permanent tool in the Chechen arsenal. At a press conference following the events of Kizlyar/Pervomaiskoe, Aslan Maskhadov and Shamil Basayev promised to wage "mass terror" on the territory of Russia.[91] The attack also showed that Chechen terrorism had become more indiscriminate. The Kizlyar/Pervomaiskoe attack followed a different pattern from Basayev's earlier differentiation between subversive action and terrorism. This time the Chechen group attempted to make their statement as dramatic as possible and therefore targeted women and children along with men and government workers. According to Raduyev, he even had a directive from

Dudayev ordering him to target civilians: "The Russian President is deliberating what to do with you. Wait for our order to start military action. Shoot civilians. There should be more casualties among women than men. Demonstrate composure."[92]

Further, Raduyev's escape showed Russia's security services in an unfavorable light. Proud of his operation, Raduyev was able to declare, "You saw for yourself the impotence of the Russian army when 180 people, with hostages and wounded men, broke through three rings of special forces and escaped from the siege."[93] Similar to Budennovsk, the hostages themselves pointed to the Kremlin's failure to protect its own citizens. The released hostages expressed anger at the Russian government for using overwhelming force and endangering their lives. As one hostage recalled, "I took up a gun and went with them [Raduyev's group] . . . because those Russian soldiers didn't look where they were shooting. They didn't think, they shot everyone."[94]

After Kizlyar/Pervomaiskoe the Russian public grew increasingly critical of Moscow's actions in Chechnya. While the Russian public became weary of Chechen terrorist attacks, Russian citizens were still a little more favorable toward Chernomyrdin's negotiations approach than toward Yeltsin's hard-line stance. An opinion poll conducted after Kizlyar/Pervomaiskoe showed that half a year later 35 percent of Russians still approved of Chernomyrdin's negotiations in Budennovsk, while 31 percent agreed with Yeltsin's decision to eliminate terrorists in Pervomaiskoe.[95] At the same time Yeltsin's approval ratings kept falling. By the end of January 1996, only 10 percent of Russians were ready to vote for Boris Yeltsin in the upcoming presidential elections.[96] Yeltsin's chances for victory were closely tied to his politics in Chechnya: his ratings began improving only by May, after the president embarked on a peace initiative with Chechnya.

In reaction to the events in Kizlyar/Pervomaiskoe, on January 17, 1996, the State Duma issued another statement criticizing Yeltsin for mishandling the Chechen crisis. To prevent similar terrorist attacks in the future, the Duma called for a political solution to the Chechen issue. Under growing pressure from both his government and the electorate, and on the verge of presidential elections, Yeltsin signed Decree 435 on March 31, 1996. The decree outlined a program for the resolution of the Chechen crisis. In this program the president envisioned a cease-fire in Chechnya, the withdrawal of federal troops, and peace negotiations. At the same time the decree also called for preparations for new elections in Chechnya—this time for members of parliament. The elections were further supposed to legitimize Zavgayev's rule in Chechnya. By creating loyal government institutions in Grozny, the Kremlin intended to pave a way to transfer the Chechen issue from the federal to the local level. Later, under President Putin, this turned into a concentrated policy of Chechenization. Therefore, it was the presidential elections campaign rather than the terrorist act of Kizlyar/

Pervomaiskoe that introduced a new wave of negotiations between Russia and Chechnya. This was also the view of the Chechen separatists. In April 1996 Shamil Basayev described Yeltsin's peace initiative as nothing more than an attempt to "freeze the war until the presidential elections."[97]

FURTHER TERRORIST TRANSFORMATIONS AND THE END OF THE FIRST WAR

With presidential elections looming in June 1996, any further hostage crises would have been devastating for Yeltsin's presidential campaign. As a result, President Yeltsin turned his full attention to the resolution of the Chechen crisis before the elections. In his announcement to run for re-election, Yeltsin stated:

> I am fully aware of the drama of our time as highlighted by the Chechen crisis. There we confronted for the first time out and out separatism that blocks any attempts to put out that seat of tension. We are all one in wanting to see that crisis resolved as soon as possible so that no danger should emanate from Chechnya for other territories of Russia and I am sure that this will happen in the coming months.[98]

For this purpose the Russian government relied on both political and military means. Parallel to Yeltsin's peace program outlined by Decree 435, Russia engaged in a continued military campaign against Chechnya. Russian warplanes continued to attack rebel positions. One of the biggest achievements of the military onslaught on Chechnya was the assassination of Ichkeriia's President Dzhokhar Dudayev. On April 21, 1996, Dudayev died in what appeared to be a Russian special operation.

On April 24, 1996, Shamil Basayev confirmed the death of his leader. Dudayev's Vice President Zelimkhan Yandarbiyev succeeded Dudayev in the role of the president. Having survived several previous assassination attempts, Dudayev was killed by a Russian missile when he was speaking on a satellite telephone. According to former officers of Russia's Main Intelligence Administration, the attack on Dudayev was planned as part of Yeltsin's presidential campaign. According to Iakovlev and Aksenov, the assassination was meant to improve Yeltsin's ratings on the verge of the elections. As the officers explained, Yeltsin paid $1 million for information on Dudayev's location.[99] While several other explanations for Dudayev's death exist, Yeltsin's ratings did indeed start to improve following the elimination of the main Chechen separatist.

After Dudayev's death Yeltsin was able to confirm that the only legitimate government in the Chechen Republic remained Doku Zavgayev's administration. The Kremlin was ready to announce victory over the breakaway republic. In Chechnya, Zavgayev declared that further negotiations were no longer necessary because the opponent had been eliminated: "the other side simply [did] not exist anymore." Zavgayev continued to describe successes against the separatists: "There are scattered groups of militants in Chechnya who are at odds with the law, the people of the Chechen republic and each other ... [The Chechen] people have understood it, people reject them, people have faith in peace zones we are forming in the territory of Chechnya."[100]

Despite the Kremlin's expectations, however, Dudayev's death did not weaken the separatists' resolve and Yandarbiyev, Dudayev's successor, continued to challenge federal troops in Chechnya. As a result, Yeltsin was pressured to take further steps toward a political settlement to the Chechen issue. In May 1996 Yeltsin made an unprecedented decision— he announced his willingness to talk to Yandarbiyev. On May 27 a Chechen delegation headed by Yandarbiyev arrived for talks in Moscow. This was the first meeting between the heads of state of Russia and self-proclaimed Ichkeriia throughout the entire first Chechen campaign. In the course of the meeting, Yeltsin and Yandarbiyev signed a cease-fire agreement.

The next day, in another pre-election stunt, Boris Yeltsin flew out to Grozny for the first time since the start of the war to demonstrate that he recognized the significance of the Chechen issue. Yeltsin was victorious. Speaking in front of federal troops, the president declared: "The war is over. You won."[101] Claiming that only small, dispersed bands of separatists were left in Chechnya, Yeltsin announced the end of the military phase of the Chechen operation and confirmed the start of the negotiations phase:

> For 18 months Russian troops have been defending the national interests of Russia, risking their lives and shedding their blood for the unity and territorial integrity of our country. They are in the forefront of the battle not only against Chechen separatists, but also against international terrorists - all those who bring death to peaceful people; all those who take sick people, children and pregnant women hostage; all those who are ready to sacrifice the entire Chechen people for their own selfish goals. Heroic soldiers have crushed the resistance of the militants, exhausted and demoralized them.[102]

On June 16, 1996, the first round of the presidential elections took place in Russia. Yeltsin gained 35.28 percent of the vote, his communist opponent Gennady Zyuganov received 32.03 percent, and General Alexander Lebed, who had demonstrated a strong pro-peace position on Chechnya, won 14.52 percent.[103] In Chechnya presidential elections were held concurrently with the Chechen parliamentary elections. According to the local electoral committee, 58 percent of registered voters voted in the parliamentary elections, and nearly 60 percent cast their votes in the presidential elections.[104] According to the official results, in Chechnya 68 percent of those who took part in the elections voted for Boris Yeltsin.[105] The OSCE monitoring group pronounced the elections in Chechnya to be "neither free nor fair."[106] Regardless, Chechnya's Moscow-backed Doku Zavgayev welcomed his newly elected parliament.

The reaction to these elections was similar to the previous reaction to the elections that brought Zavgayev to power: terrorist attacks followed. This renewed wave of terrorist attacks represented another adaptation in terrorist tactics. First, this time terrorist attacks reached the heart of Russia—Moscow. Second, these attacks were a series of explosions involving public transportation. This was a different technique from the previously employed hijackings, hostage-takings, and radiological terrorism.

The first explosion to reach Moscow took place on the very eve of the presidential elections. On June 11, 1996, an explosion occurred on the Moscow metro between the stations of Tulskaia and Nagatinskaia. While targeting the metro is a popular terrorist tactic around the world, in Moscow, the attack was the first terrorist act on the metro since the breakup of the Soviet Union and only the third in its entire history. The explosion immediately raised concerns of political terrorism. Moscow mayor Yuri Luzhkov referred to the attack as "an attempt of the reactionary forces to sabotage the elections in the capital."[107] President Yeltsin described it as a "wild barbaric act on the verge of elections [that was] aimed at destabilizing the situation in the capital, at the creation of the atmosphere of uncertainty and fear in Russia."[108] Coming days before the presidential elections, the attack immediately raised suspicions of Chechen involvement.

More terrorist attacks followed across Russia after the elections. On June 28, 1996, a bomb exploded on a bus traveling from Mineralnye Vody to Vladikavkaz through Nalchik, Kabardino-Balkaria, going off at the bus station in Nalchik. According to the Russian authorities, the attack was organized by Ruslan Khaikhoroev, a Chechen field commander. As Khaikhoroev explained, the terrorist attack was planned to create panic in the region that would demonstrate the Russian government's incompetence.[109]

According to the FSB, Ruslan Khaikhoroev was also responsible for the next wave of terrorist attacks in Moscow. Attacks on Moscow's trolleybuses followed the second round of presidential elections on July 3, 1996, in which Boris Yeltsin was re-elected president. Following his reelection, on July 12 Yeltsin signed a decree confirming the consolidation of constitutional government institutions in the Chechen Republic. In this document Yeltsin declared that the position of the head of the Chechen Republic, as well as the legislative and the executive branches, was firmly rebuilt. While Yeltsin was celebrating victory, explosions took place on Moscow trolleybuses. On July 11, 1996, an explosion struck a trolleybus on Strastnoi Boulevard. The next day another explosion took place on a trolleybus on Prospekt Mira.

These attacks indicated that Chechen terrorism had become a new reality for Moscow. As one of Moscow's counterterrorism specialists explained, "They [Chechens] cannot resist on the field of battle, so they may try to bring fear to the capital of Russia."[110] Terrorism became the means of countering Russia's military superiority on the front lines. The attacks on the Russian capital were calculated to affect Moscow's strategy on the battlefield. According to FSB officials, immediately after the first trolleybus attack, Ruslan Khaikhoroev reached out to the FSB Counterterrorism Center and claimed responsibility for the explosion. The attack was retaliation against Russia's bombardment campaign in Chechnya, and Khaikhoroev demanded that air strikes on the Chechen villages of Gekhi and Bamut be ended.[111]

Another terrorist attack was prevented in Russia's city of Voronezh. On July 19, 1996, two bombs were found in the waiting room of the railway station; the bomb detonators went off, but the bombs failed to explode. This incident became interesting in the history of Chechen terrorism because it started a wave of Chechens claiming events that were not necessarily connected to them. The already infamous Salman Raduyev took responsibility for the attempted bombing of the Voronezh railway station. However, between 1996 and 1997 Raduyev claimed responsibility for all attacks on the territory of Russia without evidence to support his claims, which undermined the credibility of his statements. Even those in the Chechen leadership tried to distance themselves from Raduyev's claims. For instance, a Chechen spokesman denied Raduyev's involvement in the Voronezh plot: "The man [Raduyev] has been through great emotional stress, has been seriously wounded and has lost relatives. That is why he made such a statement," the representative said.[112] In the future this became somewhat of a trend among Chechen separatists. At times they claimed connection to events that could work in favor of their propaganda. For instance, Shamil Basayev claimed responsibility for sinking Russia's submarine *Kursk* in 2000, the fire at TV tower Ostankino in 2000, and the fire at a Moscow theater in May 2005. According to Russian sources, these disasters were not terrorist acts.

The waves of terrorist attacks were also accompanied by Chechen successes in positional warfare. Eventually it was the takeover of Grozny that led to the signing of the peace agreement that terminated the first Chechen war. On August 6, 1996, the Chechen separatists started the operation Jihad. In the course of the operation, under the leadership of Aslan Maskhadov, 820 Chechen separatists took over Grozny. The numerically superior federal forces failed to keep the city under Russian control. Facing the pressure of military failures and a growing threat of terrorism, President Yeltsin appointed Alexander Lebed, secretary of the Security Council and presidential advisor on national security issues, as his representative in Chechnya. Under Lebed's initiative, a series of negotiations proceeded with Zelimkhan Yandarbiyev and Aslan Maskhadov. As a result of the negotiations, Lebed and Maskhadov signed the Khasavyurt Accords on August 31, 1996. The agreement effectively terminated the military campaign in

Chechnya while delaying the decision on its status until December 31, 2001. The first Chechen war was over.

TERRORISM IN THE FIRST WAR

The phenomenon of Chechen political terrorism was a direct outcome of Russia's military action in the Chechen Republic. The very first act of Chechen political terrorism came on November 9, 1991, in response to Yeltsin's first attempt to send troops to Chechnya. The second significant terrorist act perpetrated by Chechen separatists came on June 14, 1995, in response to Yeltsin's decision to tackle the issue of Chechen independence through a military approach. The 1995 attack on Budennovsk and the subsequent 1996 raid on Kizlyar/Pervomaiskoe were the most spectacular terrorist attacks of the first Chechen war. The two attacks became the biggest hostage crises in the world, with the number of hostages amounting to 2,000 people in each case. These attacks were unprecedented in Russia and set a new trend of hostage-taking raids among Chechen separatists both in the first and second Chechen conflicts.

Hostage-taking incidents, however, were not the only terrorist tactic used by the Chechen separatists. During the first Chechen war the separatist leadership made a strategic decision to adopt subversive action as a way of undermining a militarily superior Russian opponent. Terrorism thus became the chosen tool of the weaker side, and terrorist attacks ranged from plane hijackings to hostage raids to explosions on public transportation to an act of radiological terrorism. Through a diverse arsenal of terrorist tactics, Chechen separatists aimed to terminate the war in Chechnya. The demands behind these attacks included a cease-fire in Chechnya, the withdrawal of federal forces, and peace negotiations to discuss the status of the republic.

When terrorist attacks in the region failed to bring about peace in Chechnya, Chechen separatists adapted by taking terrorism to Moscow. The attacks in Moscow sent a powerful message to Russian citizens about the weakness of their own government in providing security. Strategically, attacks carried out in the Russian capital drew maximum attention to the Chechen issue, and terrorism emerged as a priority on the government's agenda. After the attacks on the Moscow trolleybuses on July 12, 1996, the Russian State Duma issued a statement expressing concerns over the growing terrorist threat in Russia. For the first time in the history of post-Soviet Russia, the Kremlin was forced to seriously consider the issue of counterterrorism. Emerging from the war with Chechnya, Russia embarked on creating a counterterrorism base, building counterterrorist legislation, and reforming counterterrorist institutions.

During the first Chechen war no specific terrorist organizations appeared for the purpose of committing terrorist attacks. Terrorist acts of the first war were committed by Chechen separatist field commanders and their battalions. Russian security services opened criminal cases against individuals responsible for terrorist attacks, such as Shamil Basayev and Salman Raduyev, but no organizational entities were designated as terrorist organizations. This feature differentiates the terrorism of the first war from that of the second. During the course of the second Chechen war, several Chechen organizations emerged that were subsequently designated as terrorist organizations by the Russian government and in the West.

The terrorism of the first Chechen campaign was widely considered to be a direct outcome of the Russian government's ineffectual handling of the Chechen issue. As one newspaper article pointed out, "Terrorists are undoubtedly criminals, but crime of this type is usually closely connected to mistakes in big politics of the state. It is produced by an unparalleled terrorist attack, planned and carried out at the federal level—that of the Chechen war."[113] The Russian population also saw clear links between the war in Chechnya and terrorism. In 1994, nineteen percent of Russians predicted terrorist acts in Moscow and other Russian cities as an outcome of the situation in Chechnya.[114] The war in Chechnya was seen as a much more significant security issue than terrorism, and later the Chechen war even became one of the justifications for starting the impeachment process against President Yeltsin.

International actors also considered the emerging terrorist threat as a corollary of the war in Chechnya. For instance, speaking after the Budennovsk attack, U.S. president Clinton stated that he disapproved of the use of terrorism and sympathized with the hostages, but at the same time he did not support Russia's action in Chechnya.[115] After the attack on Kizlyar/Pervomaiskoe, Germany and the United States both expressed concerns over Yeltsin's use of force to resolve the crisis.[116] In response to the hijacking of the *Avrasya*, a U.S. State Department representative was critical of Chechen terrorism, saying, "The entire world must condemn the Chechen insurgents for taking hostages." At the same time, however, the official linked the act of terrorism to the Chechen conflict, stating that the conflict itself could not be solved through military means: "We do not see a military solution to this problem. In our opinion, only negotiations could solve it."[117]

Thus, at the time of its inception, both domestic and foreign audiences perceived Chechen terrorism as an outcome of the Chechen war. It was seen as a domestic problem that grew out of a domestic issue. Although characterized by certain religious underpinnings, the terrorism of the first Chechen war was not explicitly religious but rather ethno-nationalist with a main goal of bringing peace to an independent Chechnya. Despite existing international links, Chechen terrorists were not perceived as members of international terrorist networks, and few references were made to the links between Chechen separatists and Osama bin Laden or Al Qaeda.

No Chechen terrorist groups were registered, as terrorist acts were planned and executed by separatist field commanders. During the first Chechen war, Russia's counterterrorism efforts were part of the military campaign and were executed under the banner of the restoration of constitutional order and the elimination of illegal armed formations in the republic. The designations "terrorist" and "separatist" were used interchangeably, and groups involved in terrorist attacks were referred to as "bands of criminals." No counterterrorist operation was announced during the first Chechen war. It was not until July 1996 that President Yeltsin first declared that Moscow needed to pay special attention to counterterrorist activities and Russia began to build its counterterrorist capabilities.

RUSSIA'S COUNTERTERRORIST RESPONSE

In Russia, Dzhokhar Dudayev often received blame for breeding terrorism in his republic. However, Moscow did not treat the first Chechen campaign as a counterterrorist operation. Instead, the military intervention was justified as an operation to restore constitutional order, since Dudayev was accused of breaching the constitution of the Russian Federation, namely the principles of constitutionalism and federalism. No counterterrorist legislation regulated the operation to restore constitutional order. Neither was a state of emergency introduced. According to the 1991 law on a state of emergency, the declaration of a state of emergency had to be approved by Russia's Federation Council. In addition, it had to be approved by the government of the republic falling under its jurisdiction. This way, a state of emergency would have added additional checks and balances on the executive decision to start military action. Such a procedure, however, could have failed in 1994 or could have added time to the planning of an operation that Yeltsin envisioned as a *blitzkrieg*. In the 1990s Yeltsin's government was critical of his decision to use military force in Chechnya. His first declaration of a state of emergency in 1991 was annulled by the Supreme Soviet. Subsequently, the Russian State Duma issued several documents urging the president to find a political solution to the Chechen crisis.

In the absence of a declaration of a state of emergency, the government relied on the Military Doctrine to justify military action. Yeltsin introduced the basic principles of the Doctrine in November 1993. According to these principles, troops could be used against illegal armed formations operating on Russian territory. The use of military force without declaration of a state of emergency was further justified by the introduction of a number of presidential decrees: 2137 (November 30, 1994), 2166 (December 9, 1994), and 2169 (December 11, 1994). Based on the principles of the Military Doctrine and presidential decrees, the troops and personnel of the Ministry of Defense, the MVD, and Federal Counterintelligence Service (renamed FSB in 1995) took part in the operation to eliminate illegal armed formations in Chechnya.

At the time of the first Chechen war, no counterterrorist legislation was in existence to justify the use of troops. Terrorism was listed as a crime under Russia's Criminal Code of 1960, which placed it under the criminal justice system. The Criminal Code was updated only in 1996. In the new version, the code included expanded provisions on terrorism. Articles 205–207 covered terrorism, terrorist acts, and hostage situations. However, even according to the new criminal code, terrorism was still under the jurisdiction of federal programs against crime. President Yeltsin signed the first terrorism-specific piece of counterterrorist legislation in Russia after the attacks on Budennovsk, Kizlyar, and Pervomaiskoe. Decree 338 came out on March 7, 1996, instructing the government to develop specific measures to fight the growing threat of terrorism in Russia.

Yeltsin's decree called for institutional reform in Russia to tackle the issue of terrorism. This reform primarily focused on the restructuring of the security agencies that grew out of the Soviet Committee for State Security, or KGB. A Department on the Fight against Terrorism already existed in 1992. After the attack on Budennovsk on June 23, 1995, Yeltsin issued Decree 633, requiring further reform of the department under the auspices of the FSB. The agency further transformed in 1997 when the Russian government created an interagency Counterterrorist Committee.

Chechen terrorism of the first Chechen war prompted the Russian government to initiate the creation of counterterrorism capabilities in the country. Aside from reforming the legislative counterterrorism base and restructuring counterterrorist institutions, Russia's responses to terrorism went through conceptual shifts during the period of the first Chechen war. Moscow's initial reaction to the first major hostage crisis in Budennovsk was negotiating with the hostage-takers. At the time Prime Minister Chernomyrdin not only agreed to negotiate with Shamil Basayev, but also adhered to the terms laid out by the Chechen separatists in exchange for a hostage release.

After the second major hostage crisis in Kizlyar, the Russian government adopted a different approach. It abandoned the idea of negotiations in order not to appear soft on terrorism. Instead, the Kremlin adopted a hard-line approach to terrorism that dictated no negotiations with terrorists would occur. Further, the Kremlin initiated the devolution of counterterrorism response, shifting responsibility from the federal to the regional level. Consequently, negotiations in Kizlyar/Pervomaiskoe took place at the level of the Dagestani government. No political terms expressed by the hostage-takers were fulfilled, as the only condition negotiated was the safe passage of Raduyev's group to Chechnya in exchange for the release of the hostages.

These changes in Russia's counterterrorism approach indicated a shift toward hard-line responses to terrorism. This shift in turn affected the future evolution of Chechen terrorism. Russia's non-negotiation stance initiated adaptations in the Chechen usage of terrorist tactics. After Kizlyar/Pervomaiskoe it became clear that the Kremlin was firm on not fulfilling terrorist demands as it did in response to Budennovsk. The Chechen separatists received the message that the use of terrorism to secure political demands would be less effective. Subsequently, the Chechen side shifted the focus of terrorist acts, using them for propaganda purposes, rather than to secure political concessions. During the second Chechen campaign hostage-taking became less frequent, while the number of bombings increased and Chechen terrorism became more indiscriminate.

3

Interwar Years: Ideological Developments behind Chechen Terrorism

POST-KHASAVYURT CHECHNYA

The Khasavyurt Accords delayed the resolution of the status of Chechnya until December 2001. In the meantime the Chechen side treated the agreement as victory. In the process of peace negotiations, Aslan Maskhadov emerged as the next leader of independent Ichkeriia. Due to Maskhadov's willingness to cooperate with Moscow, the Kremlin did not prevent his rise to power. Moreover, Moscow did not try to impose the government institutions it created in Chechnya on Maskhadov. Moscow-propped Doku Zavgayev left Chechnya after the separatist forces recaptured Grozny in August 1996, and the Kremlin did not try to bring him back. Further, Maskhadov even demanded that Moscow hand over Zavgayev to Ichkeriia authorities due to his alleged embezzlement of funds allocated in 1995–1996 to restore postwar Chechnya.[1] The Moscow-created government in Chechnya lost its relevance, and Zavgayev became persona non grata in the republic. Russia further relinquished control over Chechnya by completing the withdrawal of federal troops by December 31, 1996. Power in Grozny was transferred to the victorious separatists. The second period of contemporary de facto independence of Chechnya followed.

On January 27, 1997, Chechnya proceeded with presidential elections. A large number of international observers, including the OSCE, monitored the elections. According to the observers, aside from some minor irregularities, the elections were free and fair in accordance with international standards. As expected, Aslan Maskhadov won the elections with 59.3 percent of the vote.[2] Shamil Basayev came in second. Commenting on the elections, Basayev did not show disappointment with his defeat, saying, "I consider myself a winner all the same since we were able to hold free democratic elections without significant violations."[3] Basayev declared he was not going to continue his military career but was at the same time cautious about joining Maskhadov's government. However, he did eventually accept the position of prime minister in Maskhadov's government.

Many other government positions under the presidency of Aslan Maskhadov were filled by field commanders of the first Chechen war. Maskhadov's newly created agencies replaced the vestiges of Zavgayev's political system, and Chechnya formed its own executive, legislative, and judicial branches, as well as its own military forces. Further, in May 1997 Maskhadov created his own counterterrorist center of the Chechen Republic of Ichkeriia, which was directly answerable to the president. Maskhadov's institutions were meant to allow Ichkeriia to function as a de facto independent state.

Maskhadov's government, just like Dudayev's before him, initially enjoyed support from the Kremlin. Following the elections, President Yeltsin approved of the results by sending his congratulations to Maskhadov.[4] Russia and Chechnya embarked on further negotiations to determine the parameters of relations between the two. Even prior to his election, on November 23, 1996, Maskhadov signed a preliminary agreement with Russia's Prime Minster Chernomyrdin delineating the principles of relations between the federal center and the Chechen Republic. The agreement was a result of numerous rounds of negotiations in Moscow, Nazran, and Khasavyurt, and prepared both sides to peacefully resolve all outstanding issues, including economic aid and future cooperation. On the same day President Yeltsin confirmed his dedication to the peace process by issuing Decree 1590 outlining peaceful means of resolving all contentious issues.

In February 1997 Maskhadov created a special committee to oversee further negotiations with Russia. The committee was headed by Movladi Udugov, a Chechen chief of propaganda. The relationship between Russia and Chechnya was further consolidated with a treaty on peace and principles of relations between the two sides signed by Maskhadov and Yeltsin on May 12, 1997. In this treaty the signatories expressed a determination to never resort to a forceful solution for settling any future disputes. Both sides expressed optimism in connection to the treaty. Boris Yeltsin confirmed that Russia would "develop cooperation with the Chechen Republic only through peaceful means. This primarily concerns cooperation in the economic sphere." Aslan Maskhadov responded, "Today we showed the world that the peace process has taken place... The government of Chechnya and its President will prove to the world their competence, and there will be no place for terrorists or kidnappers in our land."[5] Following the treaty Chernomyrdin and Maskhadov reached an agreement on June 13, 1997, regarding the priority issues for cooperation between Russia and Chechnya in the spheres of banking, customs, and oil.

One of Maskhadov's priorities following the signing of the Khasavyurt Accords was external recognition of Ichkeriia's independence. Maskhadov's legitimacy as the Chechen leader was accepted not only by Russia but also by foreign countries, and Maskhadov was able to travel freely. The primary purpose of Maskhadov's trips was the opening of diplomatic missions and the seeking of humanitarian aid. The president targeted countries with a large Chechen diaspora, including Azerbaijan, Jordan, and Turkey. Among other countries he visited were Malaysia, Poland, the United Kingdom, and the United States. After his trip to the United States in 1997, Maskhadov proudly declared, "I arrived in the US having in hand a diplomatic visa and did not have to ask for Russia's opinion."[6] In 1998 while visiting Britain, Maskhadov commented on his diplomatic efforts to achieve recognition of Chechnya's independence. The president indicated he was in no rush in terms of this mission: "We are not in a hurry since we have a clear picture of what world politics is and how much space there is in it for Chechnya, striving for its independence. However, today it is necessary to use any visit, any trip, any podium to tell the truth about Chechnya."[7] During June and July 1998 Movladi Udugov further declared Chechnya's intention to seek international recognition by applying for membership in the United Nations.[8] However, despite Maskhadov's foreign policy initiatives, no country recognized Chechnya's independence during the interwar period.[9]

Domestically, Maskhadov was facing tremendous problems. His country was in ruins from the war, and he had to confront the challenge of rebuilding a war-torn Chechnya flooded with weapons. The implementation of reconstruction programs was difficult due to the lack of funds, spreading crime, and growing domestic tensions. Maskhadov expressed his determination to rebuild the republic by focusing on strengthening government institutions and the security services, decommissioning the armed forces, and stemming the proliferation of weapons in Chechnya. However, many of Maskhadov's reconstruction projects failed. Similar to the situation in 1991–1994 under Dudayev, the de facto independence years between 1996 and 1999 in Chechnya became fraught with crime, corruption, violence, abductions, warlordism, and overall economic decline.

The Chechen economic system had been destroyed by the war. Because Russia did not recognize Chechnya's independence, the federal budget included allocations to the republic as one of its 89 federal units. According to official sources, Moscow transferred 847 billion rubles of assistance to Chechnya in the first half of 1997. An additional 160 billion was supposed to be wired monthly after that.[10] However, financial transfers from Russia often fell behind schedule.[11] In the absence of official funds, Chechnya developed a shadow economy. Under these conditions illegal siphoning of oil resumed. Some accounts indicate that in 1997 around 3 tons of oil was stolen in Chechnya each day.[12]

Criminal activities spread in the republic; in particular, kidnappings became rampant. For instance, 76 kidnappings were reported in the first half of 1997 alone.[13] By early 1999 official statistics indicated that over 700 people were being held in captivity in Chechnya, with unofficial numbers ranging up to 2,000.[14] Especially popular were kidnappings of Russian journalists.[15] One kidnapping that had significant implications for the future course of events in the North Caucasus was the abduction of Russian general Gennady Shpigun on March 5, 1999. The kidnappers demanded $15 million for the general's release.[16] The general's abduction prompted radical action in Moscow as Minister of Internal Affairs Sergei Stepashin issued an ultimatum to the Chechen kidnappers. Shpigun's kidnapping became one of the reasons for Russia's intervention in Chechnya in August 1999.

Following the kidnapping of General Shpigun, in April 1999 Russia's State Duma expressed concerns over the growing crime levels in Chechnya. Maskhadov himself realized the implications of the growing criminal activities in his republic. Earlier, in June 1998, the president had imposed a state of emergency to deal with the situation. This became part of Maskhadov's crime eradication initiative known as the Sword of Justice. Further, in October 1998 Maskhadov fired his entire cabinet. This initiative to reform his government was supposed to remove criminals by introducing into the government "professionals with clean hands who had not lost the trust of people."[17] However, by December 1998 Maskhadov's administration was ready to use force against the criminal elements in his republic. As under Dudayev, clashes began occurring between Maskhadov and his opposition.

Despite securing nominal independence from Russia, Aslan Maskhadov was facing numerous problems in Chechnya. Many of the internal problems in the interwar period were caused by disagreements over the role of religion. In the 1990s Chechnya and the North Caucasus were experiencing a period of religious revival. Many new Islamic movements were introduced in the region, among which was Wahhabism. In addition, the Afghan mujahedeen who had settled in the region after the first Chechen war exerted further religious influence. The mujahedeen offered not only military training but also religious education to Chechen separatists. Wahhabi communities spread across Dagestan and began to influence the internal dynamics of Chechnya. Maskhadov was facing growing internal opposition, much of which was split on the issue of religion.

RELIGIOUS REVIVAL IN THE NORTH CAUCASUS

For centuries Islam has thrived in the North Caucasus, and today the region is home to about one fifth of all Muslims in Russia. Among the ethnic groups practicing Islam are Avars, Balkars, Chechens, Cherkess, Dargins, Ingush, Kabardins, Karachai, Kumyks, Laks, Lezgins, and many others. Islam is present in the territories of Adygea, Chechnya, Dagestan, Ingushetia, Kabardino-Balkaria, Karachaevo-Cherkessia, and even North Ossetia. Chechnya, Dagestan, and Ingushetia are predominantly Sufi, with the widespread Sufi orders of Naqshbandiyya and Qadiriyya. These territories are subject to the Shafii school of Islamic jurisprudence. The western territories of the North Caucasus inherited Islam mainly from the Ottoman Empire. As a result, they are predominantly Sunni Muslim and adhere to the Hanafi school of Islamic jurisprudence. Out of all the territories in the North Caucasus, Chechnya, Dagestan, and Ingushetia are considered to be the most devout, as over 90 percent of the population thereview themselves as religious.

Islam arrived in the North Caucasus during the eighth through eleventh centuries.[18] Dagestan became the first area to come under the influence of Islam. Here the Arab conquests of the eighth century brought an influx of Arabs, who with them imported Islam and Arabic as the language of the Quran. By the tenth to thirteenth centuries, Islam was firmly rooted in Dagestan, and by the fifteenth century it began spreading through the work of local, as opposed to foreign, agents. By the sixteenth century the Islamization of Dagestan was mainly completed, and Dagestan became a major center of Islamic learning in the North Caucasus. Arabic influences were heavily present in the area; religious education took place in madrasas (schools), the territory was divided into *jamaats* (communities), and religious life was regulated by sharia (Islamic law). Throughout the centuries, Dagestan has preserved many of these Arabic attributes. Further, the already existing Arabic base facilitated the reintroduction of Arabic influences in Dagestan in the twentieth century. As a result, following the collapse of the Soviet Union, Dagestan became the flagship of religious revival sparked by Arabic doctrines.

Islam spread through the rest of the North Caucasus after taking root in Dagestan. By the fifteenth century Islam had become a predominant faith among the Kabardin people. The majority of Cherkess peoples, who had originally turned to Christianity under Byzantine influence, converted to Islam by the sixteenth century. In the Balkar and Karachai lands, Islam appeared by the seventeenth century. By the eighteenth century Islam had arrived in North Ossetia even though the Russian Empire treated this area as a bastion of Christianity. To prevent further Islamization of this area, a decree was issued in 1744 that sent Christian missionaries to Ossetia to restore Christianity.[19] Since then North Ossetia has had the most Christian presence in the North Caucasus. Islam spread the latest, by the eighteenth century, among the Chechen and Ingush peoples.

Different branches of Islam developed in different parts of the North Caucasus. Despite such differences, however, at certain times in history

Islam served as a unifying force that brought together the diverse peoples of the Caucasus for a common cause. Islam was the consolidating element for several statehood projects; Islam united the peoples of Adyg, Chechen, Dagestani, Balkar, Cherkess, Ingush, Kabardin, Karachai, and Ossetian territories under Imam Shamil's theocratic state based on sharia that existed in the nineteenth century. In the early twentieth century Islam consolidated the lands of Chechnya, Dagestan, Kabarda, Ossetia and Ingushetia under the Emirate of the North Caucasus. Islam was also the unifying element of anti-Russian campaigns led by Sheikh Mansur, Muhammad of Yaraghi, Ghazi Muhammad, Imam Shamil, and Uzun Khadzhi. In this respect, recent developments in Islam in the North Caucasus parallel the historical processes of statehood formation, religious purification, and anti-Russian resistance in many ways.

The desire for a contemporary wave of religious revival in the North Caucasus arose during the Soviet era. Under the Soviet policy of eradicating religion, religious schools were shut down and mosques and sharia courts closed. Sheikhs, imams, and other clergy faced persecution. The elimination of religious centers under Soviet rule resulted in the decline of religious knowledge. While certain Muslim traditions in the North Caucasus were allowed in the USSR, they were celebrated for their social significance, rather than for their religious meaning. This led to the erosion of the Islamic faith, leaving several generations in the North Caucasus without much knowledge of the substance of religion. By the end of the Soviet Union, many people in the North Caucasus identified themselves as atheists or nominal Muslims who did not have a proper understanding of their religion.

For instance, on one occasion the first president of Ichkeriia, Dudayev, revealed his religious ignorance by confusing how many times per day Muslims perform prayers. Dudayev stated, "Chechens are a unique people. We love Allah so much that we are ready to pray three times a day." Yandarbiyev had to correct his president, saying, "Five, Dzhokhar, five!" To which Dudayev responded, "If necessary, we will pray five times!"[20] As a result, following the collapse of the Soviet Union, religious revival initiatives quickly filled in the religious vacuum created under the Soviet system.

In the 1990s many foreign missionaries arrived in the former Soviet Union to proselytize, and the number of new converts to different religions skyrocketed. In the North Caucasus the process of religious revival involved the reopening of mosques, religious schools, and organizations; dissemination of religious texts, including the Russian translation of the Quran; and the freedom to perform the pilgrimage to Mecca, the *hajj*. Just as with the initial wave of Islamization, in the 1990s Dagestan emerged as the religious leader in the North Caucasus. At the end of the Soviet Union, Dagestan counted only 27 mosques[21] and around 1,500 Sufi murids.[22] But by 2011 Dagestan was home to 1,276 Sunni Juma mosques; 827 neighborhood mosques; 243 prayer houses; 76 madrasas; 13 Islamic universities; and a number of Islamic cultural centers, youth groups, and religious associations.[23] The majority of pilgrims going to Mecca from Russia come from Dagestan. In comparison, by the end of the 1990s both Ingushetia and Chechnya had only around 400 mosques, Kabardino-Balkaria had 96, and Karachaevo-Cherkessia had 91.[24]

After the religious oppression of the Soviet era was lifted, new religious influences made their way to the North Caucasus. Among these movements was Salafism, which came to be known as Wahhabism in Russia. The term *Wahhabism* derives from the name of Muhammad bin Abd al-Wahhab, who partnered with Muhammad bin Saud in efforts to unify the tribes of the Arabian Peninsula during the eighteenth century. Conceptually, Wahhabism designates a branch of Sunni Islam practiced mainly in Saudi Arabia. Wahhabism descends from the Hanbali school of Islamic jurisprudence, which sets it apart from the Shafii and Hanafi schools predominant in the North Caucasus. As a result, many Wahhabi tenets at times clash with customary Islamic teachings spread in the Caucasus, especially with Sufi traditions.

Wahhabism is a puritanical form of Islam that focuses on the reformation of faith. The primary principle guiding Wahhabism is following the righteous tenets of the Islamic religion at the time of the Prophet Mohammed. Wahhabi teachings dictate return to a pure form of Islam and rejection of the impurities introduced by the erroneous interpretations of the religion since its founding. Wahhabism is preoccupied with the restoration of the oneness of God, or *tawhid*, and, as a result, it rejects the practices of the veneration of saints, shrines, or tombs as violations of this principle. As one Wahhabi adherent from Russia's Stavropol region explained, such local practices as burial following several days after death, memorial services at the house of the deceased, and the reading of the Quran at the cemetery all contradict the principle of tawhid.[25] The North Caucasus Wahhabis associate such traditions with Soviet-style Islam and aim to eradicate them, along with other "sins" brought about by Russia's rule.

In Russia the term *Wahhabism* has acquired connotations of fundamentalism, extremism, jihadism, and terrorism. And yet, similar to the emergence of Muridism in the eighteenth century, Wahhabism initially arrived in the North Caucasus as a religious revivalist movement, not necessarily one connected to violence. Organized Wahhabism in the North Caucasus originated with the Islamic Renaissance Party (IRP), which was founded in 1990. The IRP advocated for a pure form of Islam and became active mostly in Tajikistan and Dagestan. Similar to the call for religious revival under Sheikh Mansur and Mullah Muhammad of Yaraghi, Wahhabi adherents of the early 1990s called for the eradication of moral and spiritual degradation. For example, attempts were made to introduce the prohibition of alcohol, and the idea of sharia government was reintroduced once again.

Wahhabi communities, or jamaats, spread across the North Caucasus. During the 1990s in Kabardino-Balkaria, revivalist Muslim groups organized into numerous jamaats. By the mid-1990s these diverse jamaats united into a single jamaat of Kabardino-Balkaria in Nalchik under the leadership of Musa Mukozhev. Mukozhev's agenda included socio-religious revival and the fight against government corruption.[26] At the time the jamaat was not professing establishment of an Islamic state or a violent fight for independence. However, some of the members of the revivalist movement of Kabardino-Balkaria trained in Chechnya and took part in the Chechen independence campaign. These radical individuals eventually influenced the ideology of the jamaat of Kabardino-Balkaria that, during the second Chechen campaign, transformed into the radical Jamaat Yarmuk.

Karachaevo-Cherkessia also came under the influence of Wahhabi religious revival. In 1991 Muhammad Bidzhiev, an IRP member, declared the founding of the Imamate of Karachai. The imamate represented the establishment of an Islamic state in Karachaevo-Cherkessia run by sharia law. It subsequently gave rise to a network of jamaats similar to those in Kabardino-Balkaria; this movement was also nonviolent. However, Bidzhiev's movement was rather short lived. By the mid-1990s the Karachaevo-Cherkessia Islamic jamaats had transformed into more radical centers under the guidance of Ramazan Borlakov. These jamaats later led to the rise of the militant Karachaevo-Cherkessia jamaat.

In Ingushetia the spread of Wahhabism led to the establishment of its own institution of higher Islamic learning in 1995 under the leadership of Isa Tsetchoev. An Ingush mufti called Tsetchoev's education center a "breeding ground of banditism." Similarly, official accounts described Tsetchoev as the person who "introduced Wahhabism to the republic, was a recruiter for the insurgents, an extremist and an Arab spy."[27] Subsequently, Ingushetia became one of the first republics in the North Caucasus to ban Wahhabism. In 1998 the Ingush authorities shut down Tsetchoev's center. In August 1998 Ruslan Aushev outlawed Wahhabism in Ingushetia with the approval of local Muslim clergy. At the same time Aushev cooperated with the Ingush clergy to prevent the further spread of Wahhabism by co-opting some of the ideas advanced by Wahhabis. For instance, the Ingush president supported the introduction of sharia as a way to counter corruption. As Ruslan Aushev explained, sharia had always been part of life in the North Caucasus: "We have developed our customs and traditions over centuries. I have always said this. Even Lenin allowed the mountainous republic to implement sharia law. The Soviet government allowed the mountainous republic, the mountaineers, to have sharia law."[28]

Dagestan was influenced the most by Wahhabism. In 1992, in Makhachkala, Akhmad Akhtaev, an active member of the IRP, founded an organization called al-Islamiyya. The aims of al-Islamiyya included the spiritual awakening of Muslims, and the group focused on the revival of the Islamic faith. The Arabic element of Wahhabism made it especially popular in Dagestan, as it had historically been the region most influenced by Arabic culture in the North Caucasus. Wahhabi converts here included Dargins, Lezgins, and Kumyks. By 1998 there were between 2,000 and 4,000 converts.[29] However, even in Dagestan, the Wahhabi movement remained rather marginal. Geographically, it was mainly localized around the Buinaksk and Kizilyurtovsky regions. The villages of Karamakhi, Chabanmakhi, Kadar, and Chankurbe emerged as the main Dagestani Wahhabi strongholds.

The spread of Wahhabism in Dagestan was resisted by the local authorities and in December 1997 the Dagestani government issued a new law on religion that tried to limit Wahhabi activities. On September 22, 1999, Wahhabism was banned completely in the republic as an extremist activity. Due to government persecution, Wahhabi communities often clashed with the Dagestani security services, and gradually Wahhabism in the republic acquired a political agenda. Similar to the emergence of Muridism, Wahhabism transitioned from a religious revivalist movement to a movement advocating liberation from Russia. Just like Ghazi Muhammad in the nineteenth century declared jihad against Russia, the evolution of Wahhabism in the 1990s led to the emergence of calls for Dagestan's political independence. The authority of Akhmad Akhtaev was replaced by his former colleague, another Dagestani named Bagautdin Kebedov, who came to be called Bagautdin Muhammad. Bagautdin became known as a liaison between the Wahhabi communities of Dagestan and Chechnya, as well as with foreign Wahhabis.

In 1997 Bagautdin established the Islamic Jamaat of Dagestan, which pronounced the pro-Russian Dagestani government as its enemy. As Bagautdin explained, "We don't want to hold power, we want Allah to hold power. Geographical and national boundaries have no meaning for us, we work where we can. Dagestan is currently ruled from Moscow, and we do not have an Islamic society analogous to that which exists in Chechnya."[30] This way, along with religious purification of Dagestan, Bagautdin began calling for secession from Russia. In January 1998 Bagautdin issued a manifesto for the Muslim world in which he declared war on the pro-Russian government of Dagestan.[31] Dagestani Wahhabis started looking to Chechnya for inspiration in terms of the independence project. As one adherent explained, "Chechens defeated the Russians. Now it is our turn to fight for the creation of an Islamic state."[32]

In the mid-1990s Bagautdin Muhammad established close links with some of the Chechen leaders, including Shamil Basayev, Movladi Udugov, and Zelimkhan Yandarbiyev. It is through these contacts that the idea of sharia governance reached Chechnya. In fact, in December 1997 Bagautdin Muhammad moved to Chechnya, where he coordinated the spiritual education of Chechen and Dagestani separatists along with Afghan mujahedeen.

In this endeavor Bagautdin cooperated with Khattab's training center Kavkaz. The unification of the liberation movement against Russia emerged from these contacts between Chechen separatists and Dagestani Wahhabis. Just as Islam had previously rallied the peoples of the North Caucasus against the Russian conquest, the Wahhabi strand consolidated diverse groups in their strife against the Russian domination during the twentieth century in their efforts to establish an independent unified Islamic state governed by sharia.

This was the way Wahhabism arrived in Chechnya. Unlike in other areas of the North Caucasus where Wahhabism had local roots, most of the early Wahhabis in Chechnya were foreigners. Russian authorities traced the origins of Wahhabism in Chechnya to the branch of the Muslim Brotherhood that opened in Grozny in 1991.[33] Many Chechens first came in contact with Wahhabism through the activities of Afghan mujahedeen during the first Chechen war. After this the main base of Wahhabism became the village of Serzhen-Yurt—the location of Khattab's Kavkaz training center. Many Wahhabis came to Chechnya from neighboring Dagestan and other North Caucasus republics.

Many Chechens, including President Maskhadov and his supporters, were skeptical of the Wahhabi movement. Shamil Basayev spoke against Wahhabism immediately following the first Chechen war, pointing out that it was foreign to Chechen ideals. In turn, Dagestani Wahhabis were cautious toward the Chechen fight because the Chechens were Sufis. Khattab himself had referred to Sufis as enemies.[34] However, Wahhabism gradually gained support in postwar Chechnya. Wahhabi influence was primarily established through financial incentives both at the leadership and individual levels. For the Ichkeriia leadership, especially Maskhadov's opposition, foreign Wahhabis brought foreign funds for the insurgency. For individuals, Wahhabi funds became a source of income as unemployment spread. As one adherent recalled:

> For my acceptance of the new purified faith, the Arabs gave me money as a gift and told me that if I brought round two more followers, they would give me $5,000 for each of them. So I brought two of my relatives from Dagu-Barzoi. They gave them $1,000 each, and I earned $10,000.[35]

The bond between Chechen separatists and Wahhabis emerged for instrumental reasons. While in Dagestan Wahhabism primarily emerged as a theological religious revival movement, in Chechnya it took roots as an instrument for achieving political goals.

This way the movement for religious revival in the 1990s resulted in the proliferation of Wahhabi jamaats across the North Caucasus. Some of these jamaats aimed for religious purification, the establishment of "true" Islam, and social revival. Others tried to achieve the establishment of an Islamic state under sharia governance. Many jamaat members took part in the Chechen wars for independence. However, before the 2000s such initiatives were predominantly disjointed. Before the second Chechen war, the activities of the jamaats were not organized by a unified center, and most efforts remained peaceful. It was only after the beginning of the second Chechen war and the corresponding Russian counterterrorist operations that the North Caucasus jamaats began to unite around the common cause of anti-Russian jihad.

In terms of militant activity, the main product of the 1990s religious revival movement was the alliance between Chechen separatists and Dagestani Wahhabis. The Chechen-Dagestani links lay the foundation for the emergence of a unifying ideology of liberation from Russia using the slogans advanced by Wahhabi religious interpretations. Even though the union between Chechen and Dagestani rebels was rather instrumental, it was also through this alliance that the Wahhabi religious narratives influenced the Chechen independence movement. The Dagestani religious revival was also affected by Chechen militancy. These links also influenced the evolution of demands of the internal opposition to Maskhadov's regime in Chechnya. Maskhadov's opposition emerged to call for the establishment of an Islamic state, and in 1999 sharia government was proclaimed in the Chechen Republic of Ichkeriia.

MASKHADOV'S OPPOSITION

Not everybody in Chechnya welcomed the election of Aslan Maskhadov as president in January 1997. Shamil Basayev declared his intention to form the opposition immediately following the elections. Some Chechen separatists interpreted Maskhadov's readiness to negotiate with Moscow as abandonment of the separatist cause. In 1997 Maskhadov's opposition consolidated around the idea that Maskhadov did not truly represent the interests of the Chechen people. Gradually, in addition to conflicts over the meaning of the liberation struggle, the issue of religion became prominent on the agenda of Chechen self-determination. As Chechen-Wahhabi links grew, so did demands to install sharia government in independent Ichkeriia.

Opposition protests against Maskhadov's rule organized by Zelimkhan Yandarbiyev and Salman Raduyev started in Grozny in February–March 1997. By April–May 1997 the opposition camp was predominantly formed—in addition to Yandarbiyev and Raduyev, the opposition included Shamil Basayev, Arbi Barayev, and Movladi Udugov. While Basayev still occupied a post in Maskhadov's government, he was critical of the president for not being more aggressive in pushing for the de jure recognition of Chechnya's independence. According to Basayev, Maskhadov was too ready to compromise with Russia.

By the summer of 1997 it became increasingly clear that neither the West nor the Muslim world was eager to recognize Chechnya's independence against Russia's will. As a result, some Chechen separatists were ready to turn their focus back to the regional level. In their view, Chechen independence was an initial step on the way to the liberation of the entire Caucasus from Russia's rule. Consequently, some Chechen separatists engaged in projects aimed at consolidating the Caucasus into a single state, reviving the ideas of Imam Shamil and his followers. Dagestani Wahhabis provided a powerful element to further achievement of this goal—the religious quest for the Islamization of the region. Through contacts with both Dagestani and foreign Wahhabis, Maskhadov's opposition acquired religious coloring.

Trying to take advantage of the Muslim communities of Dagestan that were supportive of the Chechen cause, Movladi Udugov founded an organization called Islamic Nation. The founding conference of the organization in Grozny included 35 religious parties and movements from all over Chechnya and Dagestan. The goal behind the organization was declared to be "the unification of all the Muslims of Chechnya and Dagestan and the prevention of new wars on the territory of the North Caucasus."[36] The organization further evolved toward the aim of the "restoration of Islam [in the Caucasus] in its previous historical borders."[37] Udugov himself viewed this project as an attempt to re-create a single state, as in the era of Imam Shamil, in Chechnya and Dagestan.[38] Udugov's organization became one of the first in postwar Chechnya to imitate Imam Shamil's Imamate of the nineteenth century.

Around the same time, on August 17, 1997, Zelimkhan Yandarbiyev convened another organization—the Caucasus Confederation. The founding conference for Yandarbiyev's organization also took place in Grozny and was attended by political groups from the North Caucasus, Georgia, and Azerbaijan. The Caucasus Confederation was meant to continue the Caucasus struggle against "Russian colonialism."[39] As Yandarbiyev explained,

> The Caucasus has been oppressed for centuries by the Russian empire. It is not free yet. We have no right to pretend we see nothing around us now that we have our [Chechen] freedom at last. We can't truly be free if the rest of the Caucasus is not. All its people—the Dagestanis, Azeris, Ingushi, Georgians, Circassians, Cossacks—of whatever faith, are our brethren, we are all a single Caucasian nation... We are opening a new era in building a Common Caucasian Home free of slavery. Ichkeria plays the main role in that process, since we have shown ourselves as the most intrepid and dedicated fighters in five years of jihad.[40]

This became another anti-Russian pan-Caucasus project. As Yandarbiyev's vice chair Ali Ulkhaev indicated, the organization was prepared to overthrow Russian rule: "As long as Russian armed forces are present in the

Caucasus, no mention can even be made of any stability in the region."[41] To defend its goals, the Confederation created its own militant wing under the leadership of Mohammed Tagaev. Tagaev's group, known as the Insurgent Army of Imam Shamil, took an active role in militant activities in Dagestan during the summer and fall of 1999. Another militant group supported by Zelimkhan Yandarbiyev, the Special Purpose Islamic Regiment, emerged in 1996 headed by Arbi Barayev, and it presented another significant force against federal troops.

Both Udugov's Islamic Nation and Yandarbiyev's Caucasus Confederation initially capitalized on local Islamic movements and were cautious toward Wahhabi entities. Representatives of these organizations perceived Wahhabism as too politically extreme and therefore unappealing to local audiences.[42] For instance, one concern was that the Wahhabi rejection of elections was too foreign for local values. At the same time both the Islamic Nation and Caucasus Confederation developed closer links with Akhtaev's al-Islamiyya and Bagautdin Muhammad's organizations in Dagestan. Through these links the Chechen-Wahhabi connections consolidated and eventually led to the creation of another pan-Caucasus pro-Islamic organization.

In April 1998 a Congress of the Peoples of Chechnya and Dagestan convened in Grozny. Both Movladi Udugov and Zelimkhan Yandarbiyev took an active role in the creation of this organization, which also involved the participation of Wahhabi groups in the Caucasus. This new organization relied on the support of Khattab and his training center Kavkaz. The organization was headed by Shamil Basayev, and its goal was announced as the liberation of the Caucasus from Russia's rule and the establishment of an Islamic state in the region. The more immediate purpose of the organization was the unification of Chechnya and Dagestan as a means to foster stability in the tumultuous area.

As conflicts intensified between Dagestani Wahhabi communities and local authorities, the Congress of the Peoples of Chechnya and Dagestan turned its attention toward the liberation project in Dagestan. The Congress leadership expressed willingness to defend the interests of the Dagestani Muslim brothers against the Russian oppression. As early as May 1998 Shamil Basayev declared he was "ready to assist the people of Dagestan in their fight against the pro-Moscow government."[43] The Congress was prepared to come to the support of Dagestani Wahhabis when, in August 1998, the villages of Karamakhi and Chabanmakhi announced their sovereignty and introduced sharia law on their territory. As one of the Congress leaders stated,

> The Congress really sets as its goal demilitarization and decolonization of Dagestan and the introduction of sharia in the republic as the sole form of governance and style of life of the Muslims. In the long run that would be the unification of Chechnya and Dagestan into a single Islamic state as it

existed just recently in the last century under the Imamate of Shamil. Previously a Chechen would always say he is from Dagestan—our common motherland, and not from Chechnya. Our strife for unity and the desire to subject our life to the will of Allah by no means indicate an imminent war. We are against violence.[44]

The Congress of the Peoples of Chechnya and Dagestan came to represent the goal of resurrecting Imam Shamil's Imamate and was ready to strive for this aim militarily.

To achieve this purpose, the Congress founded several militant branches under its umbrella. The Islamic International Peacekeeping Brigade, also known as the International Islamic Battalion or International Islamic Brigade, was one such example. Basayev and Khattab referred to this force as a peacekeeping contingent ready to deploy in defense of the interests of fellow Muslims. In connection to the events in Dagestan, Basayev announced it was a "holy responsibility" of every Muslim to defend sharia.[45] As a result, Basayev was ready to deploy his peacekeeping forces in Dagestan in case of Russian military involvement in the sovereign villages. The Russian government, in turn, pronounced these groups to be terrorist organizations. The Supreme Court of the Russian Federation designated the Congress of the Peoples of Chechnya and Dagestan a terrorist organization in February 2003.

The creation of the Congress of the Peoples of Chechnya and Dagestan indicated a transition in the goals of Chechen separatists. While previously Basayev was fighting for Chechnya's independence, by 1998, under the influence of his Wahhabi allies, he became ready to defend the unity of Chechnya and Dagestan and the establishment of sharia law in the Caucasus. However, these goals were neither new nor unique in the North Caucasus. Udugov mentioned Imam Shamil in reference to his Islamic Nation; in addition, the founding members of Yandarbiyev's Caucasus Confederation referred to the 1917–1921 liberation struggle against Russia led by the Mountainous Republic and the Emirate of the North Caucasus. The members of the Congress of the Peoples of Chechnya and Dagestan recalled Imam Shamil's experiences trying to establish an Islamic state. Under Wahhabi influences, the Chechen-led organizations incorporated local historical context in their shaping of the goals and ambitions of the future struggle in the North Caucasus.

Due to the connections between his opposition and Dagestani Wahhabis, President Maskhadov was skeptical of these organizations. For instance, in Maskhadov's view, the Congress of the Peoples of Chechnya and Dagestan was a project set up to destabilize the situation in the region. According to Maskhadov, the Congress was an initiative of one of Russia's oligarchs—Boris Berezovsky—who was allegedly trying to promote anarchy in Chechnya with "Khattab's bases over here, Basayev's troops over there."[46]

As a result, Maskhadov initially condemned the organizational structures of his opposition as well as the concept of further involvement in Dagestan. However, under the growing pressure of the opposition, combined with the lack of support from the Kremlin, Maskhadov eventually embraced the religious agenda of Basayev and his team.

ISLAMIC STATE IN CHECHNYA

At the time of the declaration of independence, Chechnya was established as a secular state. However, Dzhokhar Dudayev realized the immense potential of religion as a tool for consolidating his people. As a result, he was ready to take advantage of religious symbols: on November 9, 1991, he was sworn into office on the Quran. Dudayev did not hesitate to invoke the name of Allah and encouraged his followers to wage jihad against Russia. Dudayev tasked his minister of justice Usman Imaev to work on a criminal code that would incorporate secular legal principles with sharia.[47] With the help of Sheikh Fathi in 1994–1995, Dudayev started an initiative to re-establish the system of sharia courts that had been closed down under communist rule in Chechnya. At the same time Dudayev realized Chechnya was not ready to become an Islamic state:

> The Qur'an and the imamate are holy causes, and we should not use those words in vain. There is a time for everything. There are many Muslim countries in the world, but few of them live in strict observance of Shari'a law. Besides, as we know only too well, not every Chechen is a Muslim. The roots of Islam have been badly damaged here by the communists, and we cannot restore them in an hour or even a year. I respect your insistence, but I find it premature ... So let us put our souls in order according to the Qur'an, and our lives according to the constitution.[48]

After Dudayev the religious initiative was not abandoned. The sharia courts project culminated in a decree issued by Dudayev's successor Zelimkhan Yandarbiyev in December 1996 that replaced secular courts with sharia ones. The president opened the Supreme Sharia Court, which was later confirmed by the parliament of the republic. As power in Chechnya transferred to Aslan Maskhadov in January 1997, he followed his predecessors' goal of reviving Islam in the republic. In his pre-elections speech Maskhadov indicated that he envisioned Chechnya as a state with strong Islamic traditions in the future:

> I think that a religious leader does not necessarily have to be the head of state. There is an erroneous impression that if a Constitution states that Islam is the state religion, you should not hold elections but appoint an Imam and be done with that. Islam allows for free democratic elections. But we will

delete from the Constitution all the articles that contradict our religion, customs and traditions ... In the future I see a Chechen Islamic independent state. But under no conditions will we allow Sudan or Saudi Arabia, for instance, to impose their state structures on us. We are Chechens, we have our own traditions and customs. Our daily lives are connected with Islam, we will build our own Islamic state. If I become president, there will be Islamic order in the republic, but not the same as some want to portray it—no one will cut off hands and heads. We will take the Criminal code, will figure out what is appropriate for us based on our traditions, will leave some articles that do not lead to excesses, and will transition to the rest gradually. But I consider the introduction of a sharia Criminal code wrong.[49]

In Maskhadov's vision, Chechnya was to emerge as a Muslim state with democratic institutions that would be based on the local culture and traditions and not foreign ideals such as those advocated by Wahhabis.

Loyal to his pre-election promise, Maskhadov proceeded with building his state on Sufi Islamic principles. Maskhadov closely cooperated with Akhmad Kadyrov, who had studied Sufi theology in Bukhara and Tashkent in Uzbekistan and served as a mufti of Ichkeriia. In 1997 Maskhadov amended the 1992 constitution of Chechnya to pronounce Islam as the state religion. Maskhadov was also firmly against foreign-imported Wahhabism, which caused confrontations with the opposition. He viewed Wahhabism as not only foreign but also potentially harmful. On August 13, 1997, to prevent the divisions that in Maskhadov's view Wahhabism incited, the president issued a decree banning the propaganda of any forms of Islam that promoted dissent. Mufti Akhmad Kadyrov supported Maskhadov's position on Wahhabism: "During the war in Chechnya units of volunteer Wahhabis from Arab countries came to help us. These units were very well armed and so our Chechens willingly joined them. Many of them became adherents of that doctrine [Wahhabism] and now are trying to teach us, claiming that we distort Islam."[50] As Maskhadov explained, Wahhabism remained foreign in Chechnya:

> We are Sufis, we are building a Chechen Islamic state that precludes religious extremism, fundamentalism, Wahhabism, and the like. There is no reason to scare people with this. We have always been Muslims and always will be. However, along with religion we accept all the values of democracy, freedom and equal rights. Islam, sharia—those are the values that served us even during the worst time under the communist regime. That was the only thing that helped my people to solve internal disputes. It is very difficult to instill other, secular, laws in Chechens.[51]

While he rejected Wahhabism, Maskhadov still moved, under pressure from the opposition, in the direction of accepting sharia as a form of governance. In his pre-election speech he rejected the possibility of sharia law, but by 1998 he described sharia as part of the North Caucasus heritage that could help run his state.

In Maskhadov's view, Wahhabism was closely associated with the proliferation of crime in the republic. The president described Wahhabis as "extremist forces striving to seize the state power and start a civil war in Chechnya."[52] In March–May 1998 units from Maskhadov's counterterrorist center carried out several operations against Wahhabi bases. Forces targeted a base in Urus-Martan that was known as a Wahhabi kidnapping center. In June 1998 Maskhadov declared a state of emergency as part of his anticrime initiative. Such actions led to the escalation of conflicts between Maskhadov and his opponents and on July 23, 1998, an assassination attempt was carried out against the president.

The opposition started calling for Maskhadov's resignation. Maskhadov was criticized for his misuse of power, his pro-Russian foreign policy, and his non-Islamic tendencies that violated the principles of sharia; in the view of the opposition, his secular government was contradictory to Islamic principles. The opposition blamed Maskhadov for conspiring with the Kremlin. In the view of the opposition, Maskhadov was jeopardizing the hard-won Chechen victory and was throwing away Chechnya's independence by trying to appease the Kremlin. In Movladi Udugov's words, a true Islamic state had to be based on sharia, and there was no room for "such words as president, parliament or constitution."[53] In July 1998 Shamil Basayev resigned as prime minister in Maskhadov's government. He argued,

> We are not the opposition. Maskhadov is the opposition to his people. We are not against the state and its structure, not against the existing government. Why would we be the opposition? We are being branded with another label. We are simply stating that Maskhadov is a criminal who breached the constitution and must answer according to the law.[54]

Maskhadov in turn openly called Zelimkhan Yandarbiyev an "ideational inspirator of the Wahhabi movement" in Chechnya and accused him of inciting chaos and instability in the republic.[55] By December 1998 Maskhadov was ready to use force against centers of oppositional resistance mainly located around Urus-Martan, Serzhen-Yurt, and Vedeno.

At the height of the confrontation, however, Maskhadov made a move toward appeasing his opposition. On February 3, 1999, Maskhadov issued a decree that introduced sharia law in Chechnya to "make peace and unity of the Chechen people come true, in order to implement the laws of God, guided by the Holy Quran and Sunnah."[56] The decree disbanded parliament and replaced the constitution with a new religious version modeled on Sudan's 1983 legal code. The move was accompanied by several shocking public executions in Grozny that undermined Maskhadov's standing both domestically and abroad. Maskhadov calculated that the introduction of sharia would weaken his opposition.[57] Contrary to his expectations, however, the opposition declined to cooperate and instead announced their decision to create their own Islamic Council.

The situation deteriorated further until the Russian response to the Dagestani events of summer–fall 1999 brought Maskhadov and his opposition back together. By the fall of 1999 Russian forces had returned to Chechnya. In September 1999 Prime Minister Vladimir Putin publicly questioned the legitimacy of Maskhadov's rule, thus undermining Maskhadov's standing as a leader of Chechnya. Maskhadov realized that Moscow had virtually annulled all existing agreements with Chechnya and proceeded to realign with his opposition. He declared that he would not "allow the Russian troops to march to the center of Grozny"[58] and instituted martial law in October 1999. The holy war against Russia proceeded with the participation of diverse Chechen factions, including the Wahhabis. Gradually, as the second Chechen campaign progressed, the diverse jamaats consolidated under Maskhadov's command. Among these forces also were foreign fighters.

KHATTAB AND AFGHAN MUJAHEDEEN

Russia began the second Chechen war as a counterterrorist operation against international terrorist forces harboring in Chechnya. The main basis for this claim was the presence in Chechnya of foreign fighters, predominantly the former mujahedeen who had fought against the Soviet Union in Afghanistan. The participation of Afghan mujahedeen in the Chechen struggle gave Russia reasons to claim that Chechen separatists were connected to Al Qaeda, and the leader of foreign contingents, Khattab, was Osama bin Laden's emissary. However, while many Afghan mujahedeen did indeed fight against the Russian federal troops, their precise links with Al Qaeda and Bin Laden remain convoluted. The significance of Afghan mujahedeen in the Chechen cause seems to have been somewhat exaggerated in Russian accounts.

In Russia, Samir Saleh al-Suwailem, also known as Habib Abdul Rahman, gained notoriety under the name Khattab. According to the Russian government, Khattab was an Al Qaeda leader in Chechnya who linked Chechen fighters with Bin Laden's terrorists. Khattab was portrayed as a foreign Wahhabi who radicalized the Chechen fighters to fight for a foreign cause. Despite the resultant image of Khattab as Russia's own Osama bin Laden, the available evidence suggests that his main role in Chechnya was the training of Chechen separatists in irregular warfare tactics. Khattab considered himself a military professional and left a memoir titled *The Experience of the Arab Ansar*[59] in *Chechnya Afghanistan and Tajikistan*. Khattab claimed he had come to Chechnya to support jihad: "I am not a mercenary, not a terrorist, not a hero. I am a Muslim, a simple mujahid who fights for Allah. Russia was mistreating Muslims, that is why I came to help brothers liberate themselves from the Russians. I fought with brothers in Bosnia, Tajikistan, Afghanistan. I help brothers."[60]

Born in Saudi Arabia, Khattab finished high school, after which his family wanted him to study in the United States. At that time the Soviet-Afghan war had begun in Afghanistan. In 1988 Khattab joined the ranks of Afghan Arab mujahedeen. He received training in Jalalabad camps and acquired firsthand military experience fighting the Soviets. After Afghanistan, Khattab joined the Islamic opposition in the civil war in Tajikistan. In Grozny he appeared in the winter of 1995. This is how he explained his reason for joining the Chechen struggle:

> I do not consider myself a terrorist or a leader of criminals as Russian newspapers portray me. I am simply taking part in armed struggle of Muslims with kafir, unbelievers . . . when the war started I looked at the map and saw a little spot there—Chechnya. There jihad was on in the name of Allah for the faith. Having arrived in Chechnya we saw that everyone was at war, adults, children and women. We asked them: "What are you fighting for?" They answered: "For faith!" It was enough for us, we decided to fight along with our Muslim brothers.[61]

However, due to the fact that Chechens were predominantly Sufi, and Dudayev, a former Soviet general, headed the struggle, Khattab was initially cautious in joining the Chechen separatists. As a result, he first made contact with Dagestani Wahhabis and arrived in Chechnya among their groups. In Chechnya he joined Sheikh Fathi, who at the time was the main liaison between Chechen separatists and Afghan mujahedeen.

Even though Khattab was present in Chechnya during the first war, little mention of him was made in the Russian media or by the Russian government. According to Khattab, during the first war he was a "leader of the central front with brother Shamil [Basayev]."[62] Khattab's name became known during the first war only due to his brutal attacks against federal forces, such as the one in Iaryshmardy in April 1996. He also became known for filming the attacks and posting videos on the Internet, supposedly to attract extremist sponsors.

After the first war was over, Khattab stayed in the area and even married a local Darghin woman from the Dagestani Wahhabi village of Karamakhi. As Khattab explained, it was a way to overcome any local animosity toward Afghan mujahedeen: "We married from the people here and made sure that we become relatives and kindred, so the issue was over and no one dared to do anything against us because we became relatives and kindred."[63] By 1998 Khattab had partnered with Shamil Basayev under the Congress of the Peoples of Chechnya and Dagestan and was ready to deploy his military detachments under the banner of the unified state of Chechnya and Dagestan governed by sharia. Khattab was accused of ordering the apartment bombings in Russia in the fall of 1999 and was therefore placed on Interpol's wanted list. Khattab was killed in 2002, by a poisoned letter delivered to him by a courier, in a Russian special operation.

Russian sources made a concerted effort to portray Khattab as a terrorist commissioned by Bin Laden to wage jihad against Russia. Some international sources also pointed toward a connection. For instance, a controversial declassified U.S. Defense Intelligence Agency (DIA) report of October 16, 1998, suggested that Khattab was a personal friend of Osama bin Laden. According to the report, Bin Laden specifically assigned Khattab to train international terrorists in Chechnya. However, the report contains rather superficial information and is riddled with numerous spelling mistakes, including the misspelling of Udugov's name. With no factual evidence, it can hardly be treated as solid data. Movladi Udugov called the report a "pack of lies and a gross provocation," stating that it was not the first among "claims about alleged Chechen groups in Afghanistan, Pakistan and Iraq." Udugov proceeded, "It is a known fact that neither Russians nor Americans or British have ever presented any fact substantiating their claims in this regard."[64] While both Basayev and Khattab spent time in Afghanistan, it remains unclear whether in reality they ever personally met Osama bin Laden. Basayev himself denied that either he or Khattab ever met Bin Laden.[65] As Basayev said, "If bin Laden gave me 25 million as newspapers report, why would I run around the mountains and fight the Russian soldiers? I would simply buy them off."[66]

Both Basayev and Khattab were named as terrorists in Russia. At the same time, their activities were somewhat different. Basayev was clearly involved in terrorist attacks and publicly claimed responsibility for many of them. Khattab, on the other hand, was preoccupied with militant activities that qualified as guerilla tactics at best. He was a field commander responsible for numerous raids against Russian forces, but he denied any involvement in the apartment bombings and claimed he was fighting against the Russian army, not women and children.[67] Even some Russian sources pointed out that Khattab was "no more than a military instructor, and his surreal success is mostly the result of propaganda."[68] Khattab's activities in Chechnya resembled those of mujahedeen against the Soviets in Afghanistan, and Khattab's significance in planning and carrying out terrorist attacks across Russia seems to have been somewhat overstated.

What seems to be more accurate in regards to Khattab's biography was his role in training Chechen separatists, coordinating Afghan mujahedeen, and involving himself with foreign funding for the Chechen cause. One of his most significant projects, which started during the first war and grew in the interwar years, was the training center Kavkaz, established in Serzhen-Yurt in 1995. After the first war Chechen separatists were not convinced of the finality of their victory over Russian forces, and Khattab continued running his training facilities. According to Khattab, he was training future fighters: "we are preparing the youth for the future aggression on the part of kafir so that they can survive, if only by deactivating the mines left by the Russian troops."[69] In the interwar period the system of Khattab's camps, modeled on training centers in Afghanistan and Pakistan, expanded under the umbrella of what he called the Al-Qoqaz Institute for preparing the Dawah and Duaat, or the Islamic Institute of the Caucasus—an organization reportedly established as a branch of the Muslim Brotherhood. Training camps began operating across Chechnya, Dagestan, and in Pankisi Gorge on the border with Georgia.

Early students of Khattab's camp were mostly Chechens, 60–80 percent of whom were Sufis. Even though Khattab was apprehensive of Sufis, he welcomed his students, saying, "What you have in your mind, you will answer about it before Allah. I'm only concerned about praying five times, fasting Ramadan and the Quran session in the morning, that's the most important thing for me in the camp, training and work."[70] However, to educate the fighters on matters of religion, students engaged in studies of the Quran and the Hadith, along with studies of jihad, namely the interpretations of it based on the work of Abdullah Azzam and other ideologues of Afghanistan mujahedeen. Students were also instructed on subversive action and politics.

Khattab's training system grew to include dozens of Afghan and Arab instructors. The courses ran for around three weeks, and students even received stipends in the amount of $200.[71] According to Khattab, at one point over 400 people were training in a single course. By the time of the second Chechen war, between 1,600 and 2,500 fighters had graduated from the camps.[72] Students included individuals from the North Caucasus—Dagestanis, Chechens, Ingush, Balkars, Karachai, Kabardins—as well as representatives from Central Asia, including Uzbeks and Tajiks. At one of the graduation ceremonies, Khattab left his mujahedeen with a message: "We trained you for a month in the arts of subversive action, bribery, disseminating rumors. Your goal is to spread deathly fear among those who sold Allah."[73]

It was these training facilities that spread the radicalism of Afghan mujahedeen combined with local Wahhabi teachings. New generations of fighters for Chechen independence graduated with the knowledge of religious tenets based on Wahhabism. Graduates from Khattab's centers were exposed to the idea of waging global jihad against nonbelievers. At the same time Khattab adjusted his ideology for local audiences. For example, instead of proclaiming his goal as the establishment of a global caliphate, he was content with fighting for sharia in the Caucasus. "The Caucasus is the only gateway between the West and the East—the part of the Muslim world where sharia has to rule," Khattab stated.[74] The training camps also included local ideologues who worked to prevent the ideas of global jihad from taking root in the North Caucasus. For instance, Dagestani Bagautdin Muhammad joined the system with his training camps in Urus-Martan, which allowed the ideological message that emerged before the second Chechen war to still be focused on the local project of the unification of Chechnya and Dagestan modeled on Imam Shamil's Imamate.

A further significance of Khattab in the North Caucasus was as a leader of Afghan mujahedeen. Afghan mujahedeen appeared in Chechnya during the first war, but their exact number remained controversial. According to Russian sources, foreign fighters from Afghanistan, Azerbaijan, the Baltic states, Egypt, Georgia, Jordan, Saudi Arabia, Syria, Tajikistan, Turkey, and Ukraine fought on the side of the separatists. Sergei Stepashin, the head of the FSB at the time, claimed that foreign mercenaries received $800 per day to fight for the Chechen cause.[75] However, according to alternative sources, only around 80 foreign fighters took part in the first war.[76] By the start of the second war, Russian presidential aide Sergei Iastrzhembskii claimed the Chechen forces included up to 800 foreign mercenaries.[77]

One of the first recruiters of Afghan mujahedeen to arrive in the Caucasus was Sheikh Fathi. Fathi appeared in Chechnya in the 1990s and brought the first group of Afghan mujahedeen with him. With these mujahedeen, Sheikh Fathi formed his Islamic Battalion, the leadership of which was assumed by Khattab. Using the funding he brought with him, Fathi also started organizing a system of schools and mosques. According to some sources, it was Fathi who had links with Bin Laden—he coordinated the funds received from Bin Laden through the banks of Malaysia and Indonesia.[78] After the first Chechen war Fathi's jamaats spread around Urus-Martan, Gudermes, and Vedeno. Along with Khattab, other Afghan mujahedeen participated in Fathi's network, including Abu al-Walid, Abu Omar al-Saif, and Abu Jaffar.

Abu al-Walid became another name associated with Al Qaeda in Russia. Abu al-Walid, another Saudi, also appeared in Chechnya in the 1990s. He had previously spent time in Afghanistan, where he worked in Abdulla Azzam's organizations. Al-Walid fought along with Khattab and succeeded the latter after his death in 2002. Perhaps the most famous name among foreign fighters connected to Chechnya with links to Al Qaeda remains that of Ayman al-Zawahiri. After being expelled from Sudan in 1996, Al-Zawahiri tried to enter Chechnya. In justifying his reason for going there, Al-Zawahiri envisioned the creation of a unified Islamic state and wrote that "if the Chechens and other Caucasus mujahideen reach the shores of the oil rich Caspian, the only thing that will separate them from Afghanistan will be the neutral state of Turkmenistan. This will form a mujahid Islamic belt to the south of Russia."[79] However, Al-Zawahiri was arrested by the Russian services and spent six months in a Russian jail. As an FSB spokesman explained, al-Zawahiri "had four passports, in four different names and nationalities... We checked him out in every country, but they could not confirm him. We could not keep him forever, so we took him to the Azerbaijani border and let him go."[80] After his release al-Zawahiri moved to Afghanistan.

Besides coordinating the activities of Afghan mujahedeen in Chechnya, Khattab was involved in foreign fundraising for the Chechen cause. Much of the foreign funding came from international charity organizations, with the main benefactors reportedly including Afghanistan, Kuwait, Pakistan, Qatar, Saudi Arabia, and Turkey. Some of the funding was purely humanitarian, other sources covered the expenses of Afghan mujahedeen in the Caucasus, while yet others funded religious work. Among the most active organizations in Chechnya were Saudi Igatha, Kuwaiti Jamaat al-Turath al-Islamii, and Saudi al-Haramein.[81] Khattab was responsible for bringing in Al-Haramein funding through the umbrella of the Muslim Brotherhood.[82] The group mainly channeled its funds through Azerbaijan; Baku subsequently shut down the local office.[83] U.S. Executive Order 13224 designated Al-Haramein as an entity with terrorist links. Another organization listed on the U.S. Executive Order for Al Qaeda links was the Benevolence International Foundation (BIF), a charity based in Chicago. The charity sent funds to Chechnya through Sheikh Fathi. Many other foreign organizations have also been involved in channeling money to Chechen separatists ranging from thousands to millions of dollars.[84]

Before the start of the second Chechen war, Russia tried to portray Chechnya as a safe haven for international terrorists. Al Qaeda itself showed significant interest in Chechnya. For instance, in 1997 Osama bin Laden described Chechnya as part of the struggle his Afghan mujahedeen were prepared to fight for, "their going to Bosnia, Chechnya, Tajikistan and other countries is but a fulfillment of a duty, because we believe that these states are part of the Islamic world," he said.[85] However, it seemed that the actual links between Chechen separatists and Al Qaeda were much more distant than either the Russian government or Bin Laden wanted to portray. By the start of the second Chechen war, direct contacts between Chechnya and Al Qaeda command remained controversial.

The ideological influence of Al Qaeda on the Chechen separatists through the Afghan mujahedeen also seemed quite limited. By 1999 Chechen separatists were receiving training organized by Khattab, had Afghan mujahedeen fighting among their ranks, and were collecting foreign funding for their activities. However, Chechen separatists were less inclined to participate in the global religious war than in the local independence project. The religious element of their ideology was a product of historical experiences with Islam and local religious revival rather than the Al Qaeda declaration of global jihad against nonbelievers and apostate governments. The indigenous element also prevailed in their declared goal: Chechens were willing to fight for liberation from Russia and the unification of

Chechnya and Dagestan rather than for the establishment of a global caliphate. This way, by the start of the second war, Chechen and Dagestani units were prepared to continue waging jihad against Russia rather than declaring jihad against the rest of the world.

TERRORISM AND DAGESTAN INTERVENTIONS

Similar to the years of Chechnya's de facto independence under Dudayev, the second era of de facto independence between 1997 and 1999 was not accompanied by much attention from the Kremlin. At the time Moscow was facing much internal turmoil. In 1998 Yeltsin's opposition initiated an impeachment process against the president. August 1998 brought about one of the worst economic crises in Russian history. Several prime ministers were fired before Vladimir Putin was appointed in August 1999. In the meantime the 2001 deadline stated in the Khasavyurt Accords was approaching, and the situation in Chechnya was deteriorating. Maskhadov's efforts to combat crime were ineffective, and clashes between his forces and Wahhabi groups became more frequent. Acts of terrorism resumed.

One of the most gruesome events of the interwar era that was linked to the destabilizing situation in Chechnya was the assassination of six international Red Cross personnel in Novye Atagi on December 17, 1996. The attack was immediately ascribed to Chechen separatists. In response to these allegations Chechnya's head of state security apparatus Abu Movsaev claimed that the killing was organized by Russia's FSB.[86] The FSB had supposedly committed the act to destabilize the situation in Chechnya, which would then justify the need for Russia's new intervention. This became one of a series of terrorist attacks that the Russian services ascribed to Chechen separatists, while the Chechen separatists in turn blamed the Russian services. These controversial attacks led up to the September 1999 apartment bombings that were used to justify the start of the counterterrorist operation in Chechnya, but the perpetrators remained disputed. Interestingly, in the case of the Red Cross assassination, former FSB major Aleksei Potemkin corroborated the Chechen explanation of the attack.[87] According to Potemkin, he was part of the FSB group that carried out the operation, the aim of which was to frame Chechen separatists.

In April 1997 two explosions followed: on April 23 at a railway station in Armavir and on April 28 at a railway station in Piatigorsk. The Russian authorities immediately issued a statement naming the Chechens as responsible for the explosions. According to official reports, suspicious Caucasian-looking individuals were spotted in Armavir prior to the explosion.[88] Several days after the Piatigorsk attack, two Chechens—Fatima Taimaskhanova and Aiset Dadasheva—were arrested and later convicted for carrying out the attack. As with the Red Cross assassination, the

Chechen leadership denied any connection to the explosions in Armavir and Piatigorsk, and Maskhadov's administration again claimed the terrorist acts were organized by Russia's special services.[89]

At the same time the criminal situation in Chechnya deteriorated. On May 1, 1998, Valentin Vlasov, Yeltsin's envoy in Chechnya, was kidnapped near the border with Ingushetia. President Maskhadov himself acknowledged the criminal problems in his republic, saying, "we will spare no effort in finding Vlasov ... We will also apologize to the Russian government and personally to Vlasov. The kidnapping happened on our territory, and we bear the responsibility."[90] Vlasov was released after being held in captivity for six months. The kidnappings did not stop there, and on March 5, 1999, Russian general Gennady Shpigun was abducted. After these kidnappings Moscow started actively preparing for re-engaging the military in Chechnya. It was around this time that Moscow began to secretly transfer troops to the North Caucasus to prepare for a military operation in August–September 1999.[91]

Moscow's plan for redeploying the military was greatly facilitated by the events in Dagestan. Initially it was the instability in the Wahhabi-controlled areas of Dagestan that drew the Russian military back to the North Caucasus. Clashes between the Dagestani government and Wahhabi communities had started back in the mid-1990s. In 1996 significant clashes occurred around the Wahhabi village of Karamakhi. On December 21, 1997, a group of Dagestani Wahhabis under the leadership of Bagautdin Muhammad attacked a military base in Buinaksk. Despite the fact that the raid was organized and carried out by the Dagestanis, Russian authorities blamed Khattab for orchestrating the attack. In reaction to these allegations, Shamil Basayev stated he would not send his people so far to get a "couple of tanks," and Movladi Udugov in turn blamed the raid on the Russian security services.[92] The group failed to take over the base, and Bagautdin Muhammad escaped to Chechnya, where he joined Khattab in training Chechen fighters.

On August 16, 1998, the villagers of Karamakhi and Chabanmakhi in the Kadarskii region of Dagestan declared themselves a sovereign Islamic territory and rejected Russian authority. The territory declared the implementation of sharia law and replaced the Russian security services with its own armed formations. A shura council was convened, and border checkpoints were equipped with signs saying, "Beware! Sharia law is in effect on this territory."[93] In response to the declaration of sovereignty, the government of Dagestan in Makhachkala pronounced the move "unconstitutional, presenting a security threat to Dagestan, threatening its territorial integrity, which can lead to tragic outcomes."[94] Clashes followed between Dagestani authorities and Wahhabi security formations. As a result of the clashes on August 21, 1998, Dagestani mufti Saidmagomed Abubakarov was assassinated. It was at this point that Shamil Basayev announced he was ready to defend sharia law in Dagestan with his peacekeeping forces of the Congress of the Peoples of Chechnya and Dagestan.

In early September 1998 interior minister of the Russian Federation Sergei Stepashin visited Dagestan to discuss the crisis with Wahhabi leaders. During the negotiations Stepashin was able to reach an agreement. The Russian services agreed not to continue repressive measures against Wahhabi communities, and the Wahhabis agreed to restore constitutional order on their territory. Stepashin left with a promise that "no forceful action will be taken towards individuals practicing non-traditional Islam in Dagestan. If you want to follow Islamic customs and traditions—follow them. No one will interfere."[95] The Dagestani Wahhabi communities were largely left alone for another year.

Military action in Dagestan started on August 2, 1999. In July, Bagautdin Muhammad proclaimed sharia law in the Tsumadinskii region of Dagestan along the model used in the Kadarskii region. This led to clashes between Dagestani Wahhabis and local security services, and on August 2 Bagautdin's forces entered the Tsumadinskii region. In response Moscow sent MVD divisions to Dagestan. On August 6 Dagestani Wahhabis issued a declaration of the restoration of the Islamic State of Dagestan and asked their Chechen counterparts for protection from the Russian government.[96] On August 7, to support Bagautdin's forces in Dagestan, Basayev and Khattab crossed the border into the republic.[97] Their Islamic International Peacekeeping Brigade along with Tagaev's Insurgent Army of Imam Shamil led operation Imam Ghazi Muhammad to the Tsumadinskii and Botlikhskii regions. Khattab explained that he led his forces in response to the request for help from his Dagestani partners: "The [Dagestani] government asked the Russians for help, so the brothers [Dagestani Wahhabis] asked the mujahidin for help and we entered before the Russians."[98] Basayev described this campaign in similar terms and suggested that Bagautdin's return to Dagestan was staged by the Russian security services:

> The government of the Republic of Dagestan itself insisted that Dagestanis under the leadership of Bagautdin return with their weapons from the Chechen Republic of Ichkeriia home to the Tsumadinskii region pointing to the Karamakhi dwellers as an example. They believed it and fell into a trap. We considered it our responsibility to help the encircled Tsumadinskii dwellers facing annihilation, and then later the dwellers of Karamakhi.[99]

According to the Chechen separatists, the Botlikhskii intervention was meant to distract the Dagestani security services from the Tsumadinskii region.

On August 23 Basayev and Khattab retreated back to Chechnya. On their way to Chechnya the groups were targeted by Russian aviation. Attacks were carried out in the area of the Kharami mountain pass on the border between Chechnya and Dagestan. The Russian leadership was prepared for a full-scale military intervention and declared that it "reserved the right to attack insurgent bases on the territory of any North Caucasus region, including Chechnya."[100] In Dagestan, after the departure of the Chechen groups, federal troops launched an operation to liquidate the Islamic sovereignty of the Kadarskii region that earlier had been validated by Stepashin. The operation started on August 28 and in its course Russian control over the villages of Karamakhi and Chabanmakhi was restored.

As the Russian airstrikes targeted Basayev and Khattab's groups on their way back to Chechnya, they in response promised to "take all the adequate measures."[101] This promise was interpreted as an incriminating statement linking Chechnya to an explosion in Moscow on August 31, 1999. The explosion occurred in the very center of Moscow, in the city mall Okhotnyi Riad, which is located next to the Kremlin. The explosion happened as the events in Dagestan were evolving, and the attack was immediately attributed to the Chechen separatists. After arriving at the scene of the attack, Moscow mayor Yuri Luzhkov declared, "Of course, immediately one thinks of all sorts of links with Dagestan, with Chechnya."[102] The Caucasus connection was supported by a phone call to a news agency from a so-called Khasbulat claiming that he represented an army of the liberation of Dagestan. He took responsibility for the explosion, warning that "terrorist acts in Russia will continue until the Russian army leaves Dagestan."[103] In turn, Chechen deputy prime minister Kazbek Makhashev denied Chechen involvement.[104]

On September 5 Basayev and Khattab's forces engaged in another intervention in Dagestan in an operation called Gazavat-Bek. This time the Chechen groups entered the Novolakskii district of Dagestan—a region of dispute between Chechnya and Dagestan. By September 11 the Chechen groups were forced out of the area by Russian troops. The fighting then moved to Chechnya. Parallel to the events in Dagestan, a wave of apartment bombings took place in the Russian cities of Buinaksk, Moscow, and Volgodonsk. In response to the terrorist attacks, Prime Minister Putin declared it was necessary to "strangle the vermin at the root"[105] and, promising to rid Chechnya of terrorist cells, started the second military campaign there.

APARTMENT BOMBINGS

September 1999 is sometimes referred to as the Russian equivalent of September 11, 2001. During this month Russia experienced a wave of apartment bombings in several Russian cities; hundreds of people died as a result of the explosions, and hundreds more were injured. The apartment bombings became a key element in Russia's justification for announcing a counterterrorist operation in the North Caucasus that led to the presence of federal troops first in Dagestan and then in Chechnya. The bombings rallied Russian citizens behind Prime Minister Vladimir Putin, who insisted on a forceful solution to the growing terrorist threat. The apartment bombings became the final link that connected the insurgent events in Dagestan with the threat of terrorism that was in turn traced back to Chechnya.

On September 4, 1999, an explosion took place in the city of Buinaksk in Dagestan. A bomb exploded in a car parked in front of a five-story apartment building. An entire section of the building collapsed. The attack was immediately linked to the events in the Caucasus; it was seen as a reaction of the Wahhabi rebels to the actions of federal forces in Dagestan. Basayev and Khattab were announced as the masterminds behind the attack. Following the attack a wave of anti-Wahhabi sentiment swept Dagestan. At the scene of the explosion, a woman declared, "Now I will myself take up a gun and will start killing them. Wahhabis are real beasts, and a dog deserves the death of a dog. Their nests should be eradicated from the face of the earth. If you capture someone, don't kill them but give them to us. They deserve a slow painful death."[106]

On September 8 another explosion brought down a section of a nine-story apartment building. This time the explosion took place on Gur'ianov Street in Moscow. Similar to reactions to the Buinaksk attack, the most popular explanation for the Moscow attack became the Chechen connection. The explosion was traced back to Khattab; in Chechnya, he was responsible for training students in guerilla warfare and subversive tactics.[107] As with the explosion at Okhotnyi Riad in August, after the Gur'ianov attack a news agency received an anonymous phone call confirming the Chechen connection; a person "with a Caucasus accent" informed the agency that "The events in Moscow and Buinaksk are our response to the bombardments of peaceful villages in Chechnya and Dagestan."[108]

The series of explosions continued with a terrorist attack on Kashirskoe Shosse in Moscow on September 13. This time an eight-story apartment building was completely destroyed. This attack was carried out in a way similar to the Gur'ianov Street incident: explosives were planted inside the building in a rental space on the first floor. The explosion was immediately attributed to the Islamist terrorists of Khattab, with alleged links to Osama bin Laden. Again, according to official reports, it was Khattab's training camps that were responsible for breeding the terrorists that were attacking Russia: "This is a real terrorist war," declared an FSB spokesman.[109]

Another terrorist attack was averted on September 14 when explosives were found in an apartment complex in Borisovskie Prudy in Moscow. However, this did not mark the end of the wave of terrorism. On September 16 a truck full of explosives blew up in front of a nine-story apartment complex in Volgodonsk in the Rostov region. To add further gruesomeness to the attacks, several apartment residents reported suspicious phone calls before the explosives went off that inquired, "How are you feeling before death?"[110] A government official from the Rostov region declared the explosion part of the wave of Chechen terrorism, saying, "Today the norms and rules of normal peaceful life cannot function. A Chechen trace is clearly seen in the explosion. A war was declared on us and we need to take adequate measures."[111] Following the Volgodonsk attack, an FSB spokesman stated, "We are dealing with international terrorists, with a well-prepared plan."[112] Basayev and Khattab were again named as the masterminds behind this plan.

The public reaction to the apartment bombings was similar to the American response after September 11; the people demanded justice. The majority of Russian citizens—70 percent—readily blamed Chechen terrorists for the attacks.[113] The Russian government was confident that the Chechens were responsible even before the official investigations started. The Kremlin described the wave of apartment bombings as a methodical continuation of the previously started terrorist trend. According to Prime Minister Putin, the bombings were clearly linked to previous acts of terrorism committed by Chechen separatists. He said,

> The terrorists already have many crimes on their conscience. People have been dying by their hand in the Northern Caucasus for several years now. The blasts at the Pyatigorsk railway station and the Vladikavkaz market, the acts of terror in the Moscow metro and in Buinaksk, and the latest blasts in Moscow are undoubtedly all links in the same chain.[114]

Putin described the apartment bombings as a natural outcome of the events in Dagestan and suggested that the Wahhabi instability in Dagestan and terrorist attacks in Moscow were all perpetrated by the same criminals:

> It is clear to us that both in Dagestan and in Moscow we are dealing not with individual militants but with well-trained international subversives... Those who have organized and launched this large series of ruthless acts of terrorism have far-reaching plans, they hope to build up political tensions in Russia, and their main task is to destabilize the situation in the country.[115]

In his address to the State Duma, Putin pointed out that the terrorists were challenging the very foundations of the Russian state: "By blowing up the homes of our countrymen, the bandits are blowing up government and authority—nor presidential, municipal or parliamentary authority, but authority as such in the country."[116] In regards to the perpetrators of the apartment bombings, the Kremlin clearly pointed in the direction of Basayev and Khattab.

Basayev and Khattab in turn denied any connection to the apartment bombings. The apartment bombings became the few terrorist attacks for which Basayev and Khattab vehemently denied any responsibility, as they had done with several contested attacks of the interwar years discussed earlier. Shamil Basayev claimed responsibility for many terrorist acts, including the theater hostage crisis, the assassination of Akhmad Kadyrov, and numerous bombings. He further took responsibility for infrastructure accidents that were not even acts of terrorism. He readily acknowledged he was prepared to stage terrorist attacks: "Blasts and bombs, all this will go on, of course, because those whose women and children are being killed for nothing will also try to use force to eliminate their adversaries."[117] However, in the case of the apartment bombings, he publicly denied his involvement.[118] In a 2005 interview Basayev explained that it was in the strategic interests of Moscow to blame the apartment bombings on him, saying, "[The Russian government] also pinned the bombing of houses in Moscow and Volgodonsk on us without any proof and started the war.... If I had blown up those houses, I would never deny it."[119]

Khattab also denied any links to the apartment bombings. His statements, however, were a little more contradictory. In a statement on September 13, Khattab promised, "From now on we will not only fight against Russian fighter jets and tanks. From now on, they will get our bombs everywhere. Let Russia await our explosions blasting through their cities. I swear we will do it."[120] A day later Khattab reversed his position claiming, he would not engage in acts of terrorism: "We are waging open war with armed forces and never thought of emulating those who kill peaceful sleeping civilians with their bombs and shells."[121] The Chechen separatists suggested the apartment bombings were carried out by Russia's FSB "on Putin's orders."[122]

Chechen leaders often advanced statements blaming the Russian security services for terrorist attacks. In this respect, it would be unwise to rely solely on the explanations coming from individuals involved in illegal activities against the Russian state. However, in the case of the apartment buildings, it was not only Basayev and Khattab who cast doubt on the official version of the events. Controversy arose over the Ryazan incident that led many to believe the FSB was behind the apartment bombings. After the explosion in Volgodonsk, on September 22, 1999, in Ryazan in the Moscow area, residents of an apartment complex spotted a suspicious car; its license plate was covered up with a piece of paper. Several people were unloading white bags from the car into the basement of the apartment complex. The alarmed residents called the local police, who claimed the incident was an attempted terrorist attack.

The local security experts who investigated the incident uncovered traces of the explosive hexogen in the apartment complex basement, as well as a timing mechanism among the white bags. On September 23, based on the evidence they found, the local police announced that a terrorist attack had been averted in Ryazan.[123] However, a day later, on September 24, the federal security services came out with an explanation that negated the local version. FSB head Nikolai Patrushev announced, "The incident in Ryazan was not an explosion, nor was an explosion prevented there. It was a training exercise. It was sugar there."[124] According to Patrushev, the bags were full of sugar, not explosives, and the registered traces of explosives were blamed on faulty equipment. No further information was disclosed at the time, the case of an attempted terrorist attack started by the local security services was classified, and follow-up investigations were denied.

The Ryazan incident raised suspicions about the role of the FSB in the apartment bombings. It was not clear why the FSB would contradict the account of the local security agents who were working with forensic evidence. Further questions arose about the nature and protocol of the alleged training exercise. Alternative explanations for the apartment bombings that differed from the official version of Chechen terrorism began to emerge. In August 2001 former FSB officer Aleksandr Litvinenko and historian Yuri Felshtinsky published chapters of their book *Blowing Up Russia: Terror from Within*. The book claimed an FSB conspiracy behind the apartment bombings. In March 2002 exiled Russian oligarch Boris Berezovsky circulated a documentary in London that traced the apartment bombings to the Russian security services. In reaction to these versions, polls showed that 6 percent of Russian citizens had become convinced that the FSB orchestrated the apartment bombings. Another 37 percent believed that evidence warranted further investigation into FSB's involvement in the bombings.[125]

To examine the potential FSB connection and alternative claims, State Duma deputy Sergei Kovalev, former human rights commissioner, agreed in April 2002 to head an independent investigative committee. The committee set out to inspect the apartment bombings in Moscow and Volgodonsk, and the Ryazan training exercise.[126] The committee, however, did not achieve much success in the investigation process; security services refused to cooperate with the investigation. In 2003 when Kovalev approached the FSB for information on the training exercise in Ryazan, his request was denied. Several people involved in the investigations faced harassment. In 2006 Aleksandr Litvinenko, a proponent of the belief that the FSB was responsible for the bombings, was killed. Journalist Anna Politkovskaya, who was also questioning the facts behind the attacks, was killed the same year. The committee did not produce conclusive evidence to incriminate Russia's security services.

In the meantime Moscow conducted its own official investigations into the apartment bombings. In 2000 the investigation of the Buinaksk bombing was completed. The names of eight Dagestani Wahhabis were announced in connection to the bombing: Isa Zainutdinov, Alisultan Salikhov, Magomed Magomedov, Abdulkadyr Abdulkadyrov, Ziiavudin Ziiavudinov, Zainutdin Zainutdinov, Makhach Abdulsamedov, and Magomed Salikhov. According to the prosecution, these individuals received training at Khattab's centers, where they had learned how to deal with explosives.[127] It was also alleged that the perpetrators then took part in the Wahhabi raids against the government of Dagestan in the summer of 1999. The prosecution came to the conclusion that the terrorists were acting on direct orders from Khattab.[128] The Buinaksk attack was pronounced an act of revenge organized by the Wahhabi forces in reaction to the actions of federal troops in Dagestan.

Hearings on the Moscow and Volgodonsk attacks were held behind closed doors. The process produced 90 volumes of proceedings in the criminal case, five of which were classified.[129] In the course of the hearings, the following names were made public for their alleged involvement in the Moscow bombings: Achemez Gochiiaev, Denis Saitakov, Yusuf Krymshamkhalov, and Khakim Abaev. Yusuf Krymshamkhalov, Adam Dekkushev, and Timur Batchaev were named in connection to the bombing in Volgodonsk. According to the official version, Karachai Wahhabi Achemez Gochiiaev was responsible for planning and carrying out the attacks on orders from Khattab. For this, Gochiiaev reportedly received a payment from Khattab in the amount of $2 million.[130] Allegedly under Gochiiaev's leadership, the apartment buildings were selected with the goal of inflicting the maximum number of victims. The official analysis of explosives used in Moscow and Volgodonsk also led the prosecution to Khattab's training camps, where the same explosives were found in Urus-Martan and Serzhen-Yurt. In addition, corroborating evidence was retrieved from the Shali region of Chechnya, where security services captured Chechen notes with detailed diagrams of explosive devices as well as comprehensive instructions on blowing up apartment complexes.[131]

Interestingly, despite the official version of the Chechen connection, no Chechens were tried in either case. Rather, it was Dagestani Wahhabis in the Buinaksk case and Karachai Wahhabis in the Moscow and Volgodonsk bombings. While the official explanation linked the perpetrators to Khattab and his Chechen training centers, the emergence of these individuals indicated another dangerous trend in the North Caucasus. By the start of the Dagestani operation in August 1999, Wahhabi Islamic jamaats across the North Caucasus, which arose as a result of the process of religious revival, began to radicalize and gradually accept the use of violence. Dagestani Wahhabis partnered with Chechen separatists and were ready to use violence against the secular pro-Russian Dagestani authorities. Other ethnic jamaats also became ready to support their Muslim brothers against the Russian state through violent means. For instance, Achemez Gochiiaev was connected to Ramazan Borlakov and his Wahhabi Karachaevo-Cherkessia jamaat. Gochiiaev later formed his own organization—Karachai jamaat, also known as the Muslim Society Number 3. During the counterterrorist regime announced by Putin, these entities radicalized further, consolidating around their anti-Russian sentiments. The Karachai jamaat, aside from being implicated in the apartment bombings, was later found responsible for other terrorist attacks in Russia.

PREPARING FOR THE COUNTERTERRORIST OPERATION

The apartment bombings became the last justification needed for the government to announce the regime of a counterterrorist operation. The crime, kidnappings, and terrorist attacks of the interwar years convinced Moscow of the necessity of an intervention in Chechnya. The outbreak of violence in Dagestan indicated that deep-rooted problems existed in the North Caucasus. However, the insurgent activity in Dagestan hardly qualified as acts of terrorism and did not warrant the start of a counterterrorist operation. The wave of apartment bombings not only justified such an operation but also tied together terrorism and events in Dagestan with Chechnya.

Even before the apartment bombings, following the Wahhabi attack on the Tsumadinskii region of Dagestan, the Russian government designated the clashes between Wahhabis and Dagestani security services as acts of terrorism. On August 16 the State Duma of the Russian Federation called the Dagestani intervention an "especially dangerous form of terrorism with the involvement of foreign citizens."[132] The Duma accused Chechnya of harboring and promoting terrorism. Following the outbreak of fighting in Dagestan, Putin gave an indication of a possibility of a counterterrorist operation:

> People are so fed up with confusion and laxity that many people would be prepared to accept some kind of an emergency situation. I don't think we have any grounds for introducing a state of emergency on Russian territory. As for the zone of clashes with the terrorists, a special order may be introduced there because the local bodies of power are not functioning anymore. This is clear to everyone. But we don't think even that measure is necessary so far.[133]

Accordingly, the prime minister indicated that the threat Russia was dealing with required tough countermeasures.

While justifying a counterterrorist operation in response to the skirmishes in Dagestan could have been problematic, the apartment bombings across Russia facilitated Moscow's rhetoric on the necessity of a military intervention. The bombings were used to indicate that Basayev and Khattab continued to pose a threat not only regionally but across Russia as well. In fact, President Yeltsin declared Russia was facing an international threat:

> Today our country is waging a difficult fight against international terrorism which posed a brazen challenge to the peoples of Russia. This is a fight for the life of Russians, many of whom we lost in Moscow and Dagestan, in Volgodonsk and Buinaksk. This is a fight to preserve sovereignty and

territorial integrity of the Russian Federation. At the same time, it is also part of the unified efforts of the international community to counter international terrorism... International terrorism does not have boundaries. Today it is targeting the entire world.[134]

In this way, according to Moscow, the apartment bombings became the domestic manifestation of the international terrorist threat linked to Osama bin Laden through Basayev and Khattab.

Because the Kremlin considered Basayev and Khattab responsible for both the Dagestan interventions and the apartment bombings, the Russian government traced the international terrorist threat back to Chechnya, referring to it as the "bandit hole of bloodthirsty Khattab."[135] As Prime Minister Putin explained, Chechnya was responsible for breeding terrorism: "While remaining part of the Russian territory, Chechnya today is a sort of international anomaly: a seemingly lawfully existing huge terrorist camp."[136] At this time the Kremlin publicly questioned the legitimacy of Maskhadov's rule in Chechnya as well as the significance of the Khasavyurt Accords. Maskhadov's inability to control Basayev and Khattab was interpreted as the collapse of his legitimacy. Putin described the Khasavyurt Accords, in turn, as an instrument that Chechen separatists had used to unilaterally manipulate the status of Chechnya. "A political outcome one can infer from the situation in Dagestan is that the Chechen leadership does not control the situation and cannot comply with the Khasavyurt Accords. That is why our military experts will propose our own methods on resolving the situation," Putin concluded.[137]

According to Moscow, the threat of international terrorism coming from Chechnya required a drastic solution. Following the apartment bombings the Russian government initiated police counterterrorist operations called Whirlwind and Terek all over Russia. Another operation specifically targeted foreigners; the aim of the Operation Foreigner was to register all the foreigners living in the Moscow region. As a result of this operation, many foreigners were forced to leave Russia, and many more had to register with authorities. However, such measures were seen as insufficient, and a military operation became justified as the only way to rid Chechnya of bases of international terrorism. When Chechnya's President Maskhadov insisted on a peaceful solution to the situation through mutual cooperation, he was accused of siding with terrorists. Following the apartment bombings Maskhadov sent his condolences to President Yeltsin. He condemned terrorist attacks and denied that Chechnya was involved:

In my opinion, behind these terrorist attacks are significant powers: politicians and states that are interested in destabilizing the situation in Russia. The attempt to find a "Chechen trace" in the explosions in Moscow looks foolish to say the least. Even if they had a great desire to, Chechens are physically incapable of staging terrorist attacks of such scale. One needs to look for traces in Moscow itself, and for organizers–far outside of Russia's borders. These forces, by playing the Chechen card, want to wreck Russia and establish their influence in the Caucasus.[138]

Maskhadov even offered his assistance in investigating the apartment bombings; he was ready to expel Khattab from Chechnya and offered to engage in joint action against terrorists in the North Caucasus. However, he was increasingly marginalized. In reaction to Maskhadov's offers to negotiate, Putin responded by saying that negotiations will start only "when the President of Russia will deem them necessary and when it will be beneficial for Russia."[139] The situation in Chechnya in 1999 was beginning to resemble that of 1994. Back then Dudayev, who initially had Moscow's support, became marginalized and was eventually killed in a special operation. Maskhadov, who was legitimately elected in 1997, by 1999 was essentially outside the political process, and Moscow equated him with Chechen rebels and terrorists.

The government discarded the soft approach. In Putin's eyes, it was the soft approach that had led to the growth of the terrorist danger in Russia in the first place. From his point of view negotiations in Budennovsk with terrorists back in 1995 had been a mistake; concessions to terrorists backfired by producing more terrorists. The prime minister thought that the Russian government had allowed terrorists to walk away instead of eradicating them at the root.[140] This time Putin was confident about not making the same mistake and was prepared to use military force against terrorists.

At the time alternative explanations for Putin's desire to intervene in Chechnya militarily were also voiced. Moscow's failure to reach a political agreement with Chechnya regarding its status supposedly played a role. The next presidential elections were scheduled for March 26, 2000, and Vladimir Putin's chances to win depended on his success in dealing with the situation in Chechnya. Just like in 1996, when Chechnya was a crucial issue for Yeltsin, it became the ultimate test for Vladimir Putin in terms of his ability to provide stability and security for Russia. Because Putin's chances of becoming president were at stake in Chechnya, his position on the issue was rather inflexible and was driven by his resolve to put an end to the instability in the North Caucasus. According to this explanation, it was his motivation to win presidential elections rather than the real terrorist threat in Chechnya that drove Putin's decisions.

Regardless of the possible underlying motives for starting the counterterrorist operation, unlike Yeltsin in 1994, Putin in 1999 had the Russian population's overwhelming support in deploying troops in Chechnya. Back in 1994 Yeltsin found only 30 percent of the population in favor of forcefully resolving the Chechen crisis.[141] In 1999 over 70 percent supported such a move, and 32 percent of Russians were in favor of military involvement under any circumstances. Another 40 percent supported the deployment of troops with additional measures to protect the Russian population from terrorist attacks. An overwhelming 64 percent were in favor of mass air bombings of Chechnya if terrorist attacks continued. Support of military involvement in Chechnya was undoubtedly driven by fear of terrorism; in the same survey 44 percent of Russians said they were concerned about becoming victims of terrorist attacks.[142] Fear of terrorism consolidated the Russian population behind Putin in his promise to eradicate the terrorist threat and restore stability in Russia. Russians no longer associated Chechen activities with separatism but instead viewed the separatists as international Islamist terrorists who could be defeated only through military means.

Another feature that made Putin's counterterrorist operation different from Yeltsin's war was the legal base behind it. In 1994 President Yeltsin refused to introduce a state of emergency and instead adopted several presidential decrees allowing for the use of the military force in Chechnya. This decision was widely criticized because Yeltsin's decrees, some of which were secret, were seen as inadequate for regulating a military operation. In 1999 the choice was again made against a state of emergency. Unlike Yeltsin, however, Putin had another legal instrument at his disposal—the 1998 Federal Law 130, On the Fight against Terrorism. As Putin explained, "It is my conviction that the effective application of the norms of current legislation today [Federal Law 130] makes it possible in principle to close the debate on the possible enforcement of the outdated 1991 law on the state of emergency."[143] Further, since the events in Dagestan apartment bombings and criminal activities of the interwar years were seen as evidence of the terrorist threat, the announcement of a counterterrorist operation was deemed more appropriate than a state of emergency.

Due to the terrorist nature of the threat, other existing legislation was also deemed inadequate. Russia's law on defense mainly dealt with external threats and also required the imposition of a state of emergency. The national security doctrine adopted in December 1997 was not regarded as appropriate, as it did not effectively address the issue of terrorism. In conjunction with the events in Dagestan in 1999, President Yeltsin ordered revisions to the doctrine, and a new version of the national security doctrine came out in January 2000. Similarly, the principles of the military doctrine focused on illegal armed formations and much less on terrorism. The military doctrine that was adopted in April 2000 included many more terrorism-specific provisions. The counterterrorist law, in turn, became a readily available tool for ordering the deployment of troops.

Federal Law 130 was adopted on July 25, 1998, and outlined procedures for conducting a counterterrorist operation. A counterterrorist operation was defined as

> special measures aimed at stopping a terrorist action, ensuring the security of individuals, neutralizing terrorists, and also minimizing the consequences of

terrorist action; a counterterrorist operation zone is the particular areas of land or water, vehicle, building, structure, installation, or premises and the adjoining territory or waters within which the aforementioned operation is carried out.[144]

Among the entities responsible for the fight against terrorism, the law included Russia's FSB, the MVD, the Foreign Intelligence Service, the Federal Protection Service, as well as the Ministry of Defense and the Federal Border Service. The law delineated the right to "enlist the necessary forces and resources of those federal organs of executive power that take part in the fight against terrorism."[145] This way the law effectively allowed for the use of armed forces of the aforementioned agencies in a counterterrorist zone without the declaration of a state of emergency.

Besides providing legal basis for a counterterrorist operation, the 1998 law prepared Russian institutional structures for the deployment of troops. Institutional reform was initiated in the sphere of counterterrorism, and by 1999 several new counterterrorist agencies had come into existence. The interagency Counterterrorist Committee was replaced with the new Federal Counterterrorist Committee. In June 1999 this new committee was placed under the authority of the prime minister—at the time Sergei Stepashin—which marked the start of the trend of consolidating executive control over counterterrorist activities in Russia. The FSB was also affected by institutional reform. In August 1999 the FSB Department on the Fight against Terrorism and the department on constitutional security merged into a department focused on the protection of constitutional order and the fight against terrorism. The famous special forces Alpha and Vympel became integrated into the counterterrorist system. On the eve of the counterterrorist operation in 1999, the FSB emerged as the main government institution coordinating counterterrorist activities.

In accordance with legal procedures, the second Chechen conflict began in the fall of 1999 as a counterterrorist operation.On September 23, President Yeltsin signed a secret decree—number 1255—which established a zone of a counterterrorist operation in the North Caucasus.[146] On the same day the Russian air force started the bombardment of Grozny. On September 30, Russian ground troops crossed over to the Naurskii and Shelkovskii regions of Chechnya; Russian armed forces were deployed against the "aggression of international terrorist organizations and bands of Wahhabis who [were] striving to create in the south of Russia a new Islamic state based on the principles of 'pure Islam' that would span the territory from the Caspian to the Black Sea."[147] Human rights commissioner Oleg Mironov declared the deployment of federal troops in the North Caucasus "justified and legal" in accordance with the 1998 law.[148] The second Chechen campaign had begun within the legal framework of the Russian Federation, and with the approval of the State Duma, the human rights commissioner, and a large share of the Russian population.

4

Counterterrorist Operation: The Second Chechen Campaign

COUNTERTERRORIST OPERATION BEGINS

The military phase of the counterterrorist operation in Chechnya began on September 23, 1999, as Russian forces began the bombardment of Grozny.[1] As the campaign started Prime Minister Putin made his famous promise to pursue the terrorists until final victory. "If we catch them in the toilet, we will rub them out in the outhouse," Putin declared.[2] The ground troops portion of the operation followed on September 30. Even as the troops were on their way to Chechnya, Putin firmly promised there would be no second Chechen war.[3] However, while Putin was confident that his counterterrorist operation would not turn into a war, events on the ground were eerily similar to how events unfolded during 1994–1996. Positional fighting lasted until spring 2000, when Russian troops secured control of the majority of Chechen territory. At this stage Chechen insurgents switched to guerilla tactics and ever since have engaged in unconventional warfare.

As he started the counterterrorist operation, Putin adamantly strived to avoid previous mistakes in dealing with terrorists. Favoring the forceful approach, the prime minister was ready to keep troops on the ground until the terrorist threat was completely eradicated. Putin said, "One needs to be patient and do this work—completely clear the territory of terrorists. If this work is not done today, they will come back, and all the suffered sacrifice would be in vain."[4] "Could it be better to pay them off, quit and leave?" In his view if that were the response, "the tragic events which we have suffered in Moscow and in the Rostov region, the fighting and losses which we incurred in Dagestan, would seem like a mere beginning."[5] Putin was not prepared to make any concessions to the Chechen side along the lines of the previously signed Khasavyurt Accords. Chechnya was to remain part of the Russian Federation at all costs.

Putin had learned the lessons of the first Chechen campaign. One of the most significant moves implemented by Putin in the counterterrorist operation was media control. During the first war media coverage from the front lines often portrayed the federal command in an unfavorable light. Through exposing mistakes and blunders of the command, human rights violations committed by the troops, and the abysmal conditions of the Russian soldiers, the media contributed to widely voiced criticisms of the war. Broadcasts of terrorist attacks and rescue operations often resulted in the Russian public siding with the terrorists rather than the special services. This changed during the second campaign.

To avoid negative media coverage of the second Chechen campaign, the Russian government restricted media access to the epicenter of events. In October 1999 the Russian Information Center was set up in Moscow to cover the events in the North Caucasus. This center regulated the number of news reports from Chechnya and the nature of the coverage. Another press center of the joint coalition of federal troops started functioning in Mozdok, North Ossetia. Journalist access to the front lines was restricted, as they had to acquire permission at the Mozdok center. The initiative was not new, as a similar Temporary Information Center had operated during the first war. However, between 1994 and 1996 many Russian and foreign journalists were able to travel to Chechnya independently. After 1999 such attempts became persecuted, and journalists trying to gain access to the front lines without press center permission were harassed and arrested.[6] Through such rigid control of the media, Putin was able to avoid some public criticism on the conduct of the counterterrorist operation, although the cost was freedom of information. As one might expect, Russians became increasingly disappointed in the media coverage of events in the Caucasus. In 2000 only 14 percent of Russians considered media coverage of the events in Chechnya to be objective. The majority of the population disagreed: 40 percent saw the coverage as hiding real problems and numbers, and another 38 percent considered it inadequate or superficial.[7]

Having secured control of the media, the Russian government proceeded with the military phase of the counterterrorist operation. Similar to the scenario of the first war, the fighting proceeded over control of Grozny. By February 2000 Russian forces managed to secure control of the city. Repeating Boris Yeltsin's victorious move of 1996, in anticipation of presidential elections in Russia, on March 20, 2000, Vladimir Putin visited the liberated city. After the fall of Grozny, by the spring of 2000 federal troops had taken control of the majority of Chechnya. The period of positional warfare was over; this signified the end of the military phase of the counterterrorist operation. General Troshev announced, "Today we will put an end to the efforts of eradicating bandit formations. True, it does not mean that they are completely defeated, but today solid bands no longer exist. What remains is scraps and splinters who disperse in small groups in order to save their hide."[8] Chechen separatist groups had to seek refuge in the mountainous areas. As they had failed to prevent the overwhelming military takeover of Chechnya, remaining insurgent groups abandoned positional warfare and switched to guerilla tactics; the spring of 2000 marked the return of terrorism.

As the military phase of the counterterrorist operation was declared over, the Russian side came to increasingly rely on sweep operations, or *zachistki*, which set the counterterrorist operation apart from the first Chechen campaign. In official terms zachistki referred to "special operations on checking people's residence registration and determining participants of illegal armed formations."[9] In the course of zachistki federal forces blocked a population center and carried out search operations, detaining all those suspected of terrorist links. In the period of 2000–2003, zachistki were combined with filtration camps.[10] Under such system, detained individuals were sent to specially organized camps where they were interrogated, which often included beatings and torture. The system was set up to "filter" terrorists and their supporters, as well as to collect intelligence on the rebels. Filtration camps first appeared in the 1994–1996 war. However, during the second conflict their status was institutionalized as they came to be treated as official detention centers answerable to either the Ministry of Justice or the MVD.

The Russian government avoided any negotiations with the Chechen side. In an effort to prevent a second Khasavyurt agreement, no official negotiations were held with Aslan Maskhadov. Maskhadov had insisted on negotiations before military action even started in September 1999. He had urged President Yeltsin to engage in talks in order to avoid the mistakes of 1994. However, Putin refused Maskhadov's offer at the time, claiming that the Chechen president had failed to condemn terrorism and therefore could not be negotiated with. Putin demanded that the Chechen terrorists be handed over: "First it is necessary to hand over terrorists involved in the attack on Dagestan and the bombings of Moscow, Volgodonsk and Buinaksk. Then negotiations in full force."[11] Maskhadov was blamed for inciting insurgency in Chechnya, and a criminal case was opened against him in February 2000. He was placed on the Russian federal wanted list, and his case was forwarded to Interpol to be put on the international watch list.

There were, however, several instances that raised hopes of negotiations during the second Chechen campaign, until Moscow imposed complete control over the republic with the help of Akhmad Kadyrov. After the fall of Grozny in February 2000, it became clear that the campaign was turning into an insurgency. Public support for military action in Chechnya was in sharp decline (see Figure 4.1). International actors were increasingly critical of Putin's handling of the Chechen issue. Once elections had occurred on March 26, 2000, and Putin had been elected president, the pressure of the elections was in the past. As a result, in April 2000 Putin acknowledged a possibility of negotiating with Maskhadov:

> Aslan Maskhadov is considered a criminal in Russia. He is covered by the amnesty law, to which he can apply... In general Maskhadov expresses his readiness for anything but does nothing... If Maskhadov wants negotiations, but cannot hand over bandits, we are ready to help him. Let him come out to negotiate and he can catch criminals together with us.[12]

Putin was ready to talk to Maskhadov, but such negotiations would be conducted in a limited capacity—only in order to join efforts to pursue terrorists. Political discussions on the status of the crisis were not on the agenda.

The only round of negotiations took place in November 2001, when representatives of Chechen and Russian governments met at Moscow's Sheremetyevo airport. Maskhadov's representative, Akhmed Zakayev, flew in for the talks with Viktor Kazantsev, the presidential envoy to Russia's South Federal District. These talks, however, did not have much political impact. The hardening of Putin's position on negotiations eventually finalized after the terrorist attack on a Moscow theater in October 2002. From Putin's point of view, the attack ended the possibility of any further negotiations with Maskhadov:

Figure 4.1 Russian public opinion on continued military action versus negotiations in Chechnya. (Data source: Levada Center, http://www.levada.ru/.)

Instead of negotiations, he [Maskhadov] chose the path of terror and threw his weight behind the rascals who took hundreds of hostages in Moscow on October 23. And today, after the tragic events in Moscow, I officially declare that those who choose Maskhadov, choose war. All these people, wherever they are—whether in or outside Russian territory—will be regarded as accomplices of terrorists.[13]

Maskhadov continued to be treated as a criminal, and in March 2005 he was killed after Russian security services blew up a bunker where he was hiding in Tolstoy-Yurt.

At the same time, while avoiding negotiations with the Chechen side, the Russian government implemented a strategy of Chechenization during its counterterrorist operation. Similar to previous Russian policies, including that of *korenizatsiia* during the Soviet era, Putin set out to transfer power from the federal center to local Chechen authorities in return for their loyalty to Moscow. This strategy was present in the first war when the Russian government tried to support the authority of Doku Zavgayev. Unlike in the first war, however, the Kremlin started this initiative at the very beginning of the second conflict and relied on co-opting the Chechen movement. For instance, the Kremlin tried to co-opt the Chechen separatists by offering them amnesty. One of the first declarations of amnesty was announced on December 13, 1999, by the State Duma, which encouraged insurgents to join the Chechen security forces backed by Moscow.[14]

Similar to Yeltsin's attempts to prop up a loyal Chechen administration, in October 1999 Putin turned his attention to the government structures in Chechnya. At that time in Moscow members of the 1996 legislature of the Chechen Republic tried to revive the parliament and requested assistance from the Kremlin. The Kremlin immediately recognized this institution, which further marginalized Maskhadov. Putin declared, "This is the only legislative body elected according to the law. Everything else is legitimate conditionally, as not elected according to the laws of the Russian Federation."[15]

Putin's Chechenization policy became more pronounced after he became president. At the same time it also became more centralized, which allowed Putin to focus, unhindered, on the situation in the republic. On June 8, 2000, Putin introduced direct presidential rule in Chechnya. Decree 1071 created a new administration in the Chechen Republic under the purview of the envoy of the Russian president in the South Federal District. Putin's process of Chechenization was much more concentrated than Yeltsin's. In transferring some power back to Grozny, Putin chose to do so with the help of a controversial figure: Chechen mufti Akhmad Kadyrov.

Back in 1995 under Maskhadov's rule, Akhmad Kadyrov waged jihad against Russia. However, when the counterterrorist operation started in 1999, he refused to take action against federal forces. This resulted in a split between Kadyrov and Maskhadov. Maskhadov declared Kadyrov a traitor and an "enemy number one," claiming that Kadyrov was guilty of "doing all in his powers to initiate the Russian invasion in Chechnya."[16] Putin appointed Kadyrov as head of his administration in Chechnya on June 12, 2000. This appointment was widely criticized not only by the insurgents but also by members of the local administrations. Several city and regional Chechen leaders signed a "letter of twelve" protesting the appointment.[17] Kadyrov faced several assassination attempts until his death in a terrorist attack on May 9, 2004.

In the course of the military phase of the counterterrorist operation, Russia was largely able to crush Chechen resistance through overwhelming military force. By the spring of 2000 Chechen groups had given up positional warfare and transitioned underground. The Kremlin engaged Akhmad Kadyrov in its efforts to rebuild a pro-Moscow government in the republic as it also sought to crush the resistance militarily. While Russia considered its counterterrorist operation successful, the separatist movement turned into an insurgency. At this point it crossed the border from Chechnya to other areas of the North Caucasus. In addition, it further radicalized, adjusting its goals and objectives. Terrorism returned as a widely used tactic that presents one of the biggest security challenges to Russia to this day.

PREPARING FOR TERRORISM

The apartment bombings of September 1999 were attributed to Chechen terrorists and served as a reason for Russian forces to militarily intervene in the North Caucasus. Curiously, following the start of the military operation, no further terrorist attacks took place in Russia until May 2000. In response to military action in Chechnya, Maskhadov introduced martial law on October 6, 1999, and called for jihad against Russia.[18] The struggle against Russia's military brought Maskhadov closer to his opposition. Infighting within the Chechen leadership decreased at the start of the second campaign as the conflicting factions united against the Russian invasion.

As the separatist forces were losing in positional warfare, they shifted toward a large-scale guerilla campaign. After the fall of Grozny, Maskhadov announced, "Now guerilla warfare, our warfare, is starting."[19] Maskhadov ordered his forces to disperse throughout the territory and to abandon fighting to hold positions. In respect to guerilla warfare, Maskhadov acknowledged that he was ready to target areas occupied by Russian forces as well as territories outside Chechnya.[20] With this, Maskhadov referred to a wide range of subversive action activities, not excluding renewed acts of terrorism.

Shamil Basayev confirmed Maskhadov's promise. In May 1996 when the separatists declared a switch to guerilla warfare, Basayev proclaimed the start of a subversive action campaign. In October 1999 Basayev went further and threatened a terrorist war. In Basayev's view Russia's actions in Dagestan and Chechnya deserved revenge, and he was ready to launch terrorist attacks in Russian cities. "This may happen soon. I have enough men and equipment to mount such an operation," Basayev warned. "The Russian leadership will soon have the chance to demonstrate how it combats terrorism against Russian citizens."[21]

Russia's military incursion not only radicalized Basayev's views on warfare; the presence of Russian troops also affected the insurgents' declared goals. With the start of the skirmishes in Dagestan, Basayev focused on liberating Chechnya and Dagestan from Russia. As the counterterrorist operation began, he declared his intention to take his fight to other areas of the Caucasus as well: "Caucasus is huge. Our goal is free Caucasus."[22] Russia's hard-line response to the Chechen crisis contributed to the expansion of the Chechen cause. The clashes with security services in Dagestan also led to the new goal of achieving the independence of a united state of Chechnya and Dagestan. The start of the second campaign resulted in further growth of separatist ambitions—they now encompassed the broader region of the Caucasus.

The separatists' narratives also came to rely more on religious rhetoric. In his appeal to liberate the Caucasus, Basayev was addressing sympathetic Wahhabi audiences. Back during the first war Basayev referred to himself as a warrior of Islam.[23] This time to organize joint resistance, Basayev capitalized on the Wahhabi Islamic jamaats in the North Caucasus, which were ready to support their Muslim brothers who were under attack from infidel Russians. By the early 2000s diverse Wahhabi jamaats existed in Chechnya, Dagestan, Kabardino-Balkaria, Karachaevo-Cherkessia, and other territories. Among them were the Dagestani Jennet group that later became Jamaat Shariat, Nogai jamaat, Ingush jamaat, Jamaat Yarmuk, Karachai jamaat, and others. To coordinate these diverse jamaats Basayev transformed his Congress of the Peoples of Chechnya and Dagestan into a defense council—the Supreme Military Majlis ul-Shura of the United Mujahideen Forces of the Caucasus. This organization became the precursor for the idea of a united emirate in the North Caucasus. In Russia this entity was listed as a terrorist organization in February 2003.

Further, Russia's zachistki operations contributed to the geographical spread of the insurgent movement. During the first war the major bases of Chechen separatists were located in the areas of Urus-Martan, Gudermes, and Vedeno. During the second conflict, in the course of zachistki, many of these bases and training centers in the mountains were destroyed. As a result, insurgents were forced to move and to look for alternative bases of operation. As federal control over Chechnya was restored and Kadyrov's grip on security services grew, insurgents established bases outside of Chechnya and started actively looking for new partners.

Chechen separatists intensified their quest for outside support. For example, President Maskhadov turned to the North Atlantic Treaty Organization (NATO) for assistance against Russia. Former president Zelimkhan Yandarbiyev, in turn, became disappointed in the lack of support from the West and turned to the East, namely to Taliban-controlled Afghanistan. Through Yandarbiyev's efforts Chechen rebels established official relations with Afghanistan, which culminated in the Taliban recognizing the political independence of Ichkeriia. The Taliban became the only government since that of Gamsakhurdia's Georgia to recognize Chechnya's independence. On a visit to Afghanistan in January 2000, Yandarbiyev met with Mullah Omar. In the course of the meeting, the Taliban leadership agreed to provide asylum for Chechen rebels and extended an invitation to set up a Chechen government in exile in the city of Mazar-i-Sharif.[24] Mullah Omar declared it was the Taliban's religious duty to offer assistance to their Chechen Muslim brothers.[25]

Maskhadov was very critical of Yandarbiyev's efforts to gain recognition from the Taliban. The Chechen president was concerned that the move would play into Russia's portrayal of the Chechen struggle. He said:

> The Russians want to show that we have bases there, that we receive financial aid from them, armaments too, that Afghans fight here, that Arabs fight here, that "negroes" fight here. They would be happy if weapons were sent to us from there. And you noticed correctly that today Yandarbiyev wants to look like a hero, that he forced someone to recognize the Chechen Republic of Ichkeria. At the most unsuitable moment for us ... maybe it would seem worth waiting ... at this time, it is playing into the Russians' hands.[26]

Maskhadov was correct to be concerned because the partnership with the Taliban further affected the Chechen movement by providing alternative venues for training and educating insurgents.

Reports on Chechen bases in Afghanistan remain highly contradictory, and little solid evidence exists to support any of the accounts. The Taliban officially denied any involvement with insurgent training. Maskhadov also denied the existence of bases in Afghanistan, "There are no Chechen bases in Afghanistan, or in Yemen. We don't need any bases, because during the previous war Russian generals taught our people how to fight."[27] At the same time Abdullah Abdullah, foreign minister of one of the anti-Taliban factions, claimed that "hundreds of families came from Chechnya through Pakistan and settled in Afghanistan."[28] Similarly, the Russian government reported the existence of training camps in Afghanistan. Even further, due to Taliban assistance to Chechen separatists, the Kremlin was considering a preventive move against Afghanistan. As a Kremlin spokesman explained, Russia did not "rule out the possibility of preventive strikes against Afghanistan if a real threat arises to the national interests of Russia and our allies in the region."[29]

While information on the Afghan bases remains unclear, evidence suggests that Afghan mujahedeen continued to take part in the North Caucasus insurgency during the counterterrorist operation. During the first war the mujahedeen arrived through various routes. During the counterterrorist operation such movement became more restricted and was channeled mainly through Georgia's Pankisi Gorge. The Pankisi Gorge became a major transit route for the Caucasus insurgents and for foreign mujahedeen traveling in and out of Chechnya. As such, it became a place where foreign Wahhabi influences affected the insurgents. During the first war Khattab was training predominantly Chechen fighters and had to adjust the ideological training to appeal to the locals, especially Sufis. In the second conflict, however, many fighters received training abroad, including in Afghanistan, where they were exposed to more radical Salafi jihadi ideas, such as fighting the global jihad and restoring an Islamic caliphate. As a result, the Pankisi Gorge became the transit route not only for insurgents but also for ideologies. Not surprisingly, it was the Pankisi Gorge that became the origin of one of the rising stars of Syrian jihadis, Omar al-Shishani, who joined the global jihad instead of the local North Caucasus quest.

With the Russian onslaught the insurgents were prepared to launch a new wave of terrorism. However, in contrast with the first war, the capabilities behind terrorist attacks in the second conflict broadened. The Chechen command had a larger pool of adherents to draw on—in addition to Chechens and Afghan mujahedeen, members of the North Caucasus jamaats were ready to carry out terrorist attacks against Russia. Terrorist attacks gradually spread from Chechnya to neighboring regions and beyond. In recent years the majority of terrorist attacks have taken place outside of Chechnya. The planning of terrorist attacks also became harder to detect because the insurgents had diversified their bases by moving them abroad.

The trend of orchestrating explosions continued from the previous war. Explosions took place in the North Caucasus and in Russia, including Moscow. Explosions targeted particularly crowded areas, such as city markets and public transportation systems. Often explosives were placed in trash cans. As a result, trash cans permanently disappeared from many busy parts of cities, public transportation stops, and railway stations.

A new development in explosions became the targeting of infrastructure. As the security in cities tightened, it became more difficult to carry out terrorist attacks there. In contrast, it is virtually impossible to control long stretches of pipeline or railway. In February 2004 Basayev carried out an explosion on the oil pipeline in the Moscow region. Following the attack Basayev released a video showing preparations for it. Another popular target became the railway system. While the number of casualties in such attacks was usually low, the effect on the infrastructure was much more significant, with explosions paralyzing train traffic and causing significant disruptions.

Bus and plane hijackings became much less frequent in the second conflict. As with previous hijackings, they were committed with the aim of affecting the situation in Chechnya. For example, the terrorist who hijacked a bus in Nevinnomyssk in the Stavropol region in July 2001 demanded the freedom of five Chechens who were serving sentences in prison for their participation in terrorist attacks during 1994.[30] Further, in March 2001 three Chechen terrorists hijacked a plane flying from Istanbul to Moscow. The plane was diverted to Saudi Arabia, where the terrorists demanded the withdrawal of all federal forces from Chechnya in exchange for freeing the hostages.[31] Increased security at airports as well as bus and train stations, however, disrupted the hijacking trend, bringing the number of such attacks down.

SUICIDE TERRORISM AND RUSSIA'S BLACK WIDOWS

One of the most significant developments in terrorist trends during the second Chechen campaign became Basayev's implementation of his promise to deploy suicide terrorists.[32] Basayev first mentioned suicide brigades in May 1995, but no suicide terrorist attacks were carried out during the first Chechen war. At the outset of the second conflict, Basayev warned of suicide terrorism once again. This time he prepared a unit of suicide bombers who were ready to deploy. Basayev was not bluffing. Soon after his warning the first suicide terrorist attack in Russia took place on June 6, 2000.

To carry out suicide terrorist attacks, Basayev built a special coordinating unit—the Riyad us-Saliheyn Martyrs Brigade, also known as the Islamic Brigade of Shahids. The group was formed with the participation of members of Barayev's Special Purpose Islamic Regiment and Khattab's Islamic International Peacekeeping Brigade. While the group became known to the outside world through the Dubrovka Theater attack of 2002, some reports indicate that the group might have been in existence as early as October 1999. Since its inception, the group was responsible for most of the suicide attacks until Basayev's death in 2006.

Suicide attacks have become a widely used terrorist tactic in the world.[33] Operationally, they are low cost and are comparatively easy to execute. At the same time they cast a compelling message that even death cannot prevent the movement behind the attacks. While suicide terrorist attacks have been perpetrated by non-Muslim and secular groups such as Sri Lanka's Tamil Tigers and Turkey's Kurdish Workers' Party (PKK), the phenomenon is particularly widespread among violent Islamist groups. In Islam, as in many other religions, suicide is prohibited. However, ideologues of violent jihad such as Ayman al-Zawahiri and Osama bin Laden justified suicide attacks through the concept of martyrdom. In this view martyrs, or *shahids*, do not commit suicide but become holy warriors who sacrifice themselves for faith. In this way suicide bombers are promised generous rewards from God in exchange for their sacrifice. In the North Caucasus such fundamentalist interpretations of Islam are foreign even for the locally grown Wahhabi groups. Basayev likely devised the tactic under the influence of Khattab and other Afghan mujahedeen.

While the tactic of suicide bombings brought North Caucasus terrorism closer to global jihadi movements, Basayev implemented a distinctly unique variant of suicide attacks. He deployed a female suicide unit of the Brigade of Shahids that came to be known as the Black Widows. Female suicide bombers are also not a new phenomenon in terrorism.[34] For instance, both groups mentioned earlier in this discussion—the PKK and the Tamil Tigers —have used female suicide bombers. Islamist terrorist groups, on the other hand, had not. Basayev's Black Widows became the first Islamist terrorist unit to use female suicide bombers in the name of jihad.

The participation of women in jihad is perceived as unconventional even by the standards of violent Islamist groups.[35] Traditionally, women were supposed to take a supportive role in violent jihad. Women were discouraged from joining active combat but were instead instructed to advance jihad through supporting the men. In his 1996 Declaration of War against the Americans, Osama bin Laden limited the role of women to motivating and encouraging "their sons, brothers and husbands to fight—in the cause of Allah."[36] Only under extreme circumstances did Islamist groups allow women to take an active role—for instance, when men could not perform the given task. When Hamas decided to deploy its first female suicide bomber, its spiritual leader Sheikh Yassin explained it as follows: "The fact that a woman took part for the first time in a Hamas operation marks a significant evolution ... Women are like the reserve army—when there is a necessity, we use them. Today we needed her because there are a lot of problems for a man to reach out to Israelis in the West Bank and Gaza."[37]

In the case of North Caucasus terrorism, women were not the last resort; instead, they pioneered the tactic. The very first suicide attack—on June 6, 2000—was committed by a woman, Khava Barayeva, a cousin of famous Chechen rebel Arbi Barayev, when she drove a truck loaded with explosives into a Russian police base in Alkhan-Yurt, Chechnya. This very first attack influenced jihadi jurisprudence and prompted the issuing of a *fatwa* titled "The Islamic Ruling on the Permissibility of Martyrdom Operations: Did Hawa Barayev Commit Suicide or achieve Martyrdom?"[38] It is not clear who issued this fatwa, but it covered the question of whether Barayeva was right to become a suicide bomber. The fatwa concluded that "martyrdom operations are permissible, and in fact the Mujahid who is killed in them is better than one who is killed fighting in the ranks, for there are gradations even among martyrs, corresponding to their role, action effort and risk undertaken."[39] While the fatwa did not directly tackle the issue of female suicide bombings, it gave rise to many other extremist religious rulings that encouraged women to take part in jihad. For instance, Saudi Al Qaeda cleric Yusuf al-Ayyiri wrote a piece called "The Role of Women in the Jihad against Enemies" in which he gave the example of Khava Barayeva and implicitly encouraged other women to follow it.[40]

Since then, following the North Caucasus example, many Islamist movements have used women as suicide bombers. Egyptian cleric Sheikh Yusuf al-Qaradawi encouraged Hamas women to become suicide bombers. "Committed Muslim women in Palestine have the right to participate and have their own role in jihad and to attain martyrdom," the cleric stated.[41] In 2002 Mohammed Hussein Fadlallah, one of the spiritual leaders of Hezbollah, cautiously called on women to join jihad against Israel. "It is true that Islam has not asked women to carry out jihad," he said, "but it permits them to take part if the necessities of defensive war dictate that women should carry out any regular military operations, or suicide operations."[42] Following Abu Musab al-Zarqawi's decision to make use of the tactic, Al Qaeda in Iraq has staged many female suicide bombings. In 2009 Ayman al-Zawahiri's wife Umaymah Hasan wrote a "Letter to the Muslim Sisters" in which she talked of the example of the Chechen martyred sisters and encouraged women to join the jihad.[43] In this way Basayev's use of women in suicide terrorism has inspired many other groups to implement the tactic.

In Russia, despite the commonly circulated media reports claiming that North Caucasus suicide bombers act under duress, under the influence of drugs, or for financial reasons, existing accounts of shahids illustrate that it is rather their understanding of faith that drives them to commit terrorist acts. For instance, in a letter to a friend one suicide terrorist explained her motivation as not being driven by monetary profit:

> I know that many people will not understand us, and will make accusations. But I believe, that you will understand all. Do not trust anything that will be said about us. They will say that we bargained and demanded dollars and a plane in exchange for the hostages. It's not the truth. We go on jihad. We know that all of us will die. We are ready for it. We will not bargain and we will stand to the end.[44]

Basayev's suicide brigades widely employed psychological indoctrination techniques. Suicide bombers received training and were held away from people so as not to disrupt the indoctrination effect. Shahids were usually not involved in the planning of terrorist attacks but would arrive on the scene only a few days prior to the bombings.

However, while faith indisputably has played a role in recruiting shahids, in the North Caucasus revenge seems to have been a more powerful factor. Introduced under the foreign influence, the tactic of suicide bombing was built on a local tradition of blood feud. The trademark *adat* of blood feud functions on the principle of retribution for those killed by an enemy and is still widely practiced in the North Caucasus.[45] In this respect revenge for those killed by federal forces during the two Chechen conflicts can be a powerful mechanism for recruiting suicide bombers. It has been established that the brutality of federal forces in the North Caucasus has pushed many people into the ranks of terrorists. President Maskhadov described federal troops in Chechnya acting as death squads: "Russian troops have virtually become punitive death squads that unleashed the unprecedented terror against our peaceful civilians: against women, children and the elderly."[46] As a result, as Akhmed Zakayev explained, many individuals were driven to the "extreme stage of despair" by Russia's actions and felt they no longer had anything to lose.[47] Indiscriminate zachistki operations often triggered revenge actions against Russian citizens. For instance, after the suicide bombing at Moscow metro station Avtozavodskaya in 2004, Kavkaz Center posted an anonymous message suggesting that the attack was perpetrated in revenge for a zachistka operation at Novye Aldy in Chechnya on February 5–6, 2000.[48]

Many of the Black Widows have been driven to avenge their husbands—usually insurgents killed in combat with federal forces or disappeared by security services—hence the very name given to the group by the media. For example, the suicide bomber who attacked the Moscow metro station Rizhskaia in 2004 was the widow of insurgent Idris Gloov who had been killed by the police.[49] Alla Sapyrkina, who blew herself up together with a Dagestani sheikh in 2012, lost several husbands to federal forces. Many others were motivated by seeking revenge for their relatives; Aminat Nagaeva, a suicide terrorist on plane TU-134 that was bombed in 2004, lost her brother to the Chechen wars.

Further, revenge was a key factor that led to the increase in suicide attacks in Russia. In May 2003 Shamil Basayev announced the start of a shahid operation called Boomerang. The operation was introduced in retribution for the abductions of Chechen girls by federal forces. In retaliation for such acts Basayev vowed to target Russian cities that sent military detachments to Chechnya: "On our part we pledge to hold retaliation actions deploying our *shahids* in those cities, in those regions from where come the specific military detachments, police or other security groups."[50] Operation Whirlwind-Antiterror was launched concurrently as a large-scale subversive action campaign. This campaign justified the use of any available means to target the Russian enemy until "the Chechen land is freed from Russian occupants and until the criminals are punished."[51]

As a result of these operations, the number of suicide attacks increased, and the bombings moved outside of Chechnya. The first suicide attack to take place outside of Chechnya occurred in June 2003 in Mozdok, North Ossetia. Since then the North Caucasus jamaats have been instrumental in staging suicide attacks elsewhere in the North Caucasus and the rest of

Russia. In July 2003 attacks reached Moscow when two suicide bombers exploded themselves at popular rock festival Kryl'ia. In December 2003 a suicide bomber blew herself up in front of the Moscow Hotel National. As Basayev explained, the latter bombing was supposed to strike Russia's State Duma, which is located close to the hotel.[52] In 2004 Moscow metro bombings followed at stations Avtozavodskaya and Rizhskaia. In August 2004 suicide bombers brought down planes TU-154 and TU-134 that flew out of Moscow's Domodedovo airport. Once the suicide bombings diffused from Chechnya, FSB head Nikolai Patrushev acknowledged the severity of the problem, saying, "suicide terrorism today presents an exceptional threat, this problem is urgent, and we are actively thinking of how to combat this evil."[53]

While the suicide attacks in Moscow predominantly targeted civilians, the trend did not start out this way. From 2000 to May 2003 suicide attacks exclusively targeted Russian military installations in Chechnya, government buildings, and official government representatives. Only after the start of operations Boomerang and Whirlwind-Antiterror did the suicide attacks turn against civilians. Not surprisingly, the majority of such attacks took place outside of Chechnya and aimed at causing harm to Russian citizens, as Basayev promised. While the number of suicide attacks against civilian targets increased after Basayev's death, suicide bombings to this day remain predominantly a tactic against military and government targets.

Suicide bombings continued until Basayev's death in 2006, when they sharply declined. No suicide attacks were registered in 2006, and only one took place in 2007. The number of suicide attacks picked up in 2008, but it was not until Said Buryatsky tried to revive Basayev's Riyad us-Saliheyn Martyrs Brigade that suicide attacks again became a popular method of North Caucasus terrorism. Under Buryatsky's spiritual leadership, suicide bombings transformed as a tactic. Terrorists started relying more and more on ethnic Russians to serve as shahids.

CONVERTED WAHHABI TERRORISTS

Participation of ethnic Slavs in the North Caucasus insurgency is another feature that makes the insurgency similar to other jihadi movements. Today in Syria, Iraq, and Afghanistan, we see an influx of Westerners who converted to Islam and joined the insurgencies. In the North Caucasus, a similar trend has involved ethnic Slavs. In fact, the very first terrorist attack of the second Chechen campaign reportedly involved the participation of Russians in the terrorist plot. The explosion took place in Volgograd on May 31, 2000. Several months after the explosion Russian security services apprehended six people in connection with the terrorist act. The group included individuals from the Caucasus as well as ethnic Russians.[54]

Accounts of Russian and other Slavic fighters in Chechnya first appeared during the first war. However, Russians that participated in the first campaign were predominantly mercenaries motivated by money rather than the ideology behind the insurgency. They were not converts to Wahhabism, nor were they implicated in assisting Chechen terrorist attacks. In the second conflict accounts emerged of Slavs who joined the fighting for ideological reasons; they had converted to Wahhabi Islam and embraced the ideas behind the insurgency. Many such individuals took an active role in staging terrorist attacks and recruiting terrorists, mainly suicide bombers. Others became suicide bombers themselves. Further, in more recent years recruitment of Slavs for terrorist purposes became a concerted effort on part of the insurgents.

Some ethnic Slavs joined the Wahhabi camp before the start of the counterterrorist operation. As the conflict started these individuals, under their adopted Muslim names, fought on the side of the insurgency like many other North Caucasus Wahhabis. For instance, in 2005 the Russian security services apprehended Sergei Umantsev, an ethnic Slav from central Russia. He converted to Islam in 1998 and took the name Habib.[55] At the outset of the counterterrorist operation in 1999, Umantsev joined the insurgent armed forces.

Curiously, many ethnic Slavs who embraced the insurgency had previously worked for Russian police or security services. For example, Vitalii Zagorul'ko was a police officer who secretly joined the insurgency at the age of 17. Viktor Senchenko, a native of Volgodonsk, was a graduate of the Rostov police academy and worked for the police force. In 2004 and 2005 he took part in the terrorist acts in Voronezh. Yuri Menovshchikov was a Russian paratrooper who served in the military in the North Caucasus. He was captured by the insurgents in Dagestan. In confinement he studied the Quran, converted to Islam, and subsequently switched sides to the insurgency.[56]

By the mid-2000s many ethnic Slavs had taken part in the planning and execution of terrorist attacks against fellow Slavs. This was partially caused by a switch in terrorist tactics. In its counterterrorist approach Russia had adhered to the strategy of ethnic profiling whereby security services disproportionately targeted individuals with a Caucasian appearance. As a result, it became more difficult for the North Caucasus insurgents to plan and carry out terrorist attacks in Russia without being discovered, and insurgents started actively recruiting Slavs. As the president of Russia's Institute on Religion and Politics Aleksandr Ignatenko explained, "The great dream of the 'global terrorist international' is the use of people with European appearance as shahids. Facts exist showing that Russian girls who converted to Islam are approached in mosques by recruiters with offers to take part in jihad."[57]

For the terrorist command it became important to have at their disposal individuals who could carry out the planning of terrorist attacks while raising fewer suspicions from the Russian security services. One such individual—Pavel Kosolapov—became close to Basayev. Kosolapov became the leader of an insurgent unit of Slavic saboteurs and was tasked by Basayev to carry out the next wave of terrorist attacks in Russia. Resultantly, Kosolapov's name appeared in the investigations of the Moscow region pipeline bombing of 2004, the Samara explosion of 2004, and the 2007 Nevsky Express bombing.

The Karachai jamaat became a group in the North Caucasus that especially attracted many ethnic Slavs. With their help, the group specialized in carrying out explosions across Russia. One member of the group, Nikolai Kipkeev, was implicated in staging the Moscow metro bombing at the Rizhskaia station on August 31, 2004. Kipkeev himself died during the attack while escorting the suicide bomber. Another Slavic member of the same group, Ivan Manar'in, was one of the few Russians to be arrested alive. As Manar'in explained, his motivation for joining the terrorist group was not driven by financial factors. "I can easily live on a hundred rubles[58] per day or less, and have done that many times," Manar'in confessed.[59] Accordingly, his allowance was less than $1,000 per month, and this sum had to cover rent in Moscow as well as supplies for assembling explosive devices.

Another Russian from Buryatia became an important Wahhabi leader in terms of recruiting other Russian-speaking terrorists. Aleksandr Tikhomirov became known in the North Caucasus as Said Buryatsky. He converted to Islam at the age of 15 and studied theology in several Middle Eastern institutions. In 2008 Buryatsky arrived in the North Caucasus, where he joined Doku Umarov. He explained his motivation: "After the proclamation of the Caucasus Emirate all my doubts disappeared. We have one Emir and one state. And the direct responsibility of every Muslim today is to seek Jihad and to help Jihad by word and property."[60] The impact of Buryatsky on the insurgency was not his military prowess or even the staging of terrorist attacks—he was implicated in the assassination attempt against Ingushetia president Yunus-Bek Yevkurov in 2009 and the 2009 Nevsky Express bombing. Rather, it was his Russian-language Internet propaganda targeting Muslim youths in post-Soviet states. His videos urged Muslims to join jihad in the North Caucasus. Said Buryatsky became a leading recruiter of Slavs and other Russian speakers for the North Caucasus insurgency through the Internet.

Buryatsky's method inspired others. For instance, in one of his videos Said Buryatsky encouraged women to take part in jihad.[61] His message had traction. Alena Bykova, a 19-year-old from the city of Volzhsky became radicalized mainly through the Internet. She became interested in radical Islam in 2011. Subsequently, she became involved in recruiting suicide terrorists. Following the message, many more Slavic women became suicide bombers. In February 2011 Maria Khorosheva together with her husband Vitalii Razdobud'ko blew themselves up in Dagestan. Alla Sapyrkina blew herself up in a house of a Dagestani sheikh on August 28, 2012. A former actress in a Makhachkala theater, Sapyrkina married a Wahhabi insurgent who convinced her to convert to Islam. She became a suicide bomber after her last husband was killed in a Russian special operation.

During the second Chechen campaign terrorism expanded not only geographically but ethnically as well. Many Wahhabi adherents from the North Caucasus jamaats were ready to participate in terrorist attacks against Russia. However, the participation of Slavic individuals in terrorist attacks expanded terrorist capabilities even further. Because Slavic-looking individuals were not ethnically profiled as much as individuals from the North Caucasus, Slavic plotters of terrorist attacks were able to operate with more ease. This trend has made it much harder for the Russian security services to fight terrorism and spot potential suicide bombers. Further, the radical message disseminated through the Internet has attracted many young converts to Islam and seems to be a growing threat in Russia.

RUSSIA'S BREAKING POINT: SEPTEMBER 11

In response to the wave of terrorist attacks starting in 2000, Putin pledged to reform the counterterrorist system in Russia. A number of changes followed. In 1999 the counterterrorist operation was started under the leadership of the Ministry of Defense. In early 2001 Putin decided to transfer this function from the Ministry of Defense to the FSB. On January 22, 2001, the president issued Decree 61 on counterterrorist measures in the territory of the North Caucasus of the Russian Federation. At the same time Putin reduced the number of military personnel involved in the counterterrorist operation. The era of massive military campaigns was over, and the Russian strategy shifted to more targeted special operations. These operations were conducted with the participation of the forces of the FSB, MVD, and special forces of the Ministry of Defense.

Further changes were made in Russia's legislative base. In May 2001 Putin signed a new law on the state of emergency. In contrast to the previous legislation, this law allowed for the declaration of a state of emergency in response to terrorist attacks. The law thus resolved the previous dilemmas that Yeltsin's government had to deal with when introducing troops in Chechnya. In July 2002 Putin added to his arsenal of counterterrorist tools a law on extremism. This law advanced Putin's counterterrorist campaign because it allowed for the prosecution of those who engaged in "public justification of terrorism or other terrorist activities."[62] In addition to banning vaguely defined extremist activities, the law eventually turned into an instrument used to silence opinions that contradicted official rhetoric.[63] The law helped the Kremlin solidify its narratives on the North Caucasus and counterterrorist operations.

In terms of the official narrative on Russia's actions in the North Caucasus, September 11, 2001, played a crucial role.[64] September 11 and the ensuing war on terror allowed Putin to convince not only domestic audiences but also international actors of the appropriateness of his methods against terrorism. World reactions to the attacks of September 11 allowed Putin to justify his military handling of the Chechen issue. While before September 11 Putin faced numerous criticisms from the West for his counterterrorist operation, after the start of the war on terror, Putin's tough position on the North Caucasus became widely accepted.

President Putin was the first world leader to reach President Bush after the 9/11 attacks to express his condolences. In his statement in reaction to the attacks on the United States, Putin explained that previously he had been fighting a war on terrorism alone: "The Russian Federation has been fighting international terrorism for a long time now, relying exclusively on its own resources, and it has repeatedly urged the international community to join efforts. Russia's position is unchanged: we, naturally, are still ready to make a contribution to the struggle against terror."[65] The president added, "We also believe that what is happening in Chechnya cannot be viewed out of the context of the fight against international terrorism,"[66] thus clearly linking Chechnya to such terrorist attacks as those that occurred on September 11. Following the U.S. attacks more reports appeared in Russian sources linking Chechnya to Al Qaeda and Bin Laden. The North Caucasus terrorists were portrayed as nothing less than Al Qaeda cooperatives.

While prior to September 11 Western audiences were skeptical of such portrayals, after the start of the war on terror perceptions changed. For instance, at the outset of instability in Dagestan in 1999, James Rubin, a State Department spokesman, condemned "the actions of armed groups from Chechnya against the legitimate government and peaceful residents of Dagestan."[67] At the same time, however, Rubin refused to accept the terrorist label for the insurgent groups. Following the 1999 apartment bombings in Russia, President Clinton acknowledged that Russia was justifiably engaged in counterterrorist activities but according to the U.S. president, Moscow chose "counterproductive" measures in Chechnya. At the time Clinton foresaw that Russia's methods in Chechnya would only provoke more extremism in the North Caucasus[68]—the scenario that subsequently developed. At the outset of the counterterrorist operation, the European Parliament, Organization for Security and Co-operation in Europe (OSCE), Parliamentary Assembly of the Council of Europe (PACE), International Monitory Fund (IMF), and World Bank all condemned Russia's use of military tactics.

Following September 11 many international actors accepted Russia as a partner in the war on terrorism and embraced Russia's approach to the North Caucasus. U.S. national security advisor Condoleezza Rice acknowledged after September 11 that the United States and Russia were fighting similar threats in Afghanistan and Chechnya: "We know that there are terrorists in and around Chechnya and we urge Chechen leaders to disassociate themselves from the criminals who might be found in their ranks. We cannot fight international terrorism in Afghanistan and welcome it in Chechnya."[69] The triumph of Putin's position became clear in 2002 when U.S. secretary of state Colin Powell declared that Russia was "fighting terrorism in Chechnya, there is no doubt about that."[70] After the terrorist attack in Beslan in 2004, President Bush further confirmed that the United States was "fighting international terrorism shoulder to shoulder with Russia."[71]

In a way, such a shift in international opinion was also facilitated by the information on the Al Qaeda–North Caucasus connections that emerged after September 11. The 9/11 Commission Report published details of the connections between Chechnya and the 9/11 terrorists. For instance, the principal organizer of the 9/11 attacks—Khalid Sheikh Mohammed—had previously tried to join Khattab in 1997. He was not able to reach Chechnya through Azerbaijan and went to Afghanistan instead. Others involved in staging the September 11 attacks also tried to join jihad in Chechnya. In 1999 Mohamed Atta, Marwan al-Shehhi, Ziad Jarrah, and Ramzi Binalshibh were planning their trip to Chechnya when through a "chance meeting on a train in Germany" they were diverted to Afghanistan instead.[72] The Commission Report presented further details of Saudi mujahedeen who were not successful in crossing borders to Chechnya and who then decided to join jihad in Afghanistan. Some accounts point to former Chechen mujahedeen implicated in other Al Qaeda–orchestrated attacks, such as the 2003 Istanbul bombing and the 2003 bombings in Riyadh.[73]

Further, as Operation Enduring Freedom started in October 2001 in Afghanistan, accounts emerged of Chechen insurgents fighting on the side of the Taliban. Much controversy surrounds such accounts, and solid evidence remains sparse. Reportedly, one of the groups that fought on the side of the Taliban in Afghanistan—Al Qaeda's 005 Brigade—included Chechen individuals.[74] Some reports claim that as the war started in Afghanistan, Khattab sent some of his people to fight there. Accordingly, that reduced the number of foreign mujahedeen in Chechnya, which by October 2001 supposedly was 200.[75] While no concrete evidence emerged to support these claims, such factors as Chechen-Taliban relations, the presence of Chechen training centers in Afghanistan, and the ease of crossing borders to Chechnya through the Pankisi Gorge suggest that it is possible that individuals from the North Caucasus or former mujahedeen from Chechnya reemerged in Afghanistan.

Another piece of controversial evidence for Afghanistan–North Caucasus links is presented by Russian detainees at Guantanamo. Given that no Chechens were transferred to Guantanamo from Afghanistan,[76] out of nine Russian detainees who did appear at the American base, four had connections to the North Caucasus, and several had a history of arrests in Russia for extremist activities. A native of Kabardino-Balkaria, Ruslan Odizhev received religious education in several Middle Eastern institutions. Odizhev was a friend of Anzor Astemirov, a prominent leader of the Kabardino-Balkaria jamaat.[77] Reportedly, he fought in Abkhazia in the 1990s and had encounters with Russia's FSB before leaving the republic.[78] According to Russian sources, upon repatriation from Guantanamo, Odizhev rejoined the Kabardino-Balkaria insurgency. His name appeared on a wanted list after the insurgent attack on Nalchik in October 2005. Two years later Odizhev was killed in a special operation in Kabardino-Balkaria.[79] Another Guantanamo detainee from Kabardino-Balkaria, Rasul Kudaev (also known as Abdullah Kafkas), was arrested upon his return to Russia for his alleged participation in the same raid on Nalchik in 2005.[80]

The third person, Airat Vakhitov, received religious education in Russia's Tatarstan. According to Tatarstan security services, Vakhitov was a local Wahhabi ideologue.[81] In 1998 Vakhitov traveled to Chechnya, where, according to him, he was abducted. Similar to Odizhev, Vakhitov had previous encounters with Russia's security services. He was detained in connection to the 1999 terrorist act in Moscow on Gur'ianov Street.[82] Finally, the fourth individual, Tatar Ravil Gumarov, had no firsthand experience with the North Caucasus insurgency. However, according to Russia's FSB, he made several attempts to enter Chechnya before leaving for Afghanistan.[83]

As can be seen from the discussion, the evidence of Al Qaeda–North Caucasus nexus after September 11 was no clearer than before the attacks in the United States. The evidence suggests that certain Afghan mujahedeen who had failed to join the fight in Chechnya appeared in Afghanistan. It is also suggestive of the existence of a number of individual fighters who embraced both the Caucasus jihad and Al Qaeda's ideology. However, it seems that by the mid-2000s the links remained marginal, and neither the terrorist command of the North Caucasus nor Al Qaeda implemented a concerted strategy for the fusion of the movements. After Khattab's death in 2002 his successor Abu al-Walid still adhered to the local quest for the establishment of the North Caucasus Islamic state under Basayev's command.

Despite such considerations, and the lack of solid evidence linking Osama bin Laden with Chechen terrorists, after September 11 Russia was able to convince the United States to place several Chechen entities on the terrorist lists. Despite Chechen connections to such terrorist attacks as Budennovsk, Kizlyar/Pervomaiskoe, Moscow metro attacks, and the assassination of international Red Cross personnel before September 11, no Chechen groups were designated as terrorist organizations by the United States. After September 11, following the attack on the Moscow theater, Basayev and Yandarbiyev were listed on U.S. Executive Order 23334 in 2003. The same year the Special Purpose Islamic Regiment, Islamic International Peacekeeping Brigade, and

Riyad us-Saliheyn Martyrs Brigade were listed on U.S. Executive Order 23334 and the UN list of Al Qaeda cooperatives.

Encouraged by the start of the global war on terror, the Kremlin proceeded with its counterterrorist operation in the North Caucasus with more confidence. Under the banner of the war on terror, zachistki operations continued with increased rigor. As a result, more civilians were impacted in the counterterrorist operation. According to Maskhadov's former foreign minister Ilyas Akhmadov, the start of the international campaign in Afghanistan corresponded to the period that "was the most deadly for the civilian population in Chechnya."[84] In turn, rhetoric on Al Qaeda links and stepped up violence in the region provoked Basayev to make another statement on behalf of the North Caucasus insurgency.

BASAYEV'S CLARIFICATION: DUBROVKA

To clarify the goals and tactics of the North Caucasus insurgency, Basayev masterminded another Budennovsk-style hostage raid. In response to the federal zachistki operations, artillery and air raids, and continued use of disproportionate force in Chechnya, Basayev staged the next terrorist attack to demonstrate to the Russian people what was going on in Chechnya. On October 23, 2002, a group of 40–50[85] armed Chechens from Basayev's Riyad us-Saliheyn Martyrs Brigade broke into a theater in the heart of Moscow during the performance of the musical *Nord-Ost*.[86] This time Basayev was able to plan an attack that reached Russia's own capital and took around 900 people hostage at Dubrovka in close proximity to the Kremlin. According to one of the terrorist operatives, Abu Bakar, the very location was strategically chosen as "it is in the center of the city and there were a lot of people there."[87] The gunmen booby-trapped the building, sealed off the theater, and kept everyone—including all spectators and theater personnel—inside for three days. Basayev's plan was executed by Movsar Barayev, another relative of the widely known Chechen field commander Arbi Barayev.

The raid on Dubrovka proceeded similarly to the previous attacks on Budennovsk and Kizlyar/Pervomaiskoe in 1995 and 1996. The only immediately visible difference was the presence of Black Widows among the hostage-takers. About half of the terrorists were women dressed in black clothes. Again, many of the Black Widows at Dubrovka, similar to other terrorist attacks, were widows of insurgents, including a widow of Arbi Barayev. The Black Widows were wearing suicide belts, which they were ready to activate in case the building was stormed. Based on the previous experiences, the group of terrorists anticipated the storming of the building, and the members of the group were clearly ready to become shahids.

Despite the Kremlin rhetoric on the Islamist international terrorist threat, the terrorist group at Dubrovka laid out local ethno-nationalist separatist demands consistent with the demands voiced at both Budennovsk and Kizlyar. The hostage-takers demanded the termination of the war in Chechnya, the withdrawal of federal troops, and the start of direct negotiations between Aslan Maskhadov and the Russian leadership. The terrorists ordered the termination of artillery and air raids, along with zachistki operations in Chechnya.

Another aspect of the attack that points to its intrinsically local nature was the different treatment for Russian and foreign hostages. In the initial hours of the attack, Barayev's group checked the passports of hostages to determine foreign citizens. Among the hostages were 75 foreign citizens, including individuals from the Netherlands, Germany, Australia, and the United States.[88] The terrorists immediately released all Muslim hostages and hostages from Georgia, along with 15 children.[89] The rest of the foreigners were ordered to contact their embassies to arrange for a pick-up. The hostage-takers were acting on clear orders from Basayev to not harm foreigners. As Basayev explained, "I told my men, all foreigners must be released unconditionally. That was an order. But—but you can release them, but they may not make it to safety. And it would look as if you killed them. Therefore, have every one of them call the embassies, have a car drive up to the door. Car drives up, you let them out."[90] Curiously, the Russian authorities strongly resisted the different treatment for foreign hostages, perhaps since the terrorist intention not to harm foreigners significantly undermined the official rhetoric on international Islamist terrorists with global aspirations fighting in Chechnya. The release of the foreigners eventually did not take place.

The theater raid was meant to focus attention on events in Chechnya. As one hostage later recalled, Barayev explained the attack on civilians as follows: "The war in Chechnya has been going on for many years, every day people die there ... But you [the hostages] do not get out to stage protests to stop the war! You go to theaters here while we are being killed there."[91] Barayev went on to explain that the reason for targeting innocent civilians was only due to the fact that the State Duma had tough security to penetrate. However, the terrorists expressed willingness to exchange 10 hostages for every volunteer Duma deputy. The hostage-takers promised to release 50 more people in exchange for Akhmad Kadyrov.[92]

Akhmad Kadyrov ignored the demands of the terrorists. Several Duma deputies, in turn, volunteered to negotiate with the hostage-takers. Among them were the Duma deputy from the Chechen Republic Aslambek Aslakhanov, Joseph Kobzon, Irina Khakamada, Boris Nemtsov, and Grigory Yavlinsky. Other public figures such as Evgeny Primakov, Ruslan Aushev, Alla Pugacheva, and former Soviet president Mikhail Gorbachev also volunteered to assist with negotiations. Despite such initiatives, no official negotiations were conducted with the hostage-takers. The FSB assumed a hard-line approach and instead of negotiations, the command embarked on planning a storming operation. The only offer that followed from the FSB was a safe escape route for the terrorists in exchange for the release of the hostages.[93] The hostage-takers refused, insisting on their intention to stay until their demands were met; they were willing to become shahids if necessary.

In the meantime, families and friends of the hostages received instructions during phone conversations to stage a protest against the war in Chechnya. The hostages were allowed to phone their relatives, and many expressed concerns over what would happen if the building were stormed. Based on their knowledge of how the 1995 and 1996 rescue operations had been conducted, many hostages were not hopeful.[94] Two days into the crisis, on October 25, protesters gathered close to the theater, urging the government to concede to the terms of the terrorists in order to avoid the storming of the theater at all costs. The protesters issued a petition to the president signed by over 250 people asking Putin to avoid a forceful solution.[95] No concessions followed. Instead, as the deadline for the terrorists' ultimatum approached, authorities decided to storm the theater.

The rescue operation proceeded on October 26 in two stages. During the first stage an unidentified soporific gas was pumped into the building through its ventilation system. Under the effect of the gas many people, including the terrorists, lost consciousness. That is when the second stage of storming the building with squad teams followed. Under the circumstances the use of gas was justifiable. Moreover, it was an innovative technique in Russia's handling of hostage crises. In this respect, Russia's security services followed the examples of hostage release operations throughout the world, in which gas, mostly tear gas, has been used as an effective rescue tool. For instance, tear gas was successfully used back in 1968 to free the PanAm DC6B hijacked by a U.S. marine in South Vietnam.[96]

The rescue operation in Moscow, however, failed on numerous accounts. A chemical agent of unidentified nature was used. No information was released on the exact nature of the gas. No antidote was provided to the rescue teams, and medical personnel were not informed of the use of the gas. This resulted in inadequate medical care for many hostages and a complete lack thereof in certain cases. The whole evacuation process was poorly organized and became chaotic. One eyewitness described the process as follows:

> The semi-naked bodies of unconscious hostages were piled up on the ground outside the building, where, according to a report by the Moscow Meteorological Bureau, the temperature was 1.8°C. Some of them died simply because they were laid on their backs and subsequently suffocated on their own vomit

or because their tongues were blocking their airways... there were not enough ambulances, so the hostages were transported to hospitals in ordinary city buses without the accompaniment of medical staff and without any assistance from traffic police to facilitate their rapid arrival at the hospitals. The medical staff in the hospitals were not equipped to receive so many victims, had not been informed of the properties of the narcotic gas used by the security forces and did not have appropriate equipment.[97]

The hostage crisis left 129 hostages dead. Among them, five (three of whom were not original hostages but individuals who tried to penetrate the building after the siege started) were executed by the terrorists.[98] The rest died in the course of the rescue operation or at the hospital. According to the authorities, all the terrorists, including Movsar Barayev and the Black Widows, were eliminated during the storming of the theater. As all the perpetrators were reportedly dead, no further investigations of the rescue operation were deemed necessary. The case was closed in June 2003.[99] Five Chechens were subsequently found guilty of assisting the Dubrovka terrorists: Alikhan Mezhiev, Akhyiad Mezhiev, Aslanbek Khaskhanov, Aslan Murdalov, and Khampash Sobraliev. By 2007 further investigations regarding the hostage-taking were effectively terminated.

According to the government, the rescue operation at Dubrovka was a success. However, many relatives of the deceased hostages questioned official accounts. Many of them believed some hostages died because of the effects of the unidentified gas. The government denied such a possibility but still refused to disclose details about the gas. An MVD spokesman explained, "There was information that many died of special substances (i.e., soporific gas), used in the course of the operation. That is not so." Instead, the spokesman proceeded to blame the "three days of stress, hunger, and the lack of medicinal treatment and qualified medical evaluation [in the theater]."[100]

Unsatisfied with the official explanation, some relatives started their own investigations. In November 2002 Sergei Kovalev's committee, which had been convened to examine the apartment bombings in Moscow and Volgodonsk and the Ryazan incident, decided to broaden its mandate and begin an investigation of the Dubrovka rescue operation. However, as with the investigation of the apartment bombings, the authorities were highly uncooperative. Some relatives and surviving hostages organized a class action lawsuit against the authorities for not properly disclosing information about the gas and subsequently subjecting the hostages to inadequate treatment. However, in 2003 the hearing of the case was denied by the Moscow court. Failing to find support in Russia, the group turned to the European Court of Human Rights (ECHR). In March 2012 the ECHR passed a final judgment on the case of *Finogenov and others vs. Russia*. According to the ECHR decision, the rescue operation at Dubrovka was completely justified. However, its implementation, the ECHR concluded, was not adequately prepared nor was it effectively carried out.[101]

The Dubrovka theater attack achieved the goal Basayev had hoped for: It reminded the Russian public of the war in Chechnya and once again exposed the inadequacy of the Russian response to the threat of terrorism. Having dealt with two similar cases in the past, Russia's security services still exhibited a lack of competence in rescuing people from terrorist attacks. As one woman who lost her son during the hostage crisis lamented, "I consider that our children died because of the poor organization of the rescue efforts ... I blame not only the Moscow authorities, but also the state." She continued, "I believe that the hostages died in the course of war. The war with Chechnya."[102]

COUNTERTERRORISM AFTER DUBROVKA

In response to the attack on Dubrovka, Russia moved to criminalize organizations related to Basayev. In accordance with the 1998 counterterrorist law, Russia's Office of Prosecutor General forwarded a request to the Supreme Court of the Russian Federation to list 15 organizations as terrorist groups. Along with Al Qaeda, the list included Basayev's Supreme Military Majlis ul-Shura of the United Mujahideen Forces of the Caucasus and his Congress of the Peoples of Chechnya and Dagestan. In February 2003 the Supreme Court affirmed the status of these entities as terrorist organizations.

Following the Dubrovka attack President Putin announced that "international terrorism [was] getting increasingly brazen and bloody." To counter the threat the president vowed to "respond with measures commensurate with the threat posed to the Russian Federation, and get at terrorists, those who organize crimes and their ideological and financial sponsors, wherever they may be."[103] With such a promise, Putin turned with new criticisms against Aslan Maskhadov, negating any future possibility for negotiations with the Chechen separatist leader.

While Maskhadov firmly condemned the terrorist act at Dubrovka, he in turn described the raid as a consequence of Putin's Chechen campaign: "The event that took place in Moscow is the very outcome of the horrific war that is being waged against the Chechen people. The forceful solution of the Chechen problem is impossible." Maskhadov underscored that at all times during the crisis, he had been willing to start negotiations with Putin, but it was the latter who preferred a forceful solution: "During the hostage crisis President Putin had a choice between two solutions. The first, wise, solution was to start negotiations and save the lives of hundreds of people. The second, reckless one, was to start the storm and preserve his popularity. Unfortunately, he chose recklessness."[104] To demonstrate the sincerity of his statements, Maskhadov opened a criminal case against the mastermind of Dubrovka, Shamil Basayev. Putin, however, interpreted the attack as yet another indication that Maskhadov completely lost control over his militants and concluded that any subsequent negotiations with him would be impossible.

Unlike in previous hostage crises, this time the Russian public stood behind the president. The public favored Putin's resolute stance on terrorism, and following the attack on Dubrovka support for the military involvement in Chechnya increased once again (see Figure 4.1). The number of people who trusted the president's rhetoric on international Islamist terrorism went up. In a poll conducted by the Levada Center in Moscow after the Dubrovka raid, 42 percent of respondents considered the terrorist attack to be the work of international terrorists. Almost the same number of people, 45 percent, saw the attack as a consequence of the war in Chechnya.[105] To compare, during Budennovsk the majority of people blamed Moscow for allowing the terrorist act to occur, and the majority were still against military involvement in Chechnya after the attack.

Such results demonstrated the effectiveness of Putin's control over the media as a way of promoting the official position on the course of the counterterrorist operation in the North Caucasus. Following Dubrovka, Putin proceeded to tighten such control further. The Kremlin threatened to shut down several media outlets for their coverage of the terrorist attack. For instance, the government made it clear to Russia's NTV channel that it disapproved of the information it aired.[106] Further, the Press Ministry temporarily shut down the Internet site of the radio station Ekho Moskvy for publishing the demands of the Dubrovka hostage-takers.[107] Subsequently, Russia's State Duma wanted to introduce a number of amendments to the law on mass media to restrict media coverage of terrorist attacks. President Putin vetoed the amendments, but harassment of journalists in connection with the Dubrovka attack continued. As a result, the journalists' union decided to adopt self-censorship. On April 3, 2003, the union signed a counterterrorist convention that self-regulated the coverage of terrorist acts. Accordingly, journalists could no longer interview terrorists in the course of a terrorist attack, had to avoid detailed information on the course of rescue operations, and had to be careful in terms of labels used in the coverage of terrorist attacks.[108]

Putin's further counterterrorist initiatives mainly fell under the same two categories as before. The first priority of the president was to consolidate political control over Chechnya. The second was closer coordination of military activities conducted by federal forces in the republic. In this way Putin continued Chechenization of the conflict or transferring the issue from the national to the local realm. One of Putin's biggest achievements in this sphere was holding the first referendum in Chechnya since its declaration of independence in 1991. On December 12, 2002, Putin issued

Decree 1401 in which he sanctioned a referendum in Chechnya on the issues of a new Chechen constitution as well as legislation on presidential and parliamentary elections. The referendum took place on March 23, 2003. Reportedly, almost 90 percent of the population took part.[109] Subsequently, the new constitution of the Chechen Republic, approved by 96 percent of those who took part in the referendum, came into effect.[110] Akhmad Kadyrov became acting president of the Chechen Republic. These events placed Chechnya firmly on track to become a compliant subject of the Russian Federation. From a separatist Islamic territory, Chechnya was reined back into the federal sphere and was pronounced a secular republic.

Further, the policy of Chechenization started gradually transitioning into that of Kadyrovization, as much of the control over Chechnya consolidated in Akhmad Kadyrov's hands. On October 5, 2003, Chechnya held presidential elections in which Kadyrov was affirmed as president of the republic. Kadyrov started institutionalizing his power by eliminating his Wahhabi opposition. In one of his first decrees, Kadyrov banned Wahhabism and ordered Wahhabi mosques, education centers, and religious groups to be closed down. To appeal to the locals, he began openly voicing criticisms against violations committed by federal forces in the republic. He also started demanding complete control over Chechnya's oil industry.

Perhaps the most significant step in terms of Chechnya's counterterrorist capacity was Kadyrov's building of his own security services. Through his connections with insurgents, Kadyrov was able to co-opt many former separatists like himself into his security force. The process was legalized under an amnesty announced in celebration of the passing of the new Chechen constitution. In June 2003 Russia's State Duma amnestied individuals who had taken part in the conflict in the decade between 1993 and 2003. The amnesty covered not only active insurgents but also those who already switched sides to Kadyrov's security services, as well as federal forces engaged in violations in Chechnya. The incentives of legality and more stable payments covered by the federal budget attracted many former insurgents to Kadyrov's ranks. The security apparatus was headed by Kadyrov's own son, Ramzan Kadyrov.

Akhmad Kadyrov did not stay in power long, however. He was assassinated during a terrorist attack at the Victory Parade in Grozny on May 9, 2004. Basayev claimed responsibility for the assassination. In his statement Basayev proudly declared, "Our mujahedeen successfully carried out a special operation 'Nal-17' under the campaign 'Retribution.' The sentence of the sharia court in regards to national traitors and apostates Kadyrov and Isaev [Kadyrov's head of State Council] was carried out."[111] However, Kadyrov's assassination did not stop the policy of Chechenization; Chechen minister of internal affairs Alu Alkhanov, loyal to the federal center, stepped in. Basayev tried to sabotage Alkhanov's election as well by staging a suicide bombing in Moscow at the Rizhskaia metro station on August 31, 2004.[112]

But sabotage and terrorist attacks failed to terminate the Kadyrovization policy. Ramzan Kadyrov, who had been too young to immediately succeed his father, formally became Chechen president in March 2007.

In terms of tightening control over federal forces' military activities in Chechnya, the Kremlin introduced certain changes. In addition to Kadyrov's security services, the federal center created its own special forces divisions in Chechnya. Russia's Ministry of Defense reorganized a former *spetsnaz* division, Vostok, into a battalion of the same name. The group was formed with co-opted former Chechen separatists and was headed by Sulim Yamadayev, a former Ichkeriia military member who was subsequently honored as a Hero of Russia. Another battalion, Zapad, also formed from co-opted insurgents, was led by Said-Magomed Kakiev (also a Hero of Russia). The FSB formed its own special contingent Gorets under the leadership of former separatist field commander Movladi Baisarov. The groups were especially instrumental in carrying out zachistki operations in Chechnya. All these groups eventually came in conflict with Ramzan Kadyrov's forces and were later eliminated or regrouped into other entities.

After the Dubrovka attack the Federal Counterterrorist Committee was once again affirmed as the coordinating body responsible for the oversight of counterterrorist activities of different federal agencies. The Russian government issued Decree 880 of December 10, 2002, which stated that the responsibilities of the committee included ensuring coordinated counterterrorist activities targeted at all spheres of the threat. At the same time Putin introduced changes in the control over counterterrorist operations in the North Caucasus. In June 2003 Putin issued Decree 715 on additional counterterrorist measures in the North Caucasus. The decree transferred leadership of the counterterrorist operations in the region once again. This time the FSB ceded this role to the MVD of the Russian Federation. The MVD was granted the future authority to determine the composition of joint counterterrorist forces in the North Caucasus in cooperation with the armed forces of the Russian Federation. Subsequently, in addition to the Federal Counterterrorist Committee, the MVD created its own counterterrorist agency—Center T.

Despite the evolution of Russia's counterterrorism approach after the Dubrovka attack, its impact on the actual terrorist threat proved to be rather limited. The policy of Chechenization provoked anger and resentment among the insurgents. As Basayev later explained, it was the policy of Chechenization that caused him to intensify attacks on Russia: "We actively brought military operations to the territory of Russia only in 2002, at precisely the time when they began to conduct the Chechenisation of the conflict. Chechenisation of the conflict will never work and civil war will never work because civil war occurs in a free state when free citizens fight."[113] As zachistki operations continued, in 2003 Basayev announced his operations Boomerang and Whirlwind-Antiterror, which resulted in numerous terrorist attacks across Russia. In July 2004 he warned the Russian authorities of his intention to intensify his attacks. At the time he declared that the Riyad us-Saliheyn Martyrs Brigade had "prepared a series of special operations." Basayev promised, "Our attacks will be unexpected and very painful."[114] Following his warning and around the time of presidential elections in Chechnya on August 29, 2004, the number of terrorist attacks in Russia increased. Basayev claimed responsibility for the August 24 Moscow Kashirskoe Shosse bombing, the August 24 explosions on two Russian planes, and the August 31 suicide bombing at Moscow metro station Rizhskaia.[115] However, these attacks were only the prelude to what was to come next.

BASAYEV'S NORD-WEST: BESLAN

Basayev's last significant terrorist statement before his death in 2006 became his most horrendous. September 1 is celebrated in Russia as a traditional day of knowledge and marks the opening of an academic year. Instead of a celebration, however, September 1, 2004, turned into a tragedy for Russia. On that day, a group of 30–60 armed insurgents from Basayev's Riyad us-Saliheyn Martyrs Brigade arrived in Beslan, North Ossetia.[116] The group approached city school No. 1 and ordered everyone present— 1,128 children, parents, teachers and school personnel—into the building. As an eyewitness described it, "I saw people in masks ... At first I thought it was all part of the celebrations and that these people were a special surprise. Then they began to fire shots in the air. The teachers and parents shouted 'run, run' and we did."[117] The raid left 331 people dead. Among those, more than half—186—were children.[118] Basayev proudly called the operation Nord-West, an analogy to Dubrovka's Nord-Ost.

The gunmen had arrived in North Ossetia from Ingushetia. According to Basayev, Beslan was not his preferred choice.[119] His true ambition was to stage simultaneous attacks in Moscow and Saint Petersburg. However, due to the cost of such operations, he had to settle on something closer to Chechnya, though North Ossetia was not chosen at random. Basayev's decision was driven by existing animosities between Chechens and North Ossetians. Specifically, it was North Ossetia's role in providing bases to Russia to launch military attacks on Chechnya that served as a justification for the target. "We chose Ossetia because Ossetia is Russia's fortpost in the North Caucasus, and all bad that comes to us comes from the territory of Ossetia, with the silent consent of its population," Basayev elaborated.[120] Strategically, Beslan was a convenient target because it was located close to the Ingushetia border and had less military presence than many other cities of North Ossetia.

The raid was led by Ruslan Khuchbarov, an Ingush. This was the first instance of hostage-taking being led by a non-Chechen. According to

Basayev, the total number of hostage-takers was 33. Among them were two Black Widows, two Afghan mujahedeen, as well as a number of ethnic Russians and North Ossetians. Nine Ingush and one Kabardin were also among the group.[121] The Beslan crisis demonstrated that terrorism in the North Caucasus was no longer limited to Chechens. By 2004 insurgents from the Wahhabi jamaats across the region under the leadership of the Supreme Military Majlis ul-Shura of the United Mujahideen Forces of the Caucasus had firmly joined the terrorist ranks.

The hostage crisis proceeded according to the customary scenario. The hostage-takers booby-trapped the school building and sealed off the hostages in the gym. Having learned from the Dubrovka experience, trying to preempt the potential use of gas, the terrorists destroyed the school windows. They were also equipped with gas masks. The hostages were ordered to surrender all of their cell phones and video cameras. Hostage-takers promised to blow up the building if it were stormed.

While in many respects similar to the previous hostage raids, the Beslan crisis stood out in terms of treatment of the hostages. First, the attack became the first North Caucasus–initiated terrorist attack in which hostage-takers not only captured children but also intentionally targeted them. As recently as at Dubrovka, the hostage-takers released groups of children who happened to be among the hostages. This time children were at the very heart of the plan. As Basayev explained this choice, "I figured that the more brutal I could make it, the quicker they'd get the message."[122] Further, the Beslan raid exceeded all previous raids in terms of cruelty toward the hostages. For instance, back in 1995 in Budennovsk, Shamil Basayev was known for accommodating some female hostages' requests and even allowed psychic Kashpirovsky into the building. At Dubrovka hostages were allowed to use their phones to talk freely to their friends and relatives. At Beslan, however, hostages were refused even water, food, and medicine. As per Basayev's orders, children were to receive food and water only if Putin started the withdrawal of troops from Chechnya.[123]

True to the established pattern, the hostage-takers demanded the termination of the war in Chechnya and the withdrawal of troops from the republic. The hostage-takers insisted on negotiations between Aslan Maskhadov and the Russian leadership. They also demanded to see the president of North Ossetia, Aleksandr Dzasokhov, and the head of Ingushetia, Murat Ziazikov. The authorities, however, tried to prevent the publication of these demands. Instead, they tried to persuade the hostage-takers to exchange hostages for prisoners held in detention for taking part in an insurgent raid on Ingushetia in June 2004.[124] Similar to Dubrovka, the terrorists refused to release the hostages in return for safe passage back to Chechnya.

According to Basayev, his forces arrived in Beslan "not to kill people but to stop the war."[125] As Basayev explained, Russian forces were fighting in

Chechnya "without any rules, with the direct connivance of the whole world." As a result, Russia's terrorist number one proceeded, "we are not bound by any circumstances or by anybody, and will fight by our rules, as is comfortable and beneficial for us."[126] Basayev's statements revealed that he felt forced to stage the Beslan attack because other smaller attacks had failed to achieve the desired results:

> We have not stopped directing our operations against military and political targets on Russian territory. It's just that your [one's] knowledge and our capability to conduct military action are limited. Today everywhere access to freedom of information and the free spread of information are barred to us because any journalist who asks us anything is automatically an accomplice of terrorism or something else.[127]

As a result, Basayev concluded that only through the escalation of terrorism could he affect public opinion in Russia. Further, after Beslan, Basayev even acknowledged he was a terrorist: "I admit, I'm a bad guy. A bandit, a terrorist."[128] However, he claimed, it was Russia's war in Chechnya that had led him to employ such extreme measures.

Following the start of the attack on September 1, several gunshots were exchanged. During the first day of the siege, one of the Black Widows detonated her suicide belt. A number of hostages were killed. By September 3 the authorities had managed to negotiate the evacuation of the dead bodies. What followed looked like a storming of the building. However, the versions of the events remain highly contradictory. The fighting over control of the school lasted several hours. To liberate the building Russian forces used tanks and flamethrowers, for which the government later came under severe criticism. As the terrorists retreated the fighting moved to other areas of the city. Eventually, by the end of September 3, the school building was free of the hostage-takers. The government announced that all of the terrorists had been eliminated. The only hostage-taker who was captured alive was Nur-Pasha Kulaev. He was later tried and sentenced to life in prison. Following the Beslan tragedy North Ossetia president Dzasokhov resigned from his post.

Having learned from Dubrovka, the government pursued a number of investigative initiatives to establish the facts of the attack on Beslan. On September 22 a special parliamentary committee started its analysis of the circumstances of the attack. The final report of the committee was published in December 2006.[129] It largely corroborated the official version of the events; the operations command had not planned to storm the building. Several explosions took place inside the school, in response to which the security services exchanged fire with the hostage-takers. Subsequently, hostages started fleeing the building, but terrorists fired at and killed many. The overall conclusion of the report was that the actions of federal forces were commensurate with the nature of the attack.

The parliamentary report was criticized by eyewitnesses to the event, and former hostages claimed the report did not present a true picture of the attack.[130] An alternative view was presented by one of the members of the parliamentary committee, Duma deputy Yuri Savel'ev.[131] According to his report, the explosions in the gym resulted from shots fired from the outside. In this version of the story, the storm operation was initiated by the security services, and tanks and flamethrowers were used while hostages were still in the building. Savel'iev's report thus placed responsibility for the majority of the deaths on Russian forces, not on the terrorists. It also challenged the official number of hostage-takers, indicating that some of them had managed to escape. Some of the hostages also claimed that a number of terrorists managed to escape by changing into the clothes of the hostages and blending in with the crowd. Similar to the parliamentary report, Savel'iev's account was also criticized as incomplete.

Another equally criticized account of the attack was produced by the local parliamentary committee of North Ossetia. A further investigation of the case was conducted by Russia's Office of the Prosecutor General, but this case is still ongoing, and its progress remains slow. Basayev, in turn, did not fail to offer his own account of the events. According to the mastermind of the terrorist attack himself, the personnel who came to collect the dead bodies on September 3 were in fact special forces in disguise. By Basayev's account it was these special forces that initiated the storming of the school, and the explosions came only in response to the actions of the Russian authorities.[132]

Another controversial aspect of the attack was the authorities' handling of the media. The media transmitted the information received through the operations command. The information, however, was not always accurate. For instance, the authorities insisted there were 354 hostages inside the school. Outraged by such reports, local residents produced posters that appeared in the crowd saying, "There are at least 800 people there!"[133] On the second day of the siege, journalists were asked "for some time not to send information on the events in the city to their offices or to clear their material with the operations center for the hostage release."[134] Some journalists also faced harassment on their way to cover the events in Beslan. For example, Anna Politkovskaya was poisoned by tea on the plane while she was on her way to North Ossetia. Upon arrival she had to be taken to an emergency department.[135] Journalist Andrei Babitsky was not even allowed to board the plane, as he was arrested at the Moscow airport for alleged debauchery.[136] As a result, only 13 percent of the Russian population believed the official information on the Beslan hostage crisis. Fifty-six percent believed only the partial truth was disclosed, while 22 percent were convinced that the authorities had tried to conceal the facts.[137]

Based on the lessons learned from Dubrovka, the Russian authorities did improve some aspects of handling a hostage crisis. For example, only hours into the terrorist attack, the local hospitals started getting ready to receive hostages who could require medical attention. A psychological center started operating close to the school building, offering counseling services to relatives and friends of the hostages. However, such efforts were not enough to save President Putin's ratings, which plunged in response to the Beslan tragedy to 66 percent—a record low since the poor handling of the 2000 submarine *Kursk* disaster.[138] The number of those who trusted Putin's rhetoric on international terrorism went from 42 percent at Dubrovka to 27 percent at Beslan, while 39 percent believed the attack on Beslan was an outcome of the Chechen war. Only 34 percent were generally satisfied with the hostage release operation at Beslan, compared to 78 percent at Dubrovka.[139]

COUNTERTERRORISM AFTER BESLAN

The atrocities at Beslan greatly affected public opinion both in Russia and abroad. This time excessive violence against children eroded much support for the Chechen separatist project. At an emergency meeting convened in response to Beslan, the UN Security Council strongly condemned this outrageous act of terrorism. Following the crisis Russia prompted the Security Council to adopt Resolution 1566, which became one of its strongest condemnations of terrorism since Resolution 1373, which was issued in response to September 11. This time, it was U.S. president Bush who was among the first world leaders to reach President Putin and express his support for Putin's war on terror.

Basayev himself later realized that he had probably miscalculated the effect of the Beslan raid by placing children at the epicenter of the attack. He tried to exonerate himself by blaming the massacre on Russian forces: "I thought that if we work through all options, if we don't leave the Russian leadership with a single chance for a bloodless resolution of this problem, they won't kill children."[140] He tried to justify the act through references to Russia's atrocities against Chechen children: "We regret what happened in Beslan. It's simply that the war, which Putin declared on us five years ago, which has destroyed more than 40,000 Chechen children and crippled more than 5,000 of them, has gone back to where it started from."[141] However, Basayev did not manage to restore the image of Chechen terrorism. In this respect the development paralleled a trend within Al Qaeda in precisely the same time period. In his 2005 letter to al-Zarqawi, al-Zawahiri criticized the former for the use of excessive violence, cautioning him against it because it erodes popular support.[142] The loss of popular support following Beslan is probably one of the factors that led the Chechen terrorist command to give up hostage-taking as a tactic. Since Beslan no hostage-takings have been recorded in connection to the North Caucasus.

In turn, Aslan Maskhadov distanced himself from the attack by condemning terrorism, just as he had done after Dubrovka. "It was really a tragedy, it was a blasphemy. Such methods have nothing to do with the fight of the Chechen people and Chechen Mujahideen because there is no justification to that," Maskhadov declared.[143] The Chechen president issued his condolences and apologized to the people of North Ossetia for the actions of the perpetrators, who, he acknowledged, could be Chechens. However, Maskhadov explained, such individuals did not belong to the Chechen separatist movement, "Among the Chechen resistance there is a radically minded group of people, who are convinced that fighting with Russia through conventional civilized means is useless. These people think that through metro, railway, and plane explosions, hijacking of schools—only through such means one can pressure Putin to stop this war."[144] Maskhadov, on the other hand, firmly believed that only negotiations could stop the war in Chechnya: "30 minutes are enough for the two presidents to meet and to get this bloodshed to stop, to get this terrible war to stop, to come to an agreement, i.e., to stop terrorism and blood and to stop people from suffering."[145] Maskhadov's offer remained without a response, and the Chechen president himself was killed in a special operation in March 2005.

President Putin remained resolute in his hard-line approach to terrorism. He refused to negotiate either with the hostage-takers or with separatists.[146] Following the Beslan tragedy Putin addressed the country with a statement in which he claimed, "What we are facing is direct intervention of international terror directed against Russia. This is a total, cruel and full-scale war that again and again is taking the lives of our fellow citizens."[147] Information was released by Russia's special services that the Beslan attack had been planned with the involvement of Al Qaeda.[148] To counter the growing threat, Putin initiated an overhaul of Russia's counterterrorist system.

In the political realm one of the most significant changes that followed Beslan was the elimination of elections of heads of the federal regions of the Russian Federation. As Putin explained in an address, "First of all, I consider a key factor in strengthening the state is the integrity of the executive power structure in the country."[149] To strengthen the executive, on September 13, 2004, Putin decreed that elections of governors of Russia's federal regions would be replaced by presidential appointments. In this way he substantially increased his power over the regions through instituting what came to be known in Russia as "power vertical." This system of centralized control persisted until 2012, when President Medvedev reintroduced regional direct elections. In the North Caucasus, however, the system of central control has remained. Five of the North Caucasus republics have adopted a system of parliamentary appointments that preserves the executive oversight over the process. Chechnya today remains the only republic that has so far insisted on direct elections.

In terms of the North Caucasus, Putin announced that "the fight against terror calls for a cardinal renewal of our whole policy in this region."[150] To initiate the change, in September 2004 Putin created a special committee to coordinate the activities of federal executive institutions in the South Federal District. The committee was set up to especially focus on terrorism and was tasked with developing appropriate counterterrorist approaches. The committee was headed by the presidential envoy to the South Federal District—at the time, the newly appointed Dmitry Kozak. The envoy was given the broad powers of "coordinating a number of federal civilian ministries and, in certain areas, also the military and law-enforcement bodies."[151] This way Putin assigned his trusted head of staff of the Russian government to consolidate institutions of power in the North Caucasus region under his control.

Russia's security services underwent certain restructuring. On September 13, 2004, Putin issued Decree 1167 in which he ordered his agencies to develop rigid standards for handling crisis situations. In accordance with this decree divisions of the MVD and FSB were reformed; the system of collecting intelligence was improved. A new development in the tactics of special services was the employment of counter–hostage-takings. In such operations special services captured relatives of terrorists during a terrorist attack. This was intended as a means of influencing the terrorists. For instance, in December 2004 relatives of Aslan Maskhadov were abducted and in 2005 Doku Umarov's sister was taken hostage.[152] The actions of the special forces also spread from Chechnya to the rest of the territories of the North Caucasus.

A more substantial counterterrorist reform took place in 2006. It touched upon many aspects of counterterrorist activities and remained the largest counterterrorist legislative initiative in Russia to date. Until 2006 a number of agencies—including the Ministry of Defense, the MVD, and the FSB—were involved in the fight against terrorism. Due to incomplete interagency cooperation, counterterrorist operations often suffered because of the lack of coherence among these agencies. To improve coordination among the different institutions involved in counterterrorist activities, in February 2006 the president decreed the establishment of the National Counterterrorist Center. In line with the Federal Counterterrorist Committee, the National Counterterrorist Center was created as a coordinating institution. However, unlike the Federal Counterterrorist Committee, the National Counterterrorist Center was granted the expanded authority to coordinate counterterrorist activities at all levels: federal, regional, and local. The center was also set up to coordinate the federal operations command responsible for the conduct of counterterrorist operations. The leadership of the center was assumed by the director of Russia's FSB.

In this way the National Counterterrorist Center greatly streamlined the conduct of counterterrorist operations. As FSB director Nikolai Patrushev explained, the new process created a system that was ready to be deployed at any time: "The National Counterterrorist Center is designated as an institution coordinating counterterrorist activities. Counterterrorist committees in the subjects of the Russian Federation ensure the implementation of its policies in the regions. Operations command centers at federal and regional levels then become operations centers conducting counterterrorist operations at time 'X.' "[153] As Patrushev also noted, previous experiences of conducting counterterrorist operations exposed the necessity of delineating the exact responsibilities of all the participants. For this purpose the guiding legislation on the conduct of counterterrorist operations—the 1998 counterterrorist law—was overhauled.

In March 2006 President Putin adopted a new counterterrorist law, which replaced the 1998 legislation and updated the definition of a counterterrorist operation as follows: "a complex set of special, operational-combat and army measures accompanied by the use of military equipment, armaments and special facilities which are aimed at suppressing an act of terrorism, neutralizing terrorists, ensuring the security of natural persons, organizations and institutions, as well as at reducing to a minimum the consequences of an act of terrorism."[154] The document legitimized and expanded the role of the armed forces of the Russian Federation in zones of counterterrorist operations. The armed forces now could be justifiably employed in all spheres of counterterrorism: prevention of terrorist acts, suppression of terrorism, and conduct of counterterrorist operations. Since the law came into effect, its provisions have been invoked in a number of counterterrorist operations that are routinely announced in the republics of the North Caucasus.

NEW COUNTERTERRORISM IN ACTION

Following the overhaul of the counterterrorist policies, Russia's security services were able to achieve a major success. On July 10, 2006, director of the FSB Patrushev victoriously reported to the president that Russia's terrorist number one—Shamil Basayev—had been eliminated. Putin celebrated the news as a "deserved retribution to the bandits for our children at Beslan, in Budennovsk, for all the terrorist attacks that they carried out in Moscow and other regions of Russia, including Ingushetia and the Chechen Republic."[155] Chechen president Alu Alkhanov announced that with this achievement the war on terror in the North Caucasus was over: "I consider that today can be considered a logical finish to the hardest fight against illegal armed formations that special operations, federal forces and law enforcement agencies have been conducting."[156] In the name of this success, Patrushev offered insurgents the opportunity to lay down arms and join the legitimate authority in Chechnya. In September 2006 Russia's State Duma issued another amnesty.

Basayev was undoubtedly a mastermind behind the tactic of terrorism in the North Caucasus insurgency. Under his leadership insurgents engaged in many successful terrorist operations against civilian and military targets within Chechnya, in the broader region of the North Caucasus, and throughout Russia. Under Basayev's command Chechen terrorism reached Moscow, and his people were able to stage large-scale attacks in the Russian capital such as the Dubrovka hostage crisis. With Basayev's guidance, the terrorist attacks diversified from plane hijackings to hostage-takings to explosions. He was behind implementing such innovations as radiological terrorism and female suicide bombers.

Despite such developments, however, Basayev remained firm to his original goal of liberating Chechnya from Russia. In 1991 Basayev committed his first hijacking raid to expel the Russian military from Chechnya. His last major terrorist attack, at Beslan, was committed to demand independence for Chechnya and the withdrawal of Russian troops from the republic. Along the way Basayev partnered with Khattab and adopted some Wahhabi Islamist rhetoric. He also partnered with Dagestani Wahhabis and amended his aspirations to include the liberation of Chechnya and Dagestan from Russia. However, in all his endeavors he remained true to the ideals of historical Imam Shamil: liberation from Russia, establishment of an Islamic state in the Caucasus, and the implementation of sharia. Liberation remained his priority, as he explained in a 2005 interview: "it's first and foremost a struggle for freedom . . . Shari'a comes second."[157] Basayev rejected any international goals: "We are fighting only against Rusnya,[158] and so far, only on its territory."[159] Under Basayev's leadership terrorist tactics underwent some stylistic changes, but the core of the terrorist goals remained the same.

After Basayev's death no large-scale terrorist acts similar to the hostage raids of his era were conducted. Perhaps this can be attributed to the counterterrorist reform that touched many spheres of counterterrorist activities. However, Russia's overreliance on hard-line measures in handling counterterrorist operations has resulted in the spread of the insurgency to the rest of the North Caucasus. The militant approach of Putin and Kadyrov toward Chechnya forced the insurgents to find bases of operation elsewhere, which led to the diffusion of the insurgency. By the mid-2000s Basayev wielded control of Wahhabi jamaats in the different territories of the North Caucasus. In 2005 Basayev was able to say:

> With the grace of Allah we have not only the support of the Chechen people but of all the peoples of the North Caucasus, and throughout Russian territory. This is demonstrated if only by the fact that this war, this cruel

battle has already been going for six years, and they cannot do anything with us. Over this time I have been many times in many republics of the North Caucasus, not only in Chechnya.[160]

As the geography of the insurgency spread, so did its goals. Russia's stated victory over terrorism in 2006 was premature. The Caucasus Emirate that arose in succession to Basayev's quest announced much broader goals under an organization with a less clear structure. The Russian security services had a new threat to confront.

5

The Caucasus Emirate

CONDITIONS IN THE NORTH CAUCASUS

Back in 1996 when asked if the Chechen conflict could spread, President Boris Yeltsin resolutely discounted such a possibility:

> No such danger ever existed because specific conditions that brought about the conflict in Chechnya did not exist in any of the republics neighboring on Chechnya. Neither were there any social groups there that for the sake of criminal interests would be prepared to start such conflicts. Last but not least, both the peoples and the governments of those republics did everything to prevent themselves from being drawn into the Dudayev regime's bloody ventures. As the plan of settlement in Chechnya, that I announced on March 31 of this year, is being realized, the possibility of an internationalization of that conflict will be reduced to zero altogether.[1]

However, Yeltsin's prediction turned out to be incorrect. While in 1996 conditions necessary for the spread of the insurgency might have not existed, they developed as the war in Chechnya progressed.

Over two decades of war and instability in Chechnya greatly affected the region. Neighboring republics received not only refugees but also weapons and insurgents from Chechnya. By the mid-2000s it became clear that the zones of insurgency were shared with many republics of the North Caucasus. After Beslan, President Putin initiated a transformation in the region spearheaded by the presidential envoy in the South Federal District. By then, however, the insurgent cells had already formed.

The North Caucasus republics had historically been some of the poorest regions of the Soviet Union. Since the collapse of the USSR, income levels in this region steadily fell below the Russian average (see Table 5.1). Unemployment rates in many republics also exceeded the Russian average. In a matter of a decade, from 2000 to 2010, the economic situation changed little, and some republics of the North Caucasus fell even further below the nation's average income level. Further complicating the poor economic conditions was the staggering growth of corruption across the region. Corruption impacted many spheres of life and eroded trust in government institutions. Poor socioeconomic conditions, rampant corruption, and the lack of a functioning government infrastructure, combined with persecution of the opposition and violations of religious freedoms, facilitated the spread of the insurgency from Chechnya to other regions in the North Caucasus.

Ingushetia, the poorest republic of the North Caucasus outside Chechnya, was greatly affected by political turbulence. In December 2001 Ruslan Aushev resigned his post as the president of Ingushetia. He was replaced by Murat Ziazikov, an FSB insider, whose election was surrounded by allegations of electoral fraud. In the first round of elections in April 2002, Ziazikov came second with 19.4 percent of the vote against State Duma deputy Alikhan Amirkhanov, who was leading with 31.5 percent of the vote.[2] In the second round, however, Ziazikov defeated Amirkhanov with 53 percent of the vote.[3] The opposition considered Ziazikov's victory a result of fraud and ballot stuffing.[4] Despite this, Ziazikov came to power with strong support from the presidential envoy in the South Federal District, Viktor Kazantsev, as well as Putin himself.

Under Ziazikov the situation in Ingushetia only deteriorated. Corruption reached unprecedented levels. In the first half of 2007 alone, federal audits revealed that the amount of embezzled funds reached 850 million rubles.[5] Government opposition faced persecution as Ziazikov clamped down on grassroots initiatives, such as the congress of the Ingush people. As a result, many protest activities switched venues to the Internet and social media. Ziazikov further turned on the Chechen refugee camps in Ingushetia and forced the refugees to relocate. Some refugee facilities came under attacks in *zachistki* operations.[6] The system of sharia courts functioning under Aushev in Ingushetia was dismantled, and Wahhabis were also persecuted.

In response to Ziazikov's rule, a sharia court of the Riyad us-Saliheyn Martyrs Brigade sentenced Ziazikov to death on February 27, 2004. As Basayev explained, Ziazikov was pronounced guilty of assisting Russia's genocide of the Vainakh peoples of Chechnya and Ingushetia: "Murat Ziazikov turned Ingushetia into a thoroughfare where death squads from both Chechnya and Ossetia that carry out extrajudicial killings and kidnappings of people can operate freely. In the previous year only, over 100 Chechens and Ingush disappeared on the territory of Ingushetia. Over 50 people were killed."[7] On April 6, 2004, Ziazikov was targeted in an

Table 5.1 Socio-Economic Indicators in Russia's North Caucasus and Bordering Regions in 2002 and 2010.

Region	2002				2010			
	Population (in thousands)	Average Monthly Income (in Rubles)	Gross Regional Product (in millions of Rubles)	Unemployment (percent)	Population (in thousands)	Average Monthly Income (in Rubles)	Gross Regional Product (in millions of Rubles)	Unemployment (percent)
Russia	143,097.0	3,964.1	7,830,341.5	1.8	142,914.1	18,881.0	32,072,552.0	2.1
South Federal District	21,401.3	2,648.0	607,940.5	1.9	13,853.7	15,031.0	1,988,637.6	1.4
North Caucasus Federal District	—	—	—	—	9,507.0	13,249.0	795,453.2	8.7
Adygea	444.5	2,174.2	6,804.1	2.8	440.3	12,236.0	41,439.2	2.1
Chechnya	621.0	No data	No data	No data	1,275.2	No data	64,089.7	42.7
Dagestan	2,199.9	1,787.5	31,605.7	5.8	2,981.4	15,213.0	265,092.1	3.3
Ingushetia	472.5	1,150.7	4,967.4	11.5	415.0	9,596.0	18,654.1	21.0
Kabardino-Balkaria	780.2	2,389.1	21,389.9	3.3	859.7	11,215.0	66,427.1	3.0
Karachaevo-Cherkessia	426.2	2,042.6	7,372.3	1.4	478.0	10,431.0	38,582.7	2.6
North Ossetia	676.3	2,050.0	14,685.7	1.3	712.4	13,228.0	65,140.7	3.4
Stavropol region	2,632.8	2,394.2	72,851.1	1.1	2,785.3	12,913.0	277,466.8	2.0

Data Source: Federal'naia Sluzhba Gosudarstvennoi Statistiki. Regiony Rossii. Sotsial'no-Ekonomicheskie Pokazateli – 2003g. http://www.gks.ru/bgd/regl/B03_14/Main.htm. Sotsial'no-Ekonomicheskie Pokazateli – 2011g. http://www.gks.ru/bgd/regl/B11_14p/Main.htm.

assassination attempt carried out by a suicide bomber. Despite the failed attempt Basayev swore that his forces would be persistent in executing the sharia ruling. During his presidency Ziazikov experienced several assassination attempts.

In 2008 Ziazikov was replaced with Yunus-Bek Yevkurov. Yevkurov, however, much like his predecessor, failed to significantly improve the situation in Ingushetia. In 2014 Ingushetia Duma deputy Akhmed Belkhoroev described the situation in the republic:

> The Federal Security Service is doing all it can to fight terrorism. But the government of the republic is doing nothing in this respect. There are no long-term programs for countering extremism. The republic is swamped with corruption. Neither the federal laws nor the founding law of the country are observed here. Embezzlement of budget funds is the norm. The population is unhappy with the political leadership, but peaceful protests through demonstrations and marches are not allowed. Many are dissatisfied not only among the population but also among the legislative and executive branches of the government. This leads to people loosing hope in any other ways except joining the ranks of terrorists.[8]

The deteriorating situation in Ingushetia affected many spheres of life in the republic, and the opposition was left with no outlets except for the extremist underground.

Dagestan became another insurgency hotspot in the North Caucasus due to changes in political, social, and economic structures. Putin's initiative to centralize power led to the erosion of traditional power-sharing arrangements in Dagestan. Dagestan is one of the most diverse territories in the North Caucasus, and interethnic tensions pose a serious challenge for the governance of the republic. In this respect the Dagestani authorities traditionally relied on consociational arrangements that allowed for the representation of Dagestan's largest ethno-nationalist groups in the government. Putin's "power vertical" initiative, however, interfered with the traditional consociational structures, replacing local power-sharing arrangements with directives from the Kremlin.

The erosion of political consociationalism was accompanied by a rise in corruption, crime, and lawlessness. In 2005 the head of government in Dagestan, Magomedali Magomedov, reported that over the course of eight months crime had grown at a rate of 19.6 percent compared to the previous year. In the same period the level of serious crimes increased by 18 percent, and terrorist activities grew at five times the previous rate.[9] Criminal activities were often accompanied by corruption and embezzlement. For instance, in 2010 financial audits revealed that 27 percent of the republic's budget was subject to violations.[10] By 2014 State Duma deputy Umakhan Umakhanov pronounced corruption the main security problem for Dagestan: "Unfortunately, corruption exists in many spheres of life in the republic... The structures that must fight corruption in the republic today are not working in that direction. It is hard to counter this problem even for government officials, let alone regular citizens."[11] Corruption levels reached the point that even law-enforcement structures recognized the problem. For example, in 2014 a police officer, fired for criticizing the police structure for corrupt practices, sent a petition to President Putin asking him to tackle corruption in Dagestan.[12]

The economic situation in Kabardino-Balkaria, Karachaevo-Cherkessia, and North Ossetia evolved comparatively better than it did for their eastern neighbors. At the same time, however, corruption and crime remained equally rife in the Northwestern Caucasus. Despite the fact that many of the peoples of the area—including the Balkars, Karachai, Cherkess, and Kabardins—engaged in sovereignty projects in the 1990s, the leadership of the Northwestern Caucasus historically retained more loyalty to Russia. The pro-Russian orientation of local governments, however, incited more hostilities, as many local ethno-nationalist groups still harbored anti-Russian sentiments from the Soviet-era deportation experiences of such groups as Balkars and Karachai. Not surprisingly, many of these ethnic groups presented susceptible audiences for anti-Russian insurgent recruitment. For instance, the Kabardino-Balkaria Jamaat Yarmuk became perhaps one of the most ethnically diverse insurgent groups across the North Caucasus and included representatives from the Balkars, Kabardins, Ossetians, Karachai, and even Russian Muslims.[13]

Dmitry Kozak, presidential envoy in the South Federal District, warned the government of the extent of the socio-economic and political problems.[14] In 2004 he pointed out that the region overshadowed other Russian territories in terms of corruption levels. Corruption was "pervasive in local self-governing bodies, institutions of state power, regional federal institutions and the law enforcement system," Kozak stated.[15] By 2005 Russia's president himself acknowledged the extent to which corruption was paralyzing effective governance in the region. Putin announced, "Government institutions are often used as an instrument of dishonest competition. Frankly speaking, they are being corrupted."[16] As a result, certain local and federal programs were launched to combat corruption and socio-economic problems, such as budgetary audits. However, it was not until the 2010s that a comprehensive strategy was implemented to deal with the poor socio-economic development and corrupt governance that continued to contribute to regional instability.

THE SPREAD OF THE INSURGENCY

With the presence of war in the region, poor economic conditions, rising crime, rampant corruption, political authoritarianism, and repression of religious freedoms led to the spread of the insurgency from Chechnya to other areas of the North Caucasus. As federal forces eliminated the functioning insurgent bases in Chechnya, separatist groups had to seek refuge in the neighboring republics. With the establishment of the Kadyrov regime in Chechnya, the consolidation of his security services further drove insurgents outside the zone of the counterterrorist operation there. In the meantime Wahhabi *jamaats* across the North Caucasus, sympathetic to their Wahhabi brothers, started radicalizing and turned into a significant source of support for the Chechen separatists.[17] Further, the Chechen command made a conscious decision to incite insurgent activities outside Chechnya. Around 2002, the time when Basayev declared the intensification of attacks against Russia, insurgents started carrying out active raids on the territories of the neighboring republics, including Ingushetia, Dagestan, and Kabardino-Balkaria. All these factors led to the gradual diffusion of violence in the North Caucasus, which resulted in a growing number of terrorist attacks outside Chechnya.

Ingushetia became one of the first republics in the North Caucasus to see an insurgent raid outside Chechnya since the 1999 incursion into Dagestan. Following Ziazikov's election to the presidency, a group of around 170 Chechens crossed the border from Georgia and attacked the Ingush village of Galashki on September 23, 2002, with a detachment of the Special Purpose Islamic Regiment under the command of Ruslan Gelayev. Ziazikov described the raid as an attempt to "repeat the events in Budennovsk and Pervomaiskoe," thus comparing the raid to Chechen terrorist attacks.[18] As Ingushetia's president explained, the rebels were trying to spread the insurgency to other regions of the North Caucasus, but he still promised there would be no second Chechnya in his republic.

Despite Ziazikov's promise, the situation in Ingushetia had deteriorated by the fall of 2003. On September 15, 2003, the first suicide bombing took place in the capital of the republic, killing almost 30 people. At that point Ziazikov announced that in Ingushetia there were "forces that are not satisfied with the process of stabilization in the North Caucasus. These forces would like to transfer the theater of military action to Ingushetia."[19] Ziazikov was correct in his assessment because by then a network of Wahhabi jamaats had been established in his republic.

Ethnically, the Ingush people are the closest to the Chechen ethnic group in the North Caucasus. In the 1990s many Ingush groups took part in the fighting against federal forces on the side of Dzhokhar Dudayev. These groups gave rise to the Ingush sector of the Ichkeriia Armed Forces, which later split into a system of jamaats in Ingushetia, including such branches as Jamaat Khalifat, Jamaat Taliban, and Jamaat Siddik. Individual jamaats were created in most of the cities of Ingushetia.[20] Under the leadership of Ali Taziev, also known as Magomed Evloev, Ingush forces consolidated into a system that has been referred to as the Islamic Front of Ingushetia, Islamic Movement of Ingushetia, or the Majlis of Islamic

Mujahedeen of Ingushetia. By 2004 Taziev, who came to be known as Emir Magas, received full acknowledgement from Basayev as the leader of the Ingush forces. In April 2004 Basayev appointed Taziev as emir of the Ingush jamaat. Along with Emir Magas, other prominent figures of the Ingush insurgent sector included Magomed Khashiev and Afghan mujahed Abu Dzeit.

In June 2004 the Ingush jamaat staged another significant raid on the territory of Ingushetia. In the course of operation Bekkham, insurgent forces attacked Nazran on June 21. As Aslan Maskhadov acknowledged, the raid was carried out by the Western Front of the Ichkeriia Armed Forces.[21] Shamil Basayev and Doku Umarov helped execute the raid. The forces attacked several police stations in the republic, raided warehouses, and captured weapons that they then took back to Chechnya. A number of government buildings and security services offices were destroyed. The raid was professionally planned and executed: "In the course of a few hours, several hundred men were able to disarm the republic's branch of the Ministry of Internal Affairs, destroy the local FSB branch, and blockade military units in such a way as to prevent them from moving into the center of Nazran to help."[22]

The raid was a clear attempt by insurgent forces to move the fighting from Chechnya to other territories of the North Caucasus. It achieved its goal, as President Putin announced his intention to increase the presence of troops in the North Caucasus in response to the raid. "We will increase our effort in the North Caucasus to the necessary volume. This will include the increased presence of the armed forces component," the president declared.[23] In this way the raid on Ingushetia reversed the movement of troops in the North Caucasus. Prior to the raid Moscow was withdrawing its forces from Chechnya. After the raid the federal military presence in the North Caucasus increased. Despite such measures, however, the forces of the Ingush jamaat were able to assist in the Beslan attack in September 2004.

In 2005 another organization arose in the ranks of the Ingush jamaat—the Amanat Jamaat, which was headed by Alash Daudov and another Arab mujahed, Abu Mudzhaid. An interesting feature of this specific division was its focus on developing the means for staging terrorist attacks intended to cause mass destruction. Specifically, the Ingushetia security services contended that the Amanat Jamaat was created to develop new capabilities, including the ability to stage terrorist attacks with the use of lethal poisonous agents. In one counterterrorist operation the security services retrieved chemicals, including cyanide, from Amanat jamaat hiding places.[24] The Amanat Jamaat had reanimated the weapons of mass destruction initiative started by Shamil Basayev in 1995.

By 2006 the Ingush jamaat had a well-functioning system of cells based on special operations groups. As Emir Magas explained, one of the major goals of such cells was "targeted work against specific individuals and the planning and carrying out of adequate military campaigns eliminating the set targets." The system, Emir Magas continued, became a semiautonomous network of cells. The leadership "managed to create a flexible management system where separate divisions possess maximum independence in terms of operational planning," he stated.[25] Under the leadership of Emir Magas, the Ingush jamaat became one of the strongest fighting forces in the North Caucasus. Due to his achievements, Emir Magas was appointed as military commander of the entire insurgent forces after Shamil Basayev's death.[26]

Another network of jamaats that evolved in close connections with the Chechen insurgent command emerged in Dagestan. Through frequent raids on its territory, Chechen insurgents supported the militarization of jamaats in Dagestan. In 2003 Dagestan came under another attack from the Chechen insurgents. Ruslan Gelayev, who a year earlier attacked Ingushetia, this time appeared in the Dagestani village of Shauri. Raids on Dagestan became commonplace and under the influence of militant activities in the republic, many local Wahhabi jamaats transformed into insurgent cells.

Back in the late 1990s Bagautdin Muhammad and his Islamic Jamaat of Dagestan had declared sharia law in the Kadarskii region of Dagestan. Bagautdin's close connections with Basayev and Khattab laid the framework for cooperation between Chechen and Dagestani Wahhabi groups. Bagautdin's quest for establishing an Islamic state in Dagestan was continued by Rasul Makasharipov, who led a Jennet group. In clashes with federal forces, the Jennet group was almost entirely eliminated, and its surviving members further reorganized in Jamaat Shariat. Jamaat Shariat subsequently emerged as a leader of the Dagestani front, similar to the Ingush jamaat. In 2005 Jamaat Shariat pledged allegiance to Sadulayev's command, and Makasharipov promised to continue "combat operations on the Dagestani soil against Russian invaders and [the] Dagestani puppet regime."[27]

Ideologically, Jamaat Shariat continued Bagautdin's line of effort to liberate Dagestan from Russia's oppression and establish the rule of sharia in the republic. In this goal Jamaat Shariat did not deviate from the aims declared by the historical Imam Shamil: "To answer the question what the goal of our organization (jamaat) is, we answer with Imam Shamil's words. Imam Shamil answered the question of a Russian general about what Imam Shamil wanted and was striving for—'I don't want, nor can I think of, anything more than the imposition of sharia among my Muslim brothers.'"[28] While the goals of the Dagestani Wahhabi movement did not change much, it did acquire new ideologues. Among the new generation of religious leaders in Dagestan was Iasin Rasulov, a graduate of Dagestan State University. He became a prominent ideological leader of the Dagestani jamaat and published his own thesis on jihad in the North Caucasus.[29] Similar to previous generations of Dagestani religious leaders, Rasulov was calling for jihad as a war of liberation against the Russian oppression.

In Dagestan the primary reason for the violent activities of Jamaat Shariat was corruption in the republic. The vast majority of military raids and terrorist attacks attributed to Jamaat Shariat were carried out against government officials and military personnel. For instance, one of the earlier attacks of Jamaat Shariat took place during the Victory Day parade in Kaspiisk on May 9, 2002. A large number of the victims of that terrorist attack were active duty military officers. In March 2005 Jamaat Shariat published an "execution list," naming 140 employees of the federal and local Dagestani security services that it aimed to attack.[30] True to its intention, the group has methodically targeted individuals from the list and attacked Dagestani government buildings and military installations in the republic. In April 2005 the group planted a bomb in the Makhachkala prosecutor's office. Numerous raids against police forces followed, and many government officials became assassination targets.

In one of its statements Jamaat Shariat indicated that in attacking government and security services personnel, the goal was not to target them as individuals but rather as representatives of Russian authorities in Dagestan:

> Addressing those who have not yet quit the occupational "law-enforcement agencies," we once again state that your elimination is not our goal. Our goal is to get rid of the government of infidels and to establish the rule of Allah. You became an obstacle on our way, defending with weapons this infidel order, which is fighting against Allah, your creator, and which is guilty of killing and enslaving your ancestors![31]

This statement indicates that in its fight against corrupt Dagestani authorities, Jamaat Shariat adopted a widely used jihadi justification for targeting government officials—their secular nature. In such view it becomes permissible to target government representatives because they do not abide by sharia and therefore can be subject to elimination.

Further, in response to the actions of Dagestani and federal security services, which often caused casualties among civilians, Jamaat Shariat amended its tactics, announcing it was ready to implement the same methods against its enemy. In 2005 Jamaat Shariat announced it was ready to:

1. Storm homes of infidels and traitors with all means and forces even if their children and wives happen to be there . . .
2. Destroy adult relatives of infidels . . .
3. Abduct wives and daughters of infidels.[32]

The same year Jamaat Shariat informed the Kremlin that it intended to transfer its attacks to the territory of Russia and to send its forces to

Moscow to strike there.[33] In 2007 Jamaat Shariat also promised to attack infidels during Russia's Olympic Games in 2014.[34]

Another significant raid outside Chechnya took place in Nalchik, Kabardino-Balkaria, on October 13, 2005.[35] A group of around 250 insurgents attacked the capital of the republic under guidance from Shamil Basayev. The majority of the insurgents came from local Wahhabi jamaats that had come to support the Chechen insurgency. The leader of the group, Anzor Astemirov, was a local head of the Kabardino-Balkaria jamaat. Another Kabardino-Balkaria jamaat, Yarmuk, supplied the fighters for the operation.[36] Similar to the 2004 raid on Ingushetia, the rebels attacked a number of military and government buildings and other targets. Sadulayev described the attack as "a classical sabotage operation."[37] Official sources, in turn, called the raid an attempt to change "the constitutional order of Russia, to violate its territorial integrity and to create in the territory of the North Caucasus an Islamic state."[38]

The raid on Nalchik revealed that by the mid-2000s a network of militant jamaats had consolidated in Kabardino-Balkaria. In this republic the militarization of Wahhabi groups took place under the direct influence of the Chechen insurgents. It is now known that Shamil Basayev used the republic as a safe haven.[39] At the same time local conflicts between the official Muslim boards and Wahhabi groups greatly contributed to the radicalization of Wahhabi movements in Kabardino-Balkaria. Many mosques in this region came under persecution due to disagreements between the official interpretation of Islam and Wahhabi versions. In 2000 the government of Kabardino-Balkaria adopted a law on religious groups that banned educational activities in mosques.[40] By 2003 the authorities had effectively closed down a number of mosques by allowing them to function only on Fridays and only for short periods of time.[41] By 2005 the new president of Kabardino-Balkaria, Arsen Kanokov, acknowledged that the previous administration of the republic had chosen disproportionately repressive measures to counter the spread of radicalization and violence. In an interview Kanokov explained, "Law-enforcement agencies really did act in excess... This problem cannot be solved through prohibition alone. It needs to be won through ideological means... If we do not do this, the situation will only worsen if we continue to ban their [Wahhabi] services and force them underground—where it is much harder to control them."[42]

Kanokov's summary explains how the Kabardino-Balkaria jamaat became radicalized and joined the spreading insurgency. The jamaat of Kabardino-Balkaria came into existence under the leadership of Musa Mukozhev in the 1990s. At the outset his network of loosely organized jamaats appeared in the course of the wave of religious revival, and Mukozhev's work was predominantly nonviolent. However, Mukozhev's jamaat transformed in response to repression from the authorities.[43] By the mid-2000s the Kabardino-Balkaria jamaat had become a system of insurgent cells. As Mukozhev stated in 2006, "Today the jamaat of Kabardino-Balkaria does not exist as it used to. With Allah's grace, the jamaat of Kabardino-Balkaria joined the jihad against infidels and traitors. According to the decision of the Shura, the emirs of jamaats were replaced with field commanders. Having joined jihad, we have gained true freedom."[44] Nonviolent religious activities of the Kabardino-Balkaria jamaat were replaced by militant raids and insurgent attacks.

By 2002–2003 a number of insurgent jamaats had splintered from the Kabardino-Balkaria jamaat. One of the more famous groups among them became Jamaat Yarmuk. The group was led by Muslim Ataev and was created to wage jihad against infidel government institutions imposed on Kabardino-Balkaria by Russia. In 2004 Jamaat Yarmuk published its official program. In it, the jamaat defined its goals as follows:

> We are fighting against tyrants and bloodsuckers who place the interests of their mafia clans above the interests of their own peoples. We are fighting those who are getting fat at the expense of the impoverished and scared people of Kabardino-Balkaria who were brought to their knees. We are fighting occupants and aggressors who captured the Muslim land and are abusing it.[45]

As a result, Jamaat Yarmuk joined the North Caucasus insurgency primarily to fight the pro-Russian government in the republic.

The lawlessness of security services, government corruption, and repression by the Kabardino-Balkaria authorities provided justifiable reasons for the jamaat's violent activities. Most of the terrorist acts committed by Jamaat Yarmuk involved government officials and military personnel. In specifically directing terrorist activities against such targets, Jamaat Yarmuk was similar to other regional jamaats, such as the Dagestani Jamaat Shariat. Yarmuk justified such actions as follows:

> An enemy state that is occupying our Motherland placed practicing Muslims outside the law. That is why we abrogate any responsibility before it and consider ourselves free of abiding by the laws of this enemy state. The servants of this state are collaborators of the occupation and aggression against Muslims, since they are the local channels for such policies of aggression and are the backbone of occupation. That is why their property and blood are not off limits.[46]

Because their attacks were not against individuals, but rather against the government, the leaders of Jamaat Yarmuk encouraged government officials to quit their jobs working for the occupying regime.

Similar to the religious purification movements of the eighteenth century, the Kabardino-Balkaria jamaats saw Russia not only as an occupying power but also as a cause of moral decline. For instance, Jamaat Yarmuk blamed the pro-Russian government of the republic for spreading drugs, prostitution, depravity, and alcoholism.[47] The historical roots of the perceived contemporary injustices also become clear from some of the jamaats' statements. Thus, Jamaat Yarmuk indicated that the liberation movement in Kabardino-Balkaria went back to jihad waged on the Kabarda, Balkar, Karachai, Cherkess, and Adyg territories in the nineteenth century. In this respect Jamaat Yarmuk was another jamaat in the North Caucasus that reaffirmed the aims of Imam Shamil's historical struggle. Accordingly, Jamaat Yarmuk promised "the gate of jihad will close on our land only when the rule of sharia [of 1807] is restored as the law of our life and when the occupied lands are returned to our peoples."[48]

The situation in Karachaevo-Cherkessia was similar to that in Kabardino-Balkaria, although the consolidation of insurgent jamaats started in Karachaevo-Cherkessia earlier. The Karachaevo-Cherkessia jamaats organized under the leadership of Ramazan Borlakov, who had close connections to the Chechen insurgents. Borlakov was mainly driven by the aim of establishing sharia rule for Muslims of Russia.[49] Similar to Kabardino-Balkaria, the Wahhabi Karachai jamaats came into conflict with official Muslim organizations, and by the mid-1990s the Karachai jamaats had extensively radicalized under the influence of the Chechen war. One of the best known cells, the Karachai jamaat, also referred to as the Muslim Society Number 3, splintered from Borlakov's organization under the leadership of Achemez Gochiiaev. This organization and Gochiiaev became widely known in 1999 in connection with the apartment bombings in Moscow. Since then, unlike the majority of the jamaats in the North Caucasus, the Karachai jamaat has evolved much in response to the actions of federal, rather than local, authorities in the republic.

Following news of connections between the Karachai jamaat and the Moscow bombings, both federal and local security services turned their attention to Wahhabi activities in Karachaevo-Cherkessia. With the start of the second Chechen campaign, the authorities of the republic engaged in a number of repressive measures against the Wahhabis. On December 4, 1999, the official Muslim leadership of the republic issued a statement on religious extremism and terrorism, which condemned religious ideas that contradicted the officially supported version of Islam.[50] On April 25, 2000, the government of Karachaevo-Cherkessia adopted a law on countering political and religious extremism in the republic. The law was very similar to that adopted in Dagestan in 1999 but fell short of banning Wahhabism in Karachaevo-Cherkessia. The territory of the republic subsequently became a zone of zachistki operations, which further pushed the jamaats underground.[51]

Inside Karachaevo-Cherkessia the insurgent activities of the Karachai jamaat were similar to those of other North Caucasus jamaats. The jamaat operated based on a list of government officials, security services personnel, and official religious leaders selected for targeting.[52] Terrorist attacks, however, remained rare. What made it different from many jamaats of the North Caucasus were the attacks the Karachai jamaat staged outside the republic in different cities of Russia. The jamaat specifically specialized in staging explosions. For instance, among the first attacks attributed to the group were the explosions in Mineralnye Vody and Yessentuki on March 24, 2001.[53] The peak of Karachai jamaat activities occurred around 2003–2005, when explosions took place in Krasnodar in 2003 and in Voronezh in 2004 and 2005. Among the terrorist attacks attributed to the group were the suicide bombings at the Moscow metro stations of Avtozavodskaya and Rizhskaia in 2004. Perhaps due to the increased presence of federal security services after 1999, members of Karachai jamaat had to seek hiding places outside the republic and thus had more justifications for targeting Russian cities.

The reach of Wahhabi jamaats extended even to non-Muslim areas of the North Caucasus. Thus, one of the newest insurgent formations—Kataib al-Khoul jamaat—was established in North Ossetia under the leadership of Emir Saad.[54] Despite its location, however, the jamaat drew the majority of its members from ethnic Ingush. The group claimed responsibility for attacks against the North Ossetian government and security services as well as several operations in Chechnya.[55] Another Wahhabi jamaat is connected to Russia's Stavropol region. This jamaat goes back to the first war in Chechnya when Shamil Basayev created a Nogai battalion consisting predominantly of Chechen Nogais. Basayev created this group to control the steppe districts of Chechnya and the bordering Stavropol region.[56] During the second Chechen campaign Basayev decided to revive the battalion with the assistance of Nogais from the Stavropol region. This group later became known as Nogai jamaat. Despite its name, the main bases of the jamaat were located in the Shelkovskii and Naurskii regions of Chechnya.[57]

In this way by the mid-2000s a number of insurgent Wahhabi jamaats had arisen across the North Caucasus. As seen from the earlier discussion in this chapter, most of these jamaats emerged with help from the insurgent Chechen command. Some were direct branches of Ichkeriia's armed forces. As insurgent units, the North Caucasus jamaats predominantly engaged in insurgent activities such as raids, ambushes, guerilla strikes, and direct assaults. As such, the vast majority of these attacks targeted military personnel and government officials. Terrorist attacks, mainly explosions, were a secondary tactic employed by jamaats, again predominantly against military personnel and government officials. Car bombings, similar to those that were widespread in Northern Ireland during the Troubles, became especially popular. In another tactic, jamaats staged explosions to lure security services into an ambush so that they could then attack them or stage a second explosion.

While in Chechnya the insurgency started as a separatist project, across the North Caucasus, militant jamaats arose in response to poor socio-economic conditions, lack of effective governance, widespread corruption, and the repressive policies of the local and federal authorities. Disregard for religious freedoms and persecution of Wahhabi groups led to the radicalization of many jamaats that originally emerged as alternative Islamic groups. Such policies as restricting Wahhabi education and closing down Wahhabi mosques only led Wahhabi adherents to organize clandestinely and turn to violence to protect their organizations.

The many persisting ethnic traumas in the North Caucasus also fed into the expanding numbers of the jamaats. Many jamaats traced the traumas inflicted by centuries of Russian rule back to the times of Imam Shamil. Overall, the heritage of Imam Shamil was a common theme in justification narratives advanced by the jamaats. Many North Caucasus insurgent leaders referenced the historic precedent of Imam Shamil's Islamic state in their justifications for restoring sharia in the region. At the same time, while clearly situating their struggle in the local historical context, by the mid-2000s the jamaats had adopted many stylistic frames of global jihadism. Thus, the concept of defensive jihad, widely used by Al Qaeda, was firmly adopted by the jamaats. In justifying attacks against government institutions, jamaats came to use the concept of apostate regimes. Also widely used by Al Qaeda, this concept implies that attacks against Muslim governments not based on sharia law are legitimate. Aside from such rhetoric, however, the goals of jamaats remained local with references to local roots.

CONSOLIDATION OF JAMAATS

By 2005 a system of jamaats had come into existence in the republics of the North Caucasus that supported the Chechen insurgency. Yet, the system was not unified and lacked a single command. At the same time there were multiple experiments with unification projects in the North Caucasus. The Caucasus Imamate, the Mountainous Republic of the North Caucasus, the Emirate of the North Caucasus, and the Confederation of the Mountain Peoples of the Caucasus represented both secular and theocratic statehood endeavors in the region. Since the late 1990s the Chechen leadership had introduced elements of unified cooperation through such militant formations as the Congress of the Peoples of Chechnya and Dagestan and the Supreme Military Majlis ul-Shura of the United Mujahideen Forces of the Caucasus. By 2005 enough jamaats had joined the insurgent cause to attempt another unification project. Once again the struggle against Russia's presence in the North Caucasus became the main justification behind the unification endeavor.

Shamil Basayev considered it his personal quest to continue Imam Shamil's struggle in the North Caucasus. As a result, Basayev favored the idea of the unification of the republics of the North Caucasus into a single state. In 1998 it was Basayev who headed one of the unification endeavors—the Congress of the Peoples of Chechnya and Dagestan. He envisioned the unification of the Caucasus front as a means of engaging solid resistance against Russia. Basayev, following in the footsteps of Imam Shamil, considered Islam to be a means of unification. In his view it was Islam that could consolidate the insurgency:

> Even one person is significant if he knows what to do and how to do it. Let alone entire jamaats. When one speaks of "jamaats," they mean an entire unified system. But there are different jamaats. This word is translated as "community," and any group of Muslims is a jamaat. And our superiority today—that is of the Chechen leadership—is vested in the fact that according to Sharia, Muslims of Russia and the Caucasus must help us and subordinate to us while the war is going on, whether they want it or not. And we take advantage of this for the benefit of all. And the results (Inshallah) will come.[58]

While Aslan Maskhadov adopted Islamist rhetoric under pressure from his opposition and pronounced sharia law in Ichkeriia, his struggle was resolutely ethno-nationalist separatist. Maskhadov firmly supported unification, but such unification applied to the Chechen forces. Maskhadov's efforts were meant to unify the jamaats in Chechnya:

> Actions must be organized. And for that there should be unified direction. There must be state direction. All djamaats, all emirs, all commanders should be brought under state orders and then it is necessary to start an organized war. If we bring all these things together, we have enough strength to beat the Russians in a big way. We can see this strength and we know that it exists. In order to gather them [different forces in Chechnya] under single leadership it is necessary to carry out strong policies and diplomacy with them.[59]

While supporting unification for Chechen forces, Maskhadov did not envision his project spreading to the entire North Caucasus. With Maskhadov's death in 2005, however, the same vision became possible not only for Chechnya but for the broader region. The death of the last elected president of Ichkeriia presented a political opening for insurgent forces to redefine their goals.

Aslan Maskhadov was replaced by Abdul-Halim Sadulayev. Unlike Maskhadov, Sadulayev was a renowned religious figure. He had religious education and played an active role in religious revival activities in Chechnya. Overtime Sadulayev gained widespread religious authority and in the interwar years often appeared on TV with religious sermons. Russian sources portrayed Sadulayev as an Islamist fundamentalist and extremist, and the Chechen mufti proclaimed him "Wahhabi number one."[60] Sadulayev himself, however, claimed his religious training was in the Shafii tradition practiced in the North Caucasus. He acknowledged he was familiar with the Hanbali school of

Islamic jurisprudence but remained true to the Shafii teachings because, as he explained, the "Chechens have always belonged to Imam Shafi'i."[61]

Under Sadulayev's leadership Basayev's vision was implemented in reality. Sadulayev set out with firm support for sharia law and other Islamic institutions in Chechnya. At the same time he realized the potential of the Wahhabi jamaats across the North Caucasus:

> There are Jamaats on the territory of Russia, some consisting of [ethnic] Russians, many of which have taken the oath of allegiance to me as Amir of the Majlis-ul-Shura and have directly subordinated themselves to us. There are some Muslim groups that would like to remain within Russia on the condition that their freedom of belief is observed—a freedom that is guaranteed by the Russian Federation constitution. There are such groups, but above all, it is the Chechen people who in the past have never had any desire to remain in Russia and do not have such a wish today. There are also the neighboring nations who share our demand for independence.[62]

To use this potential Sadulayev morphed the goal for independence to include Islamic unification and unified the diverse jamaats of the North Caucasus under the umbrella of the Chechen struggle. In this endeavor the Chechen forces were clearly in the lead, and under Sadulayev other jamaats became subordinated to Chechen control. The product of this project became a structured network of the North Caucasus jamaats.

In May 2005 Sadulayev issued a decree restructuring the armed forces of the Chechen Republic of Ichkeriia. In addition to the eastern, western, northern, and Grozny fronts, he created a Dagestani front and a Caucasus front. The fronts were further subdivided into 35 sectors.[63] The Caucasus front included the Ingush, Ossetian, Kabardino-Balkaria, Stavropol, Karachaevo-Cherkessia, Adyg, and Krasnodar sectors.[64] These sectors subsumed the respective jamaats on the territories of Ingushetia, Kabardino-Balkaria, Stavropol region, and Karachaevo-Cherkessia. Thus, Sadulayev's new structure had three major tiers of command, fronts, and sectors:

> As for our units, they all submit directly to the Military Council, the Ministry of Defense and the Joint Staff alike. There are no big differences between mujahideen units operating inside and outside Chechnya. We are all one unified mechanism, and all of our mujahideen are divided into fronts and sectors. Each sector and each front knows its direct Amir; each knows the objectives put before it. The Amirs of sectors and fronts are often authorized to solve many tasks. Many operations are planned and conducted in this way. We also carry out large-scale military operations, though only naturally with the authorization of the Commander-in-Chief and the Military Council of the Majlis-ul-Shura.[65]

The leadership of Ichkeriia presided over the entire structure. As Sadulayev explained, "Muslims of the Caucasus are united around the leadership of the

CRI and are waging a national-liberation struggle to decolonize the whole of the Caucasus."[66] The idea of decolonization became especially popular and in March 2006 a movement for the decolonization of the Caucasus was declared. The movement drew further on the ethnic traumas as a resource for insurgent mobilization. In its declaration the movement encouraged the peoples of the Caucasus to cooperate against the Russian occupants and support the armed struggle of the Caucasus mujahedeen.[67] Commenting on the unification of the North Caucasus jamaats under the armed forces of Ichkeriia, Basayev referred to it as a "stage of expanding jihad."[68] At this point Basayev also mentioned the idea of further consolidating the anti-Russian struggle under a single Caucasus Imamate. Unlike Maskhadov, Sadulayev supported the idea of a confederate Islamic state. In February 2006 he announced a program to unite the North Caucasus territories into a single Islamic state.[69]

While structurally Sadulayev introduced significant changes in the nature of the North Caucasus insurgency, in terms of strategy he adhered to the previously pursued directions. He viewed the 2002 decision to wage wider jihad on the territory of Russia as his plan until 2010.[70] At the same time Sadulayev inherited the movement after Beslan, when support for the Chechen cause experienced a notable decline. Taking this into consideration, Sadulayev declared that terrorist methods were unacceptable and announced a "unilateral rejection of terrorist acts."[71] "The targets of our attacks remain, as they used to be, military objects," he stated.[72] Sadulayev was true to his word; during his short presidency his armed forces mostly engaged in insurgent activities. The period between March 2005 and June 2006 had one of the lowest rates of terrorist attacks associated with the North Caucasus since the start of the second Chechen campaign.

DOKU UMAROV AND STRATEGIC CHANGES

In Russia, Umarov's name became known due to associations with the 2004 Ingushetia raid and in connection with the 2004 terrorist act in Beslan. In Chechnya, Umarov emerged as a prominent field commander who rose in the ranks to become second in command to Basayev. Umarov was born in 1964 in the Shatoi region of Chechnya. During the first Chechen war he took an active part in the separatist campaign and was subsequently appointed head of the Security Council of the Chechen Republic of Ichkeriia by Aslan Maskhadov. In 2004 he was further promoted to the position of the minister of defense in the rebel government. Under Sadulayev, Umarov became vice president of Ichkeriia and with Sadulayev's death in June 2006, he became the next leader of the insurgency. Under Umarov the North Caucasus insurgency went through significant transformations, expanding geographically and shifting ideologically. Umarov extended the struggle beyond the North Caucasus and pronounced anyone fighting against Islam as his enemy.

After succeeding Sadulayev in 2006 Doku Umarov continued the consolidation of the North Caucasus front. He went on to encourage his fellow insurgents to wage jihad against Russia: "Chechens today are not the only people fighting against the imperial ambitions of Russia. The best sons of all North Caucasus peoples rose up against the colonial dependence ... With every day the fraternity of the North Caucasus mujahedeen is gaining strength."[73] As the militant jamaats formerly loyal to Sadulayev pledged allegiance to Umarov, he expressed his intention to expand the boundaries of jihad further. Umarov no longer saw the insurgency as a regional project. Instead, he attempted to situate the North Caucasus insurgency within global Islamist movements that aimed at establishing global entities. Umarov became the first Chechen leader to expand the anti-Russian campaign beyond the territory of the North Caucasus.

On July 8, 2006, Umarov signed decrees announcing the creation of the Ural and Volga fronts of the armed forces of the Chechen Republic of Ichkeriia. Umarov decreed the formation of these fronts "in connection to the necessity to grow capabilities to counter Russia's armed aggression."[74] In this respect Russia's Muslim republics of Tatarstan and Bashkortostan presented an attractive area for Umarov. Since his declaration the North Caucasus insurgents had invested efforts in recruiting Wahhabi adherents in the Volga-Ural regions of Russia. These efforts paid off in 2010 when Vilayat Idel-Ural officially joined the North Caucasus resistance.

Umarov inherited the North Caucasus insurgency in a complex state of affairs. After the Beslan terrorist attack the separatist project lost a lot of support in the world, and sympathy from the West was much eroded. Financial support from the Muslim world also diminished. With the death of Khattab in 2002 and the start of the war in Iraq in 2003, the number of foreign mujahedeen in the North Caucasus was significantly reduced. With the departure of the foreign mujahedeen, financial channels of international support also decreased. As a result, in 2006 Umarov addressed the global Muslim community with a plea for assistance for the North Caucasus mujahedeen, asking for both moral and financial support.[75] By 2007 it became clear the movement needed to adjust its strategy to remain viable.

In early 2007 Umarov started focusing his rhetoric on jihad as a fight to protect Islam, as opposed to the traditional understanding of jihad in the Caucasus as an anti-Russian struggle. "The enemy knows that it is Islam that is our defense, our support, ally and a source from which people draw their power," Umarov declared.[76] Subsequently, in his statements Umarov started increasingly referring to Russia as the enemy of Islam. Moreover, he also started referencing Western countries as Russia's collaborators:

> Not a single country in the West or in Europe tells Russia to stop the war, to stop exterminating the people. They don't say that because they consider

Russia a strong power. Besides Russia has a lot of oil and gas that the West needs. They are perfectly aware of what is happening in Chechnya. They know about mass killings and torture of hundreds of thousands of people in Chechnya. However, oil and gas are more important than the fate of the people. This demonstrates the true nature of their "democracy."[77]

In the fall of 2007 Umarov went further and declared war on anyone who attacked Islam:

I said it before and am repeating it now. We are an integral part of the Muslim Umma. I am upset by the position of those Muslims who declare their enemies only those infidels who attacked them directly. With this they seek support and sympathy among other infidels, forgetting that all infidels are a single nation. Today our brothers are fighting in Afghanistan, Iraq, Somalia and Palestine. Everyone who attacked Muslims—no matter where—are our common enemies. Our enemy is not only Rusnya, but everyone who is waging war against Islam and Muslims. And they are our enemies first and foremost because they are the enemies of Allah.[78]

In this way for the first time in the history of the North Caucasus insurgency, Umarov declared war outside the region. He extended the list of his enemies to the West, making a strategic shift from the jihad against Russia's occupation to jihad against all enemies of Islam. This signified the transition of the insurgency from a separatist war in Chechnya to an anti-Russian struggle in the North Caucasus to a global fight against the enemies of Muslim faith.

Umarov's declaration caused an uproar not only among Western policymakers but also within the insurgent movement itself. Akhmed Zakayev, Maskhadov's close separatist ally and head of the Chechen government in exile, denounced Umarov's declaration. Zakayev challenged the legitimacy of Umarov's statement: "In the declaration made by Doku Umarov the legitimate demands of the Chechen people are transferred into the rank of the so-called international terrorism, which has nothing in common with the interests of the Chechen people or Islamic values."[79] Zakayev firmly condemned such changes and called for Umarov's resignation. The parliament of Ichkeriia backed Zakayev's request, and Zakayev appointed himself as prime minister of Ichkeriia in an effort to overthrow Umarov. However, Zakayev was based abroad, while Umarov held direct control of the insurgent forces. As a result, no coup against Umarov followed, and he pursued his declared goal of waging global jihad and became the first North Caucasus rebel to deviate from the goals established by Imam Shamil. He transformed the insurgent movement to fit the profile of an international Islamist movement—the one that Russia had been employing in reference to the insurgency since the mid-1990s.

THE CAUCASUS EMIRATE

While Doku Umarov deviated ideologically from the explicit goals of the North Caucasus insurgency, organizationally he pursued the undertakings started by his predecessors. Umarov continued the idea of a common Islamic state by announcing the formation of a theocratic entity. On October 7, 2007, Umarov proclaimed an Islamic state of the North Caucasus under the name of the Caucasus Emirate. The idea of such a state was not unique to either Umarov or Sadulayev, and the legitimacy of the new entity was explained through such historical precedents as Imam Shamil's Imamate and the 1920s Emirate of the North Caucasus.[80] The Caucasus Emirate became the continuation of the historical trend for common theocratic statehood firmly rooted in the context of the North Caucasus.

The Caucasus Emirate subsumed the militant jamaats of the North Caucasus that had earlier been integrated into the armed forces of the Chechen Republic of Ichkeriia. The jamaats were renamed into *vilayats*, or districts, which were in existence under Imam Shamil's Caucasus Imamate. Umarov further reintroduced *naibs*, or representatives, another feature of Imam Shamil's theocratic state of the nineteenth century.[81] The Emirate included the following elements:

> Vilayat Nokhchicho (Ichkeriia), the former Chechen Republic of Ichkeriia
> Vilayat Galgaiche (Ingushetia), the former Republic of Ingushetia
> Vilayat Dagestan, the former Republic of Dagestan
> Vilayat Nogai Steppe, the former Stavropol region
> United Vilayat of Kabarda, Balkaria, and Karachai, the former Republics of Kabardino-Balkaria and Karachaevo-Cherkessia
> Vilayat Iriston (Ossetia), the former Republic of North Ossetia–Alania (in May 2009 Vilayat Iriston was abolished, and its territory was subsumed in Vilayat Galgaiche)[82]

Some accounts also point to the existence of Caucasus Emirate structures in Adygea and the Krasnodar region of the South Federal District, but such accounts remain disputed. The borders of the Emirate were left intentionally undefined to allow for subsequent evolution of fronts, sectors, and jamaats.

The Caucasus Emirate changed the position of Ichkeriia as the former leader of the insurgency. While under Sadulayev, Ichkeriia was the center of the unification behind the jamaats, under Umarov this leading position was abolished. Ichkeriia became a vilayat with a status equal to other vilayats of the Caucasus Emirate.[83] Umarov thus reversed the dynamic behind the structure of the insurgency. Under Sadulayev the jamaats experienced centralization. Under Umarov the vilayats were given more autonomy, and the system became more decentralized and disjointed. This development vested more decision-making power in the vilayats and elevated the status of the North Caucasus divisions outside Chechnya. To the disappointment of Chechen ethno-nationalist separatist leaders such as Zakayev, the insurgency transitioned from a Chechen-led project to a unified North Caucasus Islamist front.

While such developments impacted the organizational structure of the insurgency, they also empowered the survivability of the North Caucasus insurgent units. Today the Caucasus Emirate resembles the cell system characteristic of many underground groups and terrorist organizations. For instance, in the decade after September 11, Al Qaeda significantly decentralized its network, making it harder for security services to track it. Cell systems, as opposed to hierarchical structures, allow for more resiliency and greater adaptability. In this way the Caucasus Emirate is much more elusive than the Chechen-led insurgency of the early 2000s. The autonomy of the North Caucasus cells promotes the fluidity of operational goals and protects the network from the shocks of losing insurgent leaders. The Internet has become crucial for coordinating activities of the cells and exchanging operational guidance. Ideology, in turn, is key to sustaining the strategic directions of the movement.

Today the ideology of the insurgent movement is highly dependent on the unifying power of the symbols of Islam. Islam played a unifying role in nineteenth-century resistance to Russian rule under the ideology of Muridism. Today the Wahhabi interpretation of Islam plays a significant role in sustaining armed resistance in the North Caucasus. The Caucasus Emirate was proclaimed as a theocratic state, and Umarov declared sharia law on its territory.[84] He thus set out to reform the existing governing institutions in accordance with sharia and announced all secular laws invalid:

> I repudiate all the infidel laws that exist in the world. I refute all the laws and systems that unbelievers set up in the lands of the Caucasus. I refute and abolish all those designations that infidels use in order to divide Muslims. I abolish all ethnic and territorial-colonial zones under the names of "North Caucasus republics," "Transcaucasus republics," and the like.[85]

Maskhadov's secular institutions were abolished. Majlis al-Shura was named the highest consultative body under the emir of the Caucasus Emirate. The supreme sharia court became the highest judiciary institution.

Thus, Doku Umarov changed both the nature and the structure of the insurgency. He changed the direction of the struggle from a focus on the North Caucasus to an orientation toward global jihad. He transformed the structure of the insurgency from a hierarchical system led by Ichkeriia to a cell network of equal partners. Among the changes introduced by Umarov, one feature that remained constant was the tactical use of terrorism against Russia.

THE CAUCASUS EMIRATE: TERRORISM

With the consolidation of the Caucasus Emirate, terrorist attacks resumed with renewed rigor. While the Caucasus Emirate predominantly engaged in insurgent activities—ambushes, raids, shootouts, and assassinations—it also relied on terrorism for propaganda effects. Umarov was prepared to wage protracted war because he realized that his forces could not withstand a direct confrontation with the superior Russian military. As Umarov noted, "We do not rush events. Time is on our side."[86] While waging this war terrorist attacks, similar to previous trends, played the role of psychological weapon meant to affect the morale of the enemy. Today terrorist attacks are often accompanied by propaganda statements that instead of media interviews are disseminated through the Internet.[87]

As opposed to earlier Chechen terrorism that relied on large-scale attacks with many civilians involved, the terrorist attacks of the Caucasus Emirate today are more focused. As discussed earlier in this chapter, they predominantly target government officials, security services, and military personnel. Since 2007 bombings using improvised explosive devices have become the main mode of terrorist operations. In this respect the method of double explosions has become a signature tactic of the North Caucasus insurgents. In such cases a second explosion, usually with a larger impact, is timed so as to affect the security services personnel who respond to the first attack.

Attacks on infrastructure have become more regular. The majority of railway attacks have affected cargo trains. At the same time some of the more widely known railway attacks involved the Nevsky Express train that travels between Moscow and Saint Petersburg. The train first came under an attack that was linked to Doku Umarov in August 2007.[88] In November 2009 the same train came under another terrorist attack for which Umarov claimed responsibility.[89] Other subversive attacks involving infrastructure targeted communications centers, electricity lines, oil and gas pipelines, and public transportation. Such attacks have a significant disruptive influence on the economy of the North Caucasus region. Kabardino-Balkaria's tourism industry has become especially affected due to the increased number of terrorist attacks.

Along with such terrorist attacks that are in line with the previous trends, the Caucasus Emirate attacks also exhibited some new trends that developed under the influence of religious ideology. Some targets today have a religious connotation, including assassinations of religious Sufi leaders. Explosions and bombings were also aimed at alcohol stores, arcades, gambling facilities, and funerals—all of which are associated with customs and traditions that are regarded as sinful under Wahhabi Islam. Many attacks have affected the service providers of "forbidden" goods and rituals, for instance, traditional healers, that are perceived as un-Islamic.

These attacks are aimed at the moral aspect of depravity associated with local secular pro-Russian governments.

Suicide bombings remain a powerful symbolic tool in the arsenal of the Caucasus Emirate. At the local level suicide bombers have targeted prominent political figures, such as Ingushetia's President Yevkurov on June 22, 2009. Many suicide bombings still occur outside the region, targeting Moscow and other cities. On March 29, 2010, suicide bombings took place in Moscow at metro stations Lubianka and Park Kultury. Responding to these attacks Umarov issued a video in which he explained that the metro bombings were in retaliation for a federal special operation in Ingushetia conducted on February 11 of the same year.[90] At the end of 2013 three suicide attacks took place in Volgograd, calling global attention to potential terrorist attacks during the Sochi Olympics. Vilayat Dagestan claimed responsibility for these attacks and warned of more terror during the Olympic Games.[91]

In 2009 the number of terrorist attacks significantly increased. This coincided with the revival of Basayev's Riyad us-Saliheyn Martyrs Brigade. In cooperation with Said Buryatsky, Umarov brought back this group to carry out retaliation campaigns against Russia:

> And if by those laws which we did not write, by the laws which were written by Taghut for itself, by kuffar for themselves, by those laws which we did not agree with and didn't sign, if we are forbidden to kill those citizens, who are so-called peaceful citizens, who provide for the army, for the FSB by their taxes, by their silence, who support that army by their approving silence, if those people are considered civilians, then I don't know, by what criteria it is judged. Therefore, insha'Allah, it is our great success that we have restored this Jamaat [Riyad us-Saliheyn], and that this Jamaat will carry out operations in the territory of Russia, and it will be our retaliatory attacks for those deeds which are committed in Caucasus.[92]

Umarov justified attacks against civilians as collaborators of the Russian regime. His offensive action campaign was meant to induce a "psychological effect, to spread fear and panic among the occupying forces so as to create conditions for the collapse of the occupying governing institutions set up by Moscow in the North Caucasus."[93]

Following the announcement, Riyad us-Saliheyn claimed responsibility for numerous terrorist attacks. Just like under Basayev, the group predominantly relied on suicide bombers. One of the most significant attacks staged by the revived group was the suicide bombing at the Moscow international airport Domodedovo on January 24, 2011. Claiming responsibility for the attack, Umarov blamed it on Putin and his lawlessness in the North Caucasus. According to Umarov, the attack on Domodedovo was in response to the torture and suffering inflicted by Russia on the peoples of the Caucasus.[94]

In February 2010 Umarov announced the expansion of the zone of offensive operations. Umarov warned of his intention to strike against cities in Russia:

> The zone of military action will expand to the territory of Russia. Praise to Allah, last year demonstrated to all those doubting—Putin, Nurgaliev—that the brigade of Riyad us-Saliheyn is truly revived and is well functioning. We are witnesses of the number of special operations the group staged within one last year. The brigade of shahids is growing with the best mujahedeen, and if Russians do not understand that war will come to their streets and houses, they are worse off for it. Blood will no longer be spilled only in our cities and villages. War will come to their cities.[95]

In this respect Umarov achieved success when he expanded the Caucasus Emirate to include Vilayat Idel-Ural in 2010. In 2012 the mujahedeen of Tatarstan renewed their pledge of allegiance to Umarov.[96] Around the same time the mujahedeen of Tatarstan claimed responsibility for the first terrorist attack against traditional Muslim clerics in Russia outside the North Caucasus.[97] On July 19, 2012, two terrorist attacks were staged in Kazan and targeted Mufti Ildus Faizov and his deputy Valiulla Iakupov. In this way North Caucasus terrorism truly expanded beyond the region.

An interesting development in the use of terrorism by the Caucasus Emirate occurred in February 2012. On February 3 Kavkaz Center published Umarov's order to avoid attacks against the Russian civilian population. The declaration followed public protests in Russia that were staged in response to the December 2011 elections to the State Duma. Umarov interpreted the protests as a sign that Russian civilians no longer supported Putin's policies. As a result, the protests signified to the insurgents that Russian citizens could be against Putin's war waged in the North Caucasus.[98] However, the moratorium was soon lifted in anticipation of the Olympic Games in Sochi in February 2014. In July 2013 Umarov declared that his initiative was interpreted as a sign of weakness by Moscow. As a result, he abandoned the moratorium and called for his followers to use all possible means to prevent the Sochi Olympic Games held on the territory where Russia had committed genocide against the peoples of the Caucasus.[99]

Despite Umarov's earlier pronouncement claiming that everyone who announced war on Muslims was his enemy, the terrorist acts of the Caucasus Emirate have been committed exclusively within Russia and against exclusively Russian targets with the exception of the Domodedovo attack committed at the international airport. No terrorist attacks have been staged in foreign countries, and Umarov was careful to distance his movement from Chechen fighters appearing in different war zones of the world. In November 2012 Umarov addressed the mujahedeen fighting in Syria, expressing his support for them. At the same time Umarov was critical of the goal of Syrian mujahedeen fighting to replace the Assad regime, implying that jihad in the Caucasus had a more legitimate cause behind it—fighting for Allah's rule in the theocratic Caucasus Emirate.[100] Further, a *fatwa* was published on insurgent websites that discouraged North Caucasus mujahedeen from going to Syria, "Jihad in Sham [Syria] is first of all the individual responsibility of the people of Sham and jihad in the Caucasus is the individual responsibility of the people of the Caucasus ... If the people of the Caucasus go to wage jihad in Sham, there will be no one left to wage jihad against Russia!"[101]

Further, following the bombing at the Boston Marathon in the United States, many news reports focused on the potential connection of the Tsarnaev brothers to the Dagestani insurgency. In response, Vilayat Dagestan published a statement clearly reminding the world that "the Caucasus mujahedeen are not engaged in military action with the United States of America." The statement continued, "we are fighting Russia, who is responsible not only for the occupation of the Caucasus but also the horrendous crimes against Muslims."[102] Despite threats to attack during the international Olympic Games, no such attacks followed. The spectrum of terrorist attacks perpetrated by the Caucasus Emirate indicates that the threat remains local and targeted against Russia. Umarov's statement on his enemies, it seems, was an attempt to appeal for international support rather than a new direction in terrorism.

The Caucasus Emirate's use of terrorism also remains highly instrumental. The North Caucasus insurgents monitor the effects produced by terrorist attacks and have amended their tactics accordingly. The latest adaptation in terrorism was announced by the new emir of the Caucasus Emirate, Ali Abu Muhammad, when he declared the termination of female suicide terrorism in June 2014. "We categorically ban our sisters from doing this [suicide terrorism] ... My order to brothers is not to use sisters for this ... It does not have any effect on infidels." Muhammad thus reversed the role of women in jihad: "It will be better if these women stay alive and raise their children in the spirit of jihad."[103] This order completed the innovative role of women in jihad in the North Caucasus by bringing them back to the traditional realm of women as supporters of, rather than active participants in, jihad. This move demonstrates that terrorism remains a tactic that changes and adapts to better serve the needs of the Caucasus Emirate and the North Caucasus insurgency.

Despite Umarov's declaration of shifting toward global jihad, links between the Caucasus Emirate and Al Qaeda remain marginal. Indisputably, a number of Chechen and North Caucasus mujahedeen joined Al Qaeda–related groups in Iraq and Syria.[104] Al Qaeda–linked Arab mujahedeen, in turn, still take part in the North Caucasus jihad. Abu Dzeit joined the Ingush jamaat, and Abu Mudzhaid was among the ranks of the Amanat Jamaat. Khattab's successors Abu al-Walid, Abu Hafs, and Muhannad continued Khattab's work of coordinating foreign mujahedeen and channeling foreign funds. However, even Abu Hafs complained of diminished international funding for the Chechen cause after the start of the war in Iraq in 2003.[105] In 2012 the Russian government also acknowledged that funding for the Caucasus Emirate had become predominantly local. Presidential envoy to the North Caucasus Federal District Aleksandr Khloponin indicated that "conversations stating that the bandit insurgency is financed from abroad is childish talk. One doesn't need to sneak abroad, it is enough to use the loopholes that exist in the District."[106] Thus, following the start of the campaign in Iraq, global support for the Caucasus Emirate declined.

Rhetoric linking the Caucasus Emirate and Al Qaeda, on the other hand, has been on the rise. Abu al-Walid's successor Abu Hafs started aligning the statements of foreign mujahedeen in the North Caucasus with the goals of global jihad. It was Abu Hafs who promised to attack American interests in Chechnya in addition to Russia.[107] The establishment of the Caucasus Emirate allowed Al Qaeda to interpret it as a way toward the creation of the global caliphate. In a statement al-Zawahiri described the Chechen movement as being driven by "the Islamic leaning of the Chechen Mujahid and their seeking to revive the Caliphate and considering themselves to be a part of it."[108] While such rhetoric is still not prevalent among the North Caucasus insurgents, younger generations of mujahedeen are increasingly exposed to such narratives through fighting outside the region in Afghanistan, Iraq, and Syria. When these fighters come back to the Caucasus, it is likely that the Al Qaeda version of jihad will prevail and will obliterate the local goals and objectives of the North Caucasus insurgency.

COUNTERTERRORISM AFTER THE CAUCASUS EMIRATE

The spread of the insurgency across the North Caucasus and the consolidation of the insurgent movement into the Caucasus Emirate prompted a number of developments in Russia's counterterrorist approach. In Chechnya the process of Kadyrovization continued with the installation of Ramzan Kadyrov in the presidential seat. In exchange for subsidies Kadyrov offered Chechnya's loyalty to Moscow. "I am not a man of the FSB or GRU, I am a man of Putin. His politics, his word, is law for me. We will follow his road," Ramzan stated.[109] Under Ramzan Kadyrov, Chechnya embarked on a reconstruction process that involved completely rebuilding Grozny. To undercut the authority of Wahhabis in his republic, Kadyrov started promoting his own version of traditional Islam, which is similar to the Soviet-supported variety. It involved a prohibition on alcohol, an Islamic dress code, and open references to polygamy.[110]

While reconstruction and social stabilization often came at the expense of freedoms and liberties,[111] Kadyrov was able to establish a firm grip on

Chechnya's security. Ramzan Kadyrov came into office bringing with him a personal security force—*kadyrovtsy*. Begun under Akhmad Kadyrov, this security apparatus consisted largely of former insurgents who had switched to the federal side. In 2006 Kadyrov further institutionalized these forces by creating battalions Iug and Sever that became formally integrated in Russia's MVD. Kadyrov's forces were instrumental in completing the counterterrorist operation in Chechnya. Putin's Chechenization policy paid off, and he was able to lift the regime of the counterterrorist operation in the republic on April 16, 2009.

The combination of stabilization and suppression seemed to have succeeded in eradicating the terrorist threat within Chechnya. Since the end of the counterterrorist operation, very few terrorist attacks have been perpetrated on the territory of the republic. At the same time, however, it seems that Kadyrov's regime pushed the insurgents out into the neighboring territories, where the majority of terrorist attacks occur today. As a result, counterterrorist operations moved into the other republics of the North Caucasus, where they are periodically announced in Dagestan, Ingushetia, Kabardino-Balkaria, Karachaevo-Cherkessia, and North Ossetia. These counterterrorist operations rely primarily on military means but are much more focused and targeted than the preceding campaign in Chechnya. The military means of addressing terrorism were further expanded upon in Russia's National Security Strategy of 2009 and the Military Doctrine of the Russian Federation of 2010.

While the military approach is still widely used against terrorism in the North Caucasus, with the change in Russia's presidential administration in 2008, the Kremlin adopted new responses to terrorism as well. President Dmitry Medvedev identified terrorism and instability in the North Caucasus as priorities for his presidency. In his presidential address Medvedev described the situation in the North Caucasus as the "most serious, domestic political problem."[112] As a result, he set out to combat the threats emanating from the region. He did deviate from Putin's insistence that the terrorist threat was imported to Russia by international terrorist organizations and acknowledged that certain internal problems had led to the proliferation of conditions ripe for terrorism. Medvedev explained,

> We understand that threats will persist if we cannot effectively counter problems that exist. They are our internal problems in the North Caucasus, such as clan politics, stealing, and bribery that is pervasive. If we fail to find the right solution to these problems we will keep fighting terrorists. And that is the outcome that eventually destabilizes the situation.[113]

With such problems in mind, Medvedev identified new directions for counterterrorism.

On October 5, 2009, President Medvedev signed the Concept on Countering Terrorism in the Russian Federation. The document not only outlined the spread of the terrorist threat but also formally acknowledged the social roots of the threat and pointed out the existing deficiencies in government responses to terrorism.[114] Consequently, the concept called for the resolution of existing grievances that were feeding into the terrorist threat and focused on improving socio-economic conditions, fostering better governance mechanisms, and countering extremist ideologies. The concept revolutionized counterterrorism in Russia through the introduction of a soft-line approach.

To address the socio-economic roots of the insurgency, and hence terrorism, in January 2010 President Medvedev segregated the North Caucasus republics into a separate North Caucasus Federal District. Moscow intended to pay better attention to developments in the North Caucasus. As head of the new district, Medvedev appointed Aleksandr Khloponin, the former governor of Russia's Krasnoyarsk region. Realizing the importance of the economic roots of the instability, Medvedev directed Khloponin to improve the socio-economic situation in the region. In September 2010 the government unveiled a strategy for the socio-economic development of the North Caucasus through 2025.[115] With Putin's return to office, more measures have been introduced to address socio-economic conditions in the turbulent region. In 2014 the Russian government created a new institution, the Ministry for the North Caucasus. The ministry was specifically designed to deal with conditions on the ground that feed into the radicalization of the North Caucasus populations.

In addition to socio-economic measures, Medvedev turned his attention to the ideological underpinnings of the insurgency. For the first time since the beginning of the insurgency, the Kremlin started re-engaging moderate Wahhabis and attempted to address the ideological aspect of the threat. The idea of decriminalizing nonviolent Wahhabism was earlier expressed by Wahhabis themselves as an alternative to Moscow's hard-line approach. As Medvedev stated, the slogan of "we will simply exterminate terrorists and the more we exterminate—the better" described a past approach to terrorism. Now, as Medvedev pointed out, "it is necessary not only to exterminate those who spread terror but also to try to educate them, reintegrate them."[116] Subsequently, federal and local governments initiated some reintegration and rehabilitation measures.

Thus, some moderate Wahhabi organizations have been allowed to function openly. For instance, in Dagestan, Magomedali Magomedov started an open dialogue with moderate Wahhabis. The authorities allowed for the creation of an association of scholars, Akhlu-Sunnah, which has subsequently called for the resolution of existing disputes through dialogue.[117] Magomedov's successor Ramazan Abdulatipov continued this line of effort. "It is necessary to engage in dialogue with those who accept dialogue.

With those who chose only the criminal way we will fight with all forces and with the entire society," Abdulatipov declared.[118] Today the Dagestani legislature is debating a proposal to abolish the 1999 anti-Wahhabi law. Other North Caucasus republics are gradually trying to adopt similar initiatives. In Kabardino-Balkaria, Arsen Kanokov attempted dialogue with underground Wahhabis and in Ingushetia, Yunus-Bek Yevkurov legalized several Wahhabi mosques. A number of rehabilitation commissions were set up in the republics with the aim of reintegrating former fighters in the society.

Such initiatives are complicated by the fact that unlike in Chechnya local authorities in other North Caucasus republics do not have complete control over security services that continue to answer to Moscow. As a result, local governments do not have leverage against the hard-line measures continued by the federal center. This situation undermines the soft-line local peacebuilding initiatives. At the same time, however, the Russian government has achieved a number of significant accomplishments in the field of counterterrorism. On February 8, 2010, Russia designated the Caucasus Emirate as a terrorist organization and subsequently persuaded the United States and the United Nations to do the same. In May 2011 the group was added to U.S. Executive Order 13224, and in July of the same year it was placed on the UN list of groups associated with Al Qaeda. In March 2010 Anzor Astemirov—a prominent leader of the Kabardino-Balkaria wing—was killed. In June 2010 Russian forces captured the leader of Ingushetia jamaat, Emir Magas. The biggest achievement has been the elimination of the founder of the Caucasus Emirate, Doku Umarov. In March 2014 the Kavkaz Center website confirmed the news of Umarov's death, stating that he became a *shahid*.[119]

6

Conclusion

North Caucasus terrorism presents an illustrative case demonstrating how terrorist movements evolve in response to counterterrorist measures and how they adapt to changing environments. Terrorism emerged in Chechnya in the early 1990s as a response to Russia's military handling of the separatist conflict there. Russia clearly had an obligation to protect its territorial integrity; however, the methods Moscow chose failed to secure peace. Instead, Russia's reliance on a military solution has caused an insurgency fraught with terrorism that has engulfed the entire region of the North Caucasus. Throughout history Russia's decisions to send troops to the North Caucasus resulted in wars, rebellions, and armed resistance. The current struggle is not an exception.

The tactic of terrorism during the first war helped the separatists secure de facto independence for Chechnya. As Russia's resolve not to grant any concessions to the separatists strengthened during the second war, so did the resolve of the Chechens to keep using the tactic of terrorism. As the fighting continued the separatists became more radical, more daring, and more convinced that terrorism was their only weapon against Russia's military superiority. In a way, Russia's persistence in using the military against Chechen separatism has led to a radicalization of terrorism that has now spread from Chechnya to neighboring republics and beyond. As the insurgency spread the objective behind terrorist attacks shifted from striving for the independence of Chechnya to the independence and unification of Chechnya and Dagestan, and later to the unification of the entire region of the North Caucasus under a theocratic state of the Caucasus Emirate.

Terrorist attacks committed by Chechen separatists during the first war and the hostage raids of the second war were staged to demand the termination of the war in Chechnya, withdrawal of Russian troops, and peace negotiations. As terrorist attacks spread across the North Caucasus during the second conflict, they became focused against local pro-Russian governments and their corrupt practices. Along the way the North Caucasus terrorist command has adopted certain global jihadi rhetoric, and today some terrorist attacks are committed in the name of religious purification, including attacks against stores selling alcohol and attacks at funeral ceremonies that are perceived as un-Islamic.

Different grievances in the North Caucasus have manifested themselves in terrorism: ethno-nationalist separatism, the drive for religious purification, and discontent with local socio-economic and political conditions that are linked to poor governance. Until 2009 Russia's primary response to such diverse issues was military force and the co-optation of local elites. The Kremlin responded to ethno-nationalist separatism by using troops to protect the constitutional order in the Russian Federation. To address the movements brought about through religious revival in the North Caucasus and those that arose in response to economic and political decline, the Kremlin again chose to use military force to stop what the Russian government described as an international Islamist terrorist threat supported by Al Qaeda and Osama bin Laden.

Only in 2009 did Moscow adopt a new counterterrorist approach—outlined in the Concept on Countering Terrorism—one that focused on the different causes behind the discontent that had pushed people to join the terrorist ranks. Since then the Russian government has engaged in focused socio-economic programs designed specifically for the North Caucasus. Around 2010 local governments started to re-engage moderate Wahhabi groups and have, to an extent, reversed some of the restrictive religious measures adopted earlier. It was also around this time that the growth of the number of terrorist attacks related to the North Caucasus was reversed (see Figure 6.1). Since then the number of terrorist acts has steadily declined. This trend might be indicative of the importance of addressing background grievances that can create conditions conducive to terrorism.

EVOLUTION OF TERRORIST TRENDS IN THE NORTH CAUCASUS

North Caucasus terrorism demonstrates how terrorist tactics evolve and adapt to changing environments. In 1995 as Chechen separatists realized they had little chance to secure victory through conventional strategy, following Basayev's initiative, they adopted terrorist tactics. Because Chechen guerillas required training in unconventional warfare, separatists welcomed assistance from Afghan mujahedeen who were ready to help their Muslim

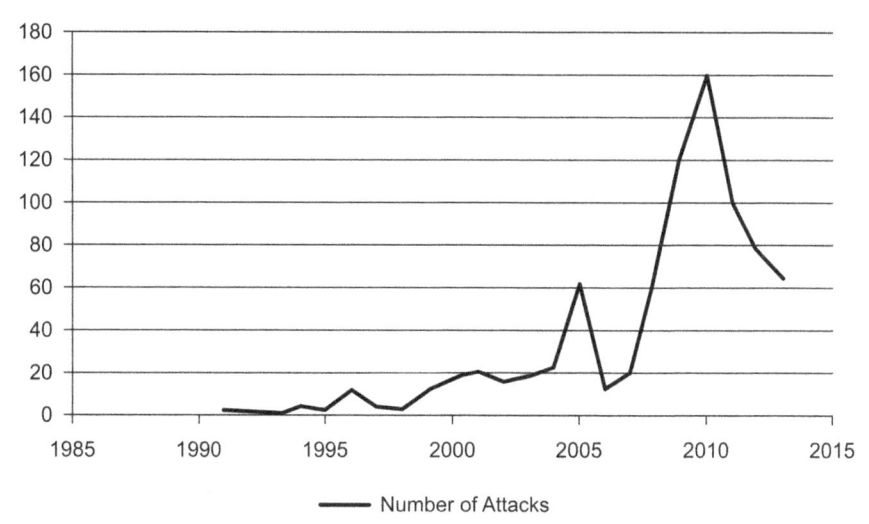

Figure 6.1 Total number of North Caucasus related terrorist attacks per year. Total number of attacks: 811 (All the charts in this chapter are compiled on the basis of the list of terrorist attacks given at the end of the book. A total of 811 terrorist attacks have been recorded by the author, and are analyzed here.)

brothers around the world after the end of the Soviet-Afghan war. Further, to preserve their foreign funding stream, the Chechen command adopted some global jihadi rhetoric but at the same time retained the local goals behind the movement. Thus, jihad in the North Caucasus has represented the struggle against Russian oppression similar to that of Imam Shamil in the nineteenth century, rather than jihad as a global war against the perceived enemies of Islam similar to that of Al Qaeda. In 2007 Doku Umarov announced that all enemies of Islam were his enemies, which brought his narratives further in line with global jihadi movements. At the same time, however, he was cautious in extending his fight beyond Russia's border. In fact, in response to the Boston Marathon bombing, the Caucasus Emirate made it clear that it was fighting solely against Russia.

In earlier years Chechen separatists experimented with international terrorism. A number of terrorist attacks involved hijacking planes and diverting them to Turkey. In 2001 a group of Chechens hijacked a plane scheduled to fly to Russia from Istanbul, Turkey. Several international terrorist attacks were committed in the name of the Chechen cause; Mohammed Tokcan acted as a terrorist advocate for the Chechen cause. Chechen separatists soon realized, however, that international terrorism did not work to their advantage, as the separatist leadership explained following Tokcan's Avrasya escapade. As a result, the Caucasus Emirate has evolved, avoiding staging terrorist attacks abroad or targeting international objects in Russia. The only terrorist attack with international connotations was the 2011 Domodedovo international airport bombing. Even as North

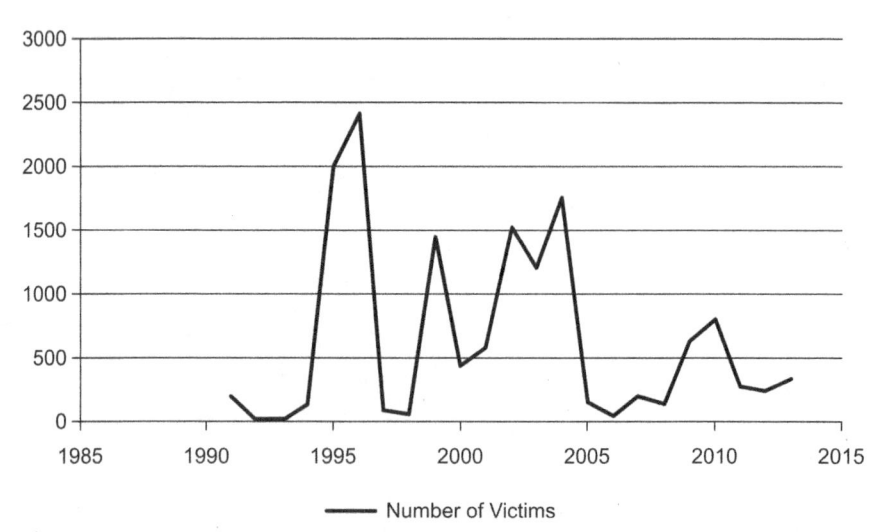

Figure 6.2 Total number of victims of North Caucasus related terrorism per year (Numbers reflect hostages, and those dead and injured during the attacks. Total number of attacks: 811.)

Caucasus links emerged in Syria, Umarov distanced his organization from individual North Caucasus mujahedeen there.

North Caucasus terrorist tactics have evolved through experimentation with many innovations. Among them have been the use of radiological terrorism and the introduction of suicide bombings. When terrorist attacks in the North Caucasus region did not produce their intended results, Chechen separatists took terrorism to Moscow in 1995. When mass terrorism started alienating supporters and sympathizers, as it did after the attack on Beslan, the terrorist command switched to smaller, but more frequent, attacks. As Figures 6.2 and 6.3 illustrate, after the attack on Beslan in 2004, the number and severity of North Caucasus terrorist attacks significantly decreased. Since then, while the number of terrorist attacks steadily grew until 2010, the number of people affected by such attacks has remained low compared to terrorist attacks prior to 2004. When Russia made it clear in 2004 that the government would not negotiate with terrorists even if schoolchildren were involved, terrorists gave up the tactic of hijackings and hostage-takings. In their place came attacks against Russia's infrastructure—railway bombings and oil and gas pipeline attacks—that significantly affect Russia's economy (see Figure 6.3). The Caucasus Emirate has increasingly relied on relatively cheap and easy to execute explosions.

As Russia's security services implemented more rigorous road checkpoint procedures, attacks further from the region became more difficult, and the terrorist command has instead relied more on attacks within the North Caucasus republics (see Figure 6.4). When Russian security services adopted ethnic profiling, disproportionately treating Caucasian-looking

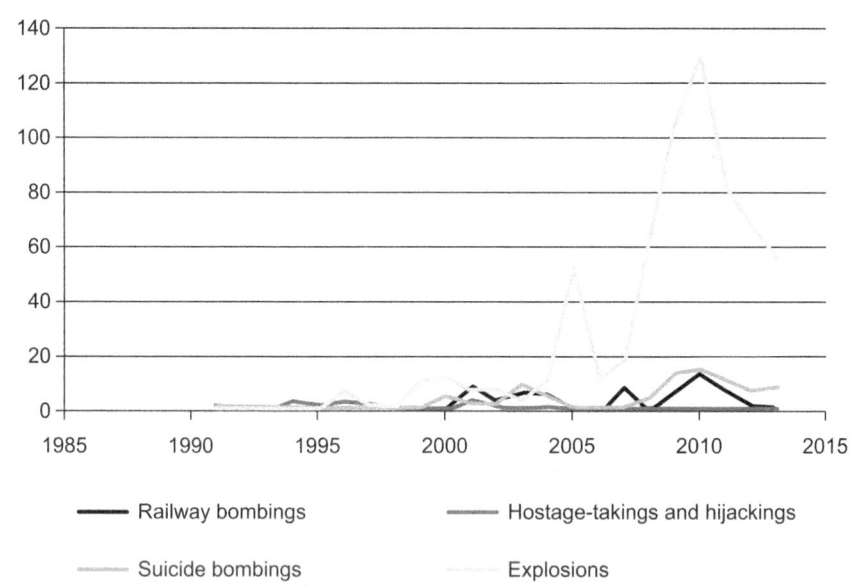

Figure 6.3 Terrorist attacks according to the type. (Total number of attacks: 809. The radiological terrorism attack and the assassination of Red Cross personnel are not included in this graph.)

people as potential terrorists, terrorists adapted by recruiting ethnic Slavs for terrorist purposes. Due to this, terrorist attacks continue to take place in Russia's capital. To compensate for the increased difficulty in personal recruitment of potential terrorists, the Caucasus Emirate has increasingly

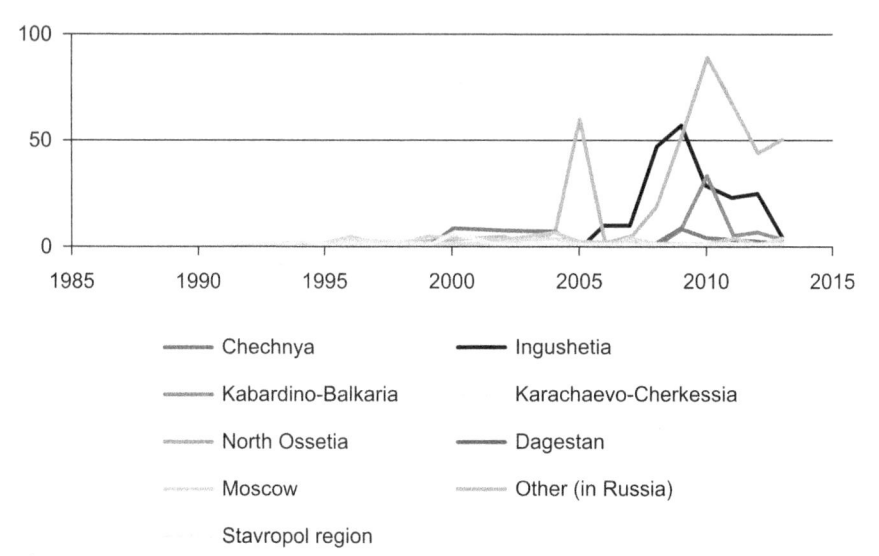

Figure 6.4 Terrorist attacks according to the region (Total number of attacks: 808. Three terrorist attacks that took place in Turkey are not shown in this graph.)

relied on online propaganda. Started by Said Buryatsky, the concerted effort in recruiting individuals through the Internet has led to the expansion of the online presence of the Caucasus Emirate. The Internet has allowed the Caucasus Emirate to expand its recruitment further to Tatarstan and Bashkortostan, and to reach radical Muslim audiences in other areas of Russia.

Poor socio-economic and political conditions in the North Caucasus and the presence of violence in Chechnya have assisted the terrorist command in recruiting more individuals to the terrorist cause. After Chechenization and Kadyrovization took root, terrorist attacks shifted from Chechnya to the neighboring republics. Since then Dagestan and Ingushetia have emerged as absolute leaders according to the number of terrorist attacks taking place there (see Figures 6.4 and 6.5). Poor socio-economic development, crime, rampant corruption, and religious persecution in these republics have contributed to the growth of discontent with local governments. Such grievances have been exploited by the Caucasus Emirate, which advertises the Islamic theocratic state as a just alternative to corrupt pro-Russian local regimes. Today Chechnya is no longer an insurgent leader. In 2014 Ali Abu Muhammad,

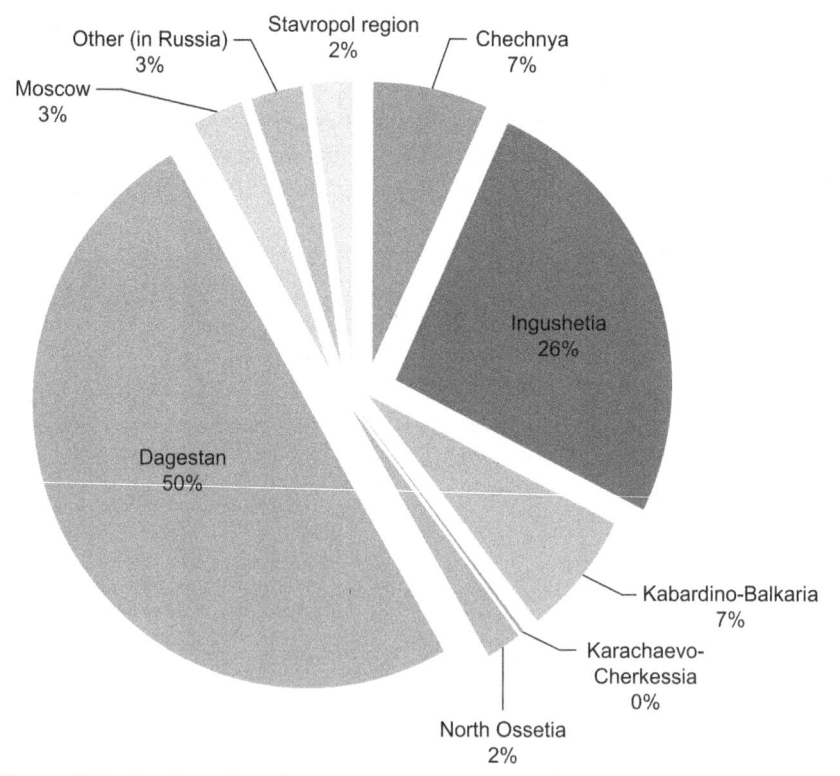

Figure 6.5 Total number of terrorist attacks per region (Total number of attacks: 808. Three terrorist attacks that took place in Turkey are not shown in this graph.)

a Dagestani, was appointed emir of the North Caucasus. He became the first non-Chechen to be appointed as the leader of the movement.

Through constant transformations the Caucasus Emirate has expanded its goals, its geography, and its appeal to different population groups. By sustaining the conditions that feed into local grievances, Moscow is failing to prevent the growth and expansion of the threat. If such conditions are not eliminated, Russia may face further radicalization of the Caucasus Emirate as North Caucasus mujahedeen start returning from Syria. Previous trends suggest that if Russia does not diversify its counterterrorist approaches and does not address the factors that push people toward terrorism in the first place, it is probably likely to face a constantly evolving, adapting, and expanding threat of terrorism.

EVOLUTION OF RUSSIA'S COUNTERTERRORISM

When post-Soviet Russia first confronted terrorism, it had neither the legal nor the political capability to counter it effectively. When North Caucasus–related terrorism first appeared as a corollary of the Chechen separatist conflict, Russia kept equating terrorism with separatism and addressed it through military means. By the start of the second Chechen conflict, Russia had developed certain counterterrorist capabilities, and the second war proceeded as a counterterrorist operation. Since then Russia has greatly expanded its arsenal of counterterrorist means; and yet such measures have failed to defeat terrorism.

During the first war Russia relied almost exclusively on military means to stem terrorism. Massive military attacks were the predominant tactic. During the second war Russia adjusted by scaling back on massive attacks, instead using more targeted operations. At the same time such tactics as *zachistki* or the use of filtration camps have proven to be counterproductive by further alienating large population groups. In this respect Russia's use of military force has not deviated from historical patterns. When General Yermolov initiated his policies of forced subjugation through military force, the Caucasus wars followed. As the Soviets turned the Red Army against the North Caucasus, the anti-Soviet revolts and uprisings of the 1930s and 1940s ensued. The contemporary wave of violence is no different from previous patterns. What is different, however, is the spillover of violence to non–North Caucasus regions and the increased circulation of mujahedeen to other conflict zones. With them, mujahedeen have brought new funding, new people, and new ideas—all of which make the contemporary conflict harder to resolve.

To complement its military approach the Kremlin has implemented the policy of co-optation of local elites. Starting as Chechenization, the policy has brought Moscow-supported government structures back to Grozny.

Further, with the help of Akhmad Kadyrov and his son, the Kremlin has been able to re-establish control over Chechnya. Through using their own security services—*kadyrovtsy*—the Kadyrovs have been able to seemingly pacify Chechnya. Ramzan Kadyrov has declared an end to the war numerous times. However, such pacification seems to be incomplete. The number of terrorist attacks in Chechnya has actually been on the rise since Ramzan Kadyrov became formal head of the Chechen Republic in 2007. The actions of kadyrovtsy differ little from those of the federal forces but are now controlled at the local level. Zachistki, counter–hostage-takings, and other actions that violate many rights of the local population keep feeding into grievances. While on the surface Kadyrovization has brought stability to Chechnya, if historical tendencies continue, this will be only a temporary respite before further unrest; Russia's previous policies of *korenizatsiia*, co-optation of local leaders, and forced integration resulted in long waves of resistance.

Since the first Chechen terrorist attack, Russia's counterterrorism has gone through remarkable changes. During the first Chechen war the Russian government had no counterterrorist legislation to regulate its counterterrorist activities. In 1998 Moscow adopted its first counterterrorist law and later replaced it with an updated piece of legislation in 2006. Throughout the years the Kremlin has restructured and reformed many institutions involved in counterterrorist efforts, including the FSB and the MVD. Over the years training of counterterrorist units has resulted in improved operations; groups Alpha and Vympel have improved their counterterrorist techniques.

Coordination and communication among the counterterrorist agencies has also improved with the creation of the National Counterterrorist Center. Military counterterrorist operations have become more professional and streamlined in their implementation. The overall counterterrorist reform that followed the 2004 Beslan attack has shifted counterterrorist operations from reliance on massive military force to more targeted and focused operations. Improvements in the conduct of counterterrorist operations have allowed the security services to achieve significant successes without causing the same number of civilian deaths as in the past; Shamil Basayev, Said Buryatsky, Anzor Astemirov, and Doku Umarov—individuals who engaged in terrorist activities against Russia—have been eliminated through special operations.

At the same time Putin's post-Beslan counterterrorist reform still adhered to the hard-line approach and was disproportionately focused on tackling the manifestations of terrorism while leaving out its causes. Until 2009 the Russian government avoided engaging with opposition groups in the North Caucasus. In fact, local governments further alienated many by shutting down community organizations and grassroots initiatives. Instead of eradicating the movement, persecution of the Wahhabi faith, including its nonviolent strands, led to its radicalization. In Dagestan, Wahhabism was banned completely, and in Chechnya, Kadyrov has introduced a state-supported version of Islam meant to replace Wahhabism. However, if one examines lessons from the history of the region, one can see the dangers of religious repression and attempts to impose a Russian version of Islam. The Russian Empire tried regulating Islam in the North Caucasus, and the Soviet Union attempted to support a Soviet version of Islam. Such efforts, however, brought about calls for religious purification that later became merged with calls for liberation from Russia.

Russia's reluctance to engage with separatist and insurgent leaders resulted in the growth and expansion of the terrorist threat. Refusing to negotiate, Russia tried to avoid the outcome brought about by negotiations with terrorists during the 1995 Budennovsk attack, not to appear soft on terrorism. At the same time it was the post-Budennovsk negotiations and rounds of negotiations that followed that allowed the sides to secure a peace agreement in August 1996. The Khasavyurt Accords did not address the status of Chechnya and, as a result, were later discarded due to their role in justifying Chechnya's de facto independence. In terms of terrorism, however, the accords seemed to be an effective tool against the threat; the interwar years of 1997 and 1998 had the lowest rate of terrorist attacks throughout the region's entire history of violence since 1994.

Since then the two drops in the numbers of terrorist attacks occurred in 2005 and 2010. The first one could arguably be attributed to the success of the post-Beslan counterterrorist reform. However, this could be an oversimplification because after Beslan the terrorist command concurrently initiated a strategic shift. Accounting for the loss of sympathy for targeting schoolchildren, Shamil Basayev switched to other insurgent activities such as military raids and avoided large-scale terrorist attacks. Because the issues contributing to terrorism remained unresolved, terrorist attacks quickly picked up pace, reaching a peak by 2010.

Since 2010 the number of terrorist attacks has been steadily declining again. This time the trend might be linked to the radical shift in Russia's counterterrorist approach. For the first time since the start of the Chechen wars, in the 2009 Concept on Countering Terrorism, President Medvedev acknowledged the need to address socio-economic and political causes that fed into the growth of terrorism. Subsequently, the Russian government introduced new economic programs, anticorruption initiatives, and political changes in the republics of the North Caucasus meant to improve local conditions and thus reduce the number of potential terrorist recruits though the elimination of grievances. Moreover, the Russian government has introduced initiatives related to engaging local moderate Wahhabis with the hope of using them to undermine extremist violent ideologies of jihadi Wahhabis.

Specifically in the North Caucasus context, the resolution of socio-economic and political grievances seems to be especially promising, as the

Caucasus Emirate effectively capitalizes on local problems for recruitment purposes. With Putin's return to the Kremlin, some of the liberalization initiatives have been reversed. For instance, in 2013 Putin replaced Magomedali Magomedov of Dagestan with Ramazan Abdulatipov. The latter has reversed some of Magomedov's reintegration initiatives, bringing back reliance on repressive measures. In the past government repression contributed to the radicalization of the insurgency in the North Caucasus and led to the increase in terrorist attacks. Pushing the insurgency further underground might produce more terrorism along with its more radicalized manifestations.

LESSONS FROM RUSSIA

The Chechen terrorist threat that has transitioned into the North Caucasus terrorist threat has remained inherently local. It has expanded geographically to Russia's Tatarstan and Bashkortostan but has been largely contained within Russia and has mainly attacked Russian targets. While the Caucasus Emirate has not yet staged attacks outside Russia or attacked other enemies of Islam as Doku Umarov had promised in 2007, North Caucasus terrorist innovations have certainly affected other terrorist groups. Moreover, the increased movement of North Caucasus mujahedeen has contributed to the exchange of tactics and ideas. Today, as the North Caucasus mujahedeen are fighting in Syria and Iraq, Russia is facing an increased threat of them returning and further changing the nature of the Caucasus Emirate.

Russia's experiences with the terrorist threat offer some valuable lessons to the global counterterrorism community. First, Russia's overreliance on the hard-line approach to terrorism has demonstrated that harsh counterterrorist measures risk further alienating the populations that might subsequently radicalize and join the ranks of terrorists. In Russia they have not only alienated groups of Chechens but also the populations of the neighboring republics that chose to follow the example set by the Chechens.

Further, Russia's overreliance on military means has left other counterterrorist spheres underdeveloped. It was only in 2009 that Russia made a strategic decision to resolve the background conditions feeding into terrorism. Such overreliance on any one counterterrorist approach leaves much room for the terrorist command to adjust and adapt—as the North Caucasus terrorists have done. The predictability of a preferred response makes it easier for terrorists to calculate their next move and keep surprising opponents. On the other hand, diversifying responses and countering the terrorist threat from different angles might reduce the space for terrorist innovations, thus depriving the terrorist command of the ability to effectively adapt.

The Russian example once again illustrates the necessity of not only combating the terrorist threat militarily but also appealing to the hearts and minds of the population. Similar to what the coalition forces have learned in Afghanistan, the hearts and minds approach is crucial in breaking the chain of support for terrorist causes. While not all research on terrorism supports the idea that socio-economic grievances are directly correlated with the terrorist threat, the case of Russia demonstrates that socio-economic factors are key for locally based terrorist groups. Because the Caucasus Emirate focuses on the establishment of a local North Caucasus state, it is local conditions the group exploits to replenish its ranks.

The North Caucasus case further demonstrates the significant predictive power of historical experiences with certain contained geographies. Similar to what the coalition forces confronted in Afghanistan—the continuities in resistance patterns to British, Soviet, and American interventions—Russia seems to be disregarding the lessons provided by history. Previously the Russian Empire and then the Soviet Union faced fierce resistance when they tried to forcefully integrate the North Caucasus through the use of military force, coerced assimilation, and scorched earth policies. Taking into consideration the significance of the deep-rooted chosen traumas inflicted by Russian rule, it is hard to foresee a quick change in local responses to the same approaches that caused such traumas throughout history.

Finally, the North Caucasus illustrates the dangers of treating such diverse challenges to the state as separatism and terrorism under a single umbrella of a war on terror. Treating such threats interchangeably does not resolve the underlying issues. As the Russian case demonstrates, substituting terrorism for separatism can further push the separatists into the illegitimate realm. During the first Chechen war domestic and international audiences, as well as the Russian government itself, saw terrorism as an outcome of Russia's handling of the separatist conflict. In the second war such distinctions became blurred, and Russia has addressed the insurgency as a terrorist threat. While intrinsically interconnected, terrorism being a tactic used by the North Caucasus insurgents, not all insurgents supported terrorist tactics during the early years of the Chechen campaign. However, Russia failed to engage such elements of the insurgency and has instead pronounced them terrorists as well. Deprived of any legal means of addressing their grievances, insurgents radicalized further, and terrorism today is no longer a by-product of Chechen separatism but has transitioned into a much bigger threat with much broader goals.

As the danger posed to the world by Al Qaeda and the like has not subsided in recent years, the global counterterrorism community should take into consideration Russia's experiences with terrorism, especially in a context in which religion has played an important role. Mistakes in counterterrorism can be costly, as terrorist movements are capable of fast adaptations—today this is the case with the Islamic State of Iraq and Syria, which has already evolved into the group known as the Islamic State. Russia, in turn, should learn from global counterterrorist practices as it faces the danger of the return of mujahedeen who are currently getting combat experiences in Syria.

Appendix A

Chechen Leaders (Dates in Power)

Leaders of Russian Administrations in Chechnya	
Doku Zavgayev	June 1989–September 1991
Doku Zavgayev	December 1995–November 1996
Akhmad Kadyrov	June 2000–May 2004
Alu Alkhanov	September 2004–February 2007
Ramzan Kadyrov	March 2007–present
Leaders of Ichkeriia	
Dzhokhar Dudayev	October 1991–April 1996
Zelimkhan Yandarbiyev	April 1995–February 1997
Aslan Maskhadov	February 1997–March 2005
Abdul-Halim Sadulayev	March 2005–June 2006
Doku Umarov	June 2006–October 2007
Emirs of the Caucasus Emirate	
Doku Umarov	October 2007–March 2014
Ali Abu Muhammad	March 2014–present

(*continued*)

Leaders of Foreign Mujahedeen in Chechnya

Khattab (Samir Saleh al-Suwailem)	January 1995–March 2002
Abu al-Walid	March 2002–April 2004
Abu Hafs al-Urduni	April 2004–November 2006
Muhannad	December 2006–April 2011
Abdulla Kurd	April 2011–May 2011

Since May 2011 the leadership has been uncertain.

Appendix B

Terrorist Attacks Associated with the North Caucasus

This list was compiled by the author based on open sources, such as news reports, government records, and other published resources. The list includes only terrorist attacks that took place and does not include attempted attacks. The list does not include activities that are not necessarily terrorist attacks but rather insurgent military raids, ambushes, assassinations, or direct assaults. For some attacks the number of victims was not published in open sources; in such cases no data is given for victims.

Date	Attack Type	Location	Victims
1991			
November 9	Hijacking, plane	Mineralnye Vody	178 hostages
1994			
May 26	Hijacking, bus	Mineralnye Vody area	30 hostages
June 28	Hijacking, bus	Mineralnye Vody area	40 hostages
July 28	Hijacking, bus	Mineralnye Vody	40 hostages, 4 dead

(continued)

Date	Attack Type	Location	Victims
1995			
June 14–19	Hostage-taking	Budennovsk	2,000 hostages; over 100 dead; over 400 injured
November 21	Radiological terrorism	Moscow, Izmailovsky Park	None
1996			
January 9–18	Hostage-taking	Kizlyar/Pervomaiskoe	2,000 hostages; over 100 dead
January 16	Hijacking, ferryboat	Trabzon, Turkey	Over 200 hostages
June 11	Explosion	Moscow, metro Tulskaia–Nagatinskaia	4 dead, 12 injured
June 28	Explosion	Nalchik bus	8 dead, 46 injured
July 11	Explosion	Moscow trolleybus, Strastnoi Boulevard	5 injured
July 12	Explosion	Moscow trolleybus, Prospekt Mira	30 injured
July 25	Explosion	Volgograd	None
August 12	Explosion	Volgograd, railway station	1 dead, 8 injured
September 16	Hijacking, bus	Makhachkala	27 hostages
November 16	Apartment bombing	Kaspiisk	69 dead
December 17	Assassination of Red Cross personnel	Novye Atagi, Chechnya	6 dead
1997			
April 14	Hijacking, bus	Makhachkala	30 hostages
April 23	Explosion	Armavir, railway station	2 dead, 20 injured
April 28	Explosion	Piatigorsk, railway station	2 dead, 30 injured
1998			
January 1	Explosion	Moscow, metro station Tretiakovskaia	3 injured

(*continued*)

Date	Attack Type	Location	Victims
June 8	Hijacking, bus	Beslan	40 hostages
1999			
March 19	Explosion	Vladikavkaz, market	64 dead, 200 injured
April 26	Explosion	Moscow, Hotel Inturist	11 injured
May 16	Explosions, 3	Sputnik, Vladikavkaz region	4 dead, 9 injured
August 31	Explosion	Moscow, Okhotnyi Riad mall	1 dead, 41 injured
September 4	Apartment bombing	Buinaksk	62 dead, 146 injured
September 4	Explosion	Makhachkala	20 dead, 60 injured
September 8	Apartment bombing	Moscow, Gur'ianov Street	106 dead, 264 injured
September 13	Apartment bombing	Moscow, Kashirskoe Shosse	124 dead, 9 injured
September 16	Apartment bombing	Volgodonsk	19 dead, 310 injured
2000			
May 31	Explosion	Volgograd	2 dead, 15 injured
June 6	Suicide bombing	Alkhan-Yurt, Chechnya	2 dead, 5 injured
July 2	Suicide bombings, 4	Argun, Gudermes, Novogroznensk, Urus-Martan	33 dead, 84 injured
July 5	Explosion	Volgograd	None
July 9	Explosion	Vladikavkaz, market	6 dead, 15 injured
August 8	Explosion	Moscow, Pushkin square underground passage	13 dead, 122 injured
August 18	Explosion	Chechnya	1 injured
October 6	Explosions, 3	Piatigorsk and Nevinnomyssk	4 dead, 40 injured
October 10	Explosion	Piatigorsk, railway station	2 dead, 10 injured

(continued)

Date	Attack Type	Location	Victims
December 8	Explosions, 2	Piatigorsk	2 dead, 26 injured
December 9	Explosion	Alkhan-Yurt, Chechnya	21 dead, 20 injured
2001			
January 15	Explosion	North Ossetia, cargo train	None
January 29	Railway bombing	Gudermes region	None
February 5	Explosion	Moscow, metro station Belorusskaya	20 injured
March 11	Railway bombing	Gudermes-Khasavyurt, cargo train	
March 15	Hijacking, plane	Istanbul, Turkey	173 hostages, 2 dead
March 19	Railway bombing	Chervlenaia station, Chechnya	
March 24	Explosions, 3	Adyge-Khabl' (Karachaevo-Cherkessia), Mineralnye Vody, Yessentuki	23 dead, 142 injured
April 9	Suicide bombing	Grozny	1 dead, 2 injured
April 10	Railway bombing	Gudermes region	None
April 23	Hostage-taking	Istanbul, Turkey, Hotel Sofitel	60 hostages
May 13	Railway bombing	Naurskaia station, Chechnya	3 injured
July 31	Hijacking, bus	Nevinnomyssk	41 hostages
August 19	Explosion	Astrakhan	3 dead, 40 injured
September 4	Railway bombing	Makhachkala region	None
September 10	Railway bombing	Argun-Khankala region, Chechnya	None
November 2	Railway bombing	Naurskii region, Chechnya, cargo train	None

(*continued*)

Date	Attack Type	Location	Victims
November 10	Explosion	Vladikavkaz, market	5 dead, 60 injured
November 29	Suicide bombing	Urus-Martan	2 dead
2002			
January 13	Explosion	Makhachkala	None
January 18	Explosion	Makhachkala	8 dead, 10 injured
January 23	Explosion	Makhachkala	1 injured
January 25	Railway bombing	Gudermes region	
February 5	Suicide bombing	Grozny	None
March 2	Railway bombing	Gudermes region	2 injured
March 21	Explosion	Makhachkala	None
April 28	Explosion	Vladikavkaz, market	7 dead, 37 injured
May 9	Explosion	Kaspiisk	43 dead, 100 injured
August 24	Railway bombing	Chechnya	None
October 10	Explosion	Grozny	25 dead
October 19	Explosion	Moscow, McDonald's restaurant	1 dead, 8 injured
October 23–26	Hostage-taking	Moscow, Dubrovka theater	Over 1,000 hostages; 130 dead
October 28	Railway bombing	Naurskii region, Chechnya	None
December 27	Suicide bombing	Grozny	72 dead, 210 injured
2003			
January 1	Railway bombing	Kizlyar region	None
May 12	Suicide bombing	Znamenskoe, Chechnya	60 dead, 250 injured
May 14	Suicide bombing	Iliskhan-Yurt, Chechnya	20 dead, 140 injured

(*continued*)

Date	Attack Type	Location	Victims
May 29	Railway bombing	Naurskii region, Chechnya	None
June 5	Suicide bombing	Mozdok	20 dead, 15 injured
June 20	Suicide bombing	Grozny	36 injured
July 5	Suicide bombing	Moscow, Tushino, concert Kryl'ia	16 dead, 48 injured
August 1	Suicide bombing	Mozdok	52 dead, 78 injured
August 18	Railway bombing	Gudermes region	None
August 25	Explosions, 3	Krasnodar, public transportation	3 dead, 30 injured
September 3	Railway bombing	Kislovodsk-Mineralnye Vody train	4 dead, 80 injured
September 15	Suicide bombing	Magas	4 dead, 29 injured
October 21	Railway bombing	Ingushetia–North Ossetia border, train Nazran-Moscow	2 injured
December 5	Suicide bombing	Yessentuki train	47 dead, 233 injured
December 9	Suicide bombing	Moscow, Hotel National	8 dead, 14 injured
December 18	Railway bombing	Chechnya	
2004			
February 6	Suicide bombing	Moscow, metro station Avtozavodskaya	41 dead, 250 injured
February 18	Explosion	Moscow region, Ramenskoe oil pipeline	
February 19	Explosion	Voronezh, public transportation	None
March 11	Explosion	Makhachkala	2 dead, 4 injured

(continued)

Date	Attack Type	Location	Victims
March 26	Railway bombing	Naurskii region, Chechnya, cargo train	None
April 4	Explosion	Dagestan, oil pipeline	
April 6	Suicide bombing	Ingushetia	6 injured
April 8	Railway bombing	Chechnya, cargo train	None
May 9	Explosion	Grozny	7 dead, including Chechen president Akhmad Kadyrov, 60 injured
May 29	Railway bombing	Vladikavkaz region, Moscow-Vladikavkaz train	1 injured
June 4	Explosion	Samara, market	11 dead, 63 injured
June 12	Railway bombing	Gudermes region, cargo train	None
July 19	Explosion	Voronezh, public transportation	1 dead, 7 injured
July 22	Explosions, 2	Dagestan	1 dead, 7 injured
July 26	Explosion	Voronezh, public transportation	11 injured
August 24	Explosion	Moscow, Kashirskoe Shosse	4 injured
August 24	Suicide bombings	Moscow, airplanes TU-154 and TU-134	89 dead
August 31	Suicide bombing	Moscow, metro station Rizhskaia	11 dead, 50 injured
September 1–3	Hostage-taking	Beslan school	1,128 hostages; 331 dead, among them 186 children
September 17	Railway bombing	Naurskii region, Chechnya, Gudermes-Mineralnye Vody cargo train	None
November 16	Railway bombing	Chechnya, Mineralnye Vody-Terek train	None

(continued)

Appendix B

Date	Attack Type	Location	Victims
2005			
January 26	Explosion	Voronezh, public transportation	None
February 11	Explosion	Makhachkala	None
February 13	Explosions, 2	Makhachkala	4 injured
March 3	Explosion	Makhachkala	3 injured
March 22	Explosion	Makhachkala	None
March 25	Explosion	Dagestan	2 injured
March 28	Explosion	Makhachkala	None
March 29	Explosion	Khasavyurt region	
April 2	Explosion	Makhachkala	None
April 4	Explosion	Makhachkala	None
April 7	Explosion	Buinaksk	None
April 8	Explosion	Dagestan	None
April 13	Explosions, 3	Makhachkala	
April 15	Explosions, 2	Makhachkala	6 injured
April 19	Explosion	Makhachkala	1 dead, 1 injured
April 22	Explosion	Makhachkala	1 dead
May 5	Explosion	Makhachkala	
May 10	Explosion	Makhachkala	1 dead, 3 injured
May 13	Explosion	Makhachkala	1 injured
May 14	Explosion	Kizlyar	None
May 19	Explosion	Buinaksk	None
May 20	Explosion	Makhachkala	2 dead, 2 injured
May 24	Explosion	Khasavyurt region	None
May 29	Explosion	Makhachkala	None
May 31	Explosion	Makhachkala	9 injured
June 3	Explosion	Makhachkala	1 injured
June 6	Explosion	Khasavyurt	
June 12	Railway bombing	Moscow region, Grozny-Moscow train	9 injured
June 24	Railway bombing	Dagestan	1 dead
June 25	Explosions, 4	Dagestan	8 injured
June 28	Explosion	Makhachkala	3 injured

(*continued*)

Date	Attack Type	Location	Victims
July 1	Explosion	Makhachkala	10 dead, 27 injured
July 5	Explosion	Makhachkala	2 dead, 2 injured
July 7	Railway bombing	Dagestan	
July 14	Explosion	Makhachkala	None
July 17	Explosion	Makhachkala	
July 24	Railway bombing	Dagestan	1 dead, 6 injured
July 26	Explosion	Khasavyurt	6 injured
July 28	Explosion	Makhachkala	2 injured
August 1	Explosion	Khasavyurt	None
August 3	Explosion	Dagestan	2 injured
August 4	Railway bombing	Dagestan	None
August 11	Explosions, 2	Buinaksk and Makhachkala	None
August 18	Explosion	Makhachkala	4 injured
August 20	Explosion	Makhachkala	3 dead, 1 injured
August 27	Railway bombing	Dagestan	None
August 30	Explosion	Makhachkala	None
September 2	Explosion	Makhachkala	4 dead, 10 injured
September 7	Explosion	Khasavyurt	1 dead
September 23	Explosion	Dagestan, oil pipeline	None
December 5	Explosion	Buinaksk	None
December 8	Railway bombing	Makhachkala	None
December 28	Explosion	Makhachkala	None
December 29	Suicide bombing	Makhachkala	1 injured
2006			
June 25	Explosion	Makhachkala	2 injured
August 10	Explosion	Nazran	1 dead, 13 injured
August 17	Explosion	Ingushetia	None
August 20	Explosion	Ingushetia	1 dead

(continued)

Date	Attack Type	Location	Victims
August 26	Explosion	Ingushetia	2 injured
September 5	Explosion	Ingushetia	None
September 6	Explosion	Ingushetia	4 dead, 4 injured
September 7	Explosion	Ingushetia	2 injured
September 13	Explosion	Ingushetia	1 injured
October 31	Explosion	Ingushetia	1 injured
November 6	Explosion	Ingushetia	3 injured
2007			
February 18	Explosion	St. Petersburg McDonald's café	6 injured
March 31	Explosion	Nazran	3 injured
April 28	Explosion	Dagestan, oil pipeline	
May 1	Explosion	Ingushetia	2 injured
May 14	Explosion	Makhachkala	1 injured
June 3	Explosion	Nazran	None
June 30	Explosion	Ingushetia	1 dead
July 18	Explosion	Ingushetia	10 injured
July 26	Explosion	Makhachkala	2 dead, 1 injured
August 13	Railway bombing	Nevsky Express train	60 injured
August 25	Explosion	Ingushetia	1 injured
August 30	Explosion	Ingushetia	None
August 31	Explosion	Nazran	4 dead
October 6	Explosion	Makhachkala	None
October 14	Explosion	Ingushetia	
October 23	Suicide bombing	Khasavyurt area	8 injured
October 31	Explosion	Tolyatti bus	8 dead, 56 injured
November 22	Explosion	Piatigorsk-Vladikavkaz bus	5 dead, 13 injured
December 5	Explosion	Ingushetia	1 injured
December 9	Explosion	Nevinnomyssk bus	2 dead, 9 injured
2008			
February 27	Explosion	Ingushetia	1 injured

(*continued*)

Date	Attack Type	Location	Victims
March 3	Explosion	Ingushetia	
March 21	Explosion	Ingushetia	None
March 24	Explosion	Nazran	4 injured
April 1	Explosion	Khasavyurt	None
April 2	Explosion	Makhachkala	1 dead
April 24	Explosion	Ingushetia	2 injured
April 27	Explosion	Khasavyurt area	1 injured
May 7	Explosion	Nazran	None
May 17	Explosion	Ingushetia	None
May 21	Explosion	Ingushetia	None
May 23	Explosion	Ingushetia	2 injured
May 25	Explosion	Makhachkala	1 injured
June 5	Explosion	Ingushetia	None
June 9	Explosion	Nazran	None
June 13	Explosion	Makhachkala	1 dead
June 21	Explosion	Dagestan	None
July 1	Explosion	Khasavyurt	None
July 5	Explosion	Khasavyurt	3 injured
July 26	Explosion	Khasavyurt	1 dead
August 11	Suicide bombing	Shali, Chechnya	
August 19	Explosion	Nazran	None
August 21	Explosion	Nazran	None
August 28	Explosion	Ingushetia	None
September 12	Explosion	Ingushetia	1 injured
September 15	Explosion	Ingushetia	2 injured
September 19	Explosion	Ingushetia	3 injured
September 22	Explosion	Ingushetia	None
September 24	Explosion	Ingushetia	None
September 27	Explosion	Makhachkala	1 dead
September 30	Suicide bombing	Nazran	4 injured
October 4	Explosions, 3	Ingushetia	None
October 10	Explosions, 3	Ingushetia	3 injured
October 16	Explosions, 3	Ingushetia	

(*continued*)

Date	Attack Type	Location	Victims
October 18	Suicide bombing	Ingushetia	
October 20	Explosion	Ingushetia	
October 22	Explosion	Makhachkala	2 injured
October 23	Explosion	Khasavyurt	4 injured
October 26	Explosions, 3	Ingushetia	4 injured
October 27	Explosion	Ingushetia	1 injured
October 28	Explosion	Ingushetia	1 dead
November 2	Explosion	Ingushetia	7 injured
November 3	Explosion	Makhachkala	4 injured
November 5	Explosion	Ingushetia	1 dead
November 6	Suicide bombing	Vladikavkaz	12 dead, 41 injured
November 13	Explosions, 2	Ingushetia	1 injured
November 14	Explosion	Nazran	None
November 18	Explosion	Makhachkala	3 injured
November 28	Explosion	Makhachkala	2 injured
November 28	Explosion	Ingushetia	None
December 4	Explosion	Khasavyurt	1 dead
December 9	Explosion	Ingushetia	
December 11	Explosion	Ingushetia	None
December 12	Explosions, 2	Ingushetia	1 injured
December 14	Explosion	Ingushetia	None
December 17	Explosions, 2	Khasavyurt	10 injured
2009			
January 2	Explosions, 2	Ingushetia	1 injured
January 4	Explosion	Khasavyurt	2 injured
January 5	Explosion	Ingushetia	None
January 6	Explosion	Makhachkala	1 dead
January 7	Explosion	Ingushetia	None
January 10	Explosion	Ingushetia	1 injured
January 13	Explosion	Makhachkala	1 injured
January 14	Explosion	Khasavyurt	1 injured
January 18	Explosion	Ingushetia	1 injured
January 22	Explosion	Ingushetia	None

(continued)

Appendix B 199

Date	Attack Type	Location	Victims
January 26	Explosion	Ingushetia	None
February 5	Explosion	Dagestan	None
February 8	Explosion	Makhachkala	1 injured
February 10	Explosion	Nalchik	1 injured
February 11	Explosion	Ingushetia	1 injured
February 18	Explosion	Ingushetia	3 injured
February 26	Explosion	Makhachkala	4 injured
February 28	Explosion	Makhachkala	None
March 3	Explosion	Ingushetia	None
March 9	Explosions, 2	Makhachkala	None
March 11	Explosion	Ingushetia	None
March 15	Explosion	Ingushetia	1 injured
March 17	Explosion	Ingushetia	None
March 23	Explosion	Makhachkala	None
March 25	Explosion	Ingushetia	1 injured
March 26	Explosion	Ingushetia	1 injured
April 5	Explosion	Nalchik	1 injured
April 5	Explosion	Khasavyurt	3 injured
April 15	Explosion	Ingushetia	None
April 17	Explosion	Nazran	None
May 1	Explosion	Khasavyurt	None
May 7	Explosion	Ingushetia	1 injured
May 11	Explosion	Nazran	3 injured
May 15	Suicide bombing	Grozny	2 dead, 5 injured
May 16	Explosion	Khasavyurt	2 injured
May 30	Explosion	Khasavyurt	None
May 31	Explosion	Makhachkala	None
May 31	Explosion	Ingushetia	3 dead
June 3	Explosion	Nazran	1 dead
June 6	Explosion	Makhachkala	1 dead
June 10	Explosion	Khasavyurt	1 injured
June 11	Explosion	Kabardino-Balkaria	
June 19	Explosion	Nazran	1 injured

(continued)

Date	Attack Type	Location	Victims
June 22	Suicide bombing	Magas area	2 dead, 2 injured
June 28	Explosion	Khasavyurt	3 injured
July 2	Railway bombing	Dagestan	1 dead
July 3	Explosion	Khasavyurt	3 injured
July 5	Explosion	Ingushetia	2 injured
July 12	Explosion	Kabardino-Balkaria	None
July 15	Explosion	Khasavyurt	None
July 21	Explosion	Dagestan	
July 22	Explosion	Ingushetia	None
July 23	Explosion	Makhachkala	
July 23	Explosions, 2	Ingushetia	None
July 25	Explosion	Ingushetia	2 injured
July 26	Suicide bombing	Grozny	5 dead
July 27	Explosion	Ingushetia	None
July 28	Explosion	Nazran	None
July 31	Explosion	Kabardino-Balkaria	None
July 31	Explosion	Khasavyurt	1 dead
August 1	Explosion	Dagestan	None
August 5	Explosion	Dagestan	4 injured
August 10	Explosions, 2	Derbent	2 dead, 1 injured
August 17	Suicide bombing	Nazran	25 dead, 262 injured
August 17	Explosion	Makhachkala	1 dead, 3 injured
August 18	Explosion	Dagestan	4 injured
August 20	Explosion	Tyrnyauz, Kabardino-Balkaria	1 dead, 1 injured
August 21	Suicide bombing	Grozny	3 dead, 2 injured
August 22	Explosion	Dagestan	2 dead
August 23	Explosion	Kabardino-Balkaria	None

(continued)

Date	Attack Type	Location	Victims
August 25	Suicide bombing	Mesker-Yurt, Chechnya	6 dead, 1 injured
August 25	Explosion	Nazran	None
August 26	Explosion	Ingushetia	2 injured
August 28	Suicide bombing	Shali, Chechnya	3 injured
September 1	Suicide bombing	Makhachkala	1 dead, 11 injured
September 1	Explosion	Ingushetia, electricity lines	
September 4	Explosion	Ingushetia	3 dead, 3 injured
September 5	Explosion	Ingushetia	1 injured
September 11	Suicide bombing	Nazran	8 injured
September 12	Suicide bombing	Grozny	3 injured
September 13	Explosion	Makhachkala	
September 14	Railway bombing	Dagestan	None
September 16	Suicide bombing	Grozny	8 injured
September 17	Explosion	Ingushetia	2 injured
September 18	Railway bombing	Ingushetia	
September 24	Explosion	Ingushetia	1 injured
September 25	Explosion	Ingushetia	None
October 1	Explosion	Makhachkala	1 dead
October 3	Explosion	Ingushetia	1 injured
October 4	Explosion	Ingushetia	1 injured
October 9	Explosion	Derbent	1 dead
October 9	Explosion	Nazran	1 dead
October 13	Explosion	Dagestan	1 injured
October 16	Explosion	Ingushetia	None
October 18	Explosion	Ingushetia	None
October 21	Suicide bombing	Grozny	5 injured

(continued)

Date	Attack Type	Location	Victims
October 22	Explosion	Ingushetia	1 dead, 2 injured
October 24	Explosion	Makhachkala	1 injured
October 25	Railway bombing	Dagestan	None
October 26	Explosions, 2	Dagestan	1 injured
October 29	Explosion	Ingushetia	2 injured
October 30	Explosion	Ingushetia	None
November 7	Explosion	Makhachkala	1 injured
November 12	Explosion	Ingushetia	1 injured
November 13	Explosion	Dagestan	
November 13	Explosion	Nazran	None
November 17	Explosion	Elbrusskii region, Kabardino-Balkaria	None
November 22	Explosion	Dagestan	1 injured
November 24	Explosion	Nazran	None
November 26	Railway bombing	Dagestan	None
November 27	Railway bombing	Nevsky Express train	27 dead, 132 injured
November 30	Railway bombing	Dagestan, train Tyumen-Baku	None
December 3	Explosion	Ingushetia	None
December 16	Explosion	Nazran	2 dead, 2 injured
December 17	Suicide bombing	Ingushetia	1 dead, 10 injured
December 22	Explosion	Dagestan	None
December 24	Explosion	Makhachkala	1 injured
December 26	Explosion	Ingushetia	None
December 28	Explosion	Makhachkala	None
December 29	Explosion	Makhachkala	1 injured
2010			
January 4	Railway bombing	Ingushetia, cargo train	
January 6	Suicide bombing	Makhachkala	5 dead, 19 injured

(continued)

Date	Attack Type	Location	Victims
January 7	Explosion	Makhachkala	None
January 12	Explosion	Dagestan, oil pipeline	
January 12	Explosion	Dagestan	None
January 18	Explosion	Ingushetia	
January 30	Explosions, 3	Ingushetia	1 injured
February 6	Explosion	Ingushetia	1 injured
February 9	Explosion	Ingushetia	None
February 10	Railway bombing	Dagestan	1 dead, 1 injured
February 14	Explosion	Dagestan	1 injured
February 19	Explosion	Nazran	2 dead, 28 injured
February 19	Explosion	Makhachkala	None
February 22	Explosions, 2	Khasavyurt and Kaspiisk	2 injured
February 23	Explosion	Makhachkala	1 injured
February 25	Explosion	Ingushetia	None
February 26	Explosion	Ingushetia	2 injured
March 1	Explosion	Ingushetia	1 injured
March 2	Explosion	Makhachkala	1 injured
March 11	Railway bombing	Dagestan	None
March 13	Explosions, 2	Makhachkala and Khasavyurt	2 injured
March 14	Explosion	Khasavyurt	3 injured
March 15	Explosion	Ingushetia	1 injured
March 20	Explosions, 3	Dagestan	1 dead, 2 injured
March 22	Explosion	Khasavyurt	None
March 23	Explosion	Ingushetia	None
March 25	Explosion	Makhachkala	None
March 29	Suicide bombing	Moscow, metro station Lubianka, metro station Park Kultury	40 dead, over 100 injured
March 31	Suicide bombing	Kizlyar	12 dead, 27 injured
April 1	Explosion	Khasavyurt region	2 dead, 1 injured

(*continued*)

Date	Attack Type	Location	Victims
April 4	Railway bombing	Makhachkala region	None
April 5	Suicide bombing	Karabulak, Ingushetia	2 dead, 2 injured
April 9	Suicide bombing	Nazran region	
April 15	Explosion	Kaspiisk	None
April 19	Explosion	Nazran	6 injured
April 20	Explosion	Makhachkala	
April 25	Explosion	Khasavyurt region	
April 29	Suicide bombing	Kazbekovsky region, Dagestan	2 dead, 17 injured
April 29	Explosion	Nalchik	2 injured
May 1	Explosion	Nalchik	1 dead, 30 injured
May 3	Explosion	Dagestan, communications point	
May 7	Railway bombing	Derbent	1 dead, 7 injured
May 7	Explosion	Derbent	2 dead, 8 injured
May 8	Explosion	Elbrusskii region, Kabardino-Balkaria	1 injured
May 8	Railway bombing	Dagestan, cargo train	None
May 9	Explosion	Nalchik	None
May 9	Explosion	Kaspiisk	
May 19	Explosion	Makhachkala	None
May 22	Explosion	Makhachkala	3 injured
May 25	Explosion	Nalchik	None
May 25	Explosion	Makhachkala	None
May 26	Explosion	Stavropol	8 dead, 42 injured
May 28	Explosion	Kaspiisk	1 dead, 1 injured
May 31	Explosion	Khasavyurt	None
June 4	Explosion	Sagopshi, Ingushetia	1 dead, 17 injured
June 7	Explosion	Dagestan	4 injured
June 8	Explosion	Makhachkala	None

(continued)

Date	Attack Type	Location	Victims
June 9	Explosion	Makhachkala	2 injured
June 12	Explosion	Kaspiisk	2 dead
June 14	Explosions, 2	Nalchik	None
June 21	Explosion	Nalchik	1 injured
June 25	Explosion	Dagestan	1 dead
June 25	Explosion	Nazran	1 injured
June 26	Explosion	Dagestan	1 dead
June 27	Explosion	Kabardino-Balkaria	None
June 27	Explosion	Ingushetia	
June 29	Railway bombing	Dagestan	None
June 30	Explosion	Nalchik region	None
June 30	Suicide bombing	Grozny	1 dead, 7 injured
June 30	Explosion	Dagestan	1 dead
July 2	Explosions, 2	Nalchik	None
July 2	Railway bombing	Dagestan, cargo train	
July 2	Explosion	Kaspiisk	None
July 3	Explosion	Kaspiisk	None
July 4	Explosion	Makhachkala	2 injured
July 6	Explosion	Baksan, Kabardino-Balkaria	None
July 6	Railway bombing	Dagestan	
July 11	Explosion	Kabardino-Balkaria	None
July 11	Explosion	Makhachkala	2 injured
July 11	Railway bombing	Dagestan, cargo train	None
July 15	Explosion	Kabardino-Balkaria	None
July 15	Railway bombing	Dagestan, cargo train	None
July 16	Explosion	Nartkala, Kabardino-Balkaria	1 dead, 4 injured

(continued)

Date	Attack Type	Location	Victims
July 21	Explosion	Kabardino-Balkaria	2 dead, 2 injured
July 23	Railway bombing	Dagestan	1 injured
July 25	Explosion	Kabardino-Balkaria	None
July 28	Explosion	Ingushetia	1 injured
July 30	Explosion	Makhachkala	1 injured
August 16	Explosions, 2	Makhachkala	None
August 17	Suicide bombing	Prigorodnii District, North Ossetia	1 dead, 3 injured
August 18	Explosion	Dagestan	None
August 21	Suicide bombing	Grozny	
August 21	Explosion	Kabardino-Balkaria	
August 23	Explosion	Dagestan	2 dead
August 27	Explosion	Dagestan	1 injured
August 29	Explosion	Kabardino-Balkaria	3 injured
August 29	Suicide bombing	Tsentoroi, Chechnya	6 dead, 18 injured
August 30	Explosions, 2	Dagestan	3 injured
August 31	Explosion	Dagestan	None
September 2	Explosion	Dagestan	1 dead
September 3	Explosion	Dagestan	None
September 5	Suicide bombing	Buinaksk region	4 dead, 35 injured
September 5	Explosion	Makhachkala	1 dead, 1 injured
September 6	Explosion	Makhachkala	1 injured
September 7	Railway bombing	Dagestan, cargo train	
September 9	Suicide bombing	Vladikavkaz	19 dead, 160 injured
September 11	Explosions, 2	Kabardino-Balkaria	5 injured
September 11	Explosion	Makhachkala	1 injured

(continued)

Date	Attack Type	Location	Victims
September 14	Explosion	Dagestan	1 injured
September 17	Explosion	Nalchik	
September 21	Explosion	Nalchik	None
September 22	Explosion	Dagestan	None
September 23	Explosion	Makhachkala	None
September 24	Suicide bombing	Nartkala, Kabardino-Balkaria	
September 24	Suicide bombing	Makhachkala	26 injured
September 24	Explosion	Makhachkala	None
September 27	Explosion	Makhachkala	None
September 29	Explosion	Kaspiisk	17 injured
September 30	Explosion	Nalchik	2 injured
October 11	Explosions, 2	Kabardino-Balkaria	4 injured
October 19	Suicide bombing	Grozny	3 dead, 17 injured
October 24	Explosions, 2	Ingushetia	7 injured
October 25	Explosion	Kabardino-Balkaria	None
November 3	Explosion	Kabardino-Balkaria	1 injured
November 4	Explosion	Dagestan	None
November 9	Explosion	Dagestan	1 injured
November 9	Explosions, 2	Ingushetia alcohol store	None
November 11	Explosions, 2	Makhachkala	
November 20	Explosion	Nazran	1 injured
November 23	Explosion	Khasavyurt	None
November 25	Explosion	Nalchik	
November 25	Explosion	Nazran	None
November 26	Explosion	Nazran	1 injured
November 27	Railway bombing	Dagestan	
November 29	Explosion	Dagestan, cellular operator	None

(*continued*)

Date	Attack Type	Location	Victims
December 3	Explosion	Kabardino-Balkaria	None
December 14	Explosion	Makhachkala	None
December 16	Explosion	Dagestan, cargo train	None
December 20	Explosion	Makhachkala	2 injured
December 22	Explosions, 2	Makhachkala	3 injured
December 23	Explosion	Nalchik	2 injured
December 27	Explosion	Nalchik	1 injured
December 28	Explosion	Makhachkala	1 injured
December 31	Explosion	Ingushetia alcohol store	1 injured
2011			
January 14	Explosion	Dagestan	4 dead, 5 injured
January 18	Explosion	Makhachkala region	None
January 20	Explosion	Khasavyurt store	None
January 23	Explosion	Ingushetia	None
January 24	Suicide bombing	Moscow, Domodedovo airport	37 dead
January 26	Explosion	Khasavyurt	4 dead, 6 injured
January 30	Explosion	Dagestan, cellular operator	
January 31	Explosion	Kabardino-Balkaria	2 injured
January 31	Railway bombing	Dagestan, cargo train	None
February 1	Explosion	Kizlyar store	3 injured
February 3	Explosion	Makhachkala	2 dead
February 3	Explosion	Ingushetia	None
February 6	Explosion	Nalchik	None
February 7	Explosion	Makhachkala	3 injured
February 7	Railway bombing	Kizlyar region, cargo train	None
February 14	Suicide bombing	Karabudakhkentskii region, Dagestan	2 dead, 27 injured

(*continued*)

Date	Attack Type	Location	Victims
February 15	Suicide bombing	Grozny	
February 16	Explosion	Kizlyar store	
February 24	Explosion	Makhachkala	None
February 26	Explosion	Makhachkala	None
March 4	Suicide bombing	Nazran	
March 7	Explosion	Buinaksk store	None
March 9	Explosion	Moscow, FSB Academy	
March 10	Railway bombing	Dagestan, cargo train	None
March 11	Explosion	Buinaksk	None
March 16	Explosion	Buinaksk	None
March 17	Explosions, 3	Magas	None
March 20	Explosion	Kabardino-Balkaria	1 injured
March 29	Explosion	Dagestan, cellular operator	None
April 2	Explosion	Ingushetia	
April 4	Explosion	Dagestan	None
April 6	Explosion	Dagestan	None
April 10	Suicide bombing	Kizlyar	
April 23	Railway bombing	Dagestan	None
April 25	Suicide bombing	Grozny	
April 25	Railway bombing	Dagestan, cargo train	
April 27	Explosions, 2	Dagestan	None
April 28	Explosion	Dagestan	None
May 3	Explosion	Moscow, police parking lot	1 injured
May 4	Explosion	Dagestan	1 dead, 1 injured
May 10	Suicide bombing	Makhachkala	2 dead

(*continued*)

Date	Attack Type	Location	Victims
May 11	Explosion	Dagestan	None
May 14	Explosion	Kaspiisk	1 injured
June 11	Explosion	Dagestan	
June 21	Explosion	Ingushetia	
June 25	Explosion	Kabardino-Balkaria	None
July 7	Explosion	Ingushetia	
July 12	Suicide bombing	Ingushetia	None
July 13	Explosion	Dagestan	None
July 15	Explosion	Dagestan	8 injured
July 18	Explosion	Kaspiisk	1 dead, 2 injured
July 21	Explosion	Dagestan	None
July 23	Explosion	Derbent	None
July 27	Explosion	Dagestan	None
August 2	Explosion	Buinaksk	3 dead
August 4	Explosions, 2	Kaspiisk and Buinaksk	None
August 8	Explosion	Dagestan	None
August 9	Explosion	Makhachkala	1 inured
August 13	Explosion	Ingushetia	
August 18	Explosion	Makhachkala	
August 21	Explosions, 2	Makhachkala	21 injured
August 23	Railway bombing	Dagestan	
August 30	Suicide bombing	Grozny	9 dead, 22 injured
August 30	Explosion	Ingushetia	1 dead
September 1	Explosions, 2	Ingushetia	2 dead, 2 injured
September 2	Explosion	Makhachkala region	1 dead, 3 injured
September 2	Explosion	Nazran	None
September 4	Explosion	Nazran	None
September 14	Explosion	Dagestan	None
September 18	Explosion	Makhachkala	
September 19	Explosion	Makhachkala	None

(*continued*)

Date	Attack Type	Location	Victims
September 21	Explosion	Makhachkala	3 dead
September 22	Explosions, 2	Makhachkala	2 dead, 54 injured
September 23	Explosions, 2	Ingushetia	None
September 27	Explosion	Ingushetia	None
September 28	Explosion	Nazran	None
September 28	Suicide bombing	Dagestan	8 dead, 6 injured
October 3	Explosions, 2	Dagestan	2 dead, 2 injured
October 6	Explosion	Nazran	None
October 11	Explosions, 2	Dagestan	None
October 12	Explosion	Makhachkala	1 injured
October 21	Explosion	Dagestan	1 dead
October 22	Railway bombing	Dagestan, cargo train	None
October 23	Explosion	Buinaksk	None
October 27	Explosion	Makhachkala	1 injured
November 15	Explosion	Nazran	None
December 6	Explosion	Dagestan	4 injured
December 12	Explosion	Kabardino-Balkaria	2 dead
December 14	Explosion	Nazran	3 injured
December 19	Suicide bombing	Karabudakhkentskii region, Dagestan	
2012			
January 6	Explosion	Makhachkala	1 injured
January 17	Explosion	Derbent	1 injured
January 21	Explosion	Dagestan	3 dead
January 28	Explosions, 2	Dagestan	1 dead, 1 injured
February 7	Explosion	Khasavyurt region	None
March 6	Suicide bombing	Karabudakhkent, Dagestan	5 dead, 2 injured
March 22	Explosion	Nazran	2 injured
March 23	Explosion	Buinaksk	2 dead
March 24	Explosion	Ingushetia	None
March 25	Explosion	Kizlyar region	None

(continued)

Date	Attack Type	Location	Victims
March 30	Explosion	Makhachkala	None
March 30	Explosion	Nazran	1 dead, 1 injured
March 31	Explosion	Ingushetia	None
April 15	Explosion	Makhachkala	2 injured
April 16	Explosions, 2	Makhachkala	2 dead
April 24	Explosion	Ingushetia	None
April 28	Explosion	Ingushetia	2 dead
May 1	Explosion	Ingushetia	None
May 1	Explosion	Buinaksk	None
May 3	Suicide bombing	Makhachkala	14 dead, over 100 injured
May 3	Explosion	Dagestan	None
May 5	Explosion	Buinaksk	None
May 18	Explosion	Dagestan, gas pipeline	
May 24	Railway bombing	Dagestan, cargo train	None
May 31	Railway bombing	Dagestan, cargo train	None
June 3	Explosion	Dagestan	None
June 4	Explosion	Nazran	None
June 5	Explosion	Nazran	None
June 9	Explosion	Kabardino-Balkaria	1 injured
June 11	Explosion	Ingushetia	None
June 17	Explosion	Buinaksk	None
June 19	Explosion	Kabardino-Balkaria	None
June 22	Explosion	Buinaksk	None
June 25	Explosion	Makhachkala	None
June 26	Explosions, 2	Dagestan	None
June 29	Explosion	Ingushetia	1 dead
July 4	Explosion	Buinaksk	None
July 12	Explosion	Buinaksk	None
July 16	Explosion	Kizlyar	None
July 17	Explosion	Ingushetia	None

(continued)

Date	Attack Type	Location	Victims
July 20	Explosion	Ingushetia	None
July 24	Explosion	Ingushetia	1 injured
July 27	Suicide bombing	Makhachkala region	
July 28	Explosion	Ingushetia	2 injured
July 29	Explosion	Ingushetia	2 dead, 1 injured
July 29	Explosion	Derbent	1 injured
August 1	Explosion	Derbent	3 injured
August 2	Explosion	Buinaksk	1 dead
August 6	Suicide bombing	Grozny	4 dead, 4 injured
August 8	Explosion	Kaspiisk	1 injured
August 14	Explosion	Buinaksk	1 dead
August 15	Explosion	Nazran	None
August 16	Explosions, 2	Derbent	None
August 19	Suicide bombing	Malgobek, Ingushetia	8 dead, 15 injured
August 20	Explosion	Kabardino-Balkaria	None
August 27	Explosion	Nazran	3 injured
August 28	Suicide bombing	Buinaksk region	7 dead, 3 injured
September 2	Explosion	Karabulak, Ingushetia	1 injured
September 5	Explosion	Ingushetia	6 dead, 1 injured
September 6	Explosion	Nazran	None
September 7	Explosion	Ingushetia	1 injured
September 14	Explosion	Kabardino-Balkaria	1 injured
October 4	Explosion	Derbent	None
October 23	Suicide bombing	Chermen, North Ossetia–Ingushetia border	1 dead, 4 injured
October 24	Explosion	Ingushetia	
October 26	Explosion	Derbent	None
November 4	Explosion	Kabardino-Balkaria	1 injured

(continued)

Date	Attack Type	Location	Victims
November 4	Explosion	Buinaksk	1 injured
November 15	Explosion	Nalchik	1 injured
November 21	Explosions, 2	Shamilkala, Dagestan	3 dead, 1 injured
December 6	Explosion	Nalchik	1 injured
December 18	Explosion	Dagestan	
2013			
January 24	Explosion	Dagestan	None
January 25	Explosions, 2	Derbent	None
January 31	Explosion	Derbent	None
February 2	Explosion	Dagestan	None
February 12	Explosions, 2	Derbent and Buinaksk	1 inured
February 14	Suicide bombing	Khasavyurt	5 dead, 5 injured
February 15	Explosion	Ekazhevo, Ingushetia	2 injured
April 3	Explosion	Bamut, Chechnya	1 dead, 3 injured
April 4	Explosion	Buinaksk	1 dead
April 8	Explosion	Buinaksk	4 injured
April 12	Explosion	Buinaksk	1 dead, 3 injured
April 12	Explosion	Ingushetia	None
April 21	Explosion	Dagestan	None
April 28	Explosion	Buinaksk	
May 1	Explosion	Makhachkala	2 dead, 2 injured
May 1	Explosion	Kabardino-Balkaria	None
May 2	Explosion	Makhachkala	None
May 17	Suicide bombing	Sunzhenskii region, Ingushetia	13 injured
May 20	Explosions, 2	Makhachkala	4 dead, 52 injured
May 25	Suicide bombing	Makhachkala	1 dead, 15 injured
May 28	Explosion	Derbent	2 injured
June 6	Explosion	Shamilkala, Dagestan	1 dead, 2 injured

(*continued*)

Date	Attack Type	Location	Victims
June 8	Explosion	Orta-Stal', Dagestan	1 injured
June 9	Explosion	Buinaksk	1 injured
June 12	Explosion	Makhachkala	None
June 19	Explosion	Kuba-Taba, Kabardino-Balkaria	
June 28	Explosion	Derbent	1 injured
July 15	Explosions, 2	Buinaksk	None
July 19	Explosion	Makhachkala region	None
August 4	Explosions, 2	Makhachkala alcohol stores	2 injured
August 18	Explosion	Dagestan	None
August 22	Explosion	Kabardino-Balkaria	None
August 28	Explosion	Dagestan	None
September 7	Explosion	Derbent	1 dead
September 10	Explosions, 2	Khasavyurt and Suleiman-Stal' region	None
September 14	Explosion	Khasavyurt	None
September 16	Suicide bombing	Sunzhenskii region, Chechnya	3 dead, 4 injured
September 23	Suicide bombing	Tabasaranskii region, Dagestan	3 dead, 15 injured
October 3	Explosion	Makhachkala	None
October 8	Explosion	Khasavyurt area	None
October 15	Explosion	Dagestan	1 dead
October 15	Explosion	Ingushetia	1 dead
October 16	Explosion	Ingushetia	1 dead, 2 injured
October 21	Suicide bombing	Volgograd bus	6 dead, 37 injured
October 24	Explosions, 2	Makhachkala and Khasavyurt area	1 dead
October 30	Explosions, 2	Makhachkala	1 dead, 17 injured
November 8	Explosion	Makhachkala store	1 dead, 1 injured

(*continued*)

Date	Attack Type	Location	Victims
November 23	Explosion	Makhachkala	1 dead
December 27	Explosion	Piatigorsk region	3 dead
December 28	Explosion	Khasavyurt area	1 dead
December 29	Suicide bombing	Volgograd, railway station	18 dead, 44 injured
December 29	Explosions, 2	Derbent	None
December 30	Suicide bombing	Volgograd trolley-bus	10 dead, 23 injured
December 31	Explosion	Khasavyurt area	1 injured
December 31	Explosion	Buinaksk	1 dead

Notes

INTRODUCTION

1. *Kavkaz Center*. 2013. "Amir IK Dokku Abu Usman Otmenil Moratorii na Operatsii v Rossii i Prizval ne Dopustit' Olimpiady v Sochi," July 3. http://www.kavkazcenter.com/russ/content/2013/07/03/98961.shtml.
2. *Gazeta.ru*. 2014. "Islamskie Boeviki Vziali na Sebia Otvetstvennost' za Vzryvy v Volgograde," January 20. http://www.gazeta.ru/social/video/islamskie_boeviki_vzyali_na_sebya_otvetstvennost_za_vzryvy_v_volgograde.shtml.
3. *BBC News*. 2014. "Olimpiiskie Komitety Evropy Poluchili Ugrozy," January 22. http://www.bbc.co.uk/russian/international/2014/01/140122_sochi_europe_olympic_committees_threats.shtml.
4. *BBC News*. 2014. "Russia Hunts Suspected Female Sochi Suicide Bomber," January 22. http://www.bbc.com/news/world-europe-25839176.
5. *Kavkaz Center*. 2007. "Ofitsial'nyi Reliz Zaiavleniia Amira Dokki Umarova o Provozglashenii Kavkazskogo Emirata," November 21. http://kavkazcenter.com/russ/content/2007/11/21/54480.shtml.
6. Lally, Kathy. 2013. "Russia Calls Boston Bombings Preventable." *Washington Post*, May 31.
7. *Kavkaz Center*. 2012. "Zaiavlenie Komandovaniia Modzhakhedov Vilaiata Dagestan IK v Sviazi s Sobytiiami v Bostone (SShA)," April 21. http://kavkazcenter.com/russ/content/2013/04/21/97502.shtml. All translations of quotations from Russian into English in this book were done by the author.
8. Rotar', Igor. 1995. "Chechnya: Po Obe Storony Fronta." *Izvestiia*, November 24.
9. Whittell, Giles. 1999. "Blast Raises Fear of a 'Holy War.'" *Times*, September 3.
10. While many disagree with the label of Wahhabism in reference to Salafism, *Wahhabism* is the term used in Russia to refer to Salafism. To avoid inconsistencies, the term *Wahhabism* will be used here.

11. *Kavkazskii Uzel.* 2014. "Infografika. Statistika Zhertv na Severnom Kavkaze s 2010 po 2013 God po Dannym 'Kavkazskogo Uzla,'" March 21. http://www.kavkaz-uzel.ru/articles/239812/.
12. *Izvestiia.* 2013. "V Novogodnem Poslanii Prezident Poobeshchal Unichtozhit' Terroristov," December 31.
13. Official Kremlin International News Broadcast. 2001. President Vladimir Putin's TV Address, September 25.
14. *The 9/11 Commission Report.* New York: W.W. Norton and Company, 165.
15. Mroue, Bassem. 2014. "Chechen in Syria a Rising Star in Extremist Group." *Associated Press*, July 3. http://bigstory.ap.org/article/chechen-syria-rising-star-extremist-group.
16. Mroue, Bassem. 2014. "Chechen in Syria a Rising Star in Extremist Group." *Associated Press*, July 3. http://bigstory.ap.org/article/chechen-syria-rising-star-extremist-group.
17. *Kavkaz Center.* 2013. "Kavkazskie Modzhakhedy v Sirii Obeshchaiut Priiti v Rossiiu i na Kavkaz," July 6. http://www.kavkazcenter.com/russ/content/2013/07/06/99026.shtml.

CHAPTER 1

1. For more detailed information on Russia's conquest of the North Caucasus, see Baddeley, John F. 1908. *The Russian Conquest of the Caucasus.* London: Longmans, Green and Co.; Piotrovskii, B. B., ed. 1988. *Istoriia Narodov Severnogo Kavkaza s Drevneishikh Vremen do Kontsa XVIII v.* Moscow: Nauka; Narochnitskii, A. L., ed. 1988. *Istoriia Narodov Severnogo Kavkaza (konets XVIII v. – 1917 g.).* Moscow: Nauka; Gammer, Moshe. 1994. *Muslim Resistance to the Tsar: Shamil and the Conquest of Chechnia and Daghestan.* London: Frank Cass; Seely, Robert. 2001. *Russo-Chechen Conflict, 1800–2000: A Deadly Embrace.* London: Frank Cass; King, Charles. 2008. *The Ghost of Freedom: The History of the Caucasus.* New York: Oxford University Press; Lieven, Anatol. 1998. *Chechnya: Tombstone of Russian Power.* New Haven and London: Yale University Press; Zelkina, Anna. 2000. *In Quest for God and Freedom: Sufi Responses to the Russian Advance in the North Caucasus.* New York: New York University Press; Gammer, Moshe. 2006. *The Lone Wolf and the Bear: Three Centuries of Chechen Defiance of Russian Rule.* Pittsburgh, PA: University of Pittsburgh Press.
2. Narochnitskii, A. L., ed. 1988. *Istoriia Narodov Severnogo Kavkaza (konets XVIIIv. – 1917 g.).* Moscow: Nauka.
3. Sokirianskaia, Ekaterina. 2012. "Ingushetiia i Chechnya: Konets Teipov." *Neprikosnovennyi Zapas*, 4, no. 84.
4. Piotrovskii, B. B., ed. 1988. *Istoriia Narodov Severnogo Kavkaza s Drevneishikh Vremen do Kontsa XVIII v.* Moscow: Nauka.
5. Gune-Yadcy, Zubeyde. 2003. "A Chechen National Hero of the Caucasus in the 18th Century: Sheikh Mansur." *Central Asian Survey* 22, no. 1: 106.
6. Sharia law was initially introduced in Dagestan by Arabs in the eighth century at the same time Islam made its way into the Caucasus. However, while sharia law spread across the region, it failed to completely replace local traditions of adat. Some areas came to be governed by sharia in civil matters and adat in criminal matters. In Dagestan, sharia influenced local jurisprudence so much that it has become virtually impossible to interpret whether adat laws reflect local traditions or are a product of the adaptation of sharia law. See Baddeley, John F. 1908. *The Russian Conquest of the Caucasus.*

London: Longmans, Green and Co; Zelkina, Anna. 2000. *In Quest for God and Freedom: Sufi Responses to the Russian Advance in the North Caucasus.* New York: New York University Press.

7. Narochnitskii, A. L., ed. 1988. *Istoriia Narodov Severnogo Kavkaza (konets XVIIIv. – 1917 g.).* Moscow: Nauka.

8. Quoted in Baddeley, John F. 1908. *The Russian Conquest of the Caucasus.* London: Longmans, Green and Co., 97.

9. Quoted in Zelkina, Anna. 2000. *In Quest for God and Freedom: Sufi Responses to the Russian Advance in the North Caucasus.* New York: New York University Press, 106.

10. Quoted in Zelkina, Anna. 2000. *In Quest for God and Freedom: Sufi Responses to the Russian Advance in the North Caucasus.* New York: New York University Press, 106.

11. Quoted in Oleinikov, D. I. 1996. "Istoricheskie Portrety. Shamil." *Voprosy Istorii,* 5: 59.

12. The definition of Muridism remains controversial. It is related to a broader debate within Islamic studies on the question of justifications for war. Many Soviet and Russian historiographers have interpreted the term at different times in history as describing religious fundamentalism, anticolonial movements, or antifeudal movements. Western scholars tend to equate Muridism with Sufi Naqshbandi order. However, not all Naqshbandi scholars supported the call to war. As a result, it would be incorrect to equate the entire Naqshbandi order with Muridism, just as today it would be incorrect to equate Salafism with violent jihadism, as not all Salafi adherents promote war. Given the ideological underpinnings of Muridism and the fact that Muridism did not have a unified backing from the representatives of the Naqshbandi order, I use the term here in reference to the ideological justifications of the nineteenth-century movement for religious revival and liberation from Russia.

13. King, Charles. 2008. *The Ghost of Freedom: The History of the Caucasus.* New York: Oxford University Press.

14. Gammer, Moshe. 1994. "The Beginnings of the Naqshbandiyya in Daghestan and the Russian Conquest of the Caucasus." *Die Welt des Islams* 34, no. 2: 204–217.

15. Quoted in Zelkina, Anna. 2000. *In Quest for God and Freedom: Sufi Responses to the Russian Advance in the North Caucasus.* New York: New York University Press, 153.

16. Baddeley, John F. 1908. *The Russian Conquest of the Caucasus.* London: Longmans, Green and Co., 147.

17. Kemper, Michael. 2002. "The Daghestani Legal Discourse on the Imamate." *Central Asian Survey* 21, no. 3: 265–278.

18. Oleinikov, D. I. 1996. "Istoricheskie Portrety. Shamil." *Voprosy Istorii,* 5: 58–76; Zelkina, Anna. 2002. "Jihad in the Name of God: Shaykh Shamil as the Religious Leader of the Caucasus." *Central Asian Survey* 21, no. 3: 249–264.

19. Quoted in Se Chzhin, Chzhun. 2010. "Sufizm na Severnom Kavkaze v XIX Veke." *Rossiiskaia Istoriia* 6: 134.

20. Narochnitskii, A. L., ed. 1988. *Istoriia Narodov Severnogo Kavkaza (konets XVIIIv. – 1917 g.).* Moscow: Nauka.

21. Zelkina, Anna. 2000. *In Quest for God and Freedom: Sufi Responses to the Russian Advance in the North Caucasus.* New York: New York University Press.

22. Zelkina, Anna. 2000. *In Quest for God and Freedom: Sufi Responses to the Russian Advance in the North Caucasus.* New York: New York University Press.

23. Narochnitskii, A. L., ed. 1988. *Istoriia Narodov Severnogo Kavkaza (konets XVIIIv. – 1917 g.).* Moscow: Nauka. A list of 16 of the districts can be found in Pokrovskii, N. 1934. "Muridism u Vlasti." *Istorik-Marksist* 2, no. 36: 30–75.

24. Baddeley, John F. 1908. *The Russian Conquest of the Caucasus*. London: Longmans, Green and Co.
25. Gammer, Moshe. 1994. *Muslim Resistance to the Tsar: Shamil and the Conquest of Chechnia and Daghestan*. London: Frank Cass, 249.
26. *Kavkazskii Uzel*. 2010. "Imam Shamil," July 19. http://www.kavkaz-uzel.ru/articles/171025.
27. Iakhiev, Said Usman. 2000. "Imam Shamil i Zikr." *NG Religii*, January 26.
28. *NG Stsenarii*. 1997. "Fenomen Shamilia," April 29.
29. Oleinikov, D. I. 1996. "Istoricheskie Portrety. Shamil." *Voprosy Istorii* 5: 58–76.
30. Adyg, Cherkess, and Circassian are often used interchangeably to designate the same identity group. Generally, Adyg (Adyghe) is the name used by the Circassian people in reference to themselves. Cherkess is a Turkic version of the designation, and Circassian, in turn, is a Westernized version of Cherkess.
31. Quoted in Richmond, Walter. 2013. *The Circassian Genocide*. New Brunswick, NJ: Rutgers University Press, 54.
32. Quoted in King, Charles. 2008. *The Ghost of Freedom: The History of the Caucasus*. New York: Oxford University Press, 97.
33. Quoted in Mamsurov, Alikhan. 2014. "O Cherkesakh, Zelenykh Lentochkakh i Kavkazskoi Voine." *BBC Russia*, May 21. http://www.bbc.co.uk/russian/blogs/2014/05/140520_blog_caucasus_war_anniversary.shtml.
34. *Kavkazskii Uzel*. 2013. "Obrashchenie Cherkesskikh Organizatsii Adygei, KChR i Krasnodarskogo Kraia k Prezidentu RF i Federal'nomu Sobraniiu RF," May 5. http://www.kavkaz-uzel.ru/articles/223778.
35. *Kavkazskii Uzel*. 2014. "Cherkesskii Vopros v Sochi: Stolitsa Olimpiady ili Zemlia Genotsida?" March 24. http://www.kavkaz-uzel.ru/articles/238010/.
36. Quoted in Mamsurov, Alikhan. 2014. "O Cherkesakh, Zelenykh Lentochkakh i Kavkazskoi Voine." *BBC Russia*, May 21. http://www.bbc.co.uk/russian/blogs/2014/05/140520_blog_caucasus_war_anniversary.shtml.
37. On chosen trauma, see Volkan, Vamik D. 1997. *Bloodlines: From Ethnic Pride to Ethnic Terrorism*. Boulder, CO: Westview.
38. Rotar', Igor'. 1995. "Chechnya: Davniaia Smuta." *Izvestiia*, October 27.
39. Saiyeva, Aminat. 2004. "... Until Not a Single Chechen Remains Alive." *Kavkaz Center*, February 25. http://www.kavkazcenter.com/eng/content/2004/02/25/2473.shtml.
40. The first capital based in Dargo in Dagestan was destroyed in the course of the Murid wars.
41. *BBC Monitoring Trans Caucasus Unit*. 2006. "Late Chechen Rebel Commander Basayev Defiant in Final Interview," July 20.
42. *Kavkaz Center*. 2006. "Imam Shamil – A Great Warrior of Islam," December 9. http://www.kavkazcenter.com/eng/content/2006/12/09/6767.shtml.
43. *Kavkaz Center*. 2008. "Movladi Udugov: 'It Is War for the Way of Life ...,'" June 27. http://www.kavkazcenter.com/eng/content/2008/06/27/9927.shtml.
44. See Marshall, Alex. 2010. *The Caucasus under Soviet Rule*. New York: Routledge; Bennigsen, Alexandre and S. Enders Wimbush. 1985. *Mystics and Commissars: Sufism in the Soviet Union*. Berkeley: University of California Press; Martin, Terri. 2001. *The Affirmative Action Empire: Nations and Nationalism in the Soviet Union, 1923–1939*. Ithaca, NY: Cornell University Press.
45. Polian, Pavel. 2007. "Kosa i Kamen': Konfliktnyi Etnos v Krepchaiushchikh Ob'iatiiakh Sovetskoi Vlasti." *Zvezda* 12: 119–150.

46. Bennigsen, Alexandre. 1983. "Muslim Guerilla Warfare in the Caucasus 1918–1928." *Central Asian Survey* 2, no. 1: 45–56.
47. Marshall, Alex. 2010. *The Caucasus under Soviet Rule.* New York: Routledge, 60.
48. Polian, Pavel. 2007. "Kosa i Kamen': Konfliktnyi Etnos v Krepchaiushchikh Ob'iatiiakh Sovetskoi Vlasti." *Zvezda* 12: 119–150.
49. Bobrovnikov, V. O. 2001. "Shariatskie Sudy i Pravovoi Pliuralizm v Sovetskom Dagestane." *Etnograficheskoe Obozrenie* 3: 80.
50. Quoted in Markedonov, Sergei. 2011. "Konflikty na Kavkaze: Sovetskaia Preliudiia." *Neprikosnovennyi' Zapas* 4: 115.
51. Polian, Pavel. 2007. "Kosa i Kamen': Konfliktnyi Etnos v Krepchaiushchikh Ob'iatiiakh Sovetskoi Vlasti." *Zvezda* 12: 119–150.
52. Bobrovnikov, V. O. 2001. "Shariatskie Sudy i Pravovoi Pliuralizm v Sovetskom Dagestane." *Etnograficheskoe Obozrenie* 3: 77–91.
53. Quoted in Bobrovnikov, V. O. 2001. "Shariatskie Sudy i Pravovoi Pliuralizm v Sovetskom Dagestane." *Etnograficheskoe Obozrenie* 3: 79.
54. Bobrovnikov, V. O. 2001. "Shariatskie Sudy i Pravovoi Pliuralizm v Sovetskom Dagestane." *Etnograficheskoe Obozrenie* 3: 77–91.
55. See Liber, George. 1991. "Korenizatsiia: Restructuring Soviet Nationality Policy in the 1920s." *Ethnic and Racial Studies* 14, no. 1: 15–23.
56. Toptygin, Aleksei V. 2002. *Neizvestnyi Beriia.* Saint Petersburg: Neva, 157.
57. For more on the deportation, see Tishkov, Valerii. 2004. *Chechnya: Life in a War-Torn Society.* Berkeley: University of California Press.
58. Marshall, Alex. 2010. *The Caucasus under Soviet Rule.* New York: Routledge, 267.
59. Sabanchiev, Kh.-M.A. 2013. "Deportatsiia Narodov Severnogo Kavkaza v 40-kh gg. XX v." *Voprosy Istorii* 11: 104–112.
60. Bugai, Nikolai F. 1990. "Iz Istorii Narodov SSSR." *Voprosy Istorii* 7: 39.
61. Marshall, Alex. 2010. *The Caucasus under Soviet Rule.* New York: Routledge, 270.
62. Sinitsyn, F. L. 2011. "Soprotivlenie Narodov SSSR Deportatsiiam (1941–1949 gg.)." *Voprosy Istorii* 2: 32–51.
63. Bugai, Nikolai F. 1990. "Iz Istorii Narodov SSSR." *Voprosy Istorii* 7: 40–42.
64. Bugai, Nikolai F. 1990. "Iz Istorii Narodov SSSR." *Voprosy Istorii* 7: 33.
65. Shevelev, Mikhail. 1996. "Shamil Basayev: 'I Hope for Peace, But I Don't Believe It.'" *Moscow News*, June 27.
66. *Kavkaz Center.* 2004. "President Maskhadov: 'No One to Rely on but God,'" February 25. http://www.kavkazcenter.com/eng/content/2004/02/25/2454.shtml.
67. Saiyeva, Aminat. 2004. "... Until Not a Single Chechen Remains Alive." *Kavkaz Center*, February 25. http://www.kavkazcenter.com/eng/content/2004/02/25/2473.shtml.
68. Ibrahim, Yusuf. 2003. "Russia Lost this War ..." *Kavkaz Center*, November 11. http://www.kavkazcenter.com/eng/content/2003/11/11/2025_print.html.
69. *Kavkazskii Uzel.* 2005. "Osetino-Ingushskii Konflikt 1992 g.: Istoki i Razvitie (po Mai 2005 goda)," September 19. http://www.kavkaz-uzel.ru/articles/81949/.
70. Batygin, Aleksandr. 1997. "Prezident po Prozvishchu 'Ded.'" *Rossiiskaia Gazeta*, November 15.
71. See Potapov, P. P. 2010. *Chechenskii Poias.* Minsk: Sovremennaia Shkola.
72. *Nezavisimaia Gazeta.* 1996. "Stanovlenie Gosudarstvennosti KBR Sviazano s Rossiei," November 23.
73. *Kavkazskii Uzel.* 2007. "Polozhenie Balkarskogo Naroda v Kabardino-Balkarskoi Respublike: Istochniki Problem i Puti ikh Preodoleniia," April 3. http://www.kavkaz-uzel.ru/articles/111075/.

74. Markedonov, Sergei. 2011. "Kabardino-Balkariia: Pogruzhenie v Turbulentnost'." *Svobodnaia Mysl'* 7: 17–30.
75. Kul'chik, Yuri. 1995. "Natsional'nye Dvizheniia v Kabardino-Balkarskoi Respublike." *Politicheskii Monitoring* 1, no. 36. http://www.igpi.ru/monitoring/1047645476/1050414836/Kabarda.htm.
76. Shapovalov, Aleksandr. 1999. "Vladimir Khubiev: 'Severnyi Kavkaz – Osobyi Region Rossii.' " *NG Regiony*, March 30.
77. *Kavkazskii Uzel.* 2001. "Magomedov Magomedali Magomedovich," May 28.
78. Aliev, Timur. 2013. "U nas Odna Sud'ba." *Rossiiskaia Gazeta*, October 11.
79. Kaenkhanov, A. 1991. "92.5 Protsenta Golosov – za Suverennuiu Ingushetiiu." *Izvestiia*, December 4.
80. Morozov, R. 1993. "Tochka Zreniia." *Argumenty i Fakty*, February 24.
81. The other republic was Tatarstan. Tatarstan later signed a federative agreement with Russia in 1994.
82. *Izvestiia.* 1996. "Tak Gotovilas' Chechenskaia Voina," October 12.
83. *Svobodnaia Gruziia.* 2002. "V Abkhazii Activno Deistvuiut Vakhkhabity i Chleny Razlichnykh Ekstremistskikh i Terroristicheskikh Grupp," March 12.
84. Aleshkin, Aleksandr. 1991. "Chetyrnadtsat' Zvezd na Zelenom." *Rossiiskaia Gazeta*, November 11.
85. Aleshkin, Aleksandr. 1991. "Chetyrnadtsat' Zvezd na Zelenom." *Rossiiskaia Gazeta*, November 11.
86. *Kommersant.* 1992. "Prezhde Vsego," March 30. http://www.kommersant.ru/doc/3953.
87. Bitsoev, Said. 2000. "Triumf i Tragediia Yusupa Soslambekova." *Novye Izvestiia*, July 28.
88. *Argumanty i Fakty.* 1992. "Vopros – Otvet," September 2.
89. Shabanov, Pavel. 2006. "Shamil', Smert' No 6," *Russkii Sever*, July 19.
90. *Krasnaia Zvezda.* 1996. "Novosti. Basayev – Prestupnik Mezhdunarodnyi," June 21.
91. Stasovskii, Anatoly, Konstantin Litvinov, and Nikolai Astashkin. 1992. "Konfederatsiia Gorskikh Narodov Kavkaza Vstupaet v Boi." *Krasnaia Zvezda*, August 27.
92. Stasovskii, Anatoly, Konstantin Litvinov, and Nikolai Astashkin. 1992. "Konfederatsiia Gorskikh Narodov Kavkaza Vstupaet v Boi." *Krasnaia Zvezda*, August 27.
93. *State Duma of the Federal Assembly of the Russian Federation.* 1994. Hearing No. 71, December 13.
94. Karapetian, Petr. 1994. "Tolstoi-Yurt ne Tol'ko Govorit, no i Pokazyvaet." *Krasnaia Zvezda*, September 1.
95. Kamyshev, Dmitry. 1997. "Dzhokhar Dudayev kak Zerkalo Russkoi Natsional'noi Politiki." *Kommersant Daily*, October 7.
96. Badasian, Edita. 2008. "Nachkebiia: Poiavlenie 'Konfederatsii Gorskikh Narodov Kavkaza' v Abkhazii Vyzyvaet Ozabochennost' v Gruzii." *Kavkazskii Uzel*, May 6. http://www.kavkaz-uzel.ru/articles/136012/.
97. Krechetnikov, Artem. 2009. "Pervaia Chechenskaia: Put' k Voine." *BBC News*, December 10.
98. The name Ichkeriia was introduced by Dudayev in January of 1994 in response to Russia adopting the new Constitution of December 1993. The Constitution listed the Chechen Republic as one of Russia's units. To differentiate his state from Russia's Chechen Republic, Dudayev adopted a new name.
99. *Rossiiskaia Gazeta.* 1991. "Chego zhe Khochet General Dudayev?" December 13.

100. Green, K. 1991. "Terrorism Threat to Yeltsin." *Sunday Mail*, November 10.
101. Murdzhikneli, Kirill. 1993. "Chechnya: Na Sem'iu? Po Avtomatu." *Krasnaia Zvezda*, August 7.
102. Murdzhikneli, Kirill. 1993. "Chechnya: Na Sem'iu? Po Avtomatu." *Krasnaia Zvezda*, August 7.
103. Ziat'kov, Nikolai. 1994. "Ruslan Khasbulatov: 'Pochemu ne Udalas' moia Missiia.'" *Argumenty i Fakty*, December 7.
104. Borovkov, A. 1992. "ChR: Komu i Dlia Chego Ostavleno Oruzhie?" *Krasnaia Zvezda*, July 1.
105. Pain, Emil, and Arkady Popov. 1995. "Rossiiskaia Politika v Chechne." *Izvestiia*, February 8.
106. Shakhrai, Sergei. 1994. "V Chechne Prozhivaet 150 Tysiach Russkikh. Chto tam, v Chechne?" *Argumenty i Fakty*, July 13.
107. Sergeev, Nikolai. 1993. "Kuda Bezhit Odinokii Volk." *Krasnaia Zvezda*, May 27.
108. Ziat'kov, Nikolai. 1994. "Ruslan Khasbulatov: 'Pochemu ne Udalas' moia Missiia.'" *Argumenty i Fakty*, December 7.
109. Pain, Emil, and Arkady Popov. 1995. "Rossiiskaia Politika v Chechne." *Izvestiia*, February 8.
110. Pain, Emil, and Arkady Popov. 1995. "Rossiiskaia Politika v Chechne." *Izvestiia*, February 8.
111. Krutikov, Evgenii. 2000. "Zhidkoe Zoloto Ichkerii." *Izvestiia*, June 7.
112. Valiuzhenich, Galina. 1994. "Pomoshch', Okazyvaemaia Oppozitsii, Otsenivaetsia v Summu Svyshe 150 mlrd. rub." *Argumenty i Fakty*, December 7.
113. Aleshkin, Aleksandr. 1993. "Dudayev Otkazalsia Delit' Vlast'." *Rossiiskaia Gazeta*, April 20.
114. *Krasnaia Zvezda*. 1993. "Osnovnye Polozheniia Voennoi Doktriny Rossiiskoi Federatsii," November 19.
115. *Rossiiskaia Gazeta*. 1994. "Chechnya: Est' li Brod v Ogne?" December 6.

CHAPTER 2

1. Astashkin, Nikolai, Anatoly Borovkov, and Vladimir Gavrilenko. 1994. "I Vnov' Dollary, Oruzhie i Vertolet." *Krasnaia Zvezda*, May 28.
2. *Moskovskie Novosti*. 1993. "Terroristicheskie Akty vo vse Vozrastaiushchikh Masshtabakh, po Mneniiu Ministerstva Bezopasnosti, Ugrozhaiut Rossii," January 10.
3. Official Kremlin International News Broadcast. 1994. Address by Boris Yeltsin, December 27.
4. Shevelev, Mikhail. 2004. "Rossiia Posle Beslana." *Moskovskie Novosti*, September 10.
5. Gartenstein-Ross, Daveed. 2006. "The Death of Shamil Basayev." *American Spectator*, July 14.
6. Avetisian, E. 2004. "Ritorika i Pravda o Terrorizme." *Respublika Armeniia*, November 12.
7. Shabanov, Pavel. 2006. "Shamil', Smert' No 6," *Russkii Sever*, July 19.
8. *Kavkazskii Uzel*. 2002. "Basayev Shamil Salmanovich (Abdallah Shamil Abu Idris)," November 14. http://www.kavkaz-uzel.ru/articles/32520/.
9. Chivers, C.J. 2004. "The Chechen's Story: From Unrivaled Guerilla Leader to the Terror of Russia." *New York Times*, September 15.

10. Chivers, C.J. 2004. "The Chechen's Story: From Unrivaled Guerilla Leader to the Terror of Russia." *New York Times*, September 15.
11. *Chechenews*. 2011. "Shamil Basayev Prizyvaet Vozrodit' Sufizm," March 23. Video. http://chechenews.com/developments/2739-1.html.
12. *BBC Monitoring Trans Caucasus Unit*. 2006. "Late Chechen Rebel Commander Basayev Defiant in Final Interview," July 20.
13. Lychkovskaia, Olga. 1998. "Basayev Gotov k Vtorzheniiu." *Bizness&Baltiia*, August 26.
14. Whittell, Giles. 1999. "Blast Raises Fear of a 'Holy War.'" *The Times*, September 3.
15. *Kavkaz Center*. 2005. "No-one Can Prevent Me from Doing what God Permits Me to Do," March 24. http://www.kavkazcenter.com/eng/content/2005/03/24/3640.shtml.
16. Basayev was delisted from the U.S. Department of State list on November 1, 2011.
17. For more on the course of the first Chechen war, see Lieven, Anatol. 1998. *Chechnya: Tombstone of Russian Power*. New Haven and London: Yale University Press; Gall, Carlotta, and Thomas de Waal. 1998. *Chechnya: Calamity in the Caucasus*. New York: New York University Press; Orlov, O.P., and A.V. Cherkasov, eds. 2010. *Rossiia-Chechnya: Tsep' Oshibok i Prestuplenii 1994–1996*. Moscow: Prava Cheloveka; Abubakarov, Taimaz. 1998. *Rezhim Dzhokhara Dudaeva: Pravda i Vymysel*. Moscow: INSAN; Evangelista, Matthew. 2002. *The Chechen Wars: Will Russia Go the Way of the Soviet Union?* Washington, D.C.: Brookings Institution Press; Akhmadov, Ilyas, and Miriam Lanskoy. 2010. *The Chechen Struggle: Independence Won and Lost*. New York: Palgrave Macmillan.
18. Mikhailov, Anatoly. 1995. "Posle Moratoriia na Iuge i Iugo-Zapade Chechni Snova Aktivizirovalis' Boevye Deistviia." *Krasnaia Zvezda*, May 16.
19. *BBC Summary of World Broadcasts*. 1995. "Dudayev Threatens to Bomb Moscow," January 16.
20. Baturin, Yuri. 1995. "Moskva-Grozny: Nuzhny Kompromissy." *Izvestiia*, June 24.
21. *BBC Summary of World Broadcasts*. 1995. "Chechens Plan to Force Russian Troops out by Guerilla War," May 10.
22. Kudriavtsev, A. 2003. "Politika, Ekonomika. Arabskie 'Afgantsy.'" *Aziia i Afrika Segodnia*, 10: 37-42.
23. Vasil'ev, Sergei. 1995. "Prostye Boeviki Daiut Otpor 'Neprimirimym.'" *Nezavisimaia Gazeta*, December 30.
24. For more on the Budennovsk terrorist attack, see Gorlov, A.G., ed. 1995. *Budennovsk: Sem' Dnei Ada*. Moscow: Kodeks.
25. *BBC Summary of World Broadcasts*. 1995. "Basayev Says No Reason Not to Trust Chernomyrdin," June 20.
26. *Kavkazskii Uzel*. 2002. "Basayev Shamil Salmanovich (Abdallah Shamil Abu Idris)," November 14. http://www.kavkaz-uzel.ru/articles/32520/.
27. See Orlov, O.P. and A.V. Cherkasov, eds. 2010. *Rossiia-Chechnya: Tsep' Oshibok i Prestuplenii 1994–1996*. Moscow: Prava Cheloveka.
28. Gritchin, Nikolai. 1995. "Banditam net Proshcheniia, no net Proshcheniia i Tem, Kto Podstavil pod Puli Mirnykh Zhitelei." *Izvestiia*, June 17.
29. Although other accounts of the Budennovsk events point out that Basayev's target was the airport in Mineralnye Vody.
30. *BBC Summary of World Broadcasts*. 1995. "Hostage Crisis in Budennovsk," June 17.

31. Hockstader, Lee. 1995. "Gunmen Hold 500 Hostages in Russian Town." *Washington Post*, June 16.
32. A type of a popular car produced by Russian VAZ automobile manufacturer.
33. *Gazeta*. 2005. "Spetsial'nyi Reportazh. Gorod-Geroi Budennovsk," June 14.
34. *Evening Standard*. 1995. "Chechens Holding 5,000 Hostages," June 16.
35. *Gazeta*. 2005. "Spetsial'nyi Reportazh. Gorod-Geroi Budennovsk," June 14.
36. Gornostaev, Dmitrii. 2000. "Voshel li Lider RF v Mirovuiu Istoriiu?" *Nezavisimaia Gazeta*, January 6.
37. *Rossiiskaia Gazeta*. 1995. "Zalozhniki Osvobozhdeny," June 20.
38. Gritchin, Nikolai. 1995. "Budennovsk Dva Mesiatsa Spustia." *Izvestiia*, August 22.
39. *Kommersant Daily*. 1998. "Khronika Odnogo Shturma," June 16.
40. *Kommersant Daily*. 1998. "Khronika Odnogo Shturma," June 16.
41. *Gazeta*. 2005. "Spetsial'nyi Reportazh. Gorod-Geroi Budennovsk," June 14.
42. York, Geoffrey. 1995. "Chechens Free Russian Hostages." *Globe and Mail*, June 20.
43. Rybakov, Yulii. 2009. "Budennovskii Krug," *Ogonek* 4, June 8.
44. Rybakov, Yulii. 2009. "Budennovskii Krug," *Ogonek* 4, June 8.
45. Rybakov, Yulii. 2009. "Budennovskii Krug," *Ogonek* 4, June 8.
46. Vandenko, Andrei. 2005. "V Rossii. Odnazhdy v Budennovske." *Itogi*, June 14.
47. *BBC Summary of World Broadcasts*. 1995. "Basayev Says No Reason Not to Trust Chernomyrdin," June 20.
48. Official Kremlin International News Broadcast. 1995. Speech by President Boris Yeltsin, June 22.
49. Kondrashev, Aleksandr. 2012. "Provaly Verkhov, a Zhertvy Nizov." *Argumenty i Fakty*, June 14.
50. Migdisova, Svetlana, Elena Petrenko, Tatiana Zakharova, Anna Vorontsova, and Dmitry Chubukov. 1995. "Posle Budennovska Rossiiane, Kak i Ranee, Polagaiut, Chto Rukovodstvo Rossii Bolee Otvetstvenno za Sluchivsheesia, Nezheli Chechenskie Lidery." *Fond Obshchestvennoe Mnenie*, June 30. http://bd.fom.ru/report/map/of19952503.
51. Migdisova, Svetlana, Elena Petrenko, Tatiana Zakharova, Anna Vorontsova, and Dmitry Chubukov. 1995. "V Techenie Trekh Nedel' Sentiabria Rossiiane Doveriali Viktoru Chernomyrdinu Chashche, Chem Borisu Yeltsinu." *Fond Obshchestvennoe Mnenie*, September 29. http://bd.fom.ru/report/cat/eltzin_/rating_eltsin/of19959902.
52. Migdisova, Svetlana, and Elena Petrenko. 1994. "Rossiiane Vozrazhaiut Protiv Uderzhivaniia Chechni s Pomoshchiu Sily." *Fond Obshchestvennoe Mnenie*, December 23. http://bd.fom.ru/report/map/of19943901.
53. Migdisova, Svetlana, Elena Petrenko, Tatiana Zakharova, Anna Vorontsova, and Dmitry Chubukov. 1995. "Tri Chetverti Respondentov Odobriaiut Nachalo Mirnykh Peregovorov Pravitel'stva Rossii s Predstaviteliami Dzhokhara Dudayeva." *Fond Obshchestvennoe Mnenie*, June 30. http://bd.fom.ru/report/map/of19952506.
54. *Deutsche Presse-Agentur*. 1995. "Dudayev Says Chechen Peace Talks Unlikely to Resolve Conflict," July 23.
55. Ianchenkov, Vladimir. 1995. "Chechnya: Mir na Poroge." *Rossiiskaia Gazeta*, August 1.
56. Rotar', Igor. 1995. "Shamil Prodolzhaet Pugat' Moskvu." *Izvestiia*, November 21.
57. *BBC Summary of World Broadcasts*. 1995. "Chechen Commander Basayev Interviewed on Elections, Village Bombing and OSCE," October 17.
58. *BBC Summary of World Broadcasts*. 1995. "Chechen Leader Basayev's Threat to Turn Moscow into 'Desert,'" October 23.

59. National Consortium for the Study of Terrorism and Responses to Terrorism (START). 2013. Global Terrorism Database. http://www.start.umd.edu/gtd/.
60. Pita, Rene, and Rohan Gunaratna. 2009. "Revisiting Al-Qa'ida's Anthrax Program." *CTC Sentinel* 2, no. 5: 10–14.
61. The 9/11 Commission Report, 380. http://www.9-11commission.gov/report/911Report.pdf.
62. *CNN World*. 2013. "Osama bin Laden Fast Facts," December 24. http://www.cnn.com/2013/08/30/world/osama-bin-laden-fast-facts/.
63. Stone, John. 2009. "Al Qaeda, Deterrence, and Weapons of Mass Destruction." *Studies in Conflict and Terrorism* 32, no. 9: 763–775.
64. Kalinina, Iuliia. 1999. "V Iadernoi Lovushke." *Moskovskii Komsomolets*, January 13.
65. *BBC Summary of World Broadcasts*. 1995. "Chechen Commander Basayev Warns Radioactive Packages Planted in Russia Ready to Explode," November 24.
66. Kalinina, Iuliia. 1999. "V Iadernoi Lovushke." *Moskovskii Komsomolets*, January 13.
67. Masiuk, Elena. 2012. "Glavnyi Vrag." *New Times*, June 25.
68. *Krasnaia Zvezda*. 1995. "Iz MChS RF. Basayev Nachal Seiat' v Moskve Radiatsiiu," November 25.
69. Specter, Michael. 1995. "Russians Assert Radioactive Box Found in Park Posed No Danger." *New York Times*, November 25.
70. Kondrashev, Aleksandr. 1996. "Podrobnosti Afer s Radioaktivnymi Materialami." *Argumenty i Fakty*, April 17.
71. Ruban, Olga. 2000. "Iadernyi Pogreb Chechni." *Moskovskii Komsomolets*, March 16.
72. Skosyrev, Vladimir. 1996. "Propazha Iadernykh Otkhodov v Chechne." *Izvestiia*, November 12.
73. Bogdanov, Vladimir. 2003. "V Londone Vziali Sled Ritsina." *Rossiiskaia Gazeta*, January 10.
74. Mikhailov, Anatoly. 1995. "Chechnya: Boeviki Stremiatsia Sorvat' Vybory." *Krasnaia Zvezda*, December 15.
75. Rotar', Igor. 1995. "Chechnya: Vybory Zakonchilis', Voina Nachinaetsia." *Izvestiia*, December 19.
76. For a detailed chronology of the Kizlyar/Pervomaiskoe raid, see Belenkin, Boris, and Aleksandr Cherkasov, eds. 1996. *Khronika Zadymleniia*. Moscow: Memorial. Also see Gorlov, A.G. 1996. *Kizlyar-Pervomaiskoe: Operatsiia bez Analogov*. Moscow: Kodeks.
77. Meek, James, and David Hearst. 1996. "Nobody Gets out Alive." *Guardian*, January 10.
78. *Krasnaia Zvezda*. 1996. "'Volki' Po-prezhnemu Smotriat v Les...," January 11.
79. Ward, Olivia. 1996. "Chechens Seize 2,000, 23 Dead as Rebels Demand Russia Pull out Troops." *Toronto Star*, January 10.
80. Meek, James, and David Hearst. 1996. "Nobody Gets out Alive." *Guardian*, January 10.
81. Dement'eva, Irina. 1996. "Desiat' Dnei Boli, Bessiliia i Pozora." *Izvestiia*, January 19.
82. Holliday, Richard. 1996. "Terror aboard Hostage Ferry." *Evening Standard*, January 17.
83. *Deutsche Presse-Agentur*. 1996. "Pro-Chechen Captors of Turkish Ferry Say Hostages Being Released," January 19.

84. *BBC Summary of World Broadcasts*. 1996. "Ferry Hijacker Agrees to Meet Reporters, End Operation in Istanbul," January 19.
85. Couturier, Kelly. 1996. "Pro-Chechen Hijackers Surrender on Ferry." *Washington Post*, January 20.
86. *St. Petersburg Times*. 1996. "Russia Abandons Hostages, Blasts Village," January 18.
87. Raduyev later became one of the few Chechen leaders captured by the Russian services. In 2001 Raduyev was sentenced for life for his terrorist activities against Russia.
88. Quoted in Belenkin, Boris, and Aleksandr Cherkasov, eds. 1996. *Khronika Zadymleniia*. Moscow: Memorial. http://www.memo.ru/hr/hotpoints/chechen/submar/.
89. *Kavkazskii Uzel*. 2013. "Terakt v Kizlyare i Pervomaiskom 9-18 Ianvaria 1996 Goda," January 18. http://www.kavkaz-uzel.ru/articles/218853/.
90. Kononenko, Vasilii. 1996. "Po Stsenariiu 'Strannykh' Boev v Gudermese." *Izvestiia*, January 10.
91. *BBC Summary of World Broadcasts*. 1996. "Chechen Commander Basayev Threatens to Bring 'Mass Terror' to Russia," January 26.
92. Iakov, Valery. 1996. "Prikaz Dudayev: 'Pogibnut' Dolzhno Bol'she Zhenshchin, Chem Muzhchin." *Izvestiia*, January 13.
93. Kuznets, Dmitry. 1996. "Chechnya's 'Lone Wolf' Vows to Fight On." *Guardian*, January 23.
94. Kuznets, Dmitry. 1996. "Chechnya's 'Lone Wolf' Vows to Fight On." *Guardian*, January 23.
95. Petrova, Anna, and Anna Vorontsova. 1996. Kazhdyi Tretii Schitaet Deistviia Chernomyrdina vo Vremia Sobytii v Budennovske Bolee Pravil'nymi, Nezheli Pozitsiiu Yeltsina vo Vremia Sobytii v Pervomaiskom. *Fond Obshchestvennoe Mnenie*, February 9. http://bd.fom.ru/report/map/of19960505.
96. Petrova, Anna, and Anna Vorontsova. 1996. "Esli by Vybory Prezidenta Sostoialis' Segodnia, to Pochti Piataia Chast' Rossiian Progolosovala by za Gennadiia Ziuganova." *Fond Obshchestvennoe Mnenie*, February 2. http://bd.fom.ru/report/map/of19960401.
97. *BBC Summary of World Broadcasts*. 1996. "Rebel Commander Basayev Demands Withdrawal of Russian Troops for Talks to Begin," April 14.
98. Official Kremlin International News Broadcast. 1996. Speech by Boris Yeltsin, February 15.
99. Baranets, Viktor. 2011. "Chechenskii Osvedomitel' Prodal Dudaeva za $1 Million." *Komsomol'skaia Pravda*, April 20.
100. *BBC Summary of World Broadcasts*. 1996. "Pro-Moscow Chechen Leader Says Rebel Side Has Ceased to Exist," April 30.
101. *Rossiiskaia Gazeta*. 1996. "Boris Yeltsin v Chechne," May 29.
102. Official Kremlin International News Broadcast. 1996. Speech by President Boris Yeltsin, May 31.
103. Kolesnikov, Andrei. 1996. "Prezidentskie Vybory-1996: Otsenki Desiat' Let Spustia." *RIA Novosti*, June 19. http://ria.ru/analytics/20060619/49733876.html.
104. *BBC Summary of World Broadcasts*. 1996. "Presidential Elections," June 17.
105. *BBC Summary of World Broadcasts*. 1996. "Election Results," June 20.
106. *BBC Summary of World Broadcasts*. 1996. "OSCE Body Says Elections in Chechnya 'Neither Free nor Fair,'" June 18.
107. *Izvestiia*. 1996. "Terakt v Moskovskom Metro Schitaiiut Politicheskim," June 13.
108. *Izvestiia*. 1996. "Terakt v Moskovskom Metro Schitaiiut Politicheskim," June 13.

109. *Kommersant.* 1996. "Zashchitnik Bamuta Obviniaetsa v Terrorizme," July 11, 1996. http://www.kommersant.ru/doc/236142.
110. Korchagina, Valeria. 1996. "Trolley Blast Called Act of Terrorism." *Moscow Times*, July 12.
111. Punanov, Grigorii, Yuri Senatorov, and Aleksandr Chuikov. 1996. "Vzryvy v Moskve i Nal'chike Organizovany Odnim Terroristom." *Izvestiia*, August 1.
112. *BBC Summary of World Broadcasts.* 1996. "Chechen Rebel Spokesman Blames Russia for Rebel Commander's Backing of Terrorism," July 26.
113. Dement'eva, Irina. 1996. "Desiat' Dnei Boli, Bessiliia i Pozora." *Izvestiia*, January 19.
114. *Izvestiia.* 1994. "Narod i Voina," December 23.
115. Nadein, Vladimir. 1995. "Lidery Mira Nastavliaiut Yeltsina, no i Sochuvstvuiut Emu." *Izvestiia*, June 20.
116. *The Australian.* 1996. "Chechen Hostage Drama Bursts Its Borders," January 18.
117. *Krasnaia Zvezda.* 1996. "SShA Osuzhdaiut Terakty Chechenskikh Boevikov," January 19.

CHAPTER 3

1. *Kommersant.* 2001. "Doku Zavgayev Vidit v Chechne Tol'ko Khoroshee," February 23. http://www.kommersant.ru/doc/169369.
2. *Kommersant Daily.* 2005. "Maskhadov Aslan Alievich," March 9.
3. Eismont, Maria. 1997. "Aslan Maskhadov ne Ostavil Shansov Sopernikam." *Segodnia*, January 29.
4. *Rossiiskaia Gazeta.* 1997. "Maskhadov Poklialsia v Vernosti Narodu ...," February 13.
5. *Rossiiskaia Gazeta.* 1997. "Podpisan Mirnyi Dogovor s Chechnei," May 13.
6. Pulina, Nataliia. 1997. "Maskhadov i v SShA Borolsia za Nezavisimost'." *Nezavisimaia Gazeta*, November 26.
7. Barban, Efim. 1998. "Maskhadov Postavil na Tetcher." *Moskovske Novosti*, March 17.
8. Charodeev, Gennady. 1998. "Grozny Sobiraetsia Podat' Zaiavku dlia Vstupleniia v OON." *Izvestiia*, July 1.
9. The only other country to recognize the independence of Chechnya since 1991 and before the 2000s was Gamsakhurdia's Georgia.
10. Shutova, Tatiana. 1997. "Razviazat' Chechenskii Uzel." *Rossiiskaia Gazeta*, August 19.
11. Chugaev, Sergei. 1997. "Yeltsin Predlagaet Maskhadovu Tatarskii Variant." *Izvestiia*, August 19.
12. Gadaborshev, Osman. 1997. "'Chernoe Zoloto' Voruiut po-Chernomy." *Rossiiskaia Gazeta*, April 11.
13. *Rossiiskaia Gazeta.* 1998. "Iz Dos'e RG: Khronika Pokhishchenii," August 23.
14. *Rossiiskaia Gazeta.* 1999. "Limit Terpeniia Ischerpan – Terrorizm Pora Obuzdat'," March 10.
15. For more on the kidnapping activities, see Tishkov, Valerii. 2004. *Chechnya: Life in a War-Torn Society.* Berkeley: University of California Press.
16. *SPB Vedomosti.* 1999. "A. Maskhadov Navodit Poriadok v Silovykh Strukturakh," March 19.
17. *Vremia.* 1998. "Aslan Maskhadov Otpravil Pravitel'stvo v Otstavku," October 2.

18. For more on Islam in the North Caucasus, see Zelkina, Anna. 2000. *In Quest for God and Freedom: Sufi Responses to the Russian Advance in the North Caucasus*. New York: New York University Press; Malashenko, Aleksei. 2001. *Islamskie Orientiry Severnogo Kavkaza*. Moscow: Gendalf; Yemelianova, Galina, ed. 2010. *Radical Islam in the Former Soviet Union*. New York: Routledge.

19. Piotrovskii, B.B., ed. 1988. *Istoriia Narodov Severnogo Kavkaza s Drevneishikh Vremen do Kontsa XVIII v.* Moscow: Nauka.

20. Koval'skaia, Galina. 1997. "Chechnya." *Itogi*, January 21.

21. Magomeddadaev, Amirkhan. 2005. "Musul'manskii Vostok i Usilenie Radikalizatsii Islama na Severnom Kavkaze." *Tsentral'naia Aziia i Kavkaz*, 1: 48-57.

22. Malashenko, Aleksei. 2001. *Islamskie Orientiry Severnogo Kavkaza*. Moscow: Gendalf.

23. Crisis Group. 2012. *The North Caucasus: The Challenges of Integration (I), Ethnicity and Conflict*. Europe Report 220, October 19, 4.

24. Malashenko, Aleksei. 2001. *Islamskie Orientiry Severnogo Kavkaza*. Moscow: Gendalf.

25. *Izvestiia*. 1998. "Kavkaz vse Bol'she Tleet Dzhikhadom," April 21.

26. See Sagramoso, Domitilla, and Galina Yemelianova. 2010. "Islam and Ethno-Nationalism in the North-Western Caucasus." In Yemelianova, Galina, ed. *Radical Islam in the Former Soviet Union*. New York: Routledge, 112–146.

27. Tlisova, Fatima. 2011. "Odnosel'chane Magomeda Evloeva ne Uvideli ego na Video s Doku Umarovym." *Golos Ameriki*, February 9. http://www.golos-ameriki.ru/content/evloev-familial-village-2011-02-09-115667449/203188.html.

28. *Ekho Moskvy*. 2008. "Kavkazskii Uzel," December 9. http://echo.msk.ru/programs/sorokina/558374-echo/.

29. Krutikov, Evgeny and Vladimir Pavlenko. 1998. "Ochistiteli Islama Gotovyk Ryvku na Sever." *Segodnia*, July 8.

30. Roschin, Mikhail. 2006. *Islam in the Northern Caucasus: Dagestan*. Washington, DC: Jamestown Foundation.

31. *Kavkazskii Uzel*. 2012. "Kebedov Bagautdin Magomedovich," March 20. http://www.kavkaz-uzel.ru/articles/203107/.

32. Rotar', Igor. 1998. "Nezavisimyi Dagestan Zhiznenno Vazhen dlia Chechni." *Nezavisimaia Gazeta*, February 12.

33. Subsequently in Russia the Muslim Brotherhood was designated in 2003 as a terrorist organization.

34. Al-Suwailem, Samir Saleh. *The Experience of the Arab Ansar in Chechnya, Afghanistan and Tajikistan. Memories of Amir Khattab*.

35. Quoted in Tishkov, Valerii. 2004. *Chechnya: Life in a War-Torn Society*. Berkeley: University of California Press, 173–174.

36. Kamyshev, Dmitrii. 1997. "Musul'mane Chechni i Dagestana Poshli v Politiku." *Segodnia*, July 18.

37. Il'in, N. 1997. "'Islamskaia Natsiia': Novaia Golovnaia Bol' dlia Rossii?" *SPB Vedomosti*, August 30.

38. *Nezavisimaia Gazeta*. 1997. "Islamizatsiia no-Chechenski," November 20.

39. Shutova, Tatiana. 1997. "Razviazat' Chechenskii Uzel." *Rossiiskaia Gazeta*, August 19.

40. Quoted in Tishkov, Valerii. 2004. *Chechnya: Life in a War-Torn Society*. Berkeley: University of California Press, 201.

41. Bagirov, M. 2000. "Chechnskie Modzhakhedy – za Kavkazskuiu Konfederatsiiu." *Zerkalo*, July 14.

42. Dunaev, Sergei. 1998. "Kavkazskie Radikaly Gotovy k Dialogu s Moskvoi." *Nezavisimaia Gazeta*, March 5.
43. Iusin, Maksim. 1998. "Basayev Gotovitsia k Novoi Voine s Rossiei." *Izvestiia*, May 23.
44. Fatullaev, Milrad. 1999. "Chechnya i Dagestan – Edinoe Gosudarstvo." *Nezavisimaia Gazeta*, May 12.
45. Lychkovskaia, Olga. 1998. "Basayev Gotov k Vtorzheniiu." *Bizness&Baltiia*, August 26.
46. Akhmadov, Ilyas, and Nicholas Daniloff. 2013. *Chechnya's Secret Wartime Diplomacy: Aslan Maskhadov and the Quest for a Peaceful Resolution*. New York: Palgrave Macmillan, Kindle Edition, Kindle Locations 2581–2582.
47. Koval'skaia, Galina. 1997. "Chechnya." *Itogi*, January 21.
48. Quoted in Tishkov, Valerii. 2004. *Chechnya: Life in a War-Torn Society*. Berkeley: University of California Press, 169.
49. *Nezavisimaia Gazeta*. 1997. "Aslan Maskhadov ne Somnevaetsia . . .," January 18.
50. Rotar', Igor. 1998. "Nezavisimyi Dagestan Zhiznenno Vazhen dlia Chechni." *Nezavisimaia Gazeta*, February 12.
51. Barban, Efim. 1998. "Maskhadov Postavil na Tetcher." *Moskovske Novosti*, March 17.
52. *Rossiiskaia Gazeta*. 1998. "Snova Gudermes v Ognennom Kol'tse," July 17.
53. Musayev, Ruslan. 1999. "Maskhadov Rivals Forge Islamic Rule." *Moscow Times*, February 10.
54. *Kommersant Daily*. 1998. "Shamil Basayev: Maskhadov – Prestupnik i Dolzhen Uiti," October 10.
55. Maksakov, Il'ia. 1998. "Stabil'nost' v Chechne pod Ugrozoi." *Nezavisimaia Gazeta*, September 29.
56. *Kavkaz Center*. 2011. "20th Anniversary of Independence of CRI. From Ichkeria to Caucasus Emirate," September 6. http://kavkazcenter.com/eng/content/2011/09/06/15148.shtml.
57. See Akhmadov, Ilyas, and Nicholas Daniloff. 2013. *Chechnya's Secret Wartime Diplomacy: Aslan Maskhadov and the Quest for a Peaceful Resolution*. New York: Palgrave Macmillan, Kindle Edition, Kindle Locations 4161–4168.
58. *Kommersant*. 1999. "Aslan Maskhadov: Rossiia uzhe Perebrala vse Sredstva Davleniia na Chechniu," September 21.
59. Afghan Ansar followed the call of Abdullah Azzam to sustain transnational brigades that would defend the interests of Muslims around the world.
60. Shermatova, Sanobar. 1998. "Ia Spokoen, Kogda pod Rukoi Patrony." *Moskovskie Novosti*, April 14.
61. Aiubov, Zamid. 1998. "Za chto Voiuet Polkovnik Khattab?" *Trud*, May 7.
62. Al-Suwailem, Samir Saleh. *The Experience of the Arab Ansar in Chechnya, Afghanistan and Tajikistan. Memories of Amir Khattab.*
63. Al-Suwailem, Samir Saleh. *The Experience of the Arab Ansar in Chechnya, Afghanistan and Tajikistan. Memories of Amir Khattab.*
64. *Kavkaz Center*. 2004. "Report about Ben Laden's Ties to Chechnya: Pack of Lies," November 20. http://kavkazcenter.com/eng/content/2004/11/20/3306.shtml.
65. *Kavkaz Center*. 2005. "No-one can Prevent me from Doing what God Permits Me to Do," March 24. http://www.kavkazcenter.com/eng/content/2005/03/24/3640.shtml.
66. Nalbandian, Zurab. 1999. "Svidetel'stvuet Pressa." *Trud*, September 24.

67. *Radio Free Europe Radio Liberty*. 1999. "Newsline," September 15. http://www.rferl.org/content/article/1141992.html.
68. Krutikov, Evgenii. 2001. "Voz'met li Khattab Grozny?" *Izvestiia*, July 7.
69. Aiubov, Zamid. 1998. "Za chto Voiuet Polkovnik Khattab?" *Trud*, May 7.
70. Al-Suwailem, Samir Saleh. *The Experience of the Arab Ansar in Chechnya, Afghanistan and Tajikistan. Memories of Amir Khattab.*
71. Ponomarev, Aleksei. 2001. "Terroristicheskii Internatsional." *Vesti Nedeli*, October 28. http://vesti7.ru/archive/news?id=254.
72. Malashenko, Aleksei and Dmitrii Trenin. 2002. *Vremia Iuga: Rossiia v Chechne, Chechnya v Rossii.* Moscow: Gendalf, 100.
73. Ianchenkov, Vladimir. 2002. "Spetsoperatsiia. Prishlo Pis'mo Khattabu." *Trud*, April 30.
74. *Svobodnaia Gruziia*. 1999. "Zaiavlenie Khattaba," November 3.
75. *Rossiiskaia Gazeta*. 1995. "Variant Byl Odin – Silovoe Davlenie," January 6.
76. Moore, Cerwyn. 2007. "The Radicalisation of the Chechen Separatist Movement: Myth or Reality?" *Prague Watchdog*, May 16. http://www.watchdog.cz/index.php?lang=1&show=000000-000004-000001-000203.
77. Akopov, Petr. 2001. "Sergei Iastrzhembskii: Naemnikov v Chechne Ochen' Malo." *Izvestiia*, October 11.
78. Shermatova, Sanobar. 1999. "Tak Nazyvaemye Vakhkhabity." *Chechnya i Rossiia: Obshchestva i Gosudarstva* 3. http://old.sakharov-center.ru/chr/chrus20_1.htm.
79. Quoted in Moore, Cerwyn, and Paul Tumelty. 2008. "Foreign Fighters and the Case of Chechnya: A Critical Assessment." *Studies in Conflict and Terrorism* 31, 423.
80. Chivers, C. J., and Steven Lee Myers. 2004. "Chechen Rebels Mainly Driven by Nationalism." *New York Times*, September 12.
81. See Khanbabaev, Kaflan. 2010. "Islam and Islamic Radicalism in Dagestan." In Yemelianova, Galina, ed. *Radical Islam in the Former Soviet Union*. New York: Routledge, 82-111; Malashenko, Aleksei, and Dmitrii Trenin. 2002. *Vremia Iuga: Rossiia v Chechne, Chechnya v Rossii.* Moscow: Gendalf.
82. Wilhelmsen, Julie. 2005. "Between a Rock and a Hard Place: The Islamisation of the Chechen Separatist Movement." *Europe-Asia Studies* 57, no. 1: 35–59.
83. *Jamestown Foundation*. 2000. "While FSB Claims Saudi-Based Islamists and Chechens," May 22. http://www.jamestown.org/single/?tx_ttnews[tt_news]=21990&tx_ttnews[backPid]=214&no_cache=1#.U6STibEtqZQ.
84. Magomeddadaev, Amirkhan. 2005. "Musul'manskii Vostok i Usilenie Radikalizatsii Islama na Severnom Kavkaze." *Tsentral'naia Aziia i Kavkaz*, 1: 48–57.
85. Chivers, C. J., and Steven Lee Myers. 2004. "Chechen Rebels Mainly Driven by Nationalism." *New York Times*, September 12.
86. *Rossiiskaia Gazeta*. 1997. "A Vot Khattab Gotovit Terroristov," January 25.
87. Shakur, A. 2010. " 'Ubiistvo po Oshibke' ili Splanirovannaia Aktsiia?" *Ekho*, November 27.
88. Riabushev, Aleksandr. 1997. "Vzryv v Armavire." *Rossiiskie Vesti*, April 25.
89. Bel'diugina, Liudmila. 1997. "Ekho Vzryva v Piatigorske." *Rossiiskaia Gazeta*, April 40.
90. Tasuyev, Alkha. 1998. "Search Goes on for Abducted Yeltsin Envoy." *Philadelphia Inquirer*, May 3.
91. Orlov, O. P., and A. V. Cherkasov, eds. 2010. *Rossiia-Chechnya: Tsep' Oshibok i Prestuplenii 1994–1996.* Moscow: Prava Cheloveka, 91.

92. Gorbanev, Dmitry, and Oleg Vladykin. 1997. "Kordon, Prozrachnyi dlia Banditov." *Obshchaia Gazeta*, December 25.

93. Shermatova, Sanobar. 1999. "Tak Nazyvaemye Vakhkhabity." *Chechnya i Rossiia: Obshchestva i Gosudarstva* 3. http://old.sakharov-center.ru/chr/chrus20_1.htm.

94. Denisov, Vitalii. 1998. "Vakhkhabity Spustili Flagi." *Krasnaia Zvezda*, August 21.

95. Igorev, Aleksandr. 1998. "Stepashin Poobeshchal ne Trogat' Vakhkhabitov." *Kommersant Daily*, September 4.

96. *Kavkaz Center*. 2011. "20th Anniversary of Independence of CRI. From Ichkeria to Caucasus Emirate," September 6. http://kavkazcenter.com/eng/content/2011/09/06/15148.shtml.

97. On the reasons for the Dagestani operation, see Malashenko, Aleksei. 2001. *Islamskie Orientiry Severnogo Kavkaza*. Moscow: Gendalf; Akaev, Vahit. 2010. "Islam and Politics in Chechniia and Ingushetiia." In Yemelianova, Galina, ed. *Radical Islam in the Former Soviet Union*. New York: Routledge, 62–81.

98. Al-Suwailem, Samir Saleh. *The Experience of the Arab Ansar in Chechnya, Afghanistan and Tajikistan. Memories of Amir Khattab*.

99. Taramov, Mairbek. 2006. "Pravda i Lozh' o Pokhode Basaeva v Dagestan." *Kavkaz Center*, January 3. http://kavkazcenter.com/russ/content/2006/01/03/40742.shtml.

100. *SPB Vedomosti*. 1999. "Dagestan: Kogda ne Ostavliaiut Vybora," August 27.

101. Ukolov, Roman, and Grigorii Sanin. 1999. "Dagestan – Moskva. Dalee Vezde . . ." *Segodnia*, September 1.

102. Rafaenko, Aleksei. 1999. "Moskva Zakhlebnetsia v Krovi?!" *Moskovskaia Pravda*, September 2.

103. Skakunov, Il'ia. 1999. "Khasbulat Vzial na Sebia 'Okhotny Riad.'" *Segodnia*, September 3.

104. *BBC News*. 1999. "Russian Media Mystified by Moscow Mall Blast," September 1. http://news.bbc.co.uk/2/hi/world/monitoring/435411.stm.

105. *Washington Post*. 1999. "World in Brief," September 17.

106. *Kommersant Daily*. 1999. "Vtoroi Front," September 7.

107. *Moskovskii Komsomolets*. 1999. "'Chernaia Metka' Khattaba," September 10.

108. Novosel'skaia, Anna, Nikitina Svetlana, and Maria Bronzova. 1999. "Vzryv Zhilogo Doma v Moskve Polozhil Konets Spokoistviiu v Stolitse." *Nezavisimaia Gazeta*, September 10.

109. Zainetdinov, Vladimir. 1999. "Terroristy Brosili Rossii Novyi Zloveshchii Vyzov." *Rossiiskaia Gazeta*, September 14.

110. Romanov, Vitalii, and Arkadii Iuzhnyi. 1999. "Kak vy Sebia Chuvstvuete Pered Smert'iu?" *Segodnia*, September 17.

111. Romanov, Vitalii, and Arkadii Iuzhnyi. 1999. "Kak vy Sebia Chuvstvuete Pered Smert'iu?" *Segodnia*, September 17.

112. *Rossiiskaia Gazeta*. 1999. "'Vikhr" Idet po Vsei Strane," September 17.

113. Kertman, G. L. 2000. "Vzryvy Zhilykh Domov: 'Moskovskii Sled?'" *Fond Obshchestvennoe Mnenie*, February 16. http://bd.fom.ru/report/map/o000601.

114. Official Kremlin International News Broadcast. 1999. Remarks by Vladimir Putin, September 14.

115. Official Kremlin International News Broadcast. 1999. Remarks by Vladimir Putin, September 14.

116. Official Kremlin International News Broadcast. 1999. Remarks by Vladimir Putin, September 14.

117. York, Geoffrey. 1999. "Guerilla Chief Links Explosions." *Globe and Mail*, September 17.
118. Wines, Michael. 1999. "Russian Denies Plan for War or Surrender in Chechnya." *New York Times*, September 20.
119. *Kavkaz Center*. 2005. "No-one Can Prevent me from Doing what God Permits Me to Do," March 24. http://www.kavkazcenter.com/eng/content/2005/03/24/3640.shtml.
120. Phillips, Hugh. 1999. "Russian Alternative in Chechnya." *Washington Post*, December 21.
121. *Nezavisimaia Gazeta*. 1999. "Khattab Otritsaet Prichasnost' k Teraktam v Moskve," September 14.
122. Stomakhin, Boris. 2002. "Putin's List." *Kavkaz Center*, April 1. http://www.kavkazcenter.com/eng/content/2002/04/01/425.shtml.
123. Voloshin, Pavel. 2000. "Chto Bylo v Ryazani: Sakhar ili Geksogen?" *Novaia Gazeta*, February 14.
124. Politkovskaya, Anna. 2005. "Nazranskii 'Sakhar.' " *Novaia Gazeta*, September 26.
125. *Levada Center*. 2002. Press-Vypusk 9, April 16. http://www.levada.ru/press/2002041600.html.
126. *Novye Izvestiia*. 2002. "Obshchestvennaia Komissiia Obsudila Osnovnye Versii Vzryvov Domov v Moskve i Volgodonske," May 29.
127. Mekhtikhanov, Albert and Gadzhimurad Radzhabov. 2005. "Za Vzryv Domov v Buinakske Nachali Sudit' Poslednego Obviniaemogo." *Izvestiia*, September 16.
128. Gomzikova, Svetlana. 2005. "Kto Vse Eto Organizoval." *Nezavisimaia Gazeta*, September 30.
129. *Pervyi Kanal*. 2004. "Na Vzryvy Zhilykh Domov Terroristam Bylo Vydeleno 2 mln. Dollarov," January 12. http://www.1tv.ru/news/other/94869.
130. Punanov, Grigorii. 2002. "Vakhkhabitskoe Podpol'e." *Izvestiia*, May 14.
131. *Federal Security Service of the Russian Federation*. 2002. "O Rezul'tatakh Rassledovaniia Riada Aktov Terrorizma," March 14. http://www.fsb.ru/fsb/press/message/single.htm!id%3D10407754@fsbMessage.html.
132. State Duma of the Russian Federation. 1999. O Situatsii v Respublike Dagestan v Sviazi s Vtorzheniem na Territoriiu Respubliki Dagestan Nezakonnykh Vooruzhennykh Formirovanii i Merakh po Obespecheniiu Bezopasnosti Respubliki Dagestan. Decree 4277-II, August 16.
133. Official Kremlin International News Broadcast. 1999. Interview with acting prime minister of the Russian Federation Vladimir Putin, August 16.
134. *Rossiiskaia Gazeta*. 1999. "Ne Otdadim Terroristam ni Piadi Nashei Zemli," December 7.
135. Iamshanov, Boris. 1999. "V Granitsakh Rossii Voiny Byt' ne Dolzhno." *Rossiiskaia Gazeta*, September 16.
136. Official Kremlin International News Broadcast. 1999. Remarks by Vladimir Putin, September 14.
137. *RIA Novosti*. 2009. "Kontrterroristicheskaiia Operatsiia v Chechne 1999-2009 gg. Spravka," March 26. http://ria.ru/defense_safety/20090326/166106234.html.
138. *Kommersant*. 1999. "Aslan Maskhadov: Rossiia uzhe Perebrala vse Sredstva Davleniia na Chechniu," September 21.
139. Vlasova, Olga. 1999. "Maskhadova Nikto ne Slyshit." *Bizness&Baltiia*, September 28.

140. Selezneva, Anna. 1999. "Khasavyurt Byl Oshibkoi." *Rossiiskaia Gazeta*, September 18.
141. *Izvestiia*. 1994. "Narod i Voina: Bol'shinstvo Protiv," December 23.
142. Vyzhutovich, Valerii. 1999. "Bombit', Vydvoriat', Arestovyvat'!" *Izvestiia*, September 28.
143. Official Kremlin International News Broadcast. 1999. Remarks by Vladimir Putin, September 14.
144. Russian Federation Federal Law 130. 1998. On the Fight against Terrorism, July 25, Article 3.
145. Russian Federation Federal Law 130. 1998. On the Fight against Terrorism, July 25, Article 11.
146. Due to the secrecy of the decree, the constitutionality of the counterterrorist operation was later questioned. In February 2002 Duma deputy Sergei Yushenkov started an initiative for the review of the decree by the Constitutional Court. The initiative was not supported by enough votes in the Duma.
147. *Rossiiskaia Gazeta*. 1999. "Za Chto Voiuet v Chechne Rossiiskii Soldat?" December 1.
148. *Rossiiskaia Gazeta*. 1999. "Obrashchenie Upolnomochennogo po Pravam Cheloveka v Rossiiskoi Federatsii O. Mironova," September 27.

CHAPTER 4

1. For more on the second Chechen campaign, see Schaefer, Robert. 2010. *Insurgency in Chechnya and the North Caucasus: From Gazavat to Jihad*. Santa Barbara: ABC-CLIO.
2. Wines, Michael. 1999. "Why Putin Boils Over." *New York Times*, November 13.
3. Berres, Leonid, and Yuri Safronov. 1999. "Potomu Chto Tak Obeshchal Sam Putin." *Kommersant*, October 1. http://www.kommersant.ru/doc/226604.
4. Berres, Leonid, and Yuri Safronov. 1999. "Potomu Chto Tak Obeshchal Sam Putin." *Kommersant*, October 1. http://www.kommersant.ru/doc/226604.
5. Wines, Michael. 1999. "Russian Denies Plan for War or Surrender in Chechnya." *New York Times*, September 20.
6. Belianchev, Aleksei, Aleksandr Chuikov, Mikhail Kliment'ev, and Dmitry Astakhov. 1999. "Spriatannaia Voina." *Izvestiia*, November 2.
7. WCIOM. 2000. "Putin. Chechnya. Belarus. NATO," February 3. http://wciom.ru/index.php?id=268&uid=498.
8. Egorov, Ivan. 2000. "Pochti Final." *Vremia MN*, March 1.
9. Memorial. 2007. "Praktika Provedeniia 'Kontrterroristicheskoi Operatsii' Rossiiskoi Federatsiei na Severnom Kavkaze v 1999-2006 gg." January 3. http://www.kavkaz-uzel.ru/articles/107436/.
10. See Memorial. 2007. "Praktika Provedeniia 'Kontrterroristicheskoi Operatsii' Rossiiskoi Federatsiei na Severnom Kavkaze v 1999-2006 gg." January 3. http://www.kavkaz-uzel.ru/articles/107436/.
11. Barakhova, Alla. 1999. "Maskhadov Poprosil Mira." *Kommersant Daily*, October 12.
12. Rashidov, Oleg. 2000. "Peregovory. Maskhadov Prosit Mira." *Komsomol'skaia Pravda*, April 22.
13. Official Kremlin International News Broadcast. 2002. Remarks by President Vladimir Putin, November 12.

14. During the first war amnesty was offered as a means of preventing future fighting rather than co-opting fighters to join the federal side.
15. *Pervyi Kanal.* 1999. "Sensatsiei Dnia Stala Vstrecha Vladimira Putina s Deputatami Chechenskogo Parlamenta Sozyva 96-go Goda," October 1. http://www.1tv.ru/news/social/114402.
16. *Pervyi Kanal.* 1999. "Aslan Maskhadov Nazval Muftiia Chechni 'Predatelem Veka,'" November 29. http://www.1tv.ru/news/polit/127283.
17. Kachmazov, Alan. 2000. "V Nagradu za Dzhikhad." *Izvestiia*, July 7.
18. *Ria Novosti.* 2009. "Kontrterroristicheskaia Operatsiia v Chechne 1999-2009 gg. Spravka," March 26. http://ria.ru/defense_safety/20090326/166106234.html.
19. Evtushenko, Aleksandr. 2000. "Aslan Maskhadov Ugrozhaet Diversiiami i Zatiazhnoi Voinoi." *Komsomol'skaia Pravda*, March 18.
20. Maksakov, Il'ia and Abdulla Dargo. 2000. "Maskhadov Ugrozhaet Partizanskoi Voinoi." *Nezavisimaia Gazeta*, February 12.
21. *The Australian.* 1999. "Chechen Rebel Warns Moscow," October 12.
22. Karush, Sarah. 1999. "Troops Mass on Chechen Border." *Moscow Times*, September 21. http://www.themoscowtimes.com/news/article/troops-mass-on-chechen-border/272215.html.
23. Rotar', Igor. 1995. "Chechnya: Po Obe Storony Fronta." *Izvestiia*, November 24.
24. *United Nations Security Council.* 2003. Security Council Committee Pursuant to Resolutions 1267 (1999) and 1989 (2011) Concerning Al-Qaida and Associated Individuals and Entities. QI.Y.106.03. Zelimkhan Akhmedovich Yandarbiev. http://www.un.org/sc/committees/1267/NSQI10603E.shtml.
25. Kramer, Andrew. 2000. "Russia Warns Afghanistan It Might Attack." *Gazette*, May 23.
26. Akhmadov, Ilyas, and Nicholas Daniloff. 2013. *Chechnya's Secret Wartime Diplomacy: Aslan Maskhadov and the Quest for a Peaceful Resolution.* New York: Palgrave Macmillan, Kindle Edition, Kindle Locations 1010-1012.
27. *Radio Free Europe Radio Liberty.* 2000. "Russia: Maskhadov Denies Chechens Training in Afghanistan," May 5. http://www.rferl.org/content/article/1094031.html.
28. *Washington Times.* 2000. "Chechen Guerrillas Are Said to Be Training in Terrorism," May 26.
29. Womack, Helen. 2000. "Russia Threatens Attack on 'Chechen Ally' Afghanistan." *Independent*, May 23.
30. Averbukh, Viktoriia, and Dmitrii Vladimirov. 2001. "Terror bez Ostanovok." *Rossiiskaia Gazeta*, August 1.
31. Diupin, Sergei, and Sergei Topol'. 2001. "Terroristicheskii Khadzh." *Kommersant Daily*, March 16.
32. For more on the North Caucasus suicide terrorism, see Reuter, John. 2004. "Chechnya's Suicide Bombers: Desperate, Devout, or Deceived?" American Committee for Peace in Chechnya; Speckhard, Anne, and Khapta Akhmedova. 2006. "The Making of a Martyr: Chechen Suicide Terrorism." *Studies in Conflict and Terrorism* 29: 429-492; Moore, Cerwyn. 2012. "Suicide Bombing: Chechnya, the North Caucasus and Martyrdom." *Europe-Asia Studies* 69, no. 9: 1780-1807.
33. For more, see Pape, Robert. 2005. *Dying to Win: The Strategic Logic of Suicide Terrorism.* New York: Random House.
34. For women in terrorism, see Cragin, Kim, and Sara A. Daly. 2009. *Women as Terrorists: Mothers, Recruiters, and Martyrs.* Santa Barbara, CA: ABC-CLIO.

35. See Cook, David. 2005. *Understanding Jihad*. Berkeley: University of California Press.
36. The fatwa is available at http://www.pbs.org/newshour/updates/military-july-dec96-fatwa_1996/.
37. Moore, Molly. 2004. "Young Mother Kills 4 at Gaza Crossing." *Washington Post*, January 15.
38. Available at http://www.religioscope.com/pdf/martyrdom.pdf.
39. "The Islamic Ruling on the Permissibility of Martyrdom Operations: Did Hawa Barayev Commit Suicide or achieve Martyrdom?" http://www.religioscope.com/pdf/martyrdom.pdf.
40. Cook, David. 2008. "Women Fighting in Jihad?" In Ness, Cindy D., ed. *Female Terrorism and Militancy: Agency, Utility, and Organization*. New York: Routledge.
41. *Middle East Quarterly*. 2004. "The Qaradawi Fatwas," 9, no. 3: 78-80.
42. *Washington Post*. 2002. "Cleric Lauds Bombings by Women," April 2.
43. Available at http://www.scribd.com/doc/25027242/A-letter.
44. Quoted in Speckhard, Anne, and Khapta Akhmedova. 2006. "The Making of a Martyr: Chechen Suicide Terrorism." *Studies in Conflict and Terrorism* 29, 447.
45. See Sokirianskaia, Ekaterina. 2012. "Ingushetiia i Chechnya: Konets Teipov." *Neprikosnovennyi Zapas*, 4(84).
46. *Kavkaz Center*. 2003. "Address by President Maskhadov to his People," December 14. http://www.kavkazcenter.com/eng/content/2003/12/14/2169.shtml.
47. Ianchenkov, Vladimir. 2003. "Kto Zatiagivaet 'Poiasa Shakhidov.'" *Trud*, July 8.
48. *Kavkaz Center*. 2004. "Blast in Moscow Metro Was Revenge for Aldy?" February 8. http://www.kavkazcenter.com/eng/content/2004/03/01/2470_print.html.
49. Siun, Iurii. 2005. "Rassledovanie." *Kommersant Daily*, June 27.
50. *Kavkazskii Uzel*. 2003. "Shamil Basayev Nachinaet Operatsiiu 'Bumerang,'" May 23. http://www.kavkaz-uzel.ru/articles/38046/.
51. *Kavkaz Center*. 2003. "Abdallakh Shamil' Beret Otvetstvennost' na Sebia," May 19. http://www.kavkazcenter.com/russ/content/2003/05/19/7550.shtml.
52. Gavrilov, Iurii. 2003. "Vzryvoopasnyi Shamil'." *Moskovskii Komsomolets*, December 25.
53. Paukov, Viktor. 2003. "Palestinskii Stsenarii dlia Chechni." *Vremia Novostei*, June 11.
54. Serenko, Andrei. 2000. "Volgogradskie Chekisty Zaderzhali Terroristov." *Nezavisimaia Gazeta*, July 22.
55. Poletaev, Vladimir. 2005. "Po Kartam Zarubezhnykh Spetssluzhb." *Rossiiskaia Gazeta*, November 9.
56. Tan'kova, Iaroslava. 2006. "Pochemu Russkie Stanoviatsia Islamskimi Terroristami." *Komsomol'skaia Pravda*, August 15.
57. Kamakin, Andrei. 2004. "Smertnyi Grekh." *Itogi*, October 5.
58. In the mid-2000s the equivalent of around $3.
59. Tan'kova, Iaroslava. 2006. "Pochemu Russkie Stanoviatsia Islamskimi Terroristami." *Komsomol'skaia Pravda*, August 18.
60. *Kavkazskii Uzel*. 2009. "Tikhomirov Aleksandr," August 27. http://www.kavkaz-uzel.ru/articles/158565/.
61. https://www.youtube.com/watch?v=8w9AFdFcj5I.
62. Russian Federation Federal Law 114. 2002. On Countering Extremist Activity, July 25, Article 1.

63. For example, see the case of Russia's human rights organization Memorial, available at http://www.memo.ru/2006/02/28/prokurat.htm.

64. For more on the role of 9/11 in Russia's war on terror, see Russell, John. 2007. *Chechnya: Russia's "War on Terror."* London: Routledge; O'Loughlin, John, Gearoid O Tuathail, and Vladimir Kolossov. 2004. "A 'Risky Westward Turn'? Putin's 9-11 Script and Ordinary Russians." *Europe-Asia Studies* 56, no. 1: 3–34.

65. Official Kremlin International News Broadcast. 2001. President Vladimir Putin's TV Address, September 25.

66. Official Kremlin International News Broadcast. 2001. President Vladimir Putin's TV Address, September 25.

67. *Rossiiskaia Gazeta*. 1999. "Amerika Osuzhdaet Deistviia Bandformirovanii na Severnom Kavkaze . . .," August 13.

68. *Rossiiskaia Gazeta*. 1999. "Klinton Znaet, kak 'Pravil'no,' Poetomu Perekhodit k Otkrytym Ugrozam," December 8.

69. Bai, Evgenii. 2001. "Kondoliza Rais: Nas Sblizila Ugroza Terrorizma." *Izvestiia*, October 16.

70. Stepanov, Georgii. 2002. "Separatisty, oni zhe Teroristy." *Izvestiia*, November 2.

71. Inozemtsev, Petr. 2004. "Glavnaia Zadacha – Spasti Zhizn' Zalozhnikov." *Izvestiia*, September 3.

72. *The 9/11 Commission Report*. New York: W.W. Norton and Company, 165.

73. Williams, Brian Glyn. 2008. "Allah's Foot Soldiers: An Assessment of the Role of Foreign Fighters and Al-Qa'ida in the Chechen Insurgency." In Gammer, Moshe, ed. *Ethno-Nationalism, Islam and the State in the Caucasus*. New York: Routledge, 169.

74. *United Nations Security Council*. 2003. Security Council Committee Pursuant to Resolutions 1267 (1999) and 1989 (2011) Concerning Al-Qaida and Associated Individuals and Entities. QE.R.100.03. Riyadus-Salikhin Reconnaissance and Sabotage Battalion of Chechen Martyrs (RSRCBCM). http://www.un.org/sc/committees/1267/NSQE10003E.shtml.

75. Akopov, Petr. 2001. "Sergei Iastrzhembskii: Naemnikov v Chechne Ochen' Malo." *Izvestiia*, October 11.

76. List of Individuals Detained by the Department of Defense at Guantanamo Bay, Cuba, from January 2002 through May 15, 2006. http://www.defense.gov/news/may2006/d20060515%20list.pdf.

77. Zhukov, A. D. 2008. *Kabardino-Balkaria: Na Puti k Katastrofe*. Moscow: Memorial.

78. Guseinov, Oleg. 2002. "Kak Stanoviatsia Talibami." *Gazeta Iuga*, December 11.

79. *Kavkazskii Uzel*. 2007. "V Kabardino-Balkarii Ubit Byvshii Uznik Guantanamo Ruslan Odizhev," June 27. http://www.kavkaz-uzel.ru/articles/117354/.

80. *Kavkazskii Uzel*. 2006. "Rasul Kudaev. Doroga v Gvantanamo," December 26. http://www.kavkaz-uzel.ru/articles/106023/.

81. *Vremia i Den'gi*. 2002. "Mama, eto ia, s Guantanamo," November 29.

82. *Gazeta*. 2005. "Airat Vakhitov – Gazete," June 28.

83. Idiatullin, Shamil'. 2002. "Tatarskii Talib Brosil Troikh Detei." *Kommersant Daily*, April 4.

84. *Jane's Islamic Affairs Analyst*. 2003. "A Light at the End of the Mountain Pass?" March 20.

85. According to official sources, all 40 terrorists were eliminated. According to Barayev, he led a group of 54 people. It is not clear which account is more accurate and whether additional terrorists managed to escape from the theater.

86. For more on the theater attack, see Dunlop, John B. 2006. *The 2002 Dubrovka and 2004 Beslan Hostage Crises: A Critique of Russian Counter-Terrorism*. Germany: Ibidem Verlag; *Memorial Pogibshykh v Nord-Oste. Kniga Pamiati*. 2011. Moscow: Nord-Ost; Dolnik, Adam, and Keith Fizgerald. 2008. *Negotiating Hostage Crises with the New Terrorists*. Westport, CT: Praeger.
87. Abdullaev, Nabi. 2002. "Picture Emerges of How They Did It." *Moscow Times*, November 6. http://www.themoscowtimes.com/news/article/picture-emerges-of-how-they-did-it/242322.html.
88. *Izvestiia*. 2002. "Shturm Zavershen, Zalozhniki Osvobozhdeny," October 26.
89. *Izvestiia*. 2002. "Terroristy Otpustili Ostal'nykh Detei, Nakhodivshikhsia v Zale," October 24.
90. *ABC Nightline Transcript*. 2005. "Reign of Terror," July 28.
91. Politkovskaya, Anna. 2006. "Nepravitel'stvennyi Doklad. 'Nord-Ost.' Neokonchennoe Rassledovanie . . ." *Novaia Gazeta*, May 15.
92. Martova, Maria. 2002. "Moment Istiny Akhmada Kadyrova." *Moskovskii Komsomolets*, October 29.
93. Politkovskaya, Anna. 2006. "Nepravitel'stvennyi Doklad. 'Nord-Ost.' Neokonchennoe Rassledovanie . . ." *Novaia Gazeta*, May 15.
94. European Court of Human Rights. 2012. Judgment on the Case of Finogenov and Others vs. Russia. Strasbourg, March 6, 11.
95. Politkovskaya, Anna. 2006. "Nepravitel'stvennyi Doklad. 'Nord-Ost.' Neokonchennoe Rassledovanie . . ." *Novaia Gazeta*, May 15.
96. Dolnik, Adam, and Richard Pilch. 2003. "The Moscow Theater Hostage Crisis: The Perpetrators, their Tactics, and the Russian Response." *International Negotiation* 8: 577–611.
97. European Court of Human Rights. 2012. Judgment on the Case of Finogenov and Others vs. Russia. Strasbourg, March 6, 6.
98. European Court of Human Rights. 2012. Judgment on the Case of Finogenov and Others vs. Russia. Strasbourg, March 6, 23.
99. *RIA Novosti*. 2003. "Dela Zakhvativshykh 'Nord-Ost' Prekrashcheny," June 2.
100. *Izvestiia*. 2002. "Shturm Zavershen, Zalozhniki Osvobozhdeny," October 26.
101. European Court of Human Rights. 2012. Judgment on the Case of Finogenov and Others vs. Russia. Strasbourg, March 6.
102. Allenova, Olga. 2003. "Nordost." *Kommersant Vlast'*, January 27.
103. Litovkin, Viktor. 2002. "Putin Declares War on Terrorism." *Moscow News*, October 30.
104. *Lenta.ru*. 2002. "Maskhadov Prizval Putina Nachat' Peregovory i Nameknul na Novye Zakhvaty Zalozhnikov," October 28. http://lenta.ru/vojna/2002/10/28/maskhadov/.
105. *Levada Center*. 2002. "Moskvichi o Zakhvate Zalozhnikov Nord-Osta," November 1. http://www.levada.ru/01-11-2002/moskvichi-o-zakhvate-zalozhnikov-nord-osta.
106. Fedotkin, Sergei. 2002. "Politicheskaia Sreda." *Rossiiskie Vesti*, November 13.
107. *Novaia Gazeta*. 2002. "Natisk na SMI v ChS," October 31.
108. *Izvestiia*. 2003. "Chto Nel'zia Pokazyvat'," April 21. http://izvestia.ru/news/275808.
109. Allenova, Olga, and Musa Muradov. 2003. "Chechnya. Dva Referenduma." *Kommersant Vlast'*, March 31.
110. Maksakov, Il'ia. 2003. "V Chechne Poiavilsia Apparat Prezidenta." *Izvestiia*, March 28.

111. Kliuev, Anton. 2004. "Basaev Vzial na Sebia Otvetstvennost' za Ubiistvo Kadyrova i Ugrozhaet Putinu," *Izvestiia*, May 18.

112. Sukhov, Ivan, and Aleksandr Shvarev. 2004. "Biudzhetnoe Poslanie Terrorista." *Vremia Novostei*, September 20.

113. *Kavkaz Center*. 2005. "Interview of Shamil Basayev to Channel 4 News," February 4. http://www.kavkazcenter.com/eng/content/2005/02/04/3500.shtml.

114. Sharov, Andrei. 2004. "Basayev Sobiralsia v Moskvu, no Doekhal do Beslana." *Rossiiskaia Gazeta*, September 18.

115. Gridneva, Marina, and Iuliia Kalinina. 2004. "Operatsiia 'Nord-Vest.'" *Moskovskii Komsomolets*, September 18.

116. According to the official reports, 34 terrorists operated in Beslan. According to the surviving hostages, the number of terrorists ranged between 60 and 70.

117. Walsh, Nick, and Zurab Timchenko. 2004. "Exchange Us for Our Children. What Are They Guilty Of?" *Guardian*, September 2.

118. Milashina, Elena. 2005. "God Posle Beslana." *Novaia Gazeta*, September 1.

119. *Kavkaz Center*. 2005. "Interview of Shamil Basayev to Channel 4 News," February 4. http://www.kavkazcenter.com/eng/content/2005/02/04/3500.shtml.

120. *Kavkaz Center*. 2005. "Interview of Shamil Basayev to Channel 4 News," February 4. http://www.kavkazcenter.com/eng/content/2005/02/04/3500.shtml.

121. Gridneva, Marina, and Iuliia Kalinina. 2004. "Operatsiia 'Nord-Vest.'" *Moskovskii Komsomolets*, September 18.

122. *ABC Nightline Transcript*. 2005. "Reign of Terror," July 28.

123. Gridneva, Marina, and Iuliia Kalinina. 2004. "Operatsiia 'Nord-Vest.'" *Moskovskii Komsomolets*, September 18.

124. Milashina, Elena. 2005. "God Posle Beslana." *Novaia Gazeta*, September 1.

125. *Kavkaz Center*. 2005. "Interview of Shamil Basayev to Channel 4 News," February 4. http://www.kavkazcenter.com/eng/content/2005/02/04/3500.shtml.

126. Page, Jeremy. 2004. "Chechen Terror Chief Organized Beslan Atrocity." *Times*, September 18.

127. *Kavkaz Center*. 2005. "Interview of Shamil Basayev to Channel 4 News," February 4. http://www.kavkazcenter.com/eng/content/2005/02/04/3500.shtml.

128. *ABC Nightline Transcript*. 2005. "Reign of Terror," July 28.

129. The report is available at http://www.pravdabeslana.ru/dokladtorshina221206.htm.

130. *Kavkazskii Uzel*. 2012. "Terroristicheskii Akt v Belane," September 1. http://www.kavkaz-uzel.ru/articles/211997/.

131. The report is available at http://www.pravdabeslana.ru/doklad/oglavlenie.htm.

132. Page, Jeremy. 2004. "Chechen Terror Chief Organized Beslan Atrocity." *Times*, September 18.

133. *Gazeta*. 2004. "Nas tam 1020 Chelovek!" September 3.

134. *Kavkazskii Uzel*. 2004. "Rabota Zhurnalistov vo Vremia Terroristicheskogo Akta v Beslane," September 29.

135. *Kavkazskii Uzel*. 2004. "Anna Politkovskaya Otravlena Neizvestnym Toksinom," September 6. http://www.kavkaz-uzel.ru/articles/61215/.

136. *Kavkazskii Uzel*. 2004. "Andrei Babitsky Obviniaet FSB v Provokatsii s Tsel'iu ne Dopustit' ego Vyleta v Beslan," September 6. http://www.kavkaz-uzel.ru/articles/61214/.

137. *Levada Center*. 2004. "Chastichnaia Pravda: Rossiiane ob Osveshchenii Sobytii v Beslane," September 16. http://www.levada.ru/16-09-2004/chastichnaya-pravdarossiyane-ob-osveshchenii-sobytii-v-beslane.

138. *Zerkalo.* 2004. "Reiting Putina Upal do Rekordnogo Urovnia za Poslednie 4 Goda," September 23.
139. Sedov L. 2004. "Obzor Sentiabr'skikh Oprosov." *Levada Center,* October 12. http://www.levada.ru/press/2004101204.html.
140. *Kavkaz Center.* 2005. "Interview of Shamil Basayev to Channel 4 News," February 4. http://www.kavkazcenter.com/eng/content/2005/02/04/3500.shtml.
141. Page, Jeremy. 2004. "Chechen Terror Chief Organized Beslan Atrocity." *Times,* September 18.
142. Gerges, Fawaz A. 2011. *The Rise and Fall of Al-Qaeda.* New York: Oxford University Press, 109.
143. *Kavkaz Center.* 2004. "President Maskhadov on the Events in Beslan," September 18. http://www.kavkazcenter.com/eng/content/2004/09/18/3209.shtml.
144. Gridneva, Marina, and Iuliia Kalinina. 2004. "Operatsiia 'Nord-Vest.' " *Moskovskii Komsomolets,* September 18.
145. *Kavkaz Center.* 2004. "President Maskhadov on the Events in Beslan," September 18. http://www.kavkazcenter.com/eng/content/2004/09/18/3209.shtml.
146. Walsh, Nick, and Zurab Timchenko. 2004. "Exchange Us for Our Children. What Are They Guilty Of?" *Guardian,* September 2.
147. Putin, Vladimir. 2004. Presidential Address, September 4. Moscow: Kremlin.
148. Perekrest, Vladimir. 2004. "Kto Stoit za Teraktom v Beslane." *Izvestiia,* September 4.
149. Official Kremlin International News Broadcast. 2004. Statement by President Vladimir Putin, September 13.
150. Official Kremlin International News Broadcast. 2004. Statement by President Vladimir Putin, September 13.
151. Official Kremlin International News Broadcast. 2004. Statement by President Vladimir Putin, September 13.
152. Soldatov, Andrei, and Irina Borogan. 2006. "Politika Rassledovaniia." *Novaia Gazeta,* January 19.
153. Iashmanov, Boris. 2006. "Antiterror po Pravu." *Rossiiskaia Gazeta,* March 21.
154. Russian Federation Federal Law 35. 2006. On Counteraction of Terrorism, March 6, Article 3.
155. *Izvestiia.* 2006. "Kto i kak Unichtozhil Shamilia Basayeva," July 10. http://izvestia.ru/news/315298.
156. *Izvestiia.* 2006. "Kto i kak Unichtozhil Shamilia Basayeva," July 10. http://izvestia.ru/news/315298.
157. *ABC Nightline Transcript.* 2005. "Reign of Terror," July 28.
158. Derogatory term used by Basayev to call Russia.
159. *Kavkaz Center.* 2005. "No-One Can Prevent Me from Doing what God Permits Me to Do," March 24. http://www.kavkazcenter.com/eng/content/2005/03/24/3640.shtml.
160. *Kavkaz Center.* 2005. "Interview of Shamil Basayev to Channel 4 News," February 4. http://www.kavkazcenter.com/eng/content/2005/02/04/3500.shtml.

CHAPTER 5

1. Official Kremlin International News Broadcast. 1996. An Interview with President Boris Yeltsin, April 30.
2. *Pervyi Kanal.* 2002. "Alikhan Amirkhanov i Murat Ziazikov Lidiruiut na Vyborakh Prezidenta Ingushetii," April 8. http://www.1tv.ru/news/polit/109825.

3. Ataev, Artur, and Milrad Fatullaev. 2002. "Ziazikov Stal-Taki Prezidentom Ingushetii." *Nezavisimaia Gazeta*, April 30.
4. Ataev, Artur, and Milrad Fatullaev. 2002. "Ziazikov Stal-Taki Prezidentom Ingushetii." *Nezavisimaia Gazeta*, April 30.
5. Fatullaev, Milrad. 2007. "Odinochestvo Murata Ziazikova." *Nezavisimaia Gazeta*, September 17.
6. *Kavkazskii Uzel*. 2004. "Ingushetia: Lager' Bezhentsev v Al'tievo Podvergsia 'Zachistke,' " June 24. http://www.kavkaz-uzel.ru/articles/57592/.
7. *Kavkaz Center*. 2004. "Ziazikova Atakovali Shakhidy 'Riyadus Salikh'iin,' " April 12. http://www.kavkazcenter.com/russ/content/2004/04/12/19663_print.html.
8. *Izvestiia*. 2014. "V Ingushetii Boeviki Pytalis' Vykrast' iz Morga Telo Svoego Glavaria," June 9.
9. Isaev, Rashid. 2005. "Korruptsiia – Soiuznik Minnoi Voiny Protiv Rossii i Dagestana." *Severnyi Kavkaz*, September 14.
10. Butrin, Dmitrii. 2011. "Dagestan Sistematiziruet Bor'bu s Korruptsiei." *Kommersant Daily*, April 27.
11. Abdurashidov, Aznaur. 2014. "Umakhan Umakhanov: 'Korruptsiia Iavliaetsia Glavnoi Ugrozoi Bezopasnosti Dagestana." *RIA Dagestan*, February 5.
12. *Kavkazskii Uzel*. 2014. "Polkovnik Politsii Poprosil Putina Rasobrat'sia s Korruptsieiv MVD Dagestana," February 28. http://www.kavkaz-uzel.ru/articles/238843/.
13. *Kavkaz Center*. 2005. "Dzhikhad v Kabardino-Balkarii Budet Prodolzhen," February 2. http://kavkazcenter.com/russ/content/2005/02/02/29800_print.html.
14. See Slider, Darrell. 2008. "Putin's 'Southern Strategy': Dmitriy Kozak and the Dilemmas of Recentralization." *Post-Soviet Affairs* 24, no. 2: 177–197.
15. *Kavkazskii Uzel*. 2004. "Dmitrii Kozak Zaiavil o Protsvetanii Korruptsii v IuFO," December 9. http://www.kavkaz-uzel.ru/articles/66082/.
16. Riskin, Andrei, and Andrei Serenko. 2005. "Dmitriia Kozaka Obvinili po Desiati Punktam." *Nezavisimaia Gazeta*, September 26.
17. See Hahn, Gordon M. 2007. *Russia's Islamic Threat*. New Haven, CT: Yale University Press.
18. Sukhov, Ivan, and Dmitry Starostin. 2002. "Dobrye Sosedi." *Vremia Novostei*, October 10. http://www.vremya.ru/print/27922.html.
19. Raskin, Aleksandr, and Viktor Paukov. 2003. "Terroristov Priniali za Kolkhoznikov." *Vremia Novostei*, September 17. http://www.vremya.ru/print/80203.html.
20. See Vachagaev, Mairbek. 2007. *The Ingush Jamaat: Identity and Resistance in the North Caucasus*. Washington, DC: Jamestown Foundation.
21. *Kavkazskii Uzel*. 2004. "Rebels Attacked Ingushetia with Maskhadov's Permission," July 27. http://eng.kavkaz-uzel.ru/articles/3505/.
22. Vachagaev, Mairbek. 2007. *The Ingush Jamaat: Identity and Resistance in the North Caucasus*. Washington, DC: Jamestown Foundation, 7.
23. *BBC News*. 2004. "Napadenie v Ingushetii: Zaderzhany Podozrevaemye," June 24. http://news.bbc.co.uk/hi/russian/russia/newsid_3835000/3835147.stm.
24. Shvarev, Aleksandr. 2005. "Proekt 'Molchanie.' " *Vremia Novostei*, May 6.
25. Borogan, Irina, and Andrei Soldatov. 2007. "Kavkazskii Front: Novaia Taktika Chuzhykh Oshibok." *Novaia Gazeta*, August 9.
26. Vachagaev, Mairbek. 2007. *The Ingush Jamaat: Identity and Resistance in the North Caucasus*. Washington, DC: Jamestown Foundation.
27. *Kavkaz Center*. 2005. "Dagestan Pledges Allegiance to Sheikh Abdul-Halim," March 15. http://www.kavkazcenter.com/eng/content/2005/03/15/3612.shtml.

28. *Kavkaz Center*. 2007. "Dzhamaat 'Shariat': Nasha Tsel' – Vosstanovlenie Islamskogo Gosudarstva," March 31. http://www.kavkazcenter.com/russ/content/2007/03/31/50294.shtml.
29. Available at http://www.kavkazcenter.com/russ/islam/jihad_in_ncaucasus/PDF_version.pdf.
30. Migalin, Sergei. 2005. "Gorod Rasstrelianykh Militsionerov." *Nezavisimaia Gazeta*, October 10. http://www.ng.ru/politics/2005-10-10/1_dagestan.html.
31. *Kavkaz Center*. 2005. "Dzhamaat 'Shariat' Soobshchaet o Boevykh Operatsiiakh v Dagestane," April 9. http://kavkazcenter.com/russ/content/2005/04/09/32537.shtml.
32. *Kavkaz Center*. 2005. "Dzhamaat 'Shariat': 'Pobeda ili Rai! Is Dvukh Luchshee!' " July 12. http://kavkazcenter.com/russ/content/2005/07/12/36015.shtml.
33. *Kavkaz Center*. 2005. "Dzhamaat 'Shariat': 'Modzhakhedy Budut Napravleny v Moskvu,' " July 2. http://www.kavkazcenter.com/russ/content/2005/07/02/35721.shtml.
34. *Kavkaz Center*. 2007. "Dzhamaat 'Shariat' Obeshchaet Atakovat' Sochi i Sinagogu v Shamil'kale," February 23.
35. For more on the insurgency in Kabardino-Balkaria, see Zhukov, A. D. 2008. *Kabardino-Balkaria: Na Puti k Katastrofe*. Moscow: Memorial.
36. *Kavkazskii Uzel*. 2013. "Napadenie na Nalchik 13-14 Oktiabria 2005 Goda," February 6. http://www.kavkaz-uzel.ru/articles/219748/.
37. *Kavkaz Center*. 2006. "Sadulayev: 'This Plan Is Meant to Last until 2010,' " July 9. http://www.kavkazcenter.com/eng/content/2006/07/09/4929.shtml.
38. *Kavkazskii Uzel*. 2013. "Napadenie na Nalchik 13-14 Oktiabria 2005 Goda," February 6. http://www.kavkaz-uzel.ru/articles/219748/.
39. *Kavkazskii Uzel*. 2004. "Shamil Basayev Dva Mesiatsa Skryvalsia v Kabardino-Balkarii," August 5. http://www.kavkaz-uzel.ru/articles/59479/.
40. Zhukov, A. D. 2008. *Kabardino-Balkaria: Na Puti k Katastrofe*. Moscow: Memorial.
41. Fatullaev, Milrad. 2003. "Mecheti Budut Otkryvat' Tol'ko po Piatnitsam." *Nezavisimaia Gazeta*, October 14.
42. *Severnyi Kavkaz*. 2005. "Zapretami Nichego ne Reshish'," October 19.
43. *Kavkazskii Uzel*. 2009. "V Kabardino-Balkarii Podtverzhdaetsia Informatsiia o Gibeli Mussy Mukozheva," May 11. http://www.kavkaz-uzel.ru/articles/154010/.
44. *Kavkaz Center*. 2006. "Musa Mukozhev: 'Vyidia na Dzhikhad, My Obreli Nastoiashchuiu Svobodu," September 23. http://www.kavkazcenter.com/russ/content/2006/09/23/47159.shtml.
45. *Kavkaz Center*. 2004. "Kabardino-Balkarskii Dzhamaat Ob'iavil Dzhikhad," August 23. http://www.kavkazcenter.com/russ/content/2004/08/23/25043_print.html.
46. *Kavkaz Center*. 2005. "Dzhikhad v Kabardino-Balkarii Obiazatelen," March 25. http://kavkazcenter.com/russ/content/2005/03/25/31816_print.html.
47. *Kavkaz Center*. 2004. "Kabardino-Balkarskii Dzhamaat Ob'iavil Dzhikhad," August 23. http://www.kavkazcenter.com/russ/content/2004/08/23/25043_print.html.
48. *Kavkaz Center*. 2005. "Dveri Dzhikhada Otkryty," January 9. http://www.kavkazcenter.com/russ/content/2005/01/09/28663_print.html.
49. Punanov, Grigorii. 2002. "Vakhkhabitskoe Podpol'e." *Izvestiia*, May 14.
50. Sagramoso, Domitilla, and Galina Yemelianova. 2010. "Islam and Ethno-Nationalism in the North-Western Caucasus." In Yemelianova, Galina, ed. *Radical Islam in the Former Soviet Union*. New York: Routledge, 136.
51. Sagramoso, Domitilla, and Galina Yemelianova. 2010. "Islam and Ethno-Nationalism in the North-Western Caucasus." In Yemelianova, Galina, ed. *Radical Islam in the Former Soviet Union*. New York: Routledge, 136.

52. Sagramoso, Domitilla, and Galina Yemelianova. 2010. "Islam and Ethno-Nationalism in the North-Western Caucasus." In Yemelianova, Galina, ed. *Radical Islam in the Former Soviet Union*. New York: Routledge, 136.
53. Vershov, Iurii. 2002. "Verdikt Vospitatel'nogo Znacheniia." *Vremia Novostei*, July 12.
54. Vatchagaev, Mairbek. 2007. "The Truth about the 'Kataib al-Khoul' Ossetian Jamaat." *North Caucasus Analysis* 8, no. 36.
55. *Kavkaz Center*. 2007. "Severnaia Osetia. Svodka Boevykh Operatsii Dzhamaata 'Kataib al Khoul," November 4. http://www.kavkazcenter.com/russ/content/2007/11/04/54134.shtml.
56. Riskin, Andrei. 2005. "Vakhkhabity Pribiraiut k Rukam Iug Rossii." *Nezavisimaia Gazeta*. http://www.ng.ru/regions/2005-02-04/4_caucasus.html.
57. Gordienko, Irina. 2011. "Chto Takoe 'Nogaiskii Dzhamaat.' " *Novaia Gazeta*, January 1.
58. *Kavkaz Center*. 2005. "Shamil Basayev: 'Segodnia Voiuet Ves' Chechenskii Narod!' " August 17. http://www.kavkazcenter.com/russ/content/2005/08/17/36759.shtml.
59. Akhmadov, Ilyas, and Nicholas Daniloff. 2013. *Chechnya's Secret Wartime Diplomacy: Aslan Maskhadov and the Quest for a Peaceful Resolution*. New York: Palgrave Macmillan, Kindle Edition, Kindle Locations 4048–4052.
60. Riskin, Andrei. 2005. "'Vakhkhabit Nomer Odin' Vozglavil Ichkeriiu." *Nezavisimaia Gazeta*, March 11.
61. *Kavkaz Center*. 2006. "Sadulayev: 'This Plan Is Meant to Last until 2010,' " July 9. http://www.kavkazcenter.com/eng/content/2006/07/09/4929.shtml.
62. *Kavkaz Center*. 2006. "Sadulayev: 'This Plan Is Meant to Last until 2010,' " July 9. http://www.kavkazcenter.com/eng/content/2006/07/09/4929.shtml.
63. *Kavkaz Center*. 2005. "Obrashchenie Prezidenta ChRI A-Kh Sadulayeva k Chechenskomu Narodu," August 19.
64. *Kavkaz Center*. 2005. "Ukazom Prezidenta ChRI Sadulayeva Sozdan Kavkazskii Front," May 16.
65. *Kavkaz Center*. 2006. "Sadulayev: 'This Plan Is Meant to Last until 2010,' " July 9. http://www.kavkazcenter.com/eng/content/2006/07/09/4929.shtml.
66. Babitsky, Andrei. 2006. "Shahid ... This Word Contains a Lot ..." *Caucasus Times*, June 29. http://www.caucasustimes.com/article.asp?id=9562.
67. *Kavkaz Center*. 2006. "Deklaratsiia Dvizheniia za Dekolonizatsiiu Kavkaza," March 6. http://www.kavkazcenter.com/russ/content/2006/03/06/42601.shtml.
68. *Kavkaz Center*. 2006. "Abdallakh Shamil' Abu-Idris: 'My Oderzahli Strategicheskuiu Pobedu,' " January 9. http://www.kavkazcenter.com/russ/content/2006/01/09/40869.shtml.
69. *Kavkaz Center*. 2006. "20th Anniversary of Independence of CRI," September 6. http://kavkazcenter.com/eng/content/2011/09/06/15148.shtml.
70. *Kavkaz Center*. 2006. "Sadulayev: 'This Plan Is Meant to Last until 2010,' " July 9. http://www.kavkazcenter.com/eng/content/2006/07/09/4929.shtml.
71. *Kavkaz Center*. 2006. "Sadulayev: 'This Plan Is Meant to Last until 2010,' " July 9. http://www.kavkazcenter.com/eng/content/2006/07/09/4929.shtml.
72. *Kavkaz Center*. 2005. "Chechnya Stalo Iadrom Vseobshchei Bor'by s Kremlevskoi Tiraniei," November 15. http://www.kavkazcenter.com/russ/content/2005/11/15/39378_print.html.
73. *Kavkaz Center*. 2006. "Dokka Umarov Vystupil s Obrashcheniem," June 23. http://kavkazcenter.com/russ/content/2006/06/23/45461.shtml.

74. *Kavkaz Center*. 2006. "President ChRI Podpisal Ukazy o Sozdanii Ural'skogo i Povolzhskogo Frontov," July 9. http://kavkazcenter.com/russ/content/2006/07/09/45779.shtml.
75. *Kavkaz Center*. 2006. "Dokka Umarov: 'Vse Resheniia Prinimaiutsia v Chechne,' " September 12. http://kavkazcenter.com/russ/content/2006/09/12/46958.shtml.
76. *Kavkaz Center*. 2007. "Dokku Umarov: 'My ne Ustanem, i Terpenie Nashe ne Issiaknet,' " February 23. http://kavkazcenter.com/russ/content/2007/02/23/49724.shtml.
77. *Kavkaz Center*. 2006. "My Nachali Bor'bus Nadezhdoi na Allakha..." August 22. http://kavkazcenter.com/russ/content/2006/08/22/46643.shtml.
78. *Kavkaz Center*. 2007. "Ofitsial'nyi Reliz Zaiavleniia Amira Dokki Umarova o Provozglashenii Kavkazskogo Emirata," November 21. http://kavkazcenter.com/russ/content/2007/11/21/54480.shtml. Umarov's declaration appeared on the Internet in October 2007. However, it was published on the Kavkaz Center website only in November.
79. *BBC News*. 2007. "Zakayev ne Priznaet Umarova Svoim Rukovoditelem," October 31. http://news.bbc.co.uk/hi/russian/russia/newsid_7071000/7071952.stm.
80. *Kavkaz Center*. 2011. "20 Let so Dnia Provozglasheniia Nezavisimosti ChRI," September 6. http://kavkazcenter.com/russ/content/2011/09/06/84937.shtml.
81. *Kavkaz Center*. 2007. "Novye Ukazy Dokki Umarova. Akhmed Evloev Naznachen Voennym Amirom," July 21. http:/kavkazcenter.com/russ/content/2007/07/21/51972.shtml.
82. *Kavkaz Center*. 2014. "7 Let so Dnia Provozglasheniia Imamata Kavkaz," July 22. http://kavkazcenter.com/russ/content/2014/07/22/105613.shtml.
83. *Kavkaz Center*. 2011. "20 Let so Dnia Provozglasheniia Nezavisimosti ChRI," September 6. http://kavkazcenter.com/russ/content/2011/09/06/84937.shtml.
84. *Kavkaz Center*. 2011. "20 Let so Dnia Provozglasheniia Nezavisimosti ChRI," September 6. http://kavkazcenter.com/russ/content/2011/09/06/84937.shtml.
85. *Kavkaz Center*. 2014. "7 Let so Dnia Provozglasheniia Imamata Kavkaz," July 22. http://kavkazcenter.com/russ/content/2014/07/22/105613.shtml.
86. *Kavkaz Center*. 2006. "Dokka Umarov: 'Chem Bol'she Liutuet Vrag – Tem My Sil'nee!' " August 6. http://kavkazcenter.com/russ/content/2006/08/06/46347.shtml.
87. See Campana, Aurelie, and Benjamin Ducol. 2014. "Voices of the 'Caucasus Emirate': Mapping and Analyzing North Caucasus Insurgency Websites." *Terrorism and Political Violence* 0: 1-22. DOI:10.1080/09546553.2013.848797.
88. Boiko, Oksana. 2009. "Ekspress Umarova." *Vzgliad*, June 30.
89. *Krasnodarskii Rabochii*. 2010. "Umarov Vzial na sebia Otvetstvennost' za Terakty v Moskve," April 2.
90. *Krasnodarskii Rabochii*. 2010. "Umarov Vzial na sebia Otvetstvennost' za Terakty v Moskve," April 2.
91. *Gazeta.ru*. 2014. "Islamskie Boeviki Vziali na Sebia Otvetstvennost' za Vzryvy v Volgograde," January 20. http://www.gazeta.ru/social/video/islamskie_boeviki_vzyali_na_sebya_otvetstvennost_za_vzryvy_v_volgograde.shtml.
92. *Kavkaz Center*. 2009. "Emir Dokka Abu Usman: 'This Year Will Be Our Offensive Year,' " May 17. http://kavkazcenter.com/eng/content/2009/05/17/10700.shtml.
93. *Kavkaz Center*. 2012. "Russkie Kafiry Priznaiut, Chto Imarat Kavkaz Stal Glavnoi Ugrozoi Imperskoi Rossii," February 7. http://kavkazcenter.com/russ/content/2012/02/07/88700.shtml.
94. *Komsomol'skaia Pravda*. 2011. "Doku Umarov Vzial na Sebia Otvetstvennost' za Vzryvy v Domodedovo," February 6.

95. *Kavkaz Center*. 2010. "Interview Amira Imarata Kavkaza Dokku Abu-Usmana," February 14. http://www.kavkazcenter.com/russ/content/2010/02/14/70668_print.html.
96. *Kavkazpress.ru*. 2012. "Mudzhakedy Tatarstana Prisiagnuli na Vernost' Doku Umarovu," July 27. http://kavkazpress.ru/archives/4286.
97. Brailovskaia, Svetlana. 2012. "Otvetstvennost' za Terakt v Kazani Vziali ' Mudzhakhedy Tatarstana.' " *Rossiiskaia Gazeta*, August 6.
98. *Kavkaz Center*. 2012. "Amir IK Dokku Abu Usman Otmenil Moratorii na Operatsii v Rossii i Prizval ne Dopustit' Olimpiady v Sochi" February 3. http://www.kavkazcenter.com/russ/content/2012/02/03/88591.shtml.
99. *Kavkaz Center*. 2013. "Amir IK Dokku Abu Usman Otmenil Moratorii na Operatsii v Rossii i Prizval ne Dopustit' Olimpiady v Sochi," July 3. http://www.kavkazcenter.com/russ/content/2013/07/03/98961.shtml.
100. *Kavkaz Center*. 2012. "Obrashchenie Amira Imarata Kavkaz Dokku Abu Usmana k Modzhakhedam Sirii," November 13. http://www.kavkazcenter.com/russ/content/2012/11/13/94315.shtml.
101. Amelina, Iana. 2014. "Siriiskie Boeviki – Sleduiushchaia Stantsiia Rossia?" *Regnum*, January 31. http://www.regnum.ru/news/polit/1761395.html.
102. *Kavkaz Center*. 2012. "Zaiavlenie Komandovaniia Modzhakhedov Vilaiata Dagestan IK v Sviazi s Sobytiiami v Bostone (SShA)," April 21. http://kavkazcenter.com/russ/content/2013/04/21/97502.shtml.
103. Abdullaev, Nabi. 2014. "Islamist Rebel Leader Renounces Female Suicide Terrorism." *Moscow Times*, June 30.
104. *Kavkaz Center*. 2013. "Statement of Emir Omar al-Chechen, Commander of Northern Directorate of Islamic State of Iraq and Sham," August 7. http://www.kavkazcenter.com/eng/content/2013/08/07/18145.shtml.
105. Khanbabaev, Kaflan. 2007. "Islamskii Radikalizm na Severnom Kavkaze." *Svobodnaia Mysl'* 3: 105–116.
106. *Stavropolye.tv*. 2012. "Khloponin Nazval Istochnik Finansirovaniia Boevikov v SKFO," February 9. http://www.stavropolye.tv/sfdnews/view/42427.
107. *Memorial*. 2006. "Bakhtiiar Akhmedkhanov. Konets Finansista," December 1. http://www.memo.ru/hr/hotpoints/caucas1/msg/2006/12/m66282.htm.
108. *Kavkaz Center*. 2014. "Sheikh al-Zawahiri: 'Lessons of Chechen Jihad for Arab Spring,' " April 20. http://kavkazcenter.com/eng/content/2014/04/20/19139.shtml.
109. *Vesti Respubliki*. 2007. "Ia Rukovoditel' Respubliki, Ia Khoziain," June 21.
110. Svinarenko, Igor'. 2009. "Vainakh i Mir." *Rossiiskaia Gazeta*, April 7.
111. See Russell, John. 2008. "Ramzan Kadyrov: The Indigenous Key to Success in Putin's Chechenization Strategy?" *Nationalities Papers* 36, no. 4: 659-687; Russell, John. 2011. "Kadyrov's Chechnya- Template, Test or Trouble for Russia's Regional Policy?" *Europe-Asia Studies* 63, no. 3: 509–528.
112. Medvedev, Dmirty. 2009. Presidential Address to the Federal Assembly of the Russian Federation, November 12. http://eng.kremlin.ru/transcripts/297.
113. *Pervyi Kanal*. 2009. "Medvedev Potreboval Priniat' Zhestkie Mery po Bor'be s Terrorizmom na Severnom Kavkaze," June 14.
114. *Rossiiskaia Gazeta*. 2009. "Kontseptsiia Protivodeistviia Terrorizmu v Rossiiskoi Federatsii," October 20.
115. *Kavkazskii Uzel*. 2010. "Strategiia Sotsial'no-Ekonomicheskogo Razvitiia Severo-Kavkazskogo Federal'nogo Okruga do 2025 Goda," October 6. http://www.kavkaz-uzel.ru/articles/175166/.

116. *Komsomol'skaia Pravda*. 2011. "Medvedev o KTO: Uzh Tochno 'Otchet Trupami' – Eto Put' v Nikuda," July 5.

117. *Kavkazskii Uzel*. 2012. "Zaiavlenie Assotsiatsii Uchenykh Akhlu-Sunna v Dagestane," August 29. http://www.kavkaz-uzel.ru/articles/211858/.

118. Aliev, Timur. 2013. "U Nas Odna Sud'ba." *Rossiiskaia Gazeta*, October 11.

119. *Kavkaz Center*. 2014. "Amir Imarata Kavkaz Dokku Abu Usman Stal Shakhidom, Inshaallakh," March 18. http://kavkazcenter.com/russ/content/2014/03/18/103603.shtml.

Selected Bibliography

Abubakarov, Taimaz. 1998. *Rezhim Dzhokhara Dudaeva: Pravda i Vymysel.* Moscow: INSAN.
Akhmadov, Ilyas, and Nicholas Daniloff. 2013. *Chechnya's Secret Wartime Diplomacy: Aslan Maskhadov and the Quest for a Peaceful Resolution.* New York: Palgrave Macmillan, Kindle Edition.
Akhmadov, Ilyas, and Miriam Lanskoy. 2010. *The Chechen Struggle: Independence Won and Lost.* New York: Palgrave Macmillan.
Baddeley, John F. 1908. *The Russian Conquest of the Caucasus.* London: Longmans, Green and Co.
Belenkin, Boris, and Aleksandr Cherkasov, eds. 1996. *Khronika Zadymleniia.* Moscow: Memorial.
Bennett, Vanora. 1998. *Crying Wolf: The Return of War to Chechnya.* London: Pan Books.
Bennigsen, Alexandre. 1967. *Islam in the Soviet Union.* New York: Praeger.
Bennigsen, Alexandre, and S. Enders Wimbush. 1985. *Mystics and Commissars: Sufism in the Soviet Union.* Berkeley: University of California Press.
Bodansky, Yossef. 2007. *Chechen Jihad.* New York: Harper Collins.
Broxop, Marie. 1996. *The North Caucasus Barrier: Russian Advance towards the Muslim World.* C Hurst & Co Publishers Ltd.
Cornell, Svante. 2001. *Small Nations and Great Powers: A Study of Ethnopolitical Conflict in the Caucasus.* New York: Routledge.
Degoev, Vladimir. 2013. *Nepostizhimaia Chechnya: Sheikh-Mansur i Ego Vremia (XVIII vek).* Moscow: Modest Kolerov.
Dolnik, Adam, and Keith M. Fizgerald. 2008. *Negotiating Hostage Crises with the New Terrorists.* Westport, CT: Praeger.
Dunlop, John B. 1998. *Russia Confronts Chechnya: Roots of a Separatist Conflict.* Cambridge: Cambridge University Press.

Dunlop, John B. 2006. *The 2002 Dubrovka and 2004 Beslan Hostage Crises: A Critique of Russian Counter-Terrorism.* Stuttgart, Germany: Ibidem Verlag.

Evangelista, Matthew. 2002. *The Chechen Wars: Will Russia Go the Way of the Soviet Union?* Washington, DC: Brookings Institution Press.

Fowkes, Ben, ed. 1998. *Russia and Chechnia: The Permanent Crisis; Essays on Russo-Chechen Relations.* London St Martin's Press.

Gall, Carlotta, and Thomas de Waal. 1998. *Chechnya: Calamity in the Caucasus.* New York: New York University Press.

Gammer, Moshe. 1994. *Muslim Resistance to the Tsar: Shamil and the Conquest of Chechnia and Daghestan.* London: Frank Cass.

Gammer, Moshe. 2006. *The Lone Wolf and the Bear: Three Centuries of Chechen Defiance of Russian Rule.* Pittsburgh, PA: University of Pittsburgh Press.

Gammer, Moshe, ed. 2008. *Ethno-Nationalism, Islam and the State in the Caucasus.* New York: Routledge.

German, Tracey C. 2003. *Russia's Chechen War.* London: Routledge.

Gilligan, Emma. 2010. *Terror in Chechnya: Russia and the Tragedy of Civilians in War.* Princeton, NJ: Princeton University Press.

Gorlov, A. G., ed. 1995. *Budennovsk: Sem' Dnei Ada.* Moscow: Kodeks.

Gorlov, A. G. 1996. *Kizlyar-Pervomaiskoe: Operatsiia bez Analogov.* Moscow: Kodeks.

Griffin, Nicholas. 2001. *Caucasus: A Journey to the Land between Christianity and Islam.* Chicago: University of Chicago Press.

Hahn, Gordon M. 2007. *Russia's Islamic Threat.* New Haven, CT: Yale University Press.

Henze, Paul B. 1995. *Islam in the North Caucasus: The Example of Chechnya.* Santa Monica, CA: RAND.

Howard, Glen E. 2011. *Volatile Borderland: Russia and the North Caucasus.* Washington, DC: Jamestown Foundation.

Hughes, James. 2007. *Chechnya: From Nationalism to Jihad.* Philadelphia: University of Pennsylvania Press.

Jaimoukha, Amjad. 2005. *The Chechens: A Handbook.* New York: Routledge.

Khodarkovsky, Michael. 2011. *Bitter Choices: Loyalty and Betrayal in the Russian Conquest of the North Caucasus.* Ithaca, NY: Cornell University Press.

King, Charles. 2008. *The Ghost of Freedom: The History of the Caucasus.* New York: Oxford University Press.

Knezys, Stasys, and Romanas Sedlickas. 1999. *The War in Chechnya.* College Station: Texas A&M University Press.

Kramer, Mark. 2005. "Guerrilla Warfare, Counterinsurgency and Terrorism in the North Caucasus: The Military Dimension of the Russian–Chechen Conflict." *Europe-Asia Studies* 57, no. 2: 209–290.

Lieven, Anatol. 1998. *Chechnya: Tombstone of Russian Power.* New Haven, CT, and London: Yale University Press.

Malashenko, Aleksei. 2001. *Islamskie Orientiry Severnogo Kavkaza.* Moscow: Gendalf.

Malashenko, Aleksei, and Dmitrii Trenin. 2002. *Vremia Iuga: Rossiia v Chechne, Chechnya v Rossii.* Moscow: Gendalf.

Markedonov, Sergey. 2010. *Radical Islam in the North Caucasus: Evolving Threats, Challenges, and Prospects.* Washington, DC: CSIS.

Marshall, Alex. 2010. *The Caucasus under Soviet Rule.* New York: Routledge.

Martin, Terri. 2001. *The Affirmative Action Empire: Nations and Nationalism in the Soviet Union, 1923–1939.* Ithaca, NY: Cornell University Press.

Matveeva, Anna. 1999. *The North Caucasus: Russia's Fragile Borderland*. London: Royal Institute for International Affairs.
Meier, Andrew. 2005. *Chechnya: To the Heart of the Conflict*. New York: W.W. Norton and Company.
Murphy, Paul J. 2004. *The Wolves of Islam: Russia and the Faces of Chechen Terror*. Washington, DC: Brassey's, Inc.
Murphy, Paul J. 2010. *Allah's Angels: Chechen Women in War*. Annapolis, MD: Naval Institute Press.
Narochnitskii, A. L., ed. 1988. *Istoriia Narodov Severnogo Kavkaza (konets XVIIIv. – 1917 g.)*. Moscow: Nauka.
Nikolaev, Yu. V., ed. 1996. *The Chechen Tragedy: Who Is to Blame?* Commack, NY: Nova Science Publishers, Inc.
Orlov, O. P., and A. V. Cherkasov, eds. 2010. *Rossiia-Chechnya: Tsep' Oshibok i Prestuplenii 1994-1996*. Moscow: Prava Cheloveka.
Piotrovskii, B. B., ed. 1988. *Istoriia Narodov Severnogo Kavkaza s Drevneishikh Vremen do Kontsa XVIII v*. Moscow: Nauka.
Politkovskaya, Anna. 2003. *A Small Corner of Hell: Dispatches from Chechnya*. Chicago: University of Chicago Press.
Potto, Vasilii. 2006. *Kavkazskaia Voina. Tom 1. Ot Drevneishikh Vremen do Yermolova*. Moscow: Tsentrpoligraf.
Richmond, Walter. 2008. *The Northwest Caucasus: Past, Present, Future*. New York: Routledge.
Richmond, Walter. 2013. *The Circassian Genocide*. New Brunswick, NJ: Rutgers University Press.
Russell, John. 2007. *Chechnya Russia's "War on Terror."* London: Routledge.
Sakwa, Richard, ed. 2005. *Chechnya: From Past to Future*. London: Anthem Press.
Schaefer, Robert. 2010. *Insurgency in Chechnya and the North Caucasus: From Gazavat to Jihad*. Santa Barbara, CA: ABC-CLIO.
Seely, Robert. 2001. *Russo-Chechen Conflict, 1800–2000: A Deadly Embrace*. London: Frank Cass.
Smith, Sebastian. 2001. *Allah's Mountains: The Battle for Chechnya*. London: I. B. Tauris Publishers.
Souleimanov, Emil. 2007. *An Endless War: The Russian-Chechen Conflict in Perspective*. Frankfurt am Main, Germany: Peter Lang Publishing.
Tishkov, Valerii. 2004. *Chechnya: Life in a War-Torn Society*. Berkeley: University of California Press.
Van Herpen, Marcel H. 2014. *Putin's Wars: The Rise of Russia's New Imperialism*. Lanham, MD: Rowman and Littlefield.
Ware, Robert Bruce, ed. 2013. *The Fire Below: How the Caucasus Shaped Russia*. New York: Bloomsbury.
Ware, Robert Bruce, and Enver Kisriev. 2010. *Dagestan: Russian Hegemony and Islamic Resistance in the North Caucasus*. New York: M. E. Sharpe.
Weismann, Itzchak. 2007. *The Naqshbandiyya: Orthodoxy and Activism in a Worldwide Sufi Tradition*. New York: Routledge.
Wood, Tony. 2007. *Chechnya: The Case for Independence*. London: Verso.
Yemelianova, Galina. 2002. *Russia and Islam: A Historical Survey*. New York: Palgrave.
Yemelianova, Galina, ed. 2010. *Radical Islam in the Former Soviet Union*. New York: Routledge.

Yermolov, Aleksei. 1991. *Zapiski A.P. Yermolova. 1798–1826 gg.* Moscow: Vysshaia Shkola.
Zelkina, Anna. 2000. *In Quest for God and Freedom: Sufi Responses to the Russian Advance in the North Caucasus.* New York: New York University Press.
Zhukov, A. D. 2008. *Kabardino-Balkaria: Na Puti k Katastrofe.* Moscow: Memorial.

WEBSITES

Kavkaz Center: http://kavkazcenter.com/eng/
Vilayat Dagestan: http://vdagestan.com/
Vilayat Galgaiche: http://hunafa.com/
Vilayat of Kabarda, Balkaria and Karachai: http://islamdin.com/

Index

Abdulatipov, Ramazan, 20, 170, 182
Abdul-Kadyr, Mullah, 4
Abkhazia, 54, 124; battalion, 24, 36; conflict in, 23–25
Abubakarov, Saidmagomed, 91
Adat, 3, 5, 12, 116, 218 n.6
Adygea, 7, 13, 71, 162
Adygs, 2–3, 72, 220 n.30; genocide, 8–9
Afghan Arabs, 40, 85. *See also* Mujahedeen
Afghanistan, 89, 112–13, 118, 123–25, 168, 183; and Basayev, 36, 86; Chechen bases in, 112; and Khattab, 85–87; mujahedeen from, 40, 84–85, 88
Akhlu-Sunnah, 170
Akhmadov, Ilyas, 125
Akhtaev, Akhmad, 74–75
Alania, 1
Algeria, 40
Alkhanov, Alu, 131, 140
Alpha group, 42–43, 46, 53, 103, 180
Al Qaeda, 116, 129, 137, 156, 163, 171; connections with North Caucasus, 84, 88–89, 122–25, 167–68; and WMD terrorism, 49–51
Amanat Jamaat, 149, 167
Amirkhanov, Alikhan, 144
Amnesty, 55, 109, 131, 141, 235 n.14

Apartment bombings, 93–101, 110, 128, 154
Army of the liberation of Dagestan, 93
Aslakhanov, Aslambek, 126
Astemirov, Anzor, 124, 152, 171, 181
Ataev, Muslim, 153
Atta, Mohamed, 123
August putsch, 25, 36
Aukhovskii district, 18
Aum Shinrikyo, 49, 51
Aushev, Ruslan, 21, 74, 126, 144
Avrasya hijacking, 54–55, 63, 175
Avturkhanov, Umar, 28
Al-Ayyiri, Yusuf, 116
Azerbaijan, 11, 69, 89, 123; conflict in Nagorno-Karabakh, 36; fighters from, 88
Azov Sea, 2
Azzam, Abdullah, 87, 230 n.59

Babitsky, Andrei, 136
Bagautdin, Muhammad, 75–76, 88, 91–92, 150
Baisarov, Movladi, 132
Bakar, Abu, 125
Baku, 2, 89
Balkar Republic, 19
Balkars, deportation of, 15–16

Barayev, Arbi, 77, 79, 115, 125
Barayev, Movsar, 125, 128
Barayeva, Khava, 115–16
Basayev, Shamil: in Abkhazia, 23–24, 54; biography, 35–38, 68, 77, 83; death, 140–42; and Imam Shamil, 10, 37, 141, 156–57; and Islam, 76, 111; and jamaats, 111, 152, 155, 159; and Khattab, 85–86, 94–96, 100; and radiological terrorism, 49–52; raid into Dagestan, 92–93; use of terrorism, 33–34, 39–40, 45, 56, 111, 114–18, 132–33, 148
Basayev, Shirvani, 48
Bashkortostan, 160, 178, 182
Bek, Gamzat, 6
Benevolence International Foundation, 89
Berezovsky, Boris, 80, 97
Beria, Lavrentiy, 15
Beslan, 123, 159–60, 176; aftermath, 137–40; raid on, 133–37; response to, 135–37, 143, 180–81
Bey, Said, 11–12
Bidzhiev, Muhammad, 74
Black Widows, 115–17, 125, 128, 134–35
Bolsheviks, 11–13, 22; October Revolution, 11
Bombings, 155; pipeline, 113, 164, 176; public transportation, 60, 62, 113, 164; railways, 113, 164, 176; as a tactic, 66, 164
Book of Mujahiddeen, 38
Boomerang, 117–18, 132
Borlakov, Ramazan, 74, 98, 154
Bosnia, 40, 85, 89
Boston Marathon, bombing of, ix, 167, 175
Botlikhskii region, 92
Budennovsk, 39; aftermath, 44–49; raid on, 41–44; response to, 42–43, 56–57, 65–66, 101, 181
Buinaksk, 91, 93–95, 98–99, 107
Burbulis, Gennadiy, 25
Buryatsky, Said, 118, 120, 165, 178, 180
Bush, George W., 122–23, 137
Bykova, Alena, 120

Caliphate: Islamic, 113; global, 87, 90, 168
Caspian Sea, 2, 37, 88, 103

Caucasian Albania, 1
Caucasus Confederation, 78–80
Caucasus Emirate: founding of, 162–63; use of terrorism, 164–68, 171, 175–79, 182
Caucasus Gubernia, 4
Caucasus Imamate, 5–11, 22, 37, 78–80, 88, 156, 162
Caucasus Wars, 4–8, 22, 179
Chabanmakhi, 75, 79, 91, 93
Chachayev, Lom-Ali, 33
Chechenization, 13, 57, 109, 130–32, 169, 178–79
Chechen Mountaineer National-Socialist Underground Organization, 14
Checheno-Ingushetia ASSR, 14–17, 21, 25–26, 28
Chechevitsa, deportation operation, 15
Chechnya, 2–3; constitution, 29, 81–83, 131; economic problems in, 27–29, 69; first war in, 29–31, 38–41, 59, 61, 106–7; independence, 21, 25–27, 67–70, 77–78, 112, 181; Islam in, 12–13, 73, 76–77, 81–84; second war in, 99–103, 105–7, 110; unification with Dagestan, 5–7, 75–80, 111, 157
Cherkess. *See* Adygs
Cherkess Republic, 20
Chernomyrdin, Viktor, 16, 42–44, 52, 65, 68–69
Ciller, Tansu, 55
Circassians. *See* Adygs
Clinton, Bill, 63, 122
Collectivization, 13–14
Concept on Countering Terrorism in the Russian Federation, 170, 174, 181
Confederation of the Mountain Peoples of the Caucasus, 21–25, 36, 156
Confederation of the Peoples of the Caucasus. *See* Confederation of the Mountain Peoples of the Caucasus
Congress of the Kabardin People, 19
Congress of the North Caucasus Peoples, 22
Congress of the Peoples of Chechnya and Dagestan, 79–80, 85, 92, 111, 129, 156–57
Congress of the United Mountain Peoples of the North Caucasus and Dagestan, 11

Cossack Line, 2
Cossacks, 2, 9, 43, 78
Council of Sheikhs and Said Bey, 12
Counter–hostage-taking, 139, 180
Counterterrorism, 62, 64–66, 129–33, 137–42, 179–82; reform, 65, 121, 132, 139–40, 168–71
Counterterrorist Committee, 65, 103
Counterterrorist operation, 140; in Chechnya, 99–103, 105–10, 169; in North Caucasus, 103, 125, 169
Crimean Khanate, 2

Dadasheva, Aiset, 90
Dagestan, 1–2, 20, 170–71, 178; insurgent raid on, 91–93; Islam in, 4, 12–13, 71–80, 180–81; radicalization in, 146, 150–52, 154
Daudov, Alash, 149
Department on the Fight against Terrorism, 46, 53, 65, 103
Deportations: rehabilitation, 17; tsarist, 8–9; World War II, 14–17, 25, 147
Deradicalization, 170–71
Derbent, 2, 7
Domodedovo airport, attack on, 165–66, 175
Dubrovka, 134–35, 137; aftermath, 129–33; raid on, 125–29; response to, 127–28, 136
Dudayev, Dzhokhar: background, 25; death, 58–59; declaring independence, 26–27; and Islamic state, 72, 81; opposition to, 28–31; as president, 27–31, 47; supporting terrorism, 39, 46, 51–52, 57, 64
Dzasokhov, Aleksandr, 134–35
Dzeit, Abu, 149, 167

ECHR (European Court of Human Rights), 128–29
Egypt, 88
Elections: in Chechnya, 26, 48, 52, 57–60, 67–68, 131, 133; in Ingushetia, 144; in regions, 138; in Russia, 53, 57, 58–60, 101, 106, 108, 166
Emirate of the North Caucasus, 11, 22, 72, 80, 156, 162
Evloev, Magomed. *See* Magas, Emir

Fadlallah, Mohammed Hussein, 116
Al-Fahd, Nasir, 50
Faizov, Ildus, 166
Fathi, Sheikh, 40, 81, 85, 88–89
Fatwa, 115, 167
Federal Border Service, 103
Federal Counterterrorist Committee, 103, 132, 139
Federal Protection Service, 103
Fedorov, Nikolai, 23
Female suicide bombers, 115–16, 167
Filatov, Sergei, 25
Filtration camps, 107, 179
Finogenov and others vs. Russia, 128
Foreign fighters, 40, 84, 88. *See also* Mujahedeen
Foreign Intelligence Service, 103
FSB (Federal Security Service): involvement in terrorism, 90, 96–97; reform, 46, 65, 103, 132, 139; role in counterterrorism, 121, 127, 132, 139–40
FSK (Federal Counterintelligence Service), 30, 46, 64

Galazov, Akhsarbek, 19, 21
Gantamirov, Beslan, 28
Gazavat, 5–8, 12, 26
Gelayev, Ruslan, 23, 148, 150
Georgia, 7, 9, 11, 15, 112, 148, 228 n.9; conflicts in, 36; fighters from, 88
Ghazi, Mullah. *See* Muhammad, Ghazi
Ghumuqi, Jamal al-Din, 6
Gitsba, Khamzat, 23, 54
Gloov, Idris, 117
Gochiiaev, Achemez, 98, 154
Gorbachev, Mikhail, 25, 126
Gorets contingent, 132
Gotsinskii, Nazhmutdin, 11
Grachev, Pavel, 39
Great Bulgaria, 1
Grozny, storming of, 30, 38–39
GTD (Global Terrorism Database), 49–50
Guantanamo, detainees from North Caucasus, 123–24
Gudermes, 88, 111
Guevara, Che, 38
Gumarov, Ravil, 124

Hafs, Abu, 167–68
Hamas, 115–16
Hanafi school, 71, 73
Hanbali school, 73, 157
Al-Haramein, 89
Hasan, Umaymah, 116
Hezbollah, 116
Hijackings, 30, 34, 60, 114, 141, 176–77
Hostage-takings, 34, 60, 62, 66, 137, 176

Iastrzhembskii, Sergei, 88
Ichkeriia, 26, 222 n.98; recognition of independence, 69, 112
Ichkeriia Armed Forces, 148–49
Idris, Abdallah Shamil Abu. *See* Basayev, Shamil
Igatha, 89
Illegal armed formations, 29–31, 39, 47, 64–65, 102
Imaev, Usman, 42, 81
Imamate of Karachai, 74
IMF (International Monetary Fund), 122
Indonesia, 88
Information Center, 106
Ingushetia, 20–21, 144–46, 148–49; Islam in, 73–74
Ingush jamaat, 111, 149–50, 167
Insurgency, 110; spread of, 147–56; transformation of, 159–61
Insurgent Army of Imam Shamil, 79, 92
Intelligence and Sabotage Battalion, 39
International Islamic Battalion. *See* Islamic International Peacekeeping Brigade
International Islamic Brigade. *See* Islamic International Peacekeeping Brigade
Internet, use for recruitment, 38, 85, 120–21, 163–64, 178
Interpol, 107
Iraq, 116, 118, 160–61, 167–68, 182, 184
IRP (Islamic Renaissance Party), 73–74
Islam, 114–16; in North Caucasus, 70–77, 163; Russia's control of, 6–7, 154, 168, 181; under Soviet rule, 12–13
Islamic Battalion, 40, 88
Islamic Brigade of Shahids. *See* Riyad us-Saliheyn Martyrs Brigade
Islamic Council, 84
Islamic Front of Ingushetia, 148
Islamic Institute of the Caucasus, 87

Islamic International Peacekeeping Brigade, 80, 92, 114, 124
Islamic Jamaat of Dagestan, 75, 150
Islamic Movement of Ingushetia. *See* Islamic Front of Ingushetia
Islamic Nation, 78–80
Islamic State, 88; in Chechnya, 77, 81–84; in Dagestan, 91–92, 150; in North Caucasus, 10, 74–76, 141, 156, 159, 162
Islamic State of Iraq and Syria, 184
Al-Islamiyya, 74, 79
Islamization, 71–72, 78
Israilov, Khasan, 14
Iug battalion, 169
Ivan IV (the Terrible), Tsar, 2
Izmailovsky Park, attack on, 50–51

Jaffar, Abu, 88
Jamaat al-Turath al-Islamii, 89
Jamaat Khalifat, 148
Jamaat Shariat, 111, 150–53
Jamaat Siddik, 148
Jamaat Taliban, 148
Jamaat Yarmuk, 74, 111, 147, 152–54
Jamaats, 40, 71, 74–77; radicalization of, 98, 113, 117–18, 121, 148–56; unification of, 111, 156–60, 162
Jennet group, 111, 150
Jihad: Dudayev declares, 26, 81; global, xiii, 87–89, 113, 161, 163, 167–68; under Imam Shamil, 10, 154, 175. *See also Gazavat*; and Kadyrov, 109; against Russia, 37, 84–90, 110, 159–61, 167; violent, 114–15, 156
Jordan, 69, 88

Kabardino-Balkaria, 15, 19–20, 22, 73–74, 147–48, 152–54, 171
Kabardino-Balkaria ASSR, 15, 20
Kabardino-Balkaria jamaat, 74, 124, 152–53
Kabardin Republic, 19
Kadarskii region, 75, 91–93, 150
Kadyrov, Akhmad, 126; and Maskhadov, 82, 109; as president, 107, 109–10, 131, 141, 148
Kadyrov, Ramzan, 131–32, 168–69, 180
Kadyrovization, 131–32, 168, 178, 180
Kadyrovtsy, 169, 180

Kakiev, Said-Magomed, 132
Kanokov, Arsen, 152, 171
Karachaevo-Cherkessia jamaat, 74, 98
Karachaevo-Cherkessia, 19–20, 73–74, 154
Karachai Autonomous Region, 15, 17
Karachai jamaat, 98, 111, 120, 154–55
Karamakhi, 75, 79, 85, 91–93
Kashpirovsky, Anatoly, 43, 134
Kataib al-Khoul jamaat, 155
Kavkaz Center website, 16, 38, 117, 166, 171
Kavkaz training center, 40, 76, 79, 86
Kazakhstan, deportation to, 15–16
Kazantsev, Viktor, 108, 144
Kebedov, Bagautdin. *See* Bagautdin, Muhammad
KGB, 65
Khadzhi, Uzun, 11, 72
Khadzhiev, Salambek, 28
Khaikhoroev, Ruslan, 60–61
Khakamada, Irina, 126
Khanate of Astrakhan, 2
Khasavyurt Accords, 61, 67–69, 90, 100, 106–7, 181
Khasbulatov, Ruslan, 27–28
Khashiev, Magomed, 149
Khattab, Amir: background, 40, 76, 84–90, 160; links with Al Qaeda, 84–85, 100; and terrorism, 91, 94–96, 98; training centers, 40, 79, 86–89
Khazar Khaganate, 1–2
Khloponin, Aleksandr, 168, 170
Khorosheva, Maria, 120
Khrushchev, Nikita, 17
Khubiev, Vladimir, 20–21
Khuchbarov, Ruslan, 133
Kidnappings, 23, 70, 91, 99, 144
Kipkeev, Nikolai, 120
Kizlyar and Pervomaiskoe: aftermath, 55–58, 65–66; raid on, 52–55; response to, 56
Kobzon, Joseph, 126
Kokov, Valery, 19, 21
Korenizatsiia, 13–14, 109, 180
Kosolapov, Pavel, 120
Kovalev, Sergei, 97, 128
Kozak, Dmitry, 139, 147
Krasnodar region, 15, 162
Kryl'ia bombing, 35, 118

Kudaev, Rasul, 124
Kulaev, Nur-Pasha, 135
Kulikov, Anatolii, 44, 47, 53
Kumyks, 3, 71, 75
Kursk, 61, 137
Kuwait, 89
Kuznetsov, Yevgeny, 45
Kyrgyzstan, deportation to, 15–16

Labazanov, Ruslan, 28
Laden, Osama bin, 22, 50, 100, 114–15; and Basayev, 37; and Khattab, 84, 86, 94; links to Chechnya, 63, 88–89, 122, 124, 174
Lashkar-e-Taiba, 49
Lebed, Alexander, 59, 61
Legislation, counterterrorist, 65, 102–3, 121, 140, 180
Luzhkov, Yuri, 60, 93

Magas, Emir, 148–50, 171
Magomedov, Magomedali, 20–21, 146, 170, 182
Majlis of Islamic Mujahedeen of Ingushetia. *See* Islamic Front of Ingushetia
Makasharipov, Rasul, 150
Malaysia, 69, 88
Mamodaev, Yaragi, 28
Manar'in, Ivan, 120
Mansur, Sheikh, 3–5, 10, 72–73
Martial law, in Chechnya, 26, 84, 110
Martyrdom, 114–16
Masiuk, Elena, 50
Maskhadov, Aslan, 61; death, 109; opposition to, 70, 77–81, 83–84; as president, 67–70, 76, 81–82, 100–101, 157; relations with foreign countries, 69, 112; and terrorism, 56, 110, 129–30, 138
Mazar-i-Sharif, 112
Media: coverage of terrorist attacks, 43, 46, 136; government control of, 53, 56, 106, 130;
Medvedev, Dmirty, 138, 169–70, 181
Menovshchikov, Yuri, 119
Metro, attacks on, 49, 60, 117–18, 131, 156, 165
Mikhailov, Vyacheslav, 47
Military agreement of 1995, 47–48

Military doctrine, 29, 64, 102, 169
Mineralnye Vody, 33, 35, 60, 155
Ministry for the North Caucasus, 170
Ministry of Defense: troops deployed, 31, 38, 64, 132; in counterterrorism, 103, 121, 139
Mironov, Oleg, 103
Mohammed, Khalid Sheikh, 123
Moscow, terrorist attacks in, 50, 60–61, 94, 113, 117–18, 125–29, 165
Mountain Autonomous Soviet Socialist Republic, 13
Mountainous Republic of the North Caucasus, 11, 22, 80, 156
Mozdok, 19, 106, 117
Mudzhaid, Abu, 149, 167
Muhajir, 9
Muhammad, Ali Abu, 167, 178
Muhammad, Ghazi, 5–6, 72, 75
Muhammad of Yaraghi, Mullah, 4–5, 72–73
Muhannad, Emir, 167
Mujahedeen, 123, 159, 160, 166–68, 179, 182; Afghan, 40, 70, 76, 84–89, 113, 124, 174; and foreign funding, 37, 88–89, 168, 179
Mukozhev, Musa, 74, 152–53
Muridism, 3–8, 73, 75, 163, 219 n.12
Muslim Brotherhood, 76, 87, 89, 229 n.33
Muslim Society Number, 3. *See* Karachai jamaat
MVD (Ministry of Internal Affairs): troops deployed, 26, 31, 38, 53, 64, 92, 121; reform, 139, 169; against terrorism, 103, 132, 180

Nagaeva, Aminat, 117
Nagorno-Karabakh, 36, 40
Naibs, 7, 162
Nalchik, 22, 74, 124, 152
Naqshband, Baha al-Din, 5
Naqshbandi order, 4–7, 71
National Congress of the Chechen People, 25–26
National Council of the Balkar People, 19
National Counterterrorist Center, 139–40, 180
National security doctrine, 102
National Security Strategy, 169

National-Socialist Party of the Caucasus Brethren, 14
NATO (North Atlantic Treaty Organization), 112
Naurskii region, 17, 103, 155
Nazis, collaboration with, 14–15
Negotiations: with Chechen side, 46–48, 61, 68, 101, 107–9; during terrorist attacks, 43–44, 53, 56, 65, 127, 129–30, 181
Nemtsov, Boris, 126
Nevsky Express, bombing of, 120, 164
Nizam, 8
NKVD, 14, 16
Nogai jamaat, 111, 155
Nord-Ost. *See* Dubrovka
Nord-West. *See* Beslan
North Caucasus: conquest of, 1–3, 9, 76; post-Soviet, 143–47; revolts in, 3–8, 10–12; Soviet era, 10–21; territorial borders in, 13, 15, 17–19
North Caucasus Federal District, 168, 170
North Caucasus Krai, 13
North Ossetia, 13, 15, 18–19, 106, 155; Islam in, 71
Novolakskii district, 18, 93
Nunn-Lugar Cooperative Threat Reduction program, 49

Odizhev, Ruslan, 124
Okhotnyi Riad bombing, 93–94
Olympics, 9, 152, 165–67
Omar, Mullah, 112
Operation Bekkham, 149
Operation Enduring Freedom, 123
Operation Foreigner, 100
Operation Gazavat-Bek, 93
Operation Imam Ghazi Muhammad, 92
Operation Jihad, 61
OSCE (Organization for Security and Co-operation in Europe), 47, 59, 67, 122
Ottoman Empire, 7, 8, 11, 71

PACE (Parliamentary Assembly of the Council of Europe), 122
Pakistan, 36, 87, 89, 112
Pamfilova, Ella, 29
Pankisi Gorge, 87, 113, 123
Patrushev, Nikolai, 97, 118, 139–40

Peace process, 47, 68–69
Pervomaiskoe. *See* Kizlyar and Pervomaiskoe
Peter the Great, 2
PKK, 54, 114–15
Politkovskaya, Anna, 97, 136
Poltoranin, Mikhail, 25
Powell, Colin, 123
Prigorodnii District, Ingushetia, 15, 17–19, 27
Primakov, Evgeny, 126
Provisional Supreme Soviet, 26
Pugacheva, Alla, 126
Putin, Vladimir: as president, 108–10, 138, 147; as prime minister, 84, 90; on terrorism, 93–95, 99–100, 105, 122–23, 129, 139–40; visit to Chechnya, 106

Qadiriyya, 37, 71
Al-Qaradawi, Yusuf, 116
Qatar, 89

Radicalization, 152, 156, 170, 173, 179–80, 182
Radiological terrorism, 49–52
Radon industrial complex, 51
Raduyev, Salman, 52–57, 61, 77, 227 n.87
Rahman, Habib Abdul. *See* Khattab, Amir
Rasulov, Iasin, 150–51
Razdobud'ko, Vitalii, 120
Reactions to terrorist attacks: domestic, 46, 57, 95, 102, 130, 136–37; international, 63, 124–25, 171
Red Cross, attack on, 90, 124
Referendum: in Chechnya, 29, 130–31; in Ingushetia, 21; in Kabardino-Balkaria, 19; in Karachaevo-Cherkessia, 20
Religious revival, 3–5, 11, 70–77, 89, 98, 152, 174
Rice, Condoleezza, 122
Riyad us-Saliheyn Martyrs Brigade, 114, 118, 125, 133, 144, 165
Romanov, Anatolii, 48
Russia-Georgia War, 9
Russian Civil War, 10, 12
Russian Empire, 9, 13, 71, 181, 183

Russian State Duma: on Chechnya, 30–31, 46, 57, 64, 70; on terrorism, 62, 99, 103, 130
Ryazan, 96–97, 128
Rybakov, Yulii, 44

Saad, Emir, 155
Sadulayev, Abdul-Halim, 157–60, 162
Al-Saif, Abu Omar, 88
Salafism, 73, 217 n.10, 219 n.12
Sapyrkina, Alla, 117, 120–21
Satuyev, Said-Ali, 33–34
Saud, Muhammad bin, 73
Saudi Arabia, 73, 82, 89, 114; fighters from, 88
Savel'ev, Yuri, 136
Senchenko, Viktor, 119
Separatism, 18, 58, 102, 174, 179, 183
September 11, 2001, 34, 93, 95, 137, 163; *Commission Report*, 49, 123; and Russia's counterterrorism, 122–24
Serzhen-Yurt, 40, 76, 83, 86, 98
Sever battalion, 169
Shafii school, 71, 73, 157–58
Shahids, 114–19, 125, 127, 171. *See also* Suicide terrorism
Shamil, Imam, 6–10, 34; legacy of, 12, 78, 141, 150, 156;
Shanibov, Musa (Yuri), 22–25
Sharia, 218 n.6; courts, 4, 12–13, 72, 81, 144, 163; in Dagestan, 91–92, 150; law, 3, 7–8, 11–12, 74, 156, 163; in North Caucasus, 4–5, 71–77, 87, 141,
Sharia Army of the Mountainous Peoples, 12
Shelkovskii region, 17, 103, 155
Sheripov, Mairbek, 14
Shia Islam, 7
Al-Shishani, Omar, xiv, 113
Shpigun, Gennady, 70, 91
Sochi, 166
Soslambekov, Yusup, 22–24, 28
South Federal District, 139, 143–44
South Ossetia, 22–23
Sovereignty campaigns, in North Caucasus, 18–21
Soviet-Afghan war, 40, 85, 175
Special Purpose Islamic Regiment, 79, 114, 124, 148
Stalin, Joseph, 10, 12, 15–16

State of emergency, in Chechnya, 26, 29–30, 33, 64, 83, 102, 121
Stavropol region, 15, 33–34, 114, 155, 158
Stepashin, Sergei, 45, 70, 88, 92–93, 103
Sudan, 82, 88
Sufism, 5, 37
Suicide terrorism, 45, 114–18, 167
Sukhumi, 22–23, 25
Sunni Islam, 7, 71–73
Supreme Military Majlis ul-Shura of the United Mujahideen Forces of the Caucasus, 111, 129, 134, 156
Supreme Soviet, 17, 26, 30, 64
Al-Suwailem, Samir Saleh. *See* Khattab, Amir
Sword of Justice, 70
Syria, 118, 184; fighters from, 88; North Caucasus mujahedeen in, 167–68, 176, 179, 182

Tagaev, Mohammed, 79
Taimaskhanova, Fatima, 90
Taimazov, Beibulat, 4
Tajikistan, 40, 73, 85; fighters from, 88
Taliban, 112, 123
Tamil Tigers, 114–15
Tatarstan, 6, 52, 222 n.81; and Caucasus Emirate, 160, 166, 178, 182; Guantanamo detainee from, 124
Taziev, Ali. *See* Magas, Emir
Teips, 1–2
Temporary Council, 29
Terek, counterterrorist operation, 100
Terrorism: as an insurgent tactic, 34, 39, 62–64, 110–14; international, 54, 100, 122–23, 129, 137, 161, 175; Slavs participating in, 118–21, 177; and subversive action, 38–39, 45, 56, 62, 110; transformations of, 56–57, 60, 113–14, 119–20, 132–33, 164–68, 174–79
Teuvazhev, Beslan, 9
Theocratic state, 7, 11, 23, 156, 162–163, 178
Tikhomirov, Aleksandr. *See* Buryatsky, Said
Tokcan, Mohammed, 54–55, 175
Training camps, 40, 87–88, 94, 98; in Afghanistan, 36, 112–13

Treaty of Gulistan, 2, 20
Troshev, Gennady, 107
Tsarnaev brothers, ix, 167
Tsetchoev, Isa, 74
Tsumadinskii region, 92, 99
Tukhums, 2
Turkey, 33–34, 69, 89, 175; fighters from, 88; terrorist attack in, 54–55

Udugov, Movladi, 68–69, 75, 77–80, 86, 91
Ukraine, 88
Umantsev, Sergei, 119
Umarov, Doku: adapting insurgency, 160–61, 175; background, 159; and Caucasus Emirate, 162–63; and terrorism, 164–67
Union of Veterans of the Confederation of the Peoples of the Caucasus, 25
United Party of the Caucasus Brethren, 14
Urus-Martan, 83, 88, 98, 111

Vakhitov, Airat, 124
Vedeno, 10, 39, 41, 83, 88, 111
Vilayat Dagestan, 165, 167
Vilayat Idel-Ural, 160, 166
Vilayats, 7, 162
Vladikavkaz, 11, 19
Vlasov, Valentin, 91
Volga-Ural regions of Russia, 160
Volgodonsk, 93–98, 107, 128
Vostok battalion, 132
Vympel group, 53, 103, 180

Al-Wahhab, Muhammad bin Abd, 73
Wahhabism, 37, 73–76, 82–83, 170, 180–81, 217 n.10; persecution of, 131, 154
Al-Walid, Abu, 88, 124, 167
War on terror, 122, 125, 137, 140, 183
Whirlwind, counterterrorist operation, 100
Whirlwind-Antiterror, 117–18, 132
WMD terrorism, 49, 149. *See also* Radiological terrorism
World Bank, 122
World War II, 14–16

Yamadayev, Sulim, 132
Yandarbiyev, Zelimkhan, 58–59, 75, 77–81, 83, 112, 124

Yassin, Sheikh, 115
Yavlinsky, Grigory, 126
Yegorov, Nikolai, 45
Yeltsin, Boris, 25–26; and Budennovsk, 42–43, 46; and elections, 53, 58–60; peace talks with Yandarbiyev, 59; policy on Chechnya, 29–31, 38–39, 47, 57–59, 61, 64–65, 102–3; visit to Chechnya, 59
Yemen, 40, 112
Yerin, Viktor, 42, 45
Yermolov, General Aleksey, 4–7, 10, 179
Yevkurov, Yunus-Bek, 120, 146, 165, 171

Zachistki, 107, 111, 125–26, 132, 179–80
Zagorul'ko, Vitalii, 119
Zakayev, Akhmed, 108, 117, 161, 163
Zapad battalion, 132
Al-Zarqawi, Abu Musab, 116, 137
Zavgayev, Doku, 25–26, 48, 52, 58–60, 67–68, 109
Al-Zawahiri, Ayman, 49, 88–89, 114, 137, 168
Ziazikov, Murat, 134, 144, 146, 148
Zikr, 8
Zyuganov, Gennady, 59

About the Author

ELENA POKALOVA, PhD, is an assistant professor of international security studies at the College of International Security Affairs of the National Defense University. Her published works include numerous articles in scholarly publications and book reviews. She holds a doctoral degree in political science from Kent State University. The views expressed in this book are those of the author and do not reflect the official policy or position of the National Defense University, the Department of Defense, or the U.S. government.